faces of change

The Belfast and Northern Ireland Chambers of Commerce and Industry 1783 — 1983

George Chambers

Garmoyle
Pool

The Flatts

Channel

Sout

COUNTY OF DOWN

Con's Water

*I certify that the foregoing is a true
and authentic copy made pursuant to
the Statute 30 & 31 Vic. Cap 70*

J Bigger La Touche

Deputy keeper of the Records.

3rd June 1874

Text Copyright © George Chambers

080442

Published by
The Northern Ireland Chamber of Commerce and Industry
22 Great Victoria Street, Belfast BT2 7BJ

Distributed by
Century Books
61-63 Donegall Street, Belfast BT1 2GS

Printed in Northern Ireland by
The Universities Press (Belfast) Ltd.
Alanbrooke Road, Belfast BT6 9HF

ISBN No. 0 901925 01 2

CONTENTS

PREFACE AND ACKNOWLEDGEMENTS

"There must be two places called Northern Ireland". That challenging epigram was coined a few years ago by an American businessman who had recognised the contrast between the hard-working and pleasant Northern Ireland of his growing experience and the strife-ridden and nasty Northern Ireland of the international news media. Now it forms the title of an audio-visual presentation commissioned by the Northern Ireland Chamber of Commerce and Industry in 1981, with generous assistance from Ulster Television Ltd. The presentation in video-cassette form is used by Northern Ireland businessmen in assisting their international customers and potential investors to form a more balanced picture of the Province. Many of those seeing it for the first time are surprised by the beauty of the scenery, by the modernity of the infrastructure, by the facilities for education and recreation, and by the richness of the industrial and commercial heritage created by hard-working and inventive people. It is my hope not only that a few readers from outside our shores may be equally surprised by this story of the long and meritorious history of the Chambers of Commerce in the North of Ireland, but also that many of our own people may be re-inspired by the recounting of the industrial and commercial achievements of our forebears. If only we who live in Northern Ireland in 1983 could in full recapture the spirit of enterprise and endeavour of those who formed the Belfast Chamber of Commerce in 1783, we could by self-help make a significant impact on the debilitating unemployment that afflicts so many of our people.

My own interest in the history of the Chamber was kindled in the years when I had the honour to be one of its office-bearers. As I approached the Presidency early in 1979 I chanced to read again the article entitled *"YOUR CHAMBER — A Short History"*, which I had seen annually in the Chamber Year Book from the early 1970s. In this fascinating little story based on the research of my good friend and colleague, Past-President James Rodgers JP, I read of the momentous meetings of the merchants of Belfast in 1783 that led to the formation of the Chamber; and I made my first acquaintance with the remarkable Waddell Cunningham, the foundation President. Indeed I was so intrigued by those glimpses of our commercial heritage and of Cunningham in particular that I made brief reference to him in my speech of acceptance of the Presidency at the Annual General Meeting on 22 March 1979; and I mentioned too that the Chamber was then entering the one-hundred-and-ninety-seventh year of its history.

That the Chamber was approching its bicentenary had been noticed too by Trevor Parkhill, Assistant Keeper in the Public Records Office of Northern Ireland, which held the documentation of the Chamber going back to 1783. And so, quite independent of my incipient interest, the Records Office in the course of the year in which I was President put a few of the more interesting documents relating to the Chamber on public display. That really whetted my appetite; and in the succeeding months I found myself going occasionally to the archives in Balmoral Avenue to delve surreptitiously for a couple of hours into the formidable mass of material that far-seeing Secretaries of the Chamber had recorded and preserved over a period of nearly two-hundred years. At that time my intention was to survey the material in a general way, so that I could stimulate interest in the bicentenary and point a potential author of a Chamber history to the riches of information that were there for the digging. But of course things turned out differently. Almost imperceptibly I became more and more involved; and eventually I came to terms with the unlikely idea that it was I in the midst of a rather busy commercial life that would try to bring the two-hundred years of Chamber history into a publication that would appear in the bicentenary year or very shortly afterwards.

What I have tried to do is to set the history of the Chamber in the context of the industrial and commercial history of the area known since 1921 as Northern Ireland. In piecing together the story of the early days I concentrated on the people involved, though that necessitated reading much more widely than in the voluminous records of the Chamber. I did that because I thought that people and their achievements as individuals would be more interesting to general readers and more inspiring to the entrepreneurs of our own generation than cold facts about economic trends established, representations made, or policies devised. Often I found remarkable parallels between the problems of the late 18th and early 19th Centuries and the problems of today. It was a time of community ferment, of political uncertainty, and of political change. It was a time too when everything depended upon the entrepreneur and his willingness to take risks in investment, in the application of new technology, in the development of new products, in exporting, and in import substitution. And so as I pursued my research and had my eyes opened to the fact that few of the problems of today and few of the solutions are fundamentally new, the words that kept coming into my mind were those of the 19th Century French writer, Alphonse Karr: *"Plus ça change, plus c'est la même chose"* — *"The more things change, the more they are the same"*.

You will have guessed that I was heading for *"The More Things Change"* as a title for the book. But as the weeks passed I began to have serious reservations about it, for I could see that it might be cynically misinterpreted. In a community that had changed so much in every decade and in the history of an organisation that had for two-hundred years been an agent of change, it would have been a travesty to imply that nothing had changed. I was therefore delighted when Gordon Duffield of Inter-City Bureaux, the Belfast-based public relations company, told me one day that he had devised the title *"Faces of Change"* for a bicentennial audio-visual that he was producing for the Chamber — and suggested diffidently that I might like to consider it for the book as well. The consideration took less than a minute, for I sensed immediately that Gordon Duffield's phrase conveyed the ethos of the book: it was to be about change manifest in different ways and at different times, and about people that brought about change. And that is how the book came to be called *"Faces of Change"*.

Before I attempt to thank all those who have helped me in the project, may I apologise to all those who may when they read the book feel aggrieved that I have dealt too scantily or not at all with a particular industry, or sector of commerce, or firm, or incident, or individual. There are three reasons for such omissions. The first is that I was under severe pressure on space and time, particularly when I came to the last two chapters, which cover the period from 1921; the second is that I tended to follow up the events and developments that were of the greatest relevance to those who were the most active in the Chamber at a particular point in time; and the third is very simply that I suffer from the human frailty of occasional forgetfulness! I do hope, therefore, that those who feel "underdone" or not done at all will be understanding of my difficulties and tolerant of my frailties!

Equally I wish to record my thanks to all those who helped with the research and with the production of the book. I am particularly indebted to Trevor Parkhill of the Public Records Office for his interest and encouragement; to Dr W A Maguire, Keeper of Local History at the Ulster Museum, for his advice and his very practical help with historic photographs; to George Thompson, Director of the Ulster Folk and Transport Museum for his personal involvement in getting things done in an unreasonable hurry; and to Robert Gowdy, the Engineer at Clifton House for providing access to the records of the old cemetery and for showing me round and answering my questions. The many "holidays" that I spent in the Public Records Office brought me into close contact with the staff there; and they could not have been more helpful. Likewise it is a pleasure to record my thanks to the staff of the Linenhall Library, the Belfast Central Library, and the two museums already mentioned. I drew heavily on a large number of previous publications listed in the Selected Sources at the end of the book; but I should like particularly to acknowledge my dependence on Dr Norman Gamble's PhD thesis about *"The business community and trade of Belfast 1767-1800"* and on Jonathan Bardon's magnificent history of the city published by

Blackstaff Press at the end of last year. In addition I wish to thank Jonathan Bardon personally for taking the time to encourage and help me in my work when he was in the throes of his own. Likewise I am deeply grateful to Desmond Miller, Chairman of the Bicentenary Committee of the Dublin Chamber of Commerce, for all his early help and advice in the light of his experiences in the commissioning of *"Princes and Pirates"*, Professor L M Cullen's splendid history of the Dublin Chamber published some months ago. It is a pleasure too to record the co-operation and help of many friends in the business community in Northern Ireland who supplied vital information and historic photographs that would not otherwise have been available to me. The staff of the Chamber were also most helpful when I called upon them. Where possible, photographs and illustrations are acknowledged as they appear in the book; but I additionally wish to thank Wilfred Green for meeting deadlines that were frequently unreasonable. Behind the whole project lay the generous and deeply appreciated underwriting and sponsorship of the Northern Bank and the understanding and support of my employers, the Milk Marketing Board for Northern Ireland, and of my executive colleagues. It is a pleasure to acknowledge too the helpfulness and professionalism of John Belshaw and the staff of Universities Press who did the lay-outs and the printing; and the devotion, cheerfulness, and encouragement of Grainger Stewart, Anne McFall, Marie Doherty, and Joan Cowan, who helped with the research, the typing and the proof-reading. That team was led by Elizabeth Bailey who also liaised with the printers: without her dedication to the task and her help in a hundred different ways, the project would not have been feasible. Finally I thank my wife and family for their toleration of my unusual life-style at the weekends and my unsociable hours in the evenings for much of the past three years. To help me get back to normal domesticity as soon as possible, our daughter Helen assisted with the proof-reading! To all those whom I have mentioned and to all those whom I ought to have mentioned, I gladly record my warmest thanks.

George Chambers

December 1983

Chapter 1

THE ORIGINS OF CHANGE

"In our opinion the establishment of a Chamber of Commerce in this town would be highly proper and great advantages may be expected therefrom."

The town was Belfast in the North-East of Ireland; the date was 20 May 1783; and the vehicle for the foregoing announcement was the Belfast News Letter which was then in its forty-seventh year. From that announcement sprang an organisation which for two-hundred years has been an agent of change in the town and city of Belfast, in the province of Ulster, and in the state of Northern Ireland. And this is its story; and the story of men and women who made it — faces that brought about change.

Although chambers of commerce were not formally established in the British Isles until the latter part of the 18th Century, the custom of groups of merchants and manufacturers meeting together from time to time to protect and promote their interests in relation to Government policies and trading opportunities is as old as business itself. In medieval times such occasional associations were formalised in the great guilds that existed in a number of the major cities of Europe; and it is notable that the foremost of the Livery Companies of the City of London in the order of civic precedence was (and is) the Mercers Company, the textile merchants. Likewise in Dublin there was a Guild of Merchants, which was represented on the Corporation and played an active part in the civic and commercial life of the city even in the 18th Century. In Dublin too there was the fascinating Ouzel Galley Society, an association of the leading merchants formed in 1705 for the administration of charitable funds retrieved from pirates, as well as for the settlement of commercial disputes and the organisation of convivial banquets. In later years (1761-1783) Dublin also had a Committee of Merchants, which co-existed with the Ouzel Galley Society and was much wider in its interests and in its membership.

From the early 1770s a similar organisation existed in Manchester, where it was known as the Committee for the Protection and Encouragement of Trade. Likewise in 1783 the merchants of Birmingham established what was known as the Birmingham Commercial Committee. The merchants of Belfast, on the other hand, relied on town meetings called at their request by the First Citizen and Chief Magistrate, who was at that time appointed by the local landlord and known as the Sovereign. Often such meetings resulted in Petitions to Parliament; and several of these are preserved by

To the Right Honble & Honble the Knights, Citizens,
& Burgesses in Parliament assembled
        The Humble Petition of the Merchants
Linen Drapers & Linen Manufacturers in & near the
Town of Belfast
Humbly Sheweth.
        That for some years past, the
Linen Manufacture of this Kingdom, has declined
most rapidly – And at present from the low prices of
every species of that Manufacture, the poorer Manufacturers, Weavers, & Spinners are reduced to very great
Wretchedness & want.   That the Legislature of Great
Britain have for many years granted a Bounty on
all Linens exported from thence, both British & Irish
not exceeding the value of 18d British ⅌ yard. – The good
effects of which, have been sensibly felt by the Manufacturers of both Countrys   That your Petitioners apprehend
if equal & similiar Bountys were granted in this
Kingdom, payable at the place of Export, it would
be a great means of encouraging considerable orders for
Linens from foreign parts as well as induce Merchants
here, to Export on their own accounts, To the great
emolument of this Country, & the revival & extension
of that staple branch of our Trade. –
                    Your Petitioners therefore
Belfast   Febr 1780   humbly hope this Honble
                    House will take the premises
                    into Consideration.

Stewart Banks
J. Waddell Cunningham   Gum McGrey   Geo Blackk   Sam Hyde
John Alexander   Tho Stewart   Jos Kibo
Thomt Greg   John Henderson   Thot Brown
                         Wm Seed   Hu Crawford   Will McConce
Jn Campbell   Robt Clerens   Jas Ferguson
John Brown   James Juffon   Tho Larson
Henry Joy   Val Jones   Robert Lylburn   George Wills Junr
Hu. Montgomery   David Tomb   Jas Patkinson
P.H. Wilson   John Rainey Robt Simmn   Jam Black
                        John Luke   Wm Brown
Alex. ory Jum   Will Boyle   Sam Robinson   Wm Hutchinson

---

*Petition to the Irish Parliament in February 1780 from the businessmen of Belfast about bounties (export subsidies)
on linen. Signatories included twenty-one who would be foundation members of the Chamber of Commerce in
1783.*
(From S Shannon Millin's "Sidelights on Belfast History" by courtesy of W & G Baird Ltd.)

reproductions in S Shannon Millin's "Sidelights on Belfast History", the originals having been destroyed in the burning of the Four Courts in Dublin in June 1922. And it was from such early attempts at business organisation that the chamber of commerce movement in Britain and Ireland sprang.

The term "chamber of commerce" for an association of merchants and manufacturers was used in other parts of the world very much earlier than in the British Isles. The "Chambre de Commerce" at Marseilles, for example, was in existence as early as 1599; but it was not until 1768, in Jersey, that the first British chamber of commerce that went by that name was formed. And another fifteen years were to elapse before the movement appeared in mainland Britain and in Ireland. Then in the course of one remarkable year — the year 1783 — chambers were established in rapid succession in Glasgow, Dublin, and Belfast; and others soon followed in Edinburgh and Leeds (1785), Manchester (1794), and Birmingham, Greenock, and Plymouth (1813).

Thus the chamber movement in Northern Ireland is sharing its bicentenary with Glasgow and Dublin. In all three areas, ambitious programmes of celebratory events have been organised and histories written. The history of the Glasgow Chamber written by Charles A Oakley, a naval architect, journalist, and Past-President deeply steeped in the tradition of the movement, was published three years early, in 1980, under the title "Our Illustrious Forbears"; and the history of the Dublin Chamber written by Dr Louis M Cullen, the distinguished Professor of Modern Irish History at Trinity College Dublin, was published in the summer of 1983 under the title "Princes and Pirates", a delightful back-reference to the origins of the Ouzel Galley Society.

Charles Oakley records that the Glasgow and District Chamber was formally established on 1 January 1783, the preparatory work having been carried out in the latter half of 1782. The prime mover was Patrick Colquhoun, who became the first Chairman (the term President was not introduced in Glasgow until 1872). Like Waddell Cunningham who became his counterpart in the Belfast Chamber later in the year, Dumbarton-born Colquhoun had begun his business career in America and was a rich man with many business and civic interests to his credit before he took up the key position in Glasgow's new commercial organisation at the age of thirty-seven. At that time tobacco and linen were two of the main business areas on Clydeside; and Colquhoun had personal interests in both.

The immediate motivation for the formation of the Glasgow Chamber, apart from the initiative and energy of its likely leader, seems to have been the fear of serious problems in the tobacco industry as the American War of Independence finally ended. Yet when the Chamber later adopted as its emblem a flying stork to symbolise the international trade of the port, the piece of vegetation that the bird was portrayed to be carrying in its beak was a sprig of flax rather than a leaf of tobacco, a salutary reminder that the linen industry was not in those days the prerogative solely of Belfast and the Lagan Valley. Within weeks of its formation the Glasgow Chamber had a membership of two-hundred-and-sixteen, a fifth of whom came from surrounding towns such as Paisley, Greenock, and Port Glasgow.

In Dublin the formation of the Chamber of Commerce in the first quarter of 1783 was a natural evolution for the Committee of Merchants, which had been in existence for over twenty years. During that time the Committee had had many notable achievements, though relationships with the Dublin Corporation and with the Irish Parliament were often strained. The Committee had also opened up lines of communication with the merchants of Cork and Belfast, the latter being particularly important because the sale of bleached linen from the North of Ireland in the Dublin markets was at that time a very significant feature in the trade of the metropolis. With a population at least ten times that of Belfast and second in the British Isles only to London, Dublin was already one of the main commercial centres in Europe, though the full development of its trade had until 1780 been inhibited by restrictions imposed by the still-superior legislature in London. Within that framework the Committee of Merchants from its formation in 1761 till its demise in 1783 to make way for the Chamber of Commerce had been continuously active in the interests of the business community not only in Dublin but also in the rest of Ireland. Its greatest achievement was to secure and finance the building of the Royal Exchange, a project that took over fifteen years of determined effort to bring to fruition. But the Committee was active too in international matters. Unbelievably, in the words of Professor Cullen's book: *"In December 1770 and February 1771 it made representations to the Lord Lieutenant regarding the embargo which had been imposed on the provision trade because of the danger of the Falklands crisis leading to war"*!

The stimulus for the progression in Dublin from a Committee of Merchants to a full-blown Chamber of Commerce came partly from a feeling of some ineffectiveness of the Committee in a particular dispute and partly from business buoyancy (possibly false hopes) arising from political change and international peace. The dispute was a long-standing one with the Revenue Commissioners about the location of the new Custom House and an associated bridge over the Liffey; the political change was the British Government's concession of Free Trade in 1780 and legislative independence for the Irish Parliament in 1782, in the face of intense pressure spearheaded by Northern activists in the Volunteer Movement; and the international peace was the ending of the American War of Independence, which brought hopes of increased trade.

It was in that context that the Committee of Merchants met in Dublin on 10 February 1783 to consider a plan for the establishment of a Chamber of Commerce. The membership fee was to be a guinea a year and membership would be open to any merchant or trader living within the city or its "dependencies". A start would be made as soon as a hundred subscriptions were obtained by two temporary treasurers; and there would then be a general meeting to ballot for a council, which would be re-elected annually. The plan was adopted; and at the subsequent general meeting on 18 March 1783 more than a hundred-and-fifty subscribers participated in the election of a council of forty-one and agreed to appoint a full-time Secretary at a salary of thirty pounds a year. Later the number of foundation subscribers increased to two-hundred-and-ninety-three; and Travers Hartley, a Presbyterian merchant who had been elected to the Irish Parliament in the previous year after long and distinguished service in the Corporation and in the Committee of Merchants, became the first President. The other office-bearers included the most senior of the Catholic merchants of the city, as well as a prominent Quaker.

News of these developments in the Irish capital spread quickly to Belfast, where it gave rise to intense discussion between the most progressive members of the business community. One such discussion was held in the Donegall Arms, the leading hostelry in the town, on 22 April 1783, just six weeks after the first general meeting of the new chamber in Dublin; and this resulted in the publication of a notice in the News Letter on 2 May:

"At a Meeting of the Merchants of Belfast held at the Donegall Arms the 22d April 1783 Mr. JAMES PARK in the Chair.

Resolved, That the Chairman do insert an advertisement in the next Belfast paper, summoning a general meeting of the Merchants of this town to be held at the Market-house, on Saturday the 3d May next, at 12 o'clock noon, for the purpose of considering the propriety of establishing a Chamber of Commerce in the town of Belfast."

The James Park who presided at that meeting and subsequently put the notice in the newspaper was a merchant engaged in "the West Indies trade". In Chamber of Commerce affairs he had but that one brief spell in the limelight, for as the story unfolded he disappeared quietly from the scene save as a foundation subscriber.

After an unexplained hiatus of sixteen days, the next decisive development took place on 19 May; and this led to an announcement in the News Letter of 20 May, repeated in the next issue four days later:

"BELFAST, 19TH MAY, 1783,

At a meeting of the Merchants of Belfast to take into consideration the propriety of establishing a Chamber of Commerce in this Town.

THOMAS GREG, Esq; in the Chair.

Resolved unanimously, That in our opinion the establishment of a Chamber of Commerce in this town would be highly proper, and that great advantages may be expected therefrom.

Resolved, That the following gentlemen be, and they hereby are, appointed a committee to digest a plan for the above purpose, and that they do report the same to a general meeting on Saturday the 24th inst. at noon, of which publick notice to be given.

Mr. Greg,	Mr. John Brown,
Mr. Cunningham,	Mr. Joy,
Mr. Thomson,	Mr. Bradshaw,
Mr. Ewing,	Any five to be a quorum.

THOMAS GREG, Chairman".

Now the initiative had passed from James Park to Thomas Greg, brother-in-law of Waddell Cunningham and one of the most enterprising and successful merchants in the town. And Greg had been provided with a committee of great talent and influence, as will be apparent from biographical material in a later chapter of the present work.

The committee obviously worked well, for within eight days it was in a position to report back to a general meeting of the merchants and traders in the Market House under the chairmanship of Waddell Cunningham. The proceedings were reported in the News Letter of 30 May, beginning with the report of the Committee:

"To the Merchants and Traders of the Town of Belfast.

The Report of your Committee appointed to digest a Plan for establishing a Chamber of Commerce in said Town.

Having taken the business to us committed under our most serious consideration, we are unanimously of opinion, that we cannot so well discharge the trust reposed in us, as by recommending to your adoption the same plan which hath been adopted by our worthy and highly respected brethren, the merchants of Dublin, with some few variations which become necessary on account of the comparative smallness of our numbers. — We therefore recommend,

That every merchant or trader resident in the town of Belfast or its vicinity, shall at anytime become and be deemed a member of said Chamber of Commerce, on paying to the treasurer for the time being one guinea; such subscribers to continue members so long as they shall respectively comply with such rules as may be established by said Chamber for its good government, and for the continuation of a fund to answer the purposes of its institution.

That a subscription be now opened for that purpose, and that such gentlemen as shall now subscribe and pay one guinea each, do appoint from among themselves a temporary treasurer to receive subscriptions; and that as soon as the subscribers shall amount to fifty, the said treasurer do call a general meeting of the subscribers by publick advertisement, at which meeting the members present shall chuse by ballot fifteen subscribers, who shall form, and be called The Council of the Chamber of Commerce, to continue in office until the first day of July, 1784; and that an annual election by ballot for such Council shall be held on every first day of July, not being Sunday, and when Sunday on the second day of July.

That it shall be the business of said Council to attend to the interests of commerce; to have a watchful attention to the proceedings of Parliament respecting trade in both kingdoms; to inspect into the method of transacting business in Belfast, and to contrive and recommend improvements therein when such shall be thought expedient; to correspond with the Council of the Chamber of Commerce in Dublin, and with any others that may be established in this kingdom, as well as, when necessary, with those that are or may be established in Great Britain.

That the said Council, for the time being, shall, by ballot, chuse from among themselves a President, Vice-President, and Treasurer.

And that the Members of the Chamber shall on every proper occasion be peculiarly intitled to the protection of the institution.

Belfast,
27th May, 1783

THOs. GREG,
Chairman of the Committee."

The report of the steering committee was "maturely considered" and adopted for immediate execution; and Waddell Cunningham was asked to act as treasurer till fifty subscriptions had been obtained, a general meeting held, and the Council elected. The speed of decision on a matter of such magnitude was indicative of the level of enthusiasm that had been kindled amongst the merchants of the town. That enthusiasm was apparent too in their last decision of the day, when it was resolved unanimously that:

". . . in our opinion similar establishments in all the principal trading towns of this kingdom might be productive of great advantage to the nation, as by that means a general union would be formed, the knowledge and experience of every intelligent trader in the various lines of commerce and manufacturers collected, and the united endeavours of the whole happily directed to the general good."

Such were the far-sighted proceedings of that historic meeting in Belfast two-hundred years ago, at which the aims of the Chamber were defined in essentially the following terms:

— to attend to the interests of commerce;
— to have a watchful attention to the proceedings of Parliament;
— to inspect into the method of transacting business in Belfast;
— to contrive and recommend improvements therein; and
— to correspond with other chambers in the North and South of Ireland and in Great Britain.

That remit was written for the conditions of 1783; but it comes remarkably close to the aims of the Chamber in 1983. Nowadays there would be a direct reference to manufacturing as well as to commerce; and the geographical scope would be Northern Ireland rather than Belfast. But otherwise Thomas Greg and his committee in May 1783 penned a charter that is not out of place in today's world.

Although the immediate stimulus for the establishment of the Belfast Chamber was the example that had been set by the merchants of Dublin some weeks previously, there were more fundamental factors in the decision. Save for the absence of a specific controversy parallel to the bridge issue in the metropolis, these were essentially the same as those that had influenced the business community in the South. They were the product of self-help and political change at home and business prospects abroad.

Many of the Belfast merchants were active in the Volunteer Movement, which had been established in 1778 for the defence of the realm but had become a powerful agent for political, social, and commercial change. As such they had played a major part in the agitation that led to the removal of some of the restrictions on Irish trade early in 1780; and they had been solidly behind Henry Grattan, the MP for the borough of Charlemont in County Armagh, when in October of the previous year his oratory had persuaded the Irish Parliament unanimously to pass a Free Trade amendment to the formal Reply to the King's Speech. *"The only means left to support the expiring trade of this miserable part of your Majesty's dominions is to open a free trade"*, Grattan had said; and a measure of free trade was indeed obtained as a result of his efforts.

Next the Volunteers, with the Belfast merchants again to the fore, had turned their attention to securing legislative independence for the Irish Parliament. So *"Liberty to those who dare contend for it"* became a popular toast in the town from 1780 onwards, though it was often tempered with *"A lasting and constitutional connection between Great Britain and Ireland"*. Yet by the autumn of 1780 the officers present at a review of twenty-four companies of the Volunteers in Newry had passed a series of resolutions that were highly critical of the British Establishment. These dealt both with their disillusionment about Free Trade and with the new issue of legislative independence for the Irish Parliament. In the historic words of one of the resolutions, this impressive gathering organised by Captain Roger Bristow and Captain Isaac Corry of Newry and with Lord Glerawly from Mountpanther near Clough in County Down as Reviewing General agreed:

"That we are firmly convinced that the Influence of the Crown has increased, is increasing, and ought to be diminished, and that the Freedom of this Country can be preserved only by the Spirit of the People and the Virtue of the House of Commons."

The agitation for legislative independence and other reforms culminated in a great convention in Dungannon on Friday 15 February 1782, involving representatives of a hundred-and-forty-three units of the Volunteers from all over Ulster, including a strong contingent from Belfast headed by Waddell Cunningham and Robert Thomson, the sugar-refiner. The resolutions passed there were soon being taken up all over Ireland; and the popular toast *"May the northern lights ever illuminate the Irish nation"* took on a new meaning. And so by the summer of 1782 the British Government, weakened by internal dissension, felt unable any longer to resist the pressure in Ireland for legislative independence; and the Irish Parliament, while remaining within the British constitutional framework, gained a degree of freedom that it had not known for two centuries. It was against that background of successful agitation through the Volunteers, of Free Trade and legislative independence secured, and of prospects opening up for a new age of commercial prosperity in Ireland that the merchants of Belfast took their far-reaching decisions in the early summer of 1783 about the constitution and role of a Chamber of Commerce.

As will be apparent from later chapters of the present work, the year 1783 itself was by no means free from political controversy. This may have been one of the reasons why the decision to form the Chamber, taken so swiftly by the merchants and traders on 27 May, was not implemented as rapidly as might have been expected. Thomas Greg's committee had envisaged that the first Council of the new organisation would hold office until 1 July 1784, which indicates that they expected it to be functioning by 1 July 1783. Exactly what did happen is not clear because the opening sixteen pages of the first minute book of the Chamber are missing; and the first surviving entry refers to a meeting of the Council held on 10 December 1783. Fortunately, however, S Shannon Millin at some time prior to the publication in 1932 of his "Sidelights on Belfast History" was permitted by the Chamber to examine the first minute book, which was then stored at the Chamber offices in Belfast and was apparently still intact. Millin was thereby able to compile a list of fifty-nine foundation members and to make a photocopy of the minutes of the first meeting of the Council held on 25 October 1783,

Minutes of the first meeting of the Council of the Belfast Chamber of Commerce.

(From S Shannon Millin's "Sidelights on Belfast History".)

both items being subsequently included in his "Sidelights". The delay from May till October was presumably due to some difficulty in collecting the requisite fifty subscriptions; and that in turn could have been due as much to the political preoccupations of the temporary treasurer, Waddell Cunningham, as to any reticence on the part of potential members.

At that first Council meeting in October 1783, Thomas Greg who had led the committee that drew up the plan for the establishment of the Chamber was again in the chair; and he was accompanied by seven of the leading businessmen of the town — Robert Getty, Henry Joy snr, Will Sinclaire, James Stevenson, David Tomb, Nat Wilson, and Robert Bradshaw of Carrickfergus Road. The only business of the meeting was to elect the first office-bearers of the Chamber; and the outcome of the ballots was that Waddell Cunningham and John Holmes were elected President and Vice-President respectively, with Robert Bradshaw as Honorary Secretary and Treasurer. For Waddell Cunningham the appointment as President was confirmation of his standing as the leading member of the business community in the North of Ireland. For Robert Bradshaw that first Council meeting marked the beginning of a period of distinguished service to the Chamber that would last for thirty-six years. And for the Chamber itself 25 October 1783 was the effective beginning of the two-hundred years of commercial history that are the essence of the present work and the reason for the celebrations that are to be held in Belfast and other centres in Northern Ireland in the autumn of 1983.

But those events back in 1783 — the events that turned out to be the origin of change for the Province of Ulster — took place in a vibrant little community clustered around a downstream crossing of the River Lagan as it meandered from Slieve Croob in County Down to Carrickfergus Lough in the Irish Sea. And this story must turn aside to look at that little town called Belfast, as it was in 1783.

Chapter 2

BELFAST IN 1783

When the Chamber of Commerce was formed in the autumn of 1783 Belfast was an important centre of international trade and a dominant influence in Irish politics. Yet it was a town of only thirteen-thousand people living within an area of about half a square mile, as illustrated in the 1791 map reproduced on the back endpaper of the present work. The limit of the area on the northern side was a little way short of the Charitable Institution's fine building, now known as Clifton House. To the east the boundary was the edge of the River Lagan, on about the present line of Donegall

The Charitable Society's Poorhouse (now Clifton House), on the northern edge of Belfast in 1783.

(From the earlist known representation of the building — a water-colour by John Nixon in the 1780s, now in the Ulster Museum.)

Quay. On the southern side there was as yet very little below the line of Castle Street and Ann Street, save for a few humble habitations in Sandy Row, which a visitor in 1780 described as ". . . *a long string of falling cabins and tattered houses, all tumbling down with a horrid aspect*". And on the western edge, domestic buildings extended only a short distance beyond the line of Millfield and Upper Library Street (then Carrick Hill) though there was an important flour mill and other industrial activity a little farther out.

There were four main routes into and out of the town which can conveniently be related to the cardinal points of the compass. The northern route led to Carrickfergus via Millfield, Carrick Hill (now Upper Library Street), and Carrickfergus Road (now North Queen Street, York Road, and Shore Road). The eastern route led to Newtownards, Ballynahinch, and Saintfield via Ann Street, the famous Long Bridge (in roughly the same position as the present Queen's Bridge) and Ballymacarrett, where the road divided for Newtownards to the east and Ballynahinch and Saintfield to the south. The Long Bridge with its twenty-one arches of hewn freestone from Scrabo had been built almost a hundred years earlier; and its stability seems to have been a constant source of worry following damage allegedly caused by the passage of the Duke of Schomberg's heavy cannon on the way to the Battle of the Boyne in 1690. Yet it was not replaced until 1842 following another bout of agitation in 1836, in which the Chamber of Commerce played a major part. The southern route out of the town also included a river crossing: this was the Salt Water Bridge over the

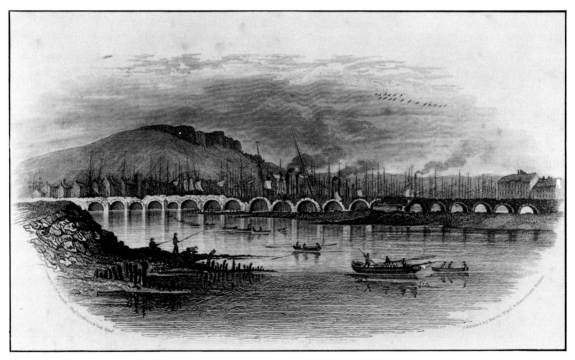

The somewhat decrepit Long Bridge, on the eastern edge of Belfast in 1783.

(After an engraving by J H Burgess — Ulster Museum.)

Blackstaff or Owenvarra River in approximately the same position as the present Boyne Bridge. The route began in the centre of the town in the area now known as Castle Place; and it ran through Castle Street into a continuation of that thoroughfare then known as Mill Street. At the western end of Mill Street the road divided, with a right incline leading to the Falls district and a sharp left along approximately the present line of Durham Street leading direct to the Salt Water Bridge and Sandy Row. Beyond Sandy Row the Blackstaff Road (now Donegall Road) went off to the right; and the main route continued through the area of the present Bradbury Place, where there was a turnpike or toll-gate. Further along, the Strand Mills (now Stranmillis) Road forked off to the left; and the spinal route to Lisburn and the south and west ran along the Malone Ridge on approximately the line of the present Malone Road. The final route out of the town was the road to Antrim; but instead of following the present line on the seaward side of the Cave Hill it ran along North Street into Peter's Hill and straight towards the high ground, on approximately the line of the present Shankill Road.

Within the town the main thoroughfare and centre of commercial life was High Street, built on the line of the River Farset which discharged into the Lagan at the eastern end of the street. Originally the carriageways and buildings had been constructed on either side of the river, which therefore ran open down the full length of the thoroughfare; but the two sides were connected by five bridges on which much of the commerce of the town was at one time conducted. As late as 1775, for example, there were occasional auctions of livestock on the Stone Bridge which crossed the river near the western end of the street; and five years earlier the Sovereign had ordered that: *"Potatoes, seeds, oats, barley, peas and beans be sold at the Market House, and in the street before it. Fresh butter, cheese, fish, pigs, geese, turkeys, hens, eggs, chickens, wild fowl, conies and other dead victual in no other place but High Street, and on the Bridges built over the River from Pottinger's Entry to the west end of the Stone Bridge, where the yarn measurers, town sergeants and overseers of the market will be, to weigh butter, count suspected yarn, oversee, and prevent disorders and disputes".* But by 1783 the river had probably been completely arched over from the western end to Skipper Street. Traditionally this difficult operation is said to have been effected "between 1770 and 1786", but the detail of a map prepared specially for a review of the Volunteers and reproduced in George Benn's first "History of Belfast" would suggest that it had been completed by the summer of 1783.

With the main dock of the town slotted into its eastern end and the Market House and the Donegall Arms Hotel on opposite sides near the other end, High Street in 1783 was invariably a hive of activity. Yet it also had on its fringes two large silent areas that were constant reminders of tragedy and mortality. Just beyond the western end of the street and running southwards to about the present line of Castle Lane lay the extensive gardens that had surrounded the great castle of the Earls of Donegall, the landlords of the town. The castle itself had been reduced to a shell by an accidental fire seventy-five years previously in which three sisters of the 4th Earl had perished. By 1783 the absentee 5th Earl's surveyor, Roger Mulholland, had begun planning a great new thoroughfare that would run due south from the western end of High Street through the neglected gardens of the castle to the front of the White Linen Hall, a large new building that was taking shape in open country about two-hundred yards outside the ramparts. In the following year Mulholland would be announcing his plans in the News Letter; and the rich and the famous would be rushing to put their names down for sites in an area that was due to become the most fashionable in town. To begin with, the new thoroughfare would be called The Flags; later it would become Linenhall Street; and ultimately it would take on the name by which it is known to this day, Donegall Place.

The other silent site on the fringe of High Street in 1783 was the Old Parish Churchyard, which fronted on to the main thoroughfare near the dock and was bounded on its other three sides by Forrest Lane, Ann Street, and Church Lane from which there was a side entrance. For several centuries this had been the site of successive Parish Churches of Belfast; but the last in that series had been taken down in 1774 because it had become unsafe. At that time St Anne's Parish Church was being erected in Donegall Street (first known as New Street) on the site occupied since the beginning of the present century by Belfast Cathedral; and when St Anne's had been consecrated in October 1776 it became the New Parish Church of Belfast. In 1783 the old churchyard in High Street was a rather neglected burial ground, which was still used for occasional interments. Fifteen years later it would receive the body of Henry Joy McCracken after he had been hanged at the front of the nearby Market House for his part in the '98 Rebellion. David Manson, the noted educationalist, would also be buried there, in a famous night-time ceremony illuminated by torchlight. And early in the 19th Century the beautiful St George's Parish Church of the present day would be raised on the site. But in 1783 it was a quiet and unlovely place of decaying headstones and thriving brambles.

The Market House was the focal point of the town. For over a century it had stood at the junction of High Street and the thoroughfare known sometimes as Corn Market (as at present) and sometimes as Shambles Street (the "shambles" referred to a slaughterhouse or meat store in the area). The junction itself was usually called Paddy Gaw's Corner, after a popular tobacconist who had a shop in the area and was well-known as a conversationalist and willing witness to innumerable legal documents. In addition to providing ground-level facilities for commercial activity the Market House (known in later years as "the Old Market House") was the first town-hall and courthouse of Belfast. It was therefore the venue for meetings of the Corporation, which consisted of the Sovereign and twelve burgesses, all of whom were in effect appointed by Lord Donegall (as were the two Members of Parliament for the borough). From the Market House the Sovereign issued a stream of orders for the regulation of the environment and trading activities of the town; and as the chief magistrate he seems also to have held court daily in an office there where agreements could be witnessed, oaths taken, and representations lodged. The old building was also the venue for town meetings, such as those held in May 1783 in connection with the formation of the Chamber of Commerce; and it had a macabre role in the administration of the harsh justice of those days, the gallows for public executions invariably being set up at the front of the building underneath the strong brackets of the town clock. Twenty-seven years previously the clock itself had been the "executioner"

The centre of Belfast in 1783 — the western end of High Street near today's Castle Place. The building second right (with projecting clock) is the Market House. On opposite side, extreme left, is the Donegall Arms Hotel. Both buildings were used for early meetings of the Chamber of Commerce.

(From a drawing of 1786 by John Nixon — Ulster Museum.)

of an innocent by-stander when its heavy dial-plate broke loose and fell to the street below. The Sovereign in 1783 was wine merchant George Black of Strand Mills; and the burgesses included Henry Joy snr, of the News Letter. Both joined the Chamber of Commerce.

Across the street from the Market House was the best-known hostelry in town, the Donegall Arms Hotel, scene of many a convivial occasion including some of the early meetings of the Council of the Chamber. The inn had been built about thirty years previously; and the proprietor in 1783 was James McKane who had bought the premises from Adrian von Brackley in 1773. The inn had facilities for dealing with quite large functions as well as with the accommodation and sustenance of individual visitors: in June 1783, for example, the 5th Earl of Donegall in his capacity as Colonel of the Belfast Battalion of the Volunteers entertained about three-hundred-and-sixty people to midnight supper there after a prolonged reception elsewhere in the town. Before the end of the century the inn was also to be host to two of the Lords-Lieutenant of Ireland; and, in the aftermath of the Rebellion in 1798, it was to be used as a temporary courthouse and prison, one of those detained there being the Rev William Steele Dickson of Portaferry, leader of the United Irishmen in Co Down, who was arrested in Ballynahinch just before the rising began. Before that, in 1786, the premises were to be extended and refurbished by James Sheridan who had entered into some form of partnership with James McKane. To the present day the windows and general facade incorporated into that renovation can be seen as part of the first and second floors of the building in High Street that was for many years the department store of John Robb & Co Ltd.

Another of the public buildings of 1783 that survives to the present day, though not so easily discernible as the upper floors of the Donegall Arms, is the Exchange with its Assembly Room on the second storey. This great solid building provided in 1769 and 1776 by Lord Donegall at a total cost of £11,000 (equivalent to at least £650,000 in modern money) stands at the junction which in 1783 was known as "the Five Corners"; and the term would still be appropriate today, for five thoroughfares converge on the area concerned, namely North Street, Donegall Street (New Street in 1783), Waring Street (Broad Street in 1783), Bridge Street, and Rosemary Street (Rosemary Lane in 1783). In 1783 the merchants of the town met daily in the Exchange to keep in touch with political and commercial news through the Newsroom and to transact business; and the Assembly Room on the upper floor was the venue for a wide range of social and cultural events, mainly in the evening. It was here that the two MPs for Belfast held *"a very elegant and crowded Ball"* in 1783 to celebrate their election. It was here too in June of that year that Lord Donegall gave a reception for his three-hundred-and-sixty guests before supper in the Donegall Arms. And it was to be here also that a famous, or infamous, Harp Festival would be held in 1792; and that Henry Joy McCracken would be tried and condemned to death in July 1798. Some twenty years later the Exchange would be converted to shops; later still the whole block would be refurbished under the guidance of Belfast's most famous architect, Charles Lanyon, to become the headquarters of the Belfast Banking Company; and finally, in 1895 it would be re-modelled again, by Lanyon's protege W H Lynn. Unfortunately these renovations, particularly that of Lynn, so modified the

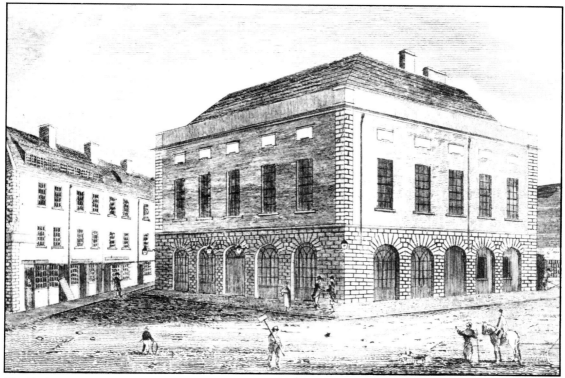

The Exchange and Assembly Room built by Lord Donegall in 1769 and 1776.

(From a contemporary engraving — Ulster Museum.)

building (which is now an office of the Northern Bank) that it is scarcely recognisable as the Exchange and Assembly Room of 1783, though the basic framework of the original building still remains and the curved beams of the famous ceiling of the upper floor can still be seen in the roof-space. But there is no trace now of the Exchange Coffee Room, the popular meeting-place used occasionally by the Chamber of Commerce in its early days.

In contrast to the Exchange and Assembly Room, the exterior of the whole front section of the Charitable Society's building at the top of Donegall Street, known since 1948 as Clifton House, is essentially the same today as it was in 1783. Opened in 1774, the Poorhouse and Infirmary as it was then known represented the fulfilment of over twenty years of voluntary work by a group of socially-conscious business and professional people in the town, amongst them several who later became prominent in the Chamber. By 1783 the institution was making a significant contribution to the relief of suffering and poverty in the urban community, though the scale of the facility was hardly commensurate with the enormity of the need. Dr R W M Strain in his admirable history of the Charitable Society published in 1961 tells of the special effort that was needed in 1783 because of shortages of food, high prices arising from poor harvests, and *"much poverty in the town"*. In addition to providing in-house medical treatment for the sick and shelter for the destitute, the Charitable Society was paying allowances to the poor outside the institution; and not only had these payments to be doubled in 1783, but the Society had also to embark on a special relief fund to purchase grain for the needy. During this period of acute misery, members of the committee of the Society, who were mostly business and professional people, went out personally into the town by districts and made payments to those who were in the greatest need, as well as taking on responsibility for the fair distribution of food supplies.

Constantly the need of the Charitable Society was for funds to carry on the work and to maintain the institution. Much of the money required for the provision of the building had been raised by lotteries; and the on-going activity was chiefly dependent on subscriptions from socially-conscious members of the business community; the proceeds of charity balls in the committee room of the institution and charity sermons in the churches of the town; and the profits from manufacturing activities undertaken by the inmates. But the great reviews of the Volunteers in the 1780s provided the Society with an additional source of income, for companies from the country areas were often billeted in the institution, and a ball for the officers and their ladies from all the units taking part in the manoeuvres was held in the committee room each evening. The accounts and minutes of the Charitable Society for the years around 1783 therefore contain entries like:

"Neat Produce of 3 Balls the time of the Review £104.4.0."

"Mr. H Joy reports that he has in his hand £53.0.2. being a benefaction bestowed on this house by the volunteer delegates at their meeting at 17th inst."

And for the visitor to the historic boardroom of Clifton House today, it requires only a short flight of imagination to have a mind's-eye picture of those glittering events of 1783 — of bright uniforms and tight hose, of swirling gowns and powdered hair piled high.

But if the Charitable Society's building has undergone little exterior modification in the course of the past two-hundred years the same fortunately cannot be said of the port of Belfast. Though the harbour of 1783 was as vital to the town of that time as the harbour of 1983 is to the city today, it was a rather primitive facility with serious limitations. The main dock was at the end of High Street, where the Albert Clock of today tilts slightly seawards as a reminder of the in-filling of the mid-19th Century and the sogginess of the underlying stratum. The quay on the northern side of the dock, known as Chichester Quay, had been constructed by Thomas Greg in 1769 in fulfilment of the conditions of his lease from Lord Donegall. Further north, near the end of Waring Street, there was Lime Kiln Dock which is covered today by Albert Square. Running south along the Lagan from the end of the Farset to the Long Bridge there was Hanover Quay in approximately the position of Donegall Quay today, though in the extensive re-modelling of the whole area in 1848/49 the quay was extended out into the river.

The problem with these facilities in 1783 was that they were three miles upstream from the deep water of the Pool of Garmoyle and could be reached only at high tide. At low tide the docks stood high and dry; and the channel wound a tortuous path to the sea through mudflats and sandbanks, its depth in midstream opposite the mouth of the Farset being only from two to four feet. The result was that much of the merchandise coming into Belfast by sea had to be trans-shipped in the Pool of Garmoyle and brought to the docks by small craft of shallow draught. Improvement of the harbour therefore became a priority objective of the Chamber of Commerce immediately after its formation; and within two years its most prominent members were to find themselves with responsibility for the project, as members of the first Harbour Corporation, usually known as the Ballast Board. Over the succeeding hundred years the development of the harbour did not always take place as quickly as many would have wished; but gradually the whole area was transformed and a splendid deep-water port created. In 1783 the value of the goods moved through the port was about £100,000 (equivalent to about £6 million in modern money): in 1983 it is likely to be of the order of £500 million.

The trade of Belfast in 1783 centred on linen, provisions, construction materials, and coal. Spinning and weaving of linen were still cottage industries; and the countryside in Counties Down and Armagh and parts of Antrim was dotted with small-holdings where the family grew flax alongside oats and potatoes. The flax was retted and dried; the fibre separated from the woody material (the "shous") by hand-flaying and spun into yarn on a foot-operated spinning-wheel; and the yarn woven into pieces of grey or brownish cloth on a handloom that usually occupied one of the rooms of the family's meagre accommodation. Once a week the weaver took his output of brown linen to the nearest market and attempted to bargain with the powerful buyers who were either bleachers or middlemen. Next the rough cloth found its way to one of the many bleaching greens that were strung out along the banks of the Upper Bann, the Lagan, and the smaller rivers flowing into Belfast. Here it was gradually transformed into white linen by the action of water and sunlight aided increasingly by chemicals. And the finished article was then either exported through the port of Belfast to Great

Britain, to America, to the Caribbean and other distant markets or (and in 1783 this was much more likely) despatched by pack horse or by horse-drawn cart to Dublin where its sale to English and foreign buyers comprised a significant part of the commercial activity of the metropolis.

But the linen trade also had enormous significance for the commercial activity of Belfast. To begin with, there was the importation and distribution of flaxseed from America and Holland; and there were fortunes to be made too by trading in the chemicals that were increasingly used in the bleaching process. So the imports of Belfast in 1783 included wood-ash (crude potash) from Dantzig and from the Mediterranean area; barilla (another crude alkali) from Alicante; sulphur from Italy for transformation to sulphuric acid in the "vitriol manufactory" of Waddell Cunningham and Thomas Greg at Lisburn; and "best powder blue" from Rotterdam and other European ports. With the exception of the sulphur which was probably imported direct by Cunningham and Greg, those materials passed through the warehouses of the Belfast merchants, who used the columns of the News Letter to advise the bleachers of what was available. Indications of price were always of a general nature; and there was obviously room for bargaining in the transactions that subsequently took place. Occasionally the goods were sold by public auction, notice again being duly given in the News Letter.

One of the venues for the sale of unbleached linen by the weavers of North Down and South Antrim was the Brown Linen Hall in Donegall Street. Provided by Lord Donegall some ten years previously, the mart of 1783 was the third that had existed in the town, its immediate predecessor having stood for about twenty years on the site occupied later by the Parish Church of St Anne's and now by Belfast Cathedral. Here on several days a week the weavers, having walked for miles with their webs of brown or greyish cloth, would congregate to bargain with the powerful bleachers or "linen drapers"; and when the deals were struck the simple country folk were paid in cash and began their journeys home, but probably not before spending part of their hard-earned rewards in one of the many taverns of the town. Dr E R R Green in his commercial history of the Lagan Valley between 1800 and 1850 records that in the neighbouring brown-linen market in Lisburn, a typical day in winter would have seen upwards of five-hundred-and-fifty weavers negotiating with some fifty buyers; and the same author in his little book dealing specifically with "Irish Linen Halls" indicates that the less frequent markets in some of the more remote country areas provided the excuse for a raucous social occasion on the previous evening. Of such events in Randalstown, for example, it was recorded that the visiting drapers *"dance in their boots and spurs to the detriment of the lady's aprons, but as the destruction of the aprons increases the demand for fine linen, the patriotic ladies do not complain"*!

The year 1783 saw a significant development in another facet of the linen industry in Belfast. This was the building of the White Linen Hall on the site occupied since the beginning of the present century by the City Hall; and the purpose was to provide a local venue for the sale of bleached linen, in replacement of the long-standing practice of sending it off laboriously to factors in Dublin. A building fund was launched in mid-

November 1782; and by the end of that year more than £17,000 (over a million in today's money) had been promised. The subscribers included many who would join the Chamber of Commerce in the course of the following twelve months; and the list was topped by the Stewart brothers of Ballydrain and Wilmont who each contributed £300. This magnificent response enabled the work to begin early in 1783, following the appointment of a project committee at a meeting in the Town Hall on 20 December 1782. Seven of the thirteen members of that committee would become foundation members of the Chamber some months later, including the omnipresent Waddell Cunningham. Robert Thomson of Jennymount, who managed a sugar refinery in Rosemary Lane, was given the job of recruiting the tradesmen and purchasing the building materials; and soon it was time to lay the foundation stone. The ceremony, one of the most remarkable ever seen in Belfast, took place on 28 April 1783, when the stone was laid by John Brown of Peter's Hill, one of the richest of the linen drapers.

The odd feature of the proceedings that day was that John Brown occupied the centre of the stage not as a member of the Corporation (he became one later) or as High Sheriff of County Antrim (an office that he held that year) but as Worshipful Master of a famous masonic lodge in the town. The Sovereign, George Black, and the burgesses were also present; but it was the masonic lodge in full regalia that commanded the attention of the spectators. It was the lodge too that provided an interesting object to be built into the foundations; namely a hermetically-sealed glass tube containing a scroll referring to Volunteer influence on political events. Whoever found the scroll (it was recovered in 1896 when the White Linen Hall was being demolished to make way for the City Hall) would be reminded that: *". . . by the firmness and unanimity of the Irish Volunteers, this Kingdom (long oppressed) emerged from a state of slavery, and was fully and completely emancipated."* And to cap these extravagant words the lodge confirmed its commitment to the project by presenting *"one hundred guineas to the managers of this building, and five guineas to the workmen as an encouragement to them to push it forward with alacrity"*! But it was all too much for one old "worshipful brother" by the name of Joseph Clotworthy, for as the ceremony approached its climax he keeled over and died, giving rise to a masonic funeral in the town two days later.

The provision trade was another important element in the commercial activity of Belfast in 1783. The commodities exported included butter (about seven-hundred tons a year), salted beef (around thirteen thousand barrels a year), salted pork (about ten thousand barrels a year), salted herrings from Donegal, and salmon from the River Bann. The destination of nearly all the butter, about 85% of the pork, and about 80% of the beef was Great Britain; but there was also significant trade with the West Indies, particularly Antigua, and other distant customers. The salted herrings went mostly to the West Indies as food for the slaves in the sugar plantations. In return for the provisions, the vessels that ventured to the Caribbean came back to Belfast months later laden with rum and crude sugar as raw material for the little refineries in Rosemary Lane and Waring Street. But that was not the only source of intoxicating liquors: there was brandy and wine from France, gin from Holland, fortified wine from Madeira, port from Portugal, and sherry from Spain. Indeed from an examination of the import statistics dug out by Dr Norman Gamble for his PhD thesis to Trinity College Dublin (which became available for public inspection in January 1983) it would seem that Belfast and the area served by its merchants consumed in 1783 about eighty-thousand gallons of rum, sixty-thousand gallons of brandy, and fifteen-thousand gallons of gin, on top of locally-produced and imported ales and whiskies. And along with the spirits and wines from France and from the Iberian Peninsula came grapes and raisins, prunes and figs, oranges and lemons.

Salt too was an important import, for it was needed not only as a domestic condiment but also and in much greater quantity as a preservative for provisions that were to be exported or stored. And Dr Gamble's graphs indicate that Belfast in 1783 imported about sixty-thousand bushels (probably about three-thousand tons) of salt both from Cheshire and from the Iberian Peninsula; but part of that may have been rock salt as a raw material for the salt-extraction process that was then being carried on at the seaward end of Waring Street by James Munfoad, later to become famous as Secretary and Treasurer for over thirty years both of the Linen Hall Library and of one of the Rosemary Street churches. Munfoad's salt extraction process would be commended today by the Department of Economic Development; for, unbelievably, it was based on the use of waste-heat from a nearby lime-kiln.

But the importation and extraction of salt were by no means the only business adjuncts of the provisions trade. Around the centre of the town there were several markets where agricultural commodities were bought from producers for re-sale or further preparation. For example in the Smithfield area there was a livestock market where cattle and pigs from the surrounding countryside or from the backyard hovels of the town were sold to the butchers of Hercules Street, the forerunner of Royal Avenue. This narrow thoroughfare, named after Hercules Langford of Crumlin, was a hive of odoriferous activity; for within a stretch of about five-hundred yards it had three slaughter-houses, thirty-three butcher's shops, two soap and candle boilers, a tan-yard, and a bird shop, as well as four taverns, three basket-makers, a clog factory, a nail foundry, and several cork cutters! The tan-yard and the soap and candle-makers were using hides and surplus fat from the slaughtered cattle; and their activities and similar operations elsewhere in the town also required the importation of large quantities of bark as a natural tanning agent together with supplementary quantities of tallow from sources as distant as St Petersburg (now Leningrad). According to the News Letter of 14 November 1783 the untreated hides cost from twenty-eight to thirty-five shillings a hundredweight; and the tallow about five-shillings "per foot", the explanation of the unit not being immediately clear!

Likewise there was a butter market in one of the lanes off High Street, where farmhouse butter (valued at fifty-seven shillings a hundredweight in 1783) was assembled and weighed in its wooden firkins prior to despatch; and many an argument took place about the accuracy of the weighing, the quality of the butter, and the tightness of the staves in the firkins (the concern was that the firkins should "hold pickle", that is not allow the preserving brine to leak out). So the cattle industry of 1783 was exporting its product as prepared beef and utilising the by-products locally, objectives that have only in recent years been re-attained in the cattle industry of the 20th Century; and the dairy industry of 1783 was exporting butter to England and to the West Indies and was building up a reputation for quality and fair-dealing in both markets, just as the dairy industry of 1983 is trying to do today.

In the same way as the food-processing industry of 1983 gives rise to employment in the manufacture of packaging materials, so the provisions trade of 1783 gave employment in Belfast to over a hundred-and-sixty coopers, for almost everything was stored and moved in wooden barrels or firkins. Often the wood for the shaped staves or the finished staves themselves were imported from Scandinavia or from the West Indies. In addition there was a large requirement for metal hoops and nails, which were made locally from iron imported from the Baltic region. In 1783 such activities together with the requirements of Stewart Hadskis' foundry in Hill Street gave rise to total imports of iron which Dr Gamble puts at about three-hundred tons. Hadskis, who had been operating in Hill Street from about 1760, was most enterprising in the jobs that he would tackle; and in the News Letter of 7 November 1783 he was advertising the availability of vats of up to 950-gallon capacity for bleachers, brewers, and candle-makers together with *"Pots, Griddles, Smoothing-irons, and every other article in the Cast Iron Way"*. Likewise Benjamin Edwards, who had been managing a glassworks near Coalisland until 1776, now had his own ambitious works at the County Down end of the Long Bridge, soon to be challenged commercially by a second manufacturer, John Smylie & Co.

These and other industrial activities together with domestic heating gave rise to the importation of large quantities of coal from England, supplemented from 1783 onwards by supplies from Scotland. In that year total coal imports through the port of Belfast were about fifteen-thousand tons; and the annual quantity would more than double in the course of the succeeding ten years. Substantial imports of coal also took place through Newry, which at that time was a large and bustling port comparable to Belfast. The price of coal in Belfast in November 1783 was fifteen shillings a ton.

Though linen manufacture based on home spinning and weaving still dominated the textile industry of Belfast in 1783, the introduction of factory-based cotton-spinning was well underway. The process had been introduced on a small-scale as "work therapy" for the younger inmates of the Poorhouse four or five years earlier; and by 1783 preparations were being made for that operation to be expanded, co-incident with its transfer to a disused sugar-house in Rosemary Lane. In April Nicholas Grimshaw, a Lancastrian who had advised on the Poorhouse project and was later described as *"the father of cotton manufacture in this country"*, joined with Nathaniel Wilson in a major cotton-spinning factory at Whitehouse; and several other entrepreneurs were beginning to experiment with mixed cotton/linen yarns. Meanwhile domestic weaving of cotton yarns was beginning to develop in the urban environment, in the tiny homes of Sandy Row and in the entries off North Street and Smithfield. And since these activities were based on raw material from the West Indies and the American mainland, "cotton wool" soon featured prominently in the import traffic of the port. So too did Russian hemp, which was the main raw material for one of the town's oldest industries, the manufacture of canvas and cordage for its intrepid mariners. But the brigs in which they ventured across the oceans of the world were generally not constructed in Belfast at that time, for it would be another nine years before William Ritchie, the father of shipbuilding in the North of Ireland, would arrive from Ayrshire with a few craftsmen and begin work on the County Antrim side of the Lagan in what is now the Corporation Street area.

In contrast with the relatively late arrival of shipbuilding, paper manufacture in Belfast began early. It was in the hands of the Joy family who had a picturesque paper-mill in the Cromac area, coinciding roughly with the Gasworks end of Ormeau Avenue today. Opened in 1767, the mill was powered by water from a large dam on the Blackstaff or Owenvarra River as it flowed towards its junction with the Lagan. A pleasant country walk known as "The Mall" led from the centre of the town to the mill dam, through the site on which the White Linen Hall would shortly be built; and in December 1783 someone had occasion to give notice in the News Letter that the disfigurement of this public amenity would not be tolerated:

"As the practice of drying cloaths on each side of the mall is (for many reasons) very disagreeable to the Ladies and Gentlemen who frequent that walk, the public are desired to take notice that if such custom is persisted in, the hedges will be positively sprinkled with vitriol which will effectively distroy any cloaths spread upon them".

One wonders what would have happened to the hedges! Further south lay Cromac Wood which was segmented by three intersecting driveways or "passes", one of which was approximately on the line now followed by Donegall Pass. The raw material for the coarse type of paper made in the mill was linen rags collected from all over the North of Ireland, an early example of waste utilisation. The output of the mill was neither suitable in quality nor sufficient in quantity to meet more than a fraction of the growing paper requirements of the region. The local product was therefore used for newsprint and wrapping paper; and there were substantial imports of other types from England and from Scandinavia.

The remaining industries of the town included shoemaking, flour milling and baking, brewing, tobacco processing, watchmaking, and the manufacture of brick, all aimed at supplying requirements of the local population. The shoemaking was based on supplies of leather from the many local tanneries; and there were several large firms in the trade. The only flour mill operating close to the town in 1783 was situated on the River Farset in the Falls area, reflected to this day in the name Millfield. The ubiquitous Waddell Cunningham was one of the proprietors; and part of the output was used in an associated bakery. Flour was also brought into the town from Comber and Crumlin; and there would shortly be a new flour mill in Ballymacarrett. Grain for flour manufacture was frequently imported from America; and wheat was fetching eleven shillings a hundredweight in the Belfast market in November 1783. The brewing industry was more fragmented in that the town was served not only by three specialist breweries each with its own maltings but also by a number of independent maltsters who supplied raw materials to the inns to enable them to brew their own ales. The tobacco industry was based on American leaf, though for legal reasons it had to be either imported via a port in Great Britain or smuggled. In Belfast it was processed by a number of small firms into snuff, twist, and other smoking products. The town had several watchmakers, the best known being Thomas McCabe, whose name will come up again in the present work. The manufacture of fired bricks from suitable clays had been well developed for several decades; and there were a number of brickworks around the town. When the Charitable Society's building was being erected twelve years previously, several brickmakers had been engaged to make up to half-a-million bricks on the site, using raw materials from a nearby clay-pit. In 1783 as the town moved into a phase of rapid development, the permanent brickworks were busy; and there was a strong demand for lime, sand, and the full range of timbers imported from Scandinavia, Russia, and North America.

Most of the industrial and trading activities of the town involved the merchant class who would form the backbone of the Chamber of Commerce. They were entrepreneurs to a man, prepared to engage in any kind of import or export business or new manufacture that seemed to offer opportunities for profit. In the local market they acted both as wholesalers and as retailers; but there was also a well-developed and separate retailing class concentrated in the central streets of the town. There were to be found the grocers, butchers, fruiterers, bakers, spirit merchants, tobacconists, drapers, milliners, hosiers, shoemakers, jewellers, ironmongers, and chandlers; and none was more important than the chandler, for candles were almost the only source of light for the long dark evenings, as Dr William Drennan dramatically recorded for posterity in a letter written to his mother in September 1783. He had been awakened by a burst of heat on the top of his head, which turned out to be due to a fire in his night-cap, the tassle having swung into the candle as he unbuckled his shoe! By day Dr Drennan would have worn a tricorn hat, a powdered periwig, a lace cravat, a colourful waistcoat, a long coat probably trimmed with braid, tight trousers, hose stockings to the knee, and buckled black shoes. The ladies of the period wore colourful and bouffant long dresses with elaborate feathery hats perched on top of hair held high by a mixture of flour, grease, and the skill of the hairdresser, who was another important member of the high-street community. Further glimpses of the fashion scene are provided by Brigid Wilson's advertisements in the News Letter. Widow of Robert Wilson, she was primarily a retailer of carpets, beddings, and other fabrics, but she also catered for the fashion-conscious ladies of the town. So in December 1783 she was making it known that she had *"lately laid in a great variety of goods suitable to the season, chiefly consisting of gown and cloak sattins, Tabbinets and Poplins of the most fashionable colours, Calicoes, Muslins, Modes, Laces etc"*.

Behind the wholesale and retail trade of the town there was as yet relatively little development of the supporting services which later generations have regarded as indispensable. A bank had been established in Belfast over thirty years earlier by Daniel Mussenden, James Adair, and Thomas Bateson; but it had operated only for six years. Since that time all transactions whether in home or in overseas trade, in wholesale or in retail, had had to be conducted either in cash or by barter. Provision for the establishment of the Bank of Ireland had been made in February 1782 by an act of the Irish Parliament; but it would be June 1783 before the bank opened its doors in Dublin and another forty years before it established a branch in Belfast. There were plans to open a Discount Office in association with the new White Linen Hall; but it would be May 1785 before that would be fully operational and it was intended only to facilitate the linen trade. Likewise the concept of insurance against risks of various kinds was only just beginning to be accepted. In 1782 a group of sugar refiners and bakers in London had formed the New Fire Office, which would become the Phoenix Assurance Company; but it would be twenty-eight years before the company appointed an agent in Belfast. Meanwhile in 1783 the Dublin Insurance Company already had no less than three agents in the town; and businessmen were beginning to use their services and those of the General Insurance Company, services that were to be put to the test two years later when there was a serious fire at the sugar refinery in Waring Street. But it would be six years after that before the first locally-based insurance company, involving several prominent members of the Chamber of Commerce, would begin operations in the town. On the other hand, personal life insurance societies had been in existence in Belfast and other centres in the North of Ireland from the early 1770s. Thus in 1783 some elements of the commercial infrastructure were in place, but many remained to be developed under the stimulus of the upsurge in trade and industry that began at that time.

Communications too were poised for much-needed development. The busy commercial life of Belfast was to a considerable extent dependent upon the transmission of information between sellers and buyers; and market intelligence was as important then as it is today, though it would not have been recognised by that name. For many years the News Letter, established in 1737 by old Francis Joy (and as such, the oldest surviving English-language newspaper in Europe and probably in the world), had fulfilled several important roles within the commercial scene. Through its twice-weekly issues, each bearing the publication dates both of the previous issue and of the current one, it provided not only a comprehensive background on world events and parliamentary proceedings, but also a fairly complete picture of shipping movements into and out of the port of Belfast. Furthermore it was almost the only advertising medium of the day; and its columns abounded with commercial announcements both from the wholesale merchants and from retailers. The paper was distributed not only in Belfast but also over most of the area that now comprises Northern Ireland, as well as into a number of counties that are now part of the Irish Republic; and by 1794 the circulation was said to be over three-thousand-two-hundred. Outside Belfast the paper was distributed by men or boys travelling on horseback; and in October 1783, persons interested in carrying it to Donaghadee, Ballywalter, and Portaferry (a fair step on horseback!) were invited to apply to H & R Joy, the sons of Francis who had taken over on his early retirement to Randalstown. The year 1783 also saw the launch of a second newspaper in the town, the Belfast Mercury or Freeman's Chronicle printed by John Tisdall & Co in an office near the Exchange. The Mercury, which may have been edited behind the scenes by the colourful Amyas Griffith (of whom more later), was a strong advocate of the Volunteer influence on Irish politics; but it ceased publication after about three years. The Newsroom of the Exchange, where the merchants congregated daily to read notices and swop news and views, also played an important part in the communication process.

Unfortunately communication by letter was not easy in the Belfast of 1783. The bill for the establishment of the Irish Post Office became law that year; and the Council of the Chamber would soon be addressing itself frequently to the problem of improving postal communications now that the Irish Parliament had power in the matter. A rudimentary postal service had existed from the beginning of the century or earlier; but it was based on post-messengers travelling irregularly and hazardously on horseback between the major towns such as Belfast, Dublin, Newry, and Carrickfergus. Furthermore those who were expecting letters had to go along to the local customs officer to collect them. During this period postal communications with Great Britain and further afield were dependent on a small open boat that crossed when it could from Donaghadee to Portpatrick in Scotland. Attempts had been made in the middle of the century to establish regular coach services between Belfast and Dublin; and the state of the roads and the hazards of the journey were such that a round trip with only one day for business in Dublin took at least a week. By 1783 there was a much-improved regular service between Newry and Dublin; but the connection to Belfast would until two years later be dependent on the traveller's being able to hire a post-chaise, at very great cost. Despite intense pressure from the Chamber and others there would not be a daily mail coach between Belfast and Dublin till 1790. In these circumstances the chief modes of locomotion in 1783 were on foot, on horseback (including pillion for the ladies), by hired post-chaise or individually-owned carriage, by hackney cars in the immediate environs of the town, and by sedan chair within the town.

For goods traffic within Ireland the options available in 1783 were coastal vessels, the inland waterways, horse-drawn wagons or carts, and the very popular pack-horse. The string of little ports on the eastern seaboard between Cork in the south and Londonderry in the north were connected by small sailing ships specialising in this trade; and there were also occasional sailings from Belfast to ports in the West of Ireland. For inland traffic as far as Sprucefield, just beyond Lisburn, the so-called "Lagan Navigation" could be used. This consisted of the navigable parts of the Lagan and a series of "collateral cuts" by-passing the sections where navigation would have been hazardous or impossible. Stimulated by the success of the canal from Newry to the River Bann opened in 1742, the waterway from Belfast to Lisburn had been constructed over a period of seven years from 1756, and had been opened with great jollification almost exactly twenty years before the formation of the Chamber, on 8 September 1763. Fortified by food of every description eased down by twelve different wines and with a band on board playing *"popular airs"*, the great and the good of Belfast had on that day travelled along the new navigation on a fifty-ton lighter, the LORD HERTFORD; and on arrival in Lisburn the chief guest had according to the report in the News Letter of the following day *"instructed his agent to supply barrels of ale for those of the townspeople who wanted to drink his health"*. Two years later the navigation had been extended to Sprucefield; but a further fourteen years were to elapse before it was possible, with the aid of a large grant from Lord Donegall, to contemplate pushing the canal through from Sprucefield to Lough Neagh to open up the Tyrone coalfields and facilitate inland trade generally. A year before the Chamber was formed a new engineer from Lancashire, Richard Owen, had been appointed to undertake this great project; and just as the Chamber got underway he was advertising in the News Letter for workmen to help him with the task. Around Belfast and on the difficult road to Dublin, Ramadge's carts were also much used at this time for the movement of goods; and there was the long tradition of sending finished linen to the Dublin market by pack-horse, traffic that would shortly dwindle as selling operations were transferred to the White Linen Hall then being built in Belfast.

But if the people of Belfast in 1783 were concerned about their means of communication with the rest of Ireland and with the outside world, they had at least equal reason to be concerned about the need for improvement of living conditions and the general environment of the town. It was only three years previously that a Scottish visitor had written of his surprise, on a Sunday morning, at *"beholding piles of dunghills made up through the middle of the whole town from one end to the other"*, hopefully residues from the streetmarkets of the previous Friday; and it was by no means unknown for pigs from the backyard styes to be found roaming the streets. The Sovereign did his best to improve things by a string of edicts about cleaning up the pavements, about trading in the properly appointed place, about desisting from throwing rubbish into the watercourses, and so on; but he was very short of enforcement staff, and progress was slow. Fifteen years previously the Sovereign of the day had himself become embroiled in the street scene by shooting a couple of roaming pigs and offering thirteen pence apiece to any of his fellow townsmen who did likewise!

And while the merchants built their fine new houses and the retailers lived in reasonable comfort over their shops, a high proportion of the population eked out a miserable existence in dank and overcrowded hovels that were a breeding ground for disease, a situation exacerbated by shortages of food and clean water. The Charitable Society was active in trying to improve the water supply, many of the old wooden pipes laid down over the previous hundred years having become leaky and contaminated; and water carts had begun to re-appear on the streets. Street-lighting was also woefully inadequate. An attempt had been made in the middle 1760s to institute a reasonable lighting system; but by 1783 many of the lamps could no longer be used. Within two years the Sovereign would therefore be making an order requiring householders to place lighted candles in their front windows when the fire alarm was raised at night, so that the firemen could see to get their rudimentary equipment to the scene of the fire. Then as now there was also trouble with vehicles parked in the wrong places. Father James O'Laverty in his wonderfully detailed "Historical Account of the Diocese of Down and Connor" tells of the "car-men" of the day leaving their "cars" (wagons, carts, coaches) parked in public places at night *"whereby people fall over them, breaking their legs or arms"*; and he records that the "traffic wardens" of the day had the back-up of a mandatory fine of ten shillings per offence!

Education was in short supply, save in the hard school of experience. From around the middle of the previous century, the Donegall family had made a number of attempts to maintain a community Latin school; and several of the clerics of the town gave private tuition or ran small classes in their homes. For the sons and daughters of the rich there was also the option of attending David Manson's famous school in Donegall Street, an institution that was well in advance of its time in terms of the scope and liberality of the education offered and the emphasis placed on recreation. Manson had come to Belfast from Cairncastle near Larne about 1752; and he had dabbled successfully in small-scale brewing before establishing his school in an entry off High Street between 1755 and 1760. It had proved popular with the rich merchants and professional people of the town; and the pupils in due course included the sons and daughters of the Joys, the McCrackens, the Templetons, and other notable families that would be at the centre of the radical movement at the end of the 18th Century. By 1783 the school had for fifteen years been housed in a new building in Donegall Street, near the Brown Linen Hall; and David Manson had for four years been a freeman of the town, in recognition of his unique contribution to educational development.

But soon there would be another educational development, also in Donegall Street, that would long out-live Manson and his pupils; namely the establishment in 1785 of the Belfast Academy, destined many decades later to have the "Royal" accolade and to become one of the most important grammar schools in the region. Meanwhile for those with money and a mathematical bent there was William Dineen's "Mathematical School-Room" in Skipper's Lane, which in September 1783 extended its activities to provide evening classes in *"Arithmetic, Euclid's Elements of Geometry, Trigonometry, Geography and the Use of the Globe's, Conic Sections, Algebra and Fluxions, together with Book-keeping, Mensuration, Surveying, Guaging, Navigation, Dialling, Gunnery, and Fortification, all in the most correct manner."* But for a high proportion of the children of Belfast in the late 18th Century and through much of the 19th as well, education was limited to what the parents could impart in the tender years; and by the age of ten or eleven the children were at work from dawn to dusk for a shilling or so a week. Obviously advanced education was scarcer still — indeed it was non-existent in Belfast — and young men aspiring to medicine, the church, or the law went to one of the Scottish universities or (less frequently) to Trinity College Dublin, which at that time was already within eight years of its bicentenary.

In contrast with its relative dearth of educational facilities, Belfast in 1783 was not short of churches or of religious fervour and doctrinal difference. The ancient Episcopal tradition, invigorated by the influence of the ruling family and the preponderance of Anglicans amongst the earliest settlers, was represented by the Parish Church of St Anne's in Donegall Street, opened in 1776. The vicar was the Rev William Bristow who had also been the last incumbent of the old parish church in High Street, which early in the next century would be replaced by St George's. Before that, Bristow would have become Sovereign of the town on eleven separate occasions; and his brother, Skeffington Gore Bristow, would have begat James Bristow (1796-1866) who would also become famous, as a director of the Northern Bank for thirty-eight years and President of the Chamber of Commerce on three separate occasions. In 1783 the Rev William Bristow and his parishioners headed by Lord Donegall constituted the Establishment of the town; but from the middle of the century, that

Establishment had been under increasing pressure from the mostly-Presbyterian, mostly-radical, and mostly-merchant middle-class that had been sucked in from the Scottish settlements in Down and Antrim as the industry and commerce of the town burst into life.

To cater for the spiritual needs and differing dogmas of the Presbyterians there were no less than three churches in Rosemary Lane and one in Berry Street. The first of the Rosemary Lane churches was the mother church of Presbyterianism in Belfast, with a history stretching back to 1642 when a detachment of Scottish troops had been stationed in the town and had worshipped in the Presbyterian tradition. The year 1783 was as notable for that congregation as it was for the Chamber of Commerce, for it

First Presbyterian Church in Rosemary Lane, re-built in 1783. The building in the background is the Meeting House of the Second Congregation.

(From an engraving by J Thomson — Ulster Museum.)

was on 1 June 1783 that their beautiful new church replacing an older one on the same site was opened for worship. This was the church which John Wesley six years later described as *"the completest place of worship I have ever seen"*; and it was the church which still stands proudly in Rosemary Street today, with its exterior heavily altered but with much of its elliptical interior essentially the same as when it was opened in 1783. Seventy-six years earlier the First Congregation had divided amicably, under pressure of increasing numbers; and its off-spring, the Second Congregation, had built a new church cheek by jowl with the original (years later it would have Waddell Cunningham and Thomas Greg as two of its three trustees). Both of these congregations under the leadership of their ministers, the Rev James Crombie of First (who became Dr Crombie in September 1783 and the first principal of the Academy two years later) and the Rev James Bryson of Second (who was prominent in the Volunteers), had taken up the "non-subscription" or "New Light" position in the first of the series of doctrinal controversies that beset Presbyterianism in the 18th and 19th Centuries; that is they opposed compulsory subscription to the Westminster Confession of Faith. This had led to the establishment of the Third Congregation as a breakaway, in the "Old Light" or subscription tradition; and to the opening of a third church (the "New Erection") in Rosemary Lane in 1722. Sixty-one years later the effective minister of that church was a fiercely-radical young Dubliner by the name of Sinclare Kelburn; and his congregation included the McCrackens, the Neilsons, and the Simms brothers, families that would all have representation in the Chamber and become deeply immersed in the republican movement before the end of the century. Worship there within the mainstream of Presbyterianism would continue till 1941 when the old church would be destroyed in a German air-raid; and the congregation would after almost two hundred years in the centre of the town move out to the North Circular Road to merge with Ekenhead in the new congregation of Rosemary. Meanwhile the other two congregations in Rosemary Lane would become Unitarian, with First remaining in its beautiful church of 1783 and Second moving to Elmwood Avenue at the end of the 19th Century to become All Souls. And by that time the town's fourth Presbyterian congregation of 1783, the Seceders in Berry Street, would also have moved first to Linenhall Street (in 1839) and later to the Crescent (in 1887). They too were a manifestation of differences within Presbyterianism, the Seceders having refused to abide by an Act of 1712 that had denied congregations the right to choose their own ministers. And the Seceders in turn had split into Burghers and Anti-Burghers on the basis of acceptance or rejection of the propriety of the oath administered to the burgesses in several of the borough towns in Scotland. Thus in the words of Alex Blair in his history of First Kilraughts there was in the Presbyterianism of those days *"a tendency to make things of no vital importance matters of principle and conscience"*.

Unlike the Presbyterians the Catholics of Belfast in 1783 were few in number but united in doctrine. They did not as yet have a church in the town; and occasional masses were celebrated in the open air at Friar's Bush on the Strand Mills Road or in a private home in the Castle Street area or in an old shed in Mill Street. For the particularly pious there was also the option of walking or riding out to Hannahstown or Derriaghy where there were long-established Catholic churches. But soon there would be an easier way to exercise their faith; for in the previous year the leaders of the Catholic community in the town had secured a suitable site for a church in Crooked (now Chapel) Lane, and building was already underway. On 30 May 1784 the new place of worship, known as St Mary's, would be opened; and the ceremony would be the occasion for one of the most remarkable displays of religious tolerance ever seen in Belfast. Under the command of Captain Waddell Cunningham the Belfast companies of the Volunteers, having opened their ranks to Catholics just a few days previously, would march to the new chapel in full regalia; and provide a guard of honour for the appreciative parish priest, Father Hugh O'Donnell from the Glens. And in company with many other members of the Protestant community the Volunteers would also attend the opening mass and contribute handsomely to the building fund. Indeed it would emerge that almost half of the total cost of that first Catholic church in Belfast had been provided by the Protestants of the town; and Father O'Donnell *"excited by the attendance of so respectable a Protestant audience on Sunday last"* would write appreciatively in the newspapers of *"that mark of regard that would never be effaced."*

Religious tolerance was apparent too in the relationships between the various denominations of Protestantism, which included a few Baptists, a very few Quakers, and a growing number of Methodists. John Wesley, the founder of Methodism, had been a frequent visitor to Belfast from the mid-1750s; and it was usual for him to be granted the use of the Episcopal and Presbyterian churches in the town when the Market House was unavailable or conditions were unsuitable for preaching outdoors at the Linen Hall. His journal includes many fascinating references to those missionary visits to Belfast (and Lisburn), which continued until a year or two before his death in 1791 at the age of eighty-eight; but there is none more poignant than the entry made after a visitation in 1785: *"I often wonder that among so civil a people we can do but little good"*. Wesley's cynicism then or in his oft-repeated observation that *"they care for none of these things"* was not fully justified; for by the end of his life, his preaching in Belfast had borne fruit and there would be a Methodist church in the town and a Methodist flame alighted in the community that would burn undiminished to the present time. But in another sense his cry of 1785 could be the cry of a British politician in Northern Ireland in the 1970s or the 1980s: *"I often wonder that among so civil a people we can do but little good"*. But there is hope in the story too, for John Wesley in the end did get his converts and did establish institutions that lasted!

The political issues of 1783 also have a familiar ring: parliamentary reform, equality of opportunity for the Catholic community, devolution of greater powers to a "local assembly" (the Irish Parliament in Dublin), and the improvement of industry and commerce by the removal of artificial barriers to trade. As outlined in the opening chapter of the present work the previous three years had seen substantial progress on devolution and free trade, under the influence of the Volunteer movement; and the emphasis was now switching to electoral reform and Catholic Emancipation. In the electoral system of the day the franchise was limited to the burgesses or freemen, who comprised only a tiny proportion of the population; and the selection of candidates was vested in the patronage of the nobility. Flushed with their success on legislative independence and the removal of trade barriers, the Volunteers in 1783 were therefore campaigning vigorously for more democracy and greater accountability in the representation of the people; and the summer and autumn of that year were filled with meetings, petitions, conventions, and reviews aimed in the long-term at general reform and in the short-term at the election of independent candidates to the Irish Parliament for a new session beginning in October.

From the newspapers of the period it is clear that many of the merchants who in May had decided to form the Chamber of Commerce were deeply involved also in the political events of that busy summer; and there can be little doubt that that was the reason that the Chamber did not get off the ground as quickly as had been intended. For example at least ten of the foundation members headed by Waddell Cunningham were signatories to an important public notice published in the News Letter on 15 July, summoning the inhabitants of the town to a meeting in the Market House *"to determine whether you will at the approaching election vote for or support any candidate who will not make, subscribe, and publish a Declaration that he will in all cases vote and act in Parliament agreeable to the instruction he may, from time to time, receive from his constituents"*. And the influence of the Belfast merchants was again apparent in the second of the great Volunteer conventions held in Dungannon, on 8 September 1783, when it was resolved: *"That freedom is the indefeasible birthright of Irish men and Britons; derived from the author of their being; and of which, no power on earth, much less a delegated power, hath a right to deprive them"*; and *"That the present imperfect representation and the long duration of parliaments are unconstitutional and intolerable grievances"*.

But by now the Establishment was fighting back more effectively; and independent candidates made little headway in the elections that autumn. Nor did a great National Convention of the Volunteers in Dublin in November succeed in pressurising the Irish Parliament in the direction either of Parliamentary Reform or of Catholic Emancipation. Thus by the end of 1783, when Waddell Cunningham himself was chosen to contest an election in Carrickfergus in the following year, the power of the Volunteers was beginning to fade, their military role having also become less important with the ending of the American War and the return of large numbers of regular troops to garrison duties in Ireland.

While all the high-minded political debate rumbled on in the Volunteer conventions, in the town meetings, and in the drawing rooms of the middle and upper classes, the more humble people of the town had other problems on their minds. Food was in short supply because of poor harvests, and grain was being imported for charitable distribution. Though the price of bread was carefully controlled by the Sovereign, it took the whole of a labourer's daily wage — about sixpence in old money — to buy a two-pound white loaf or a three-pound wheaten. Hours of work were long; and environmental conditions in industry were often unpleasant and dangerous. Just how dangerous was well illustrated by a news report of 23 September 1783 about a boy of fourteen being pulled into the machinery of the flour mill in the Falls area and crushed to death. The report concluded coldly: *"This accident it is to be hoped will prevent future misfortunes of a similar kind, by showing the necessity of caution in such places."* But nowhere was there the slightest suggestion that the proprietor of the mill had any responsibility in the matter.

Though most people were poor and undernourished, insobriety was prevalent and immorality abounded, especially in and around a group of taverns near the Charitable Society's building, in what is now the North Queen Street area. Separations and elopements were quite common; and aggrieved husbands frequently revealed all in the columns of the News Letter, warning everyone that they were no longer responsible for the debts of their estranged wives. Some of those who eloped no doubt joined the constant stream of emigrants to North America, which promised much for those who survived the appalling conditions that prevailed on many of the hundred or more emigrant ships that left Belfast and Newry each year to face the Atlantic gales. Both for the emigrants aboard ship and for those who stayed at home in the crowded quarters of the labouring classes, there was a constant risk of catching the latest fever; and life expectancy was low. Robberies both on the highway and from the homes of the well-to-do occurred frequently, despite the fact that the perpetrators could be hanged. The News Letter of 15 August 1783 carried a report of the public hanging of three robbers in Dublin a few days previously, the youngest being a boy of fourteen. And there was barbarism too in the most popular amusements of the day — cock-fighting and bull-baiting.

But interest in cock-fighting was not confined to the poorer classes. On the contrary, it was also a significant past-time of the rich, with substantial sums being wagered on the results. Meanwhile the ladies engaged in what the prolific letter-writer Mrs McTier described as *"an eternal round of cards"*. In the evenings the cards could continue in mixed company; and Mrs McTier's brother, Dr William Drennan, wrote of parties in his home in Newry for *"whist, punch, and oysters"*. The theatre too was well established; and Mrs Sarah Siddons, the most accomplished actress of the day, would soon be enthralling Belfast audiences with her performances, to the point where Waddell Cunningham (in the words of the observant Mrs McTier) *"rubbed his legs and changed his posture"* as a mark of appreciation! There were also occasional musical performances in the Market House and in the Assembly Room at the Exchange; and personal involvement in music was one of the principal forms of recreation. Music had a place too in the activities of the Volunteers, for many companies had their own bands to head their parades and stir the onlookers. But the Volunteers were equally well known for their gargantuan dinners in the Donegall Arms and their elegant dances in the Assembly Room and in the boardroom of the Charitable Society. And if the subsequent indisposition lasted for more than a day or two, it was off to the country for "the cure" — a pint or two of goat's whey at Dundrum or Magilligan!

Such then was the political, commercial, and social environment into which the Belfast Chamber of Commerce was launched in the autumn of 1783. And 1783 really was a remarkable year. It was the year when the influence of the Volunteers peaked and began to decline; it was the year when the building of the White Linen Hall commenced, signalling a new-found spirit of independence in commerce; it was the year in which the Bank of Ireland and the Order of St Patrick were instituted; it was the

Plate VI of the famous Hincks prints, depicting spinning, reeling, and boiling of linen yarn in a domestic setting.
(From an engraving by Wm Hincks 1783 — Linenhall Library.)

year in which the incipient cotton industry began to gather momentum; it was the year in which plans were laid for the building of the Ballycopeland Windmill and the Temple of the Winds at Mountstewart; it was the year when William Hincks produced his remarkable series of original engravings on the various aspects of the linen industry, currently being promoted as prints by the Linenhall Library; and it was the year of Waddell Cunningham, landowner, businessman, politician, part-time soldier, and President-elect of the Belfast Chamber of Commerce — a "captain of change".

Chapter 3

CAPTAIN OF CHANGE: WADDELL CUNNINGHAM

"A man famous in those days as a most patriotic and enterprising citizen." Such were the words used in 1917 by D J Owen, historian of the port of Belfast, in referring to Waddell Cunningham's appointment in 1785 to the port's first controlling body, the Belfast Harbour Corporation, subsequently known as the Ballast Board. And these words were but the echo of those used almost forty years earlier by George Benn in his second history of Belfast when he too referred to Waddell Cunningham as *"this patriotic and enterprising citizen"*. More fundamentally, the words used on Cunningham's mausoleum in Knockbreda Cemetry and in his obituary in the News Letter in December 1797 leave little doubt that he was the most remarkable man of his generation in the North of Ireland in terms of the scope and intensity of his activities — in business, in Volunteering, in politics, in charitable work, and in the church.

But in the local history of the period and its subsequent analysis there are suggestions too that there was a darker side to Cunningham's nature and to his success in accumulating wealth. In her correspondence with her brother Dr William Drennan, the redoubtable Mrs Martha McTier gave a hint of this when she wrote in 1788: *"I would shudder if WC's interest, ambition, and therefore inclination and abilities were combined against me"*. And she was more explicit and more waspish when she wrote later of the allegedly feigned regard of Cunningham's nephews, the younger Batts, for their *"cunning dark-souled Uncle"* as he neared the end of his days and thought about will-making. The cynic may say that Waddell Cunningham's fault was that he was highly successful and accumulated great wealth; and the moralist will point to his alleged involvement in privateering, in smuggling, in land-grabbing, perhaps even in the slave business, and ignore the proven record of his enormous enterprise and sterling service to the community; but the realist will recognise that like many great men he was a complex amalgam of saint and sinner, with the balance tilted quite strongly in the saintly direction.

Waddell Cunningham's ancestors came from Scotland to settle in the Killead district of County Antrim in the middle of the 17th Century. When Cromwell was in power and had a scheme to translate the most prominent Presbyterians from Ulster to Munster, the Cunninghams were on the list to go; but somehow the move was evaded and they remained in the county of their adoption. At the beginning of the next century John Cunningham married a Miss Waddell from Island-derry near Dromore in County

Down; and they raised a large family in a typical Ulster farmhouse in the townland of Ballymacilhoyle, which is also in the parish of Killead, near the shores of Lough Neagh. The family included a daughter Jane who would marry a Robert Douglas and go to live in Belfast; a son Charles who would also move to Belfast, to manage a small sugar refinery in Waring Street; another son Daniel who would ultimately become a sea captain sailing the oceans of the world; and the youngest son, born in 1729, on whom ultimately his sister Jane and his brothers Charles and Daniel would all depend for a living. He was given his mother's family name as a first name; so he became Waddell Cunningham.

Waddell Cunningham (1729-1797). First President of the Belfast Chamber of Commerce (1783-1790).
(From a painting by R Home — Ulster Museum)

As the last son of a large family the young Cunningham had no prospect of a living on the ancestral farm at Ballymacilhoyle. He therefore emigrated to America at an early age and began a commercial career, probably with a company that had trading connections with Belfast. By 1756, at the age of twenty-seven, he owned at least one sailing ship, which was engaged in the logwood trade out of Honduras in Central America; and he was a businessman of sufficient substance to become a partner in a New York trading company with Thomas Greg of Belfast, Hamilton Young, and Robert Ross Waddell who was probably his cousin. It was in 1756 too that the Seven Years War was formally declared; and those who would cast doubts on the business ethics of Waddell Cunningham would suggest that as the war escalated in the Americas and opportunities for privateering against French and Spanish shipping off the coast of Canada and in the Caribbean began to arise, the man from Ballymacilhoyle soon learned how to take his chances. And he certainly took his chances seven years later, at the end of the war, when he acquired a substantial estate in the Caribbean island of Dominica as that territory passed from Spain to Britain under the Treaty of Paris.

But Dominica and its notorious trading port of Monte Cristi were by no means unfamiliar to Cunningham, for he had had an agent there throughout the war and had allegedly engaged in what Dr Norman Gamble in his PhD thesis describes as *"rather dubious trade"*. By the end of the war he had also, by whatever means, become the largest shipowner in the port of New York, a quite remarkable distinction for a man of thirty-four years of age who had started out in life with so few resources. He had also built up an extensive experience in international trade, particularly in the Caribbean; and he had acquired a base in Dominica — his "Belfast Estate" as he called it — which he would retain for the rest of his life. Thus endowed he returned to Belfast in 1765 at the age of thirty-six to begin the second phase of his career, a phase that would take him to the very forefront of the business community in the North of Ireland.

But before applying himself fully to the commercial life of the developing town, the rich young bachelor had some personal business to transact under the watchful eye of the Vicar of Belfast, the Rev William Tisdall. On 9 November 1765, in the old Parish Church in High Street, he married Margaret Hyde, daughter of Samuel Hyde of Hydepark and sister of Mrs Elizabeth Greg, the wife of his long-standing business partner Thomas Greg. The Gregs had been married for seventeen years; and Thomas Greg had been trading through Waddell Cunningham's office in New York for much of that time. It is highly likely, therefore, that it was the Gregs that brought Cunningham into contact with Margaret Hyde; and that it was the prospect of wedding-bells back home that determined the principle and the timing of Cunningham's unusual move from New York to Belfast in 1765.

The marriage took place within months of his return; and it was the second such occasion for the Hydes that year, for their third daughter Hannah had married Captain Robert Batt at the end of July. In that way Cunningham was brought into contact with the family that would provide one of his successors in business leadership a generation later; for Robert and Hannah Batt were to have a son, Narcissus, who in the fullness of time would become almost as famous as the man from Ballymacilhoyle. But all that was in the distant future; and the newly-wed Cunninghams went to live in a large house at the southern end of Hercules Lane, now Royal Avenue. The house, with its business premises at the back and its extensive grounds stretching northwards, occupied the sites now covered by St Mary's Hall, the Reform Club block, and the Northern Ireland head office of Allied Irish Banks, the beautiful old building provided for the Provincial Bank in 1868 by the famous architect W J Barre.

The building that stood on that town-centre site in 1765 was no classic; but it was one of the largest in the town and it was destined to be Waddell Cunningham's home for the rest of his life, save for a period in 1771 when it was being restored after a serious fire. And it was very much a working home, for many of Cunningham's commercial activities were conducted from the site; and the house itself was used extensively for business and political entertaining. But unfortunately the extensive gardens never reverberated with the uninhibited laughter of children at play; for the Cunninghams were not to be blessed with a family and that was destined to give rise to a serious inheritance problem later.

Between the marriage in High Street in 1765 and the occurrence of the inheritance problem on Cunningham's death thirty-two years later lay a bewildering career, bewildering in its diversity, its complexity, and its intensity. Yet it did not begin all that auspiciously, for one of his earliest and most ambitious projects was also one of his least successful: that was the manufacture of sulphuric acid in a factory on the Lagan at Lisburn, where he was in partnership with his brother-in-law Thomas Greg. The provision and equipping of the factory on a three-acre island site between the River Lagan and an adjacent stretch of canal cost about £3,500 (equivalent to around a quarter of a million today). The expertise too was costly; and the transport of bulky raw materials from Italy and of coal from Britain also mitigated against competitiveness and viability. Yet the project typified the business spirit of the age generally and of Cunningham and Greg in particular: the bleachers needed sulphuric acid, it was being imported, it could instead be made in Ulster. It was, wrote Cunningham in an advertisement in the News Letter of 30 June 1772, "a work evidently of national advantage, though those engaged in it have hitherto sustained loss."

But by that time the "vitriol manufactory" as it was called was only a tiny segment of the business activities of Cunningham and his brother-in-law. At the centre of those activities was a highly successful import/export business in which they were again in partnership; and in their premises in Hercules Lane at the back of Cunningham's home they stocked an unbelievable array of goods from many parts of the world. There was rum from Antigua; herrings from Sweden; hemp from St Petersburg; timber from Memel; brandy from France; almonds from Jordan; gin from Holland; and the whole panoply of physical and chemical aids for the bleacher from Dantzig, Spain, and America. And that was only one side of the business; for the ships that brought those goods to Belfast were increasingly owned by Cunningham and Greg themselves, and they would leave a few days later laden with provisions, linen, and bright-eyed Ulster emigrants seeking a better life in America.

As their wealth grew, Waddell Cunningham and Thomas Greg began to look for new areas in which to deploy their capital. In 1769 Cunningham tried to acquire the leasehold of some seven-thousand acres of land in the Coleraine area, which would have given him a handsome return in annual rents; but he was outbid. In the following year, however, both he and Thomas Greg entered into an arrangement with Lord Donegall under which for ready money they each in effect acquired the leasehold of several hundred acres of land in South Antrim over the heads of sitting tenants who were in difficulty in paying their rents. Soon there was talk of evictions; and the small farmers sought to protect their interests by forming militant agrarian societies, the most powerful of which was the "Hearts of Steel". To these societies the appearance on the disputed land of cattle belonging to the Belfast merchants was a provocative act; and their response was to engage in surreptitious attacks on the grazing herds with a view to maiming a few of the animals.

For one such attack on cattle belonging to Thomas Greg, a Templepatrick man was arrested on 21 December 1770 by Waddell Cunningham (probably as an officer of the pre-1778 Volunteers) and taken to Belfast where he was lodged in the main military barracks in the town. Two days later, on a Sunday morning just before Christmas, over a thousand members of the Hearts of Steel from a wide area of South Antrim around Templepatrick marched on Belfast with a motley array of weapons and laid siege to the barracks where the prisoner was detained. As they waited for the official response to their demand for his release, a splinter group went to Waddell Cunningham's home in Hercules Lane, broke in, and began damaging the furniture and fittings. Just as they had been dissuaded from further destruction by a mediator who promised to plead their cause at the barracks, the gates of that establishment were flung open and a group of soldiers dashed out and opened fire on the crowd, killing five almost immediately and seriously injuring many more. In the subsequent melée, Cunningham's house was set on fire and shots were discharged into the home of Thomas Greg; and order was restored only by the release of the prisoner.

A decisive moment in the Hearts of Steel riot in Belfast on Sunday 23 December 1770, as troops emerge from the barracks and open fire. The rioters subsequently burned Waddell Cunningham's home.
(From a drawing by J W Carey — Linenhall Library)

For the damage to his house and personal effects Cunningham was awarded £737:16s:7d by the Irish Parliament in November of the following year; and the incident seems to have had no effect on his acquisition of the leaseholds of land around Belfast, for there are later references to his having the use of land in the Springfield area (where he had a bleaching green) and to his selling substantial tracts of land both in County Antrim and in County Down. For example in 1783 he sold land in the Ballypalady district of County Antrim to two of his tenants on generous terms; and in 1791 he sold three townlands on the eastern side of the Lagan near Belfast to David Ker, who was at that time building up his huge estates in County Down.

Meanwhile Cunningham had been adding steadily to his own business interests. He had become the leading partner in the New Sugar House in Waring Street, where his main associates were John Campbell and the trusted Thomas Greg. Though it was still called "New" this little refinery employing about ten people had been in existence from 1704; and the significance of its name was that there was an even earlier refinery operating in the town, the Old Sugar House in Rosemary Lane established in 1683. The New Sugar House was managed for a time by Waddell Cunningham's brother Charles, who died in 1769; and it is likely that in the years following Waddell's return to Belfast in 1765 the refinery drew at least part of its raw material (muscovado sugar) from his Dominican estate. Cunningham also became a partner in John Smylie & Co, the Ballymacarrett glassmakers, and in John Cranston & Co, who were maltsters and brewers in Barrack Street. In the Cranston establishment his initial holding was £1000, a very substantial sum in those days. Flourmilling too attracted his interest; and in 1779 he took over the tenancy of Lord Donegall's old grinding-mill on the banks of the Farset to the west of the town, in partnership with William Harrison who had been a clerk in the estate office. Later they also became involved in baking; and they continued these operations for the best part of ten years.

During the same period another of Cunningham's major activities was the export of salted herrings from Donegal to the West Indies. In this operation his chief associate was again Thomas Greg; and they were jointly responsible for opening up the Donegal and North Sligo fisheries in the mid-1770s. In the West Indies the herrings were used mainly as cheap food for the slaves working in the sugar-cane plantations. To the same area Cunningham also exported pack horses and mules bred by small farmers around Belfast in response to his newspaper advertisements. Quick to recognise every new business opportunity, he became involved too in the direct importation of American tobacco when a change in the law removed the earlier requirement to import via Great Britain. And he was even prepared to act as an estate agent from time to time; as evinced by his involvement in the letting of a new windmill and other property at Kairny (now Kearney) near Portaferry just as the Chamber of Commerce got underway in October 1783. "She will have two running mill-stones, one for oats, the other for hard grain, in a good wheat country", read the advertisement in the News Letter; and it added predictably: "None but solvent bidders need offer".

Waddell Cunningham himself was always a very solvent bidder; and there can be no doubt about his commercial acumen or his devotion to the accumulation of wealth. It is less easy, however, to be unequivocal about the ethics of every part of his mercantile activity. Reference has already been made to his alleged involvement in privateering in the Caribbean and off the North American coast during the Seven Years War. The evidence on this is sketchy; but there is no doubt that during the next international conflagration, the American War of Independence (1775-1783), he had one of his sailing ships fitted out with twelve light guns which could be used either defensively or offensively. Incongrously the name of the ship was PEACE AND PLENTY; and she was involved in at least one fire-fight with a French vessel. This took place in 1779 and it resulted in the death of five members of Cunningham's crew; but whether the PEACE AND PLENTY was using its guns offensively or defensively at the time remains a matter of doubt. There is doubt too about what really was going on when customs officers in 1785 found a shipload of tobacco belonging to Cunningham and his business associates anchored in Strangford Lough when it was supposed to be on its way to Norway, having earned a "drawback" or export subsidy for diverting away from an over-supplied Ulster market. But the most fascinating doubt of all is about Cunningham's alleged promotion of a scheme to establish a slave-trading company in Belfast along lines said to have been adopted by the merchants of Bristol.

In 1926, some one-hundred-and-forty years after the slave-ship episode reputedly occurred, the story was the subject of sharp exchanges in the columns of the Belfast Telegraph between the two leading amateur historians of the day, S Shannon Millin and Francis J Bigger. Afterwards Millin published a pamphlet entitled "Was Waddell Cunningham, Belfast Merchant, a Slave Ship Projector?", which argued convincingly that the story was a fabrication and that Cunningham was entirely innocent. The core of the indictment of Cunningham was a drawing published in 1896 by another amateur historian, Robert M Young, in his book "Old Belfast". This was captioned: *"Thomas McCabe denouncing Waddell Cunningham's proposed Slave Ship Company in the Old Exchange 1786"*; and the text stated that McCabe (who was a well-known watchmaker and political activist in the town) has been responsible for thwarting a Cunningham-inspired slave-ship scheme by a powerful speech to the merchants in the Exchange culminating in the words: *"May God wither the hand, and consign the name to eternal infamy, of the man who will sign that document"*, the document being the prospectus for the company.

In his very cogent analysis of the story, Shannon Millin contended that it was based solely on a contribution submitted by a relative of Thomas McCabe to Dr R R Madden, historian of the United Irishmen, for his volume of lives published in 1846, ie sixty years after the incident allegedly took place. Millin further pointed out that even in that contribution there was no reference to the reputed involvement of Waddell Cunningham as the chief advocate of the slave-ship scheme; and he deduced that that twist to the story had been introduced by R M Young himself, only at the end of the 19th Century. However Millin appears to have missed the fact that Dr Drennan in a letter to his sister dated 17 May 1806 referred to his having lately received a letter from Thomas McCabe about McCabe's having damned an association planned by Waddell Cunningham for carrying on the slave trade from Belfast, by writing in the proposal book the words: *"May G... eternally damn the soul of the man who subscribes the first guinea!"*. So a substantial element of doubt remains about whether the Belfast merchants did discuss such a venture and whether Cunningham was its chief architect.

But if there are doubts about a few of Cunningham's mercantile ventures, there are no doubts whatsoever about his public services to the town. Within a year or two of his return from New York, he had become a leading member of the Second Presbyterian Congregation in Rosemary Lane, with the result that when Lord Donegall granted a long lease to the church in 1767 he was named as a trustee. He also represented the congregation on the first controlling body of the Belfast Charitable Society after its incorporation in June 1774; and he was present at the inaugural meeting in the Market House a few weeks later. Thus began a long association with the work of the Society reflected in his annual subscription of five guineas, his occasional gifts of food from the provisions department in Hercules Lane, his help with the financing and organisation of special efforts to relieve starvation (as in January 1783), and his bequest of £200 in his will, with another £100 to follow on the death of his wife.

Though he and his wife had no children themselves Cunningham seems also to have taken a close interest in the education and training of young people; and he was closely associated with the Rev Dr Crombie in the establishment of the Academy in Donegall Street in 1785. With fellow merchant Robert Getty he was responsible too for an arrangement in which the Second Congregation trained and clothed a group of children from the Poorhouse to sing in the church choir. And his support for the religious institutions of the town extended beyond his own congregation, for his name occurs in the list of subscribers to the building fund of the First Church in 1783; and it was he who gave the lead to his fellow Presbyterians in helping the Catholics of the town to defray the cost of erecting St Mary's in 1784.

Cunningham became massively involved too in the public life of the community. This began with his answering the call to arms in March 1778 as the country faced the threat of invasion arising from the ramifications of the American War of Independence. Though he was almost fifty years of age at the time, this tireless doyen of the commercial world rapidly became the most active and influential of the Belfast Volunteers, taking over the command of the famous First Company from Captain Stewart Banks, as Banks became Sovereign for the sixth time. In due course this led Cunningham into politics; but first there was soldiering to be done, and he played a leading part in the great training exercises that characterised the early years of the Volunteers. Moreover he was under fire on at least one occasion, when he and his company marched twenty miles into the country with small arms and cannon to assist the Sheriff of County Antrim in executing a writ that was being opposed by force of arms. But by 1780 the political facet of Volunteering was coming to the fore; and Cunningham presided at a great Volunteer convention in Belfast in May that year which petitioned Henry Grattan on Free Trade, legislative independence, and parliamentary reform. Two years later Cunningham was one of the Belfast delegates to the historic Convention of Dungannon; and he was appointed to an inner group charged with progressing the far-reaching resolutions hammered out during that momentous day in February 1782. Thus his place at the centre of Volunteer politics was secured; and his standing as a provincial leader recognised.

It was against that background of great commercial success, of self-less community service, and of almost universal recognition as a gifted leader that Waddell Cunningham in 1783 found himself drafted first as chairman of the project committee of the White Linen Hall and then as foundation President of the Chamber of Commerce. But there were nevertheless doors that were shut to him: the doors that could be opened only by Lord Donegall. He was never to be appointed a burgess of the town, so he could never become Sovereign though he was in many ways admirably suited to the post. And Lord Donegall chose also to ignore a petition from a number of prominent inhabitants requesting that Cunningham be nominated for one of the Belfast seats in a new Irish Parliament which was due to assemble in October 1783. That in turn led Cunningham to put his hat in the ring when a Carrickfergus seat became vacant shortly afterwards; and in the first six weeks of 1784, he was embroiled in a bitter election against an Establishment candidate, which resulted in a clear-cut victory for the Belfast merchant despite all the exertions of the nobility on behalf of his opponent (who was a son of the Lord Chancellor). *"The Friends of Liberty are fully gratified in the Success of the man of their choice"*, wrote the Dublin Evening Post; and the man of their choice duly took his seat in the Parliament in Dublin on 5 March 1784. Amongst those who welcomed him was the MP for Lisburn, William Todd Jones. *"He brings a fund of mercantile knowledge into this house"*, said Mr Jones. But the House was not to have the benefit of that mercantile knowledge for long; for the defeated candidate at Carrickfergus brought forward a petition to unseat the new MP on the grounds that the voters had been corrupted by Cunningham's associates from the business community in Belfast, who had poured into the ancient County Antrim borough to lend a hand to their champion.

Though the evidence of corruption was scant the petition was upheld and Cunningham was unseated, with the result that by March 1785 he was before the voters of Carrickfergus again in a fresh election. This time his opponent was a burgess of Belfast who had been appointed to that office by Lord Donegall; and Cunningham's election address was unbridled in its references to the nobility. After outlining his own political principles of Parliamentary Reform and so on, he wrote: *"Thus driven out of Parliament without disgrace or crime I once more throw myself on your virtue, on your public spirit, on your honour, on the regard to the independence of your Corporation, and to your dearest interests and those of your posterity. Preserve the character you have gained . . . . The same interest will be employed against you, and the same arts practised as before. Whoever be that instrument, it will be managed by the same lordly hand, supported by the same lordly power, and directed to the same infamous end — that of enslaving you and destroying the rights of your Constitution for Ever"*.

But all the rhetoric was not enough: Cunningham was defeated by a narrow majority and the "lordly power" regained supremacy. Whether Cunningham's campaign in the first election did involve bribery and corruption, as was alleged, is another of those fascinating features of his life and times that remain to be further researched. But for Cunningham himself the position was clear: all that his supporters had done was to spend fifty pounds on a celebratory dinner **after** the election! *"I had given a moderate* *entertainment to some poor electors after they had polled",* wrote Cunningham; and posterity is again left with just a shade of doubt.

Despite the heavy demands of Volunteering, parliamentary politics, his many business interests, and his involvement in the building of the White Linen Hall, Cunningham was by no means just a figure-head as President of the Chamber in its early years. In the fifteen months covering the two Carrickfergus elections separated by his spell in Parliament, this incredibly busy man presided at twelve of the twenty-six meetings of the Council of the Chamber; and he also undertook a number of executive tasks on behalf of the organisation such as drafting petitions and corresponding with the customs authorities and with merchants in mainland ports about duties and other regulations affecting trade.

Meanwhile the building of the White Linen Hall had been completed; and the bleachers were beginning to sell their wares there rather than in Dublin. That gave rise to a need for an organisation that would pay cash against bills drawn on Dublin; and the outcome was the establishment in May 1785 of a discount office, with Cunningham as the leading light and first subscriber. And when the members of the new Belfast Harbour Corporation were named in an Act of Parliament a few months later, Cunningham again headed the list save for one or two ex-officio members. Above all he continued to command the confidence of his colleagues in the business community, for he remained President of the Chamber till the beginning of 1792. By that time he had been running his own bank for three or four years in association with William Brown, John Campbell, and Charles Ranken; and in order to conform with a law forbidding bankers to have other business interests he had, as he put it, *"retired from mercantile life"* — but it was a busy retirement.

Cunningham's Bank closed its doors for the last time on 31 December 1793. Throughout its existence it had been in competition with Ewing's Bank ("The Bank of the Four Johns"), which preceded it by a couple of years and outlived it by about five. From April 1793 there had been further competition from the newly-established Belfast Discount Company, a successor to the Belfast Discount Office of 1785. Whether it was the effects of this competition, or a desire to get back to the cut and thrust of trade, or some other factor that caused Waddell Cunningham to withdraw from banking is not certain. But the most likely explanation is that his business was simply the victim of recessionary circumstances, the severity of which was indicated by a Government loan of £200,000 to industry and commerce throughout Ireland, with £30,000 coming to Belfast through the agency (would you believe it) of Waddell Cunningham.

The crisis in industry and commerce arose from the outbreak of war with France at the beginning of 1793; and the business community was reasonably pleased by the Government's rapid reaction and by Cunningham's initiative in getting a proportion of the aid to Belfast quickly. But the restless Dr Drennan (then practising in Dublin) was sceptical, for he wrote to his sister: *"How it can make the shuttle . . . go more briskly . . . is hard to say while the natural vent of the goods in foreign parts is kept shut by the war and while at the same time England is disburthening her glutted market . . . at an underselling rate into our market when she cannot dispose of her goods abroad".* And he went on to suggest remedies that have a familiar ring in the recessionary circumstances of 1983. Indigenous industry should be saved by protective duties; and import substitution must be the order of the day!

But Dr Drennan's restlessness ran much deeper than his apparent concern about commercial questions, for he had long been convinced that the salvation of Ireland in terms of Parliamentary reform and Catholic Emancipation lay in complete separation from England; and he was at that time a key figure in the Society of United Irishmen which was gradually taking over the radical cause from the Volunteers. Disappointed when their reasoned arguments to the authorities began to fail from about 1783 onwards, Waddell Cunningham and the other leaders of Volunteer politics for a time went with the mood of increasing radicalism, though they had doubts about the timing if not the principle of Catholic Emancipation. When the very militant Wolfe Tone visited Belfast in October 1791 in connection with the formation of the First Society of United Irishmen in the town, Cunningham met him over dinner in the home of Samuel and Martha McTier; and Tone subsequently recorded in his journal that they had had *"a furious battle, which lasted two hours, on the Catholic question".*

Yet it was the same Cunningham who presided at a lively meeting of radical spirits in the Exchange on 9 July 1792 when the decision was taken to organise a huge demonstration five days later to mark Bastille Day, the anniversary of the

Waddell Cunningham's First Belfast Company of the Volunteers parading in High Street on 14 July 1792 in celebration of the anniversary of the start of the French Revolution.
(From a 19th Century impression by J W Casey — Ulster Museum)

commencement of the French Revolution. And the very first item in the published report of that meeting over Cunningham's signature was to the effect that his beloved First Belfast Company of the Volunteers had decided to wear the green cockade, a symbol of Irish nationalism, when they took part in the Bastille Day parade a few days later. But Cunningham personally had deep doubts about where it was all leading; and when Wolfe Tone visited Belfast again in the autumn of 1792 and took part in an evening of revelry with an extreme radical flavour he recorded in his journal on the following day: *"Everybody as happy as a King except Waddell, who looks like the devil himself"*. Tone had discovered the deep divisions in radicalism that existed in Belfast at the time; and Waddell Cunningham epitomised a group — albeit a minority group — in the Presbyterian merchant class that wanted Parliamentary Reform urgently and Catholic Emancipation gradually but was not prepared to allow either to lead them into armed rebellion against the Crown.

By 1793 Cunningham was entering the twilight of his life. He was no longer involved in the Chamber of Commerce; the Volunteers which had taken up so much of his time for fifteen years were proscribed in March; and his bank was not doing well. After the bank closed in December, he tried to make a come-back into his trading company in Hercules Lane, where business colleagues headed by his sister Jane Douglas (wife of Robert Douglas, his personal clerk) had been holding the fort while he was legally excluded by his involvement in banking. But his re-involvement in the old trading activities was minimal; and he became largely dependent on a good staff headed by Campbell Sweeney, whom he had taken on in 1794 to manage the business. He was now over sixty-five years of age and his health began to fail, the enormous physical and mental exertions of his middle life having taken their toll.

Cunningham's wife was deeply worried about the inheritance, for she was conscious of his huge fortune and of his reluctance to leave her in sole control of his business empire. She therefore tried to bring her nephews, the sons of Captain Robert Batt and her sister Hannah, into the picture; and they responded readily by paying inordinate attention to their rich uncle as his health showed signs of deteriorating. But Waddell would have none of it; for he had been offended by an earlier refusal of the Batts to take his favourite nephew, James Douglas, into partnership, especially when he heard that old Mrs Batt had said that the reason was that *"her sons had never been connected with any but of good character"*. And the wily old merchant reacted decisively by disinheriting his own wife save for a life interest in the house in Hercules Lane and naming as the chief beneficiary that self-same James Douglas, the twenty-three-year-old son of his sister Jane. The final will was made early in December 1797 and Cunningham died a few days later, on Friday 15 December. His possessions in Belfast were said to be worth about £60,000, equivalent to over £3 million today; and that excluded the estate in Dominica. So young James Douglas became a very rich man, for he inherited everything save for a few small bequests to charity, £2,000 to Cunningham Greg (son of Waddell's old business partner, who had died the previous year), and immediate possession of the house in Hercules Lane. The house too became his in April 1808 when the widow died; and it was promptly sold to William Tennent, another rising star in the business world.

On Monday 18 December 1797 the earthly remains of Waddell Cunningham were laid to rest in the historic graveyard at Knockbreda Parish Church, which had been built about fifty years previously. The cortege was accompanied by the Belfast and Castlereagh Yeoman Cavalry and by the Belfast Yeoman Infantry; for as the country drifted towards the tragedy of June 1798, the aged Cunningham like many other old liberals had "declared for the King" and joined the yeomanry. But on that crisp day just a week before Christmas the yeomanry were, in the words of the News Letter, accompanied by *"a great concourse of other inhabitants"*; for the North of Ireland had lost one of its most famous sons. In the earlier years there may have been occasional doubts, some genuinely held, some perhaps motivated by petty jealousies. But in December 1797 everyone recognised that a truly remarkable man had gone; and the obituary in the News Letter was unreserved in its praise. It spoke of his energy, his ardour, his enterprising genius, the hospitality of his home, his public service — all fairly conventional and expected tributes. But it included too a few challenging thoughts about what Waddell Cunningham meant to many of the ordinary people of Belfast: *"The poor man and the industrious mechanic may long regret his decease — as the one was sure of relief and the other of employment from him"*.

The Cunningham mausoleum in Knockbreda Churchyard.
(Photo by Peter Houston 1983)

Not surprisingly, the old warrior's heir James Douglas named a son Waddell Cunningham Douglas; and when the infant died at the age of five months he re-used the name for another son, who soldiered in the 17th Lancers and lived to the ripe old age of eighty-six. Both were interred in the Cunningham mausoleum in Knockbreda churchyard. But in the old Shankill graveyard, far removed from Knockbreda, an exact namesake of Waddell Cunningham was buried in 1870 at the age of seventy-eight. The name is an unusual one; and it is tempting to speculate that in 1792 that second Waddell Cunningham was the bouncing baby son of a workman or clerk who had been befriended or given employment by the illustrious original, the man from Ballymacilhoyle.

So the Belfast Chamber of Commerce had a remarkable man as its first President, a man of many parts, a man who brought about change; and in 1783 that man presided over a colourful and sparkling assembly of fifty-eight merchants and professional men, many of whom were almost equally remarkable in their talents and their attainments. And of such is our industrial and commercial heritage. They were merchants of change.

Chapter 4

MERCHANTS OF CHANGE:
THE FOUNDING FATHERS

Though he had many other things on his mind, Waddell Cunningham did a good job in channelling the enthusiasm of May 1783 into paid-up subscriptions of a guinea each by the middle of October. There is some doubt about the precise number of members that he attracted — the distinguished antiquarian S Shannon Millin said sixty-six, but recorded the names of only fifty-nine — and there is now nothing that can be done to clarify the issue, because of the loss of the opening pages of the first minute book. Millin's list, published in 1932 in his "Sidelights on Belfast History", was presumably based on personal inspection of the Chamber records, for he acknowledged that he was afforded that facility; and the minute book must have been complete at that time for Millin photocopied the record of the first Council meeting and reproduced it in his book. The present author has therefore used Millin's list as the sole surviving record of the foundation members of the Chamber, save that he has taken a "Samuel Sinclaire" on that list to be the very famous Will Sinclaire, there being no further evidence of the involvement of a Samuel but abundant evidence of the deep involvement of Will. In addition he has chosen to spell Robert Thomson's surname without a "p" since that version occurs more frequently in Chamber records and contemporary writings.

Whether in 1983 or 1783, organisations consist of people; and great achievements depend totally on the enterprise and effort of individuals. The fifty-eight individuals who joined Waddell Cunningham in the Belfast Chamber of Commerce in 1783 made it into an effective organisation for upholding the interests of the business community and promoting change; but they contributed much more to the whole community by their enterprise as individuals in their own businesses. In the difficult circumstances of Northern Ireland in 1983, the nine-hundred or so businessmen and women who now comprise the Northern Ireland Chamber of Commerce and Industry and the many hundreds more who are members of the twenty-five affiliated Chambers up and down the country, of the thriving Junior Chamber movement, and of the Chambers of Trade are the successors to the men of 1783 and the very backbone of the whole community. As they face their problems and as they seek new opportunities to improve their own businesses, to broaden the industrial base, to penetrate new markets, to bring employment to more of our people, and to increase the spending power and quality of life of the whole community, they may derive some inspiration and some encouragement from the business achievements and the community involvements of the men of 1783 in the much more difficult circumstances of that time. It is in that hope that the lives of all fifty-nine of the foundation members have been researched and the following biographical notes written. They vary greatly in length and in the amount of detail that they contain; and that is a reflection only of what was available in the many possible sources covered. Hopefully that variability of content will also be a stimulus to further research.

THOMAS ANDREWS

By a happy coincidence the alphabetical first of the founding fathers was a member of a family that is still associated with the Chamber today — a family that over a period of three-hundred years has contributed more than most to honest business endeavour, to social and technological progress, and to basic human decencies in the North of Ireland. He was an Andrews of Comber: Thomas Andrews (1747-1809), son of John (1719-1808) and brother of Michael (1788-1870) and of James (1762-1841). And it was that James Andrews whose great-grandson, John Miller Andrews, one-hundred-and-fifty-three years later became President of the Chamber just four years before becoming the second Prime Minister of Northern Ireland; and whose great-great-grandson, Sir John Andrews, has been a member of the modern Chamber for many years. Indeed there is a second strand to the thread of continuity for it was a nephew of Thomas Andrews, the foundation member, who in 1878 with his two sons formed the milling business of Isaac Andrews & Sons which is also still in membership of the Chamber today; and that family too provided a President of the Chamber in the person of David Andrews in 1963. So no-one will be surprised that when Thomas Andrews joined the Chamber in 1783 his main business interests were in linen and flour, with diversification provided by occasional puncheons of *"very fine Antigua rum"!*

After a spell in the family business in Comber, which was then concerned both with linen bleaching and with flour milling, Thomas Andrews in 1781 set up on his own account as a linen draper and flour merchant in Thompson's Court off Donegall Street in Belfast. He bought brown linen in the markets; sent it to Comber for bleaching; and sold it either independently or through the channels then being used by his father. In addition the carts needed for the linen traffic brought flour from the mill in Comber, which he sold in Belfast on a commission basis. In November 1783, for example, he was advertising in the News Letter that he was *"as usual, largely supplied with first, second, and third flour of the best quality, fresh and sweet from the Comber mills".* The different grades related to the meshes of the cloth sieves used in the sifting process; and there was a substantial price differential between the finest grade and the third, which was really like wheaten meal. As Thomas frequently indicated in his correspondence with the mill in Comber, the main demand was for second grade. It is also worth noting that at that time the finest grade was by no means white, for almost a hundred-and-twenty years were to elapse before another Andrews discovered and patented a process for bleaching flour with nitrogen peroxide. That was Sydney Andrews, author subsequently of the family history "Nine Generations", published in 1958.

Like most of the merchants in Belfast, Thomas Andrews became involved in the liberal movement at the end of the 18th Century. When the Volunteers were re-formed in 1778, his father John Andrews had raised and equipped a company in Comber. The unit was known as the Comber Rangers and its officers included Thomas Andrews and his brother James, both as lieutenants. Later when he moved to Belfast Thomas was still known as "Lieutenant Andrews"; and he was so recorded in the 1782 membership list of a famous masonic lodge, reproduced by S Shannon Millin in his "Sidelights". In December of the following year his was the second of thirty-five signatures on a public call to the people of Belfast for "a very general meeting of the Inhabitants" to progress the campaign for proper representation of the people in Parliament — a meeting which the people were assured would involve "every thing dear to Freemen". It is not known whether Thomas Andrew's radical views went so far as to lead him into the Society of United Irishmen, though it is known that his father in Comber was involved for a time but withdrew as the movement went underground and headed for rebellion.

In the difficult years that followed the Rebellion, Thomas Andrews got into severe financial difficulty and was rescued with great generosity and considerable risk by his father. For Thomas the experience must have been traumatic, for he was by then a prominent figure in the community whose lifestyle implied considerable business success. He had subscribed £100 (around £6,000 in modern money) to the fund for the establishment of the White Linen Hall; he had been appointed a Justice of the Peace for County Antrim; and he was chairman of a committee concerned with public kitchens to relieve famine in the town. Though he was never able to repay his father's generosity in financial terms, it saved him from ruin and he repaid in terms of subsequent business stability and restored standing in the community. By 1804, for example, he was presiding at meetings of the linen merchants of the town and was obviously back to the very centre of his trade. When he died five years later at the age of sixty-two his obituary in the News Letter contained a warm tribute to his service as a magistrate, a tribute that would just as well fit many another Andrews of Comber before and since. "His strict sense of justice", wrote that correspondent of 1809, "was ever tempered by the milder dictates of Heaven-born humanity".

WILLIAM AUCHINLECK
William Auchinleck was involved in the tobacco trade in partnership with David Dinsmore and Samuel Jameson. According to an announcement in the News Letter, Dinsmore (who was also a foundation member of the Chamber) withdrew from the partnership in August 1783; and the business was continued as Jameson & Auchinleck for "the manufacturing of Tobacco in all its branches". In later years, William Auchinleck also became involved in the brewing industry, as a partner in John and Thomas Cunningham's malting house and brewery in Chapel Lane. There he had a stake of only £50, equivalent to about £3,000 in modern money. This partnership, which involved total capital of £1,500 from sixteen subscribers, was registered in October 1807 as the New Brewery Company; and it took over existing premises and equipment from the Cunninghams.

Auchinleck too was involved in the Volunteers. He had joined the First Belfast Company in March 1778; and his name appeared on a very early nominal roll of the company as a private in the "Second Division" — No 2 Platoon in the military parlance of today — whose officer was Waddell Cunningham, then a lieutenant. A William Auchinleck, probably this one but possibly his son, was a member of the Committee of the Linenhall Library in 1805 and was described in John Anderson's 1888 history of the library as "author of *Interest Tables* and other mercantile works".

NARCISSUS BATT

The distinction of being the youngest of the foundation members goes to Narcissus Batt (1767-1840); for if the recorded year of his birth is correct he was only sixteen when the Chamber was formed. But he was destined to become one of the most distinguished and faithful members in the two-hundred years of its history, achieving enormous success in business and serving the organisation in various capacities over a period of almost forty years (sixteen of them as Vice-President and one as President). The minute books of the early 19th Century contain many examples of his copper-plate handwriting; together with the sad message received by the Council on 14 October 1821 *"begging to decline the honour of President of the Chamber"* for a second term.

Descended from an old Cornish family settled in Wexford in the 17th Century, he was the eldest of five sons of Captain Robert Batt (lately of the 18th Regiment) and his wife Hannah, who was a daughter of Samuel Hyde of Hydepark, himself another foundation member of the Chamber. And since Samuel Hyde's other two daughters were married to Waddell Cunningham and Thomas Greg, also foundation members of the Chamber as was Thomas Greg's son Cunningham, early meetings of the new body must have seemed to the young Narcissus Batt rather like a family gathering at Hydepark. And to compound the intermeshing, Narcissus himself some ten years later married another of his full cousins, Thomas Greg's daughter Margaret!

The key to Narcissus Batt's involvement in the Chamber at such an early age lay in the fact that his father having inherited the family lands in Wexford in 1779 had moved back to that part of the country to supervise his inheritance and had died in Waterford in the year that the Chamber was formed. This left Narcissus as the eldest son of a young family to carry on the business that Captain Batt had been forced to start in Belfast eighteen years previously as a condition of his marriage to Hannah Hyde, the Hydes having insisted that he turned immediately from soldiering to commerce. The complexity of that business and the enterprise of the young man who was at the helm in 1783 are well illustrated by an advertisement that he placed in the News Letter in December 1787, when he had just turned twenty:

"Narcissus Batt is now landing of the John, from Leghorn and Malaga, a quantity of Mountain Wine, Sicily Barilla of the first quality and Brimstone. He is well supplied with Claret, Port, Sherry, Madeira and Canary Wine in wood and bottle, old spirit, rum, brandy and gineva, essence of spruce, Spermaceti Oil, Bergen Deals, Ridge and Scue stone, all of which he will dispose of on the most reasonable terms at his stores in Linenhall Street."

The indicated location of his stores is a reminder that the Batt connection had a great liking for the fashionable new thoroughfare leading from "The Parade" (later Castle Place) to the front of the White Linen Hall. Known first as "The Flags" and then as Linenhall Street, this historic thoroughfare laid out about 1784 did not acquire the name Donegall Place until about twenty years later. But from its earliest years many of the most successful business families in the town sought to make their homes there; and no less than four of the five sons of Captain Robert Batt were sufficiently prosperous to be living in that costly street in the first decade of the 19th Century. Narcissus owned the most elegant home in the area, Donegall House, which he had purchased from the 2nd Marquis of Donegal when his Lordship was moving to Ormeau; and from its commanding position on the corner opposite to the present site of Robinson & Cleaver's department store, he could look towards The Parade and see the homes of brother Thomas at No 4, brother Samuel at No 6, and brother the Rev William near Fountain Street. These were the nephews whom Mrs McTier in a letter to her brother accused of having taken such a keen interest in the health and affairs of their Uncle Waddell Cunningham in his last years, only to be totally rebuffed in his will.

Narcissus Batt's fourth and youngest brother, Robert, had been his partner in the import/export business from about the turn of the century; but tragedy struck in 1811 when Robert died at the age of twenty-eight. By that time Narcissus had become one of the best known businessmen in the town with interests in salt extraction, sugar refining, and ropemaking; and three years previously he had become involved in the enterprise that was to dominate the remainder of his commercial life. This was "The Belfast Bank" launched in 1808 as Gordon & Co with an office at the corner of Callendar Street, near the present site of the fine old building that used to be the Water Office and is currently being adapted to become an extension of the Marks & Spencer store. Narcissus Batt's partners in that great venture were John Holmes Houston and two old friends who had joined the Chamber with him in 1783, David Gordon (the senior partner) and Hugh Crawford. Some nineteen years later this bank merged with the Commercial Bank to form the Belfast Banking Company, with headquarters in Waring Street. And after a fascinating history so well told by Noel Simpson in his book "The Belfast Bank: 1827-1970", that institution ultimately became part of the Northern. So the threads of the banking story begun by Narcissus Batt and his colleagues in the first decade of the last century have continued unbroken to the present day.

The name of Batt is also commemorated in and around the Parish Church of Drumbo, for Mr and Mrs Narcissus Batt and their family of two sons and two daughters moved from Donegall Place to Purdysburn House about 1811; and some years later they began a long association with Drumbo Parish Church, having previously worshipped in St George's in High Street. The family therefore featured prominently in J F Rankin's delightful history of the Drumbo Parish published in 1982: and there are family memorials both in the church and in the churchyard. But the move to Purdysburn was by no means a total retirement; for Narcissus continued to be active in the Chamber and in banking for at least another ten years. In addition he was Chairman of the Belfast Harbour Corporation in 1816; began a massive re-building and extension of Purdysburn House about 1820; acquired extensive lands both in the area of his magnificent home and in South Down between Hilltown and Warrenpoint; and was appointed High Sheriff of Belfast in 1835.

When he died a very rich man in 1840 he was the subject of a glowing obituary in the News Letter which referred to his philanthropy and to his business success, but particularly to his part in introducing *"those liberal yet safe and judicious principles of Banking, which so peculiarly characterise this portion of Ireland"*. Such then were the achievements and the worth of that founding father of the Chamber who when he joined in 1783 was unique only for his youth and unusual only as a member of the Established Church amongst a host of Presbyterian radicals! (Incidentally his wife was a Presbyterian who peculiarly maintained a close connection with the First Congregation in Rosemary Street in her married life and was recorded in the annals of that church as a "constituent" as late as December 1831.)

GEORGE BLACK

It must have been regarded as a triumph for the organisers when George Black was persuaded to become a foundation member of the Chamber; for he was at that time Sovereign of the town and indeed had occupied that prestigious office on four other occasions over the previous eleven years. Furthermore his brother Samuel had been Sovereign on three occasions during the same period, so the Blacks had something of a monopoly of the office in those years. They were kinsmen (some say brothers) of the famous Scottish chemist Professor Joseph Black (1720-1790); and George Black had his main residence at Strand Mills, which was then a rolling country glade about two miles south of the built-up area.

But the Blacks had much wider territorial interests, for the family owned a number of estates in the Bordeaux region of France, where George and Samuel and at least one other brother and one sister were born and spent their early years before coming to Belfast for schooling. Afterwards George was apprenticed to Daniel Mussenden, who had extensive business interests in Belfast in the middle of the 18th Century before retiring to an estate near Hillsborough. Samuel Black became a linen draper; and the sister, Catherine, married Francis Turnley of Newtownards who subsequently became a well-known businessman in Belfast with a particular interest in land development and property ownership. George Black too had a hand in estate management for he acted as agent for the dynastic Macartney family in connection with their lands in the Ballymena area. But his main business activity was the importation of wine from the family estates in Bordeaux, using his own fleet of ships built and operated under the supervision of his senior shipmaster, Captain John McCracken, father of Henry Joy McCracken.

Subsequent to his joining the Chamber in 1783, George Black's high standing in the town was confirmed by his becoming in 1784 one of the four original lessees of the site on which the White Linen Hall was subsequently built (another was his brother-in-law Francis Turnley); his being appointed Sovereign for the sixth time, in 1785; and his becoming a foundation member of the Harbour Corporation in the same year.

Nevertheless his relationship with the Chamber was not always a happy one; for after having worked in 1784 as a key member of a small committee set up to study the feasibility and cost of deepening the harbour, he refused in the following year to see the project through by going to Dublin to make representations on behalf of the Chamber to the appropriate authorities there, *"not thinking the money raised adequate to his Expences"*. Since a subsequent minute asks posterity to note well that *"the money collected was £23:11:9½"* (which was about a quarter of many a professional man's annual earnings in those days) George Black was either a hard man in financial matters despite his great possessions or a very expensive traveller — probably both. For a man who thought so much about money his later years must have been frustrating and depressing, for in 1791 he invested £1,000 in John Cranston & Co, porter brewers in Barrack Street; and five years later he was describing the venture as a total failure that had consumed the whole of his life's savings.

JOHN BOYLE

When John Boyle joined the Chamber in 1783 he was in partnership with Waddell Cunningham in the import/export business in Hercules Lane. The breadth of that business was illustrated by two advertisements that appeared in the News Letter in the summer of that year: the goods on offer ranged from rosin to rum, from French Brandy to Alicant Barilla, from bundles of reeds for weavers to barrels of flour for bakers. And when Waddell Cunningham retired *"from mercantile life"* in December 1788 to meet the legislative requirements of his entry into banking, John Boyle continued the business in partnership with Cunningham's sister, Jane Douglas. The company engaged too in coastal shipping between Belfast and Dublin; and Boyle himself took substantial shares in several other businesses in Belfast from 1790 onwards. For example he invested £300 in John Smylie & Co, glassmakers, when that partnership was reorganised in September 1791; and fifteen months later he became involved with Narcissus Batt and Thomas Lyons in Robert Wilson & Co, cotton spinners and bleachers, to the tune of £1,000. In later life he had even more extensive involvements in the industrial activity of the town, for by the turn of the century he had acquired from Waddell Cunningham's heir, James Douglas, the interests that the old entrepreneur had held in sugar refining, ropemaking, and muslin weaving.

As with so many of the most successful merchants in Belfast, John Boyle's huge business interests did not prevent his becoming deeply involved in the political and social turmoil of his generation. He joined the First Belfast Company of the Volunteers in March 1778 and was posted to the "Light Infantry Division" under the command of David Tomb who would join the Chamber with him five-and-a-half years later. More significantly he was one of the original proprietors of the Northern Star, the fiercely radical newspaper of the United Irishmen which first appeared on 4 January 1792 and continued despite increasing harassment by the authorities until its offices were sacked by the Monaghan Militia on 19 May 1797. As Jonathan Bardon wrote in his great work on the history of Belfast published last year: *"It was a curious sectarian warfare: the largely Catholic militia acted for the crown in taking vengeance on the Protestant republicans of Belfast"*. And John Boyle, extensive merchant and shipowner, substantial investor and financial organiser through the Discount Office, freemason and part-time light infantryman, Council member of the Chamber in 1792/93, was one of those Protestant and Presbyterian republicans.

WILLIAM BOYLE

Whether the two Boyles who joined the Chamber at the beginning were father and son, brothers, cousins, or more distant kinsmen is not immediately apparent. What is apparent, however, is that William did not have as many involvements in the business life of the community as John. He appears to have been engaged in the export of provisions and the import of flaxseed and the barter goods of the Caribbean area, rum and sugar. Around the time that the Chamber was formed he also began a brewing business in North Street in premises that he had bought some fourteen years previously. Apart from this the records show that like most of the radical merchants of the day he was an avid signer of petitions to Parliament and requisitions to the Sovereign. And so his signature appears in a strong clear hand as "Willm Boyle" on documents dealing with such diverse subjects as the importation of flaxseed (1777), the state of the linen industry (1780), the briefing of public representatives in liberal principles (1781), and the proposed legislative union of Great Britain and Ireland (1800).

ROBERT BRADSHAW

The Robert Bradshaw who joined the Chamber in 1783 and served it faithfully till his life's end some thirty-six years later was one of the busiest and most distinguished men of his generation. The name occurs so frequently and in such diverse connections over a period of forty-five years from 1775 onwards that many a student of Belfast history must have wondered how many Robert Bradshaws were active in commerce and politics at that time. In fact there were two, who are distinguished (unfortunately not always) as "Robert Bradshaw of Milecross near Newtownards" and "Robert Bradshaw of Carrickfergus Road Belfast". The former was involved in the linen business; was a member of the initial project committee of the White Linen Hall in 1783; and is recorded as having erected a Scottish-type flax-scutching mill at Milecross some thirty-five years later, with the aid of a grant from the Linen Board. But it was the latter, the Robert Bradshaw of Carrickfergus Road, that joined the Chamber in 1783 and was at or near the centre of so many organisations and events in Belfast for almost four decades. This Robert Bradshaw seems to have been an early example of the adage that if you want a job well done you give it to a busy man. For in the midst of many other demanding activities he found time to be Honorary Secretary of the Chamber for the first ten years; to serve on Council and as occasional scribe for a period of five years in the first decade of the 19th Century; and finally to become the longest-serving President in the history of the organisation, his period of office extending from 1807 until the year of his death, which was almost certainly 1820. He was then succeeded by another of the men of 1783, Narcissus Batt, who had been the Vice-President for the whole of this marathon presidency and indeed for three years before it as well.

But when Robert Bradshaw joined the Chamber in the Autumn of 1783 all that was in the future. In the distant past was his English ancestry; in the more immediate past was his becoming a foundation member and Ensign of the First Belfast Company of the Volunteers in March 1778; and in the present were his thriving business as a merchant in Ann Street, his country home on the Milewater stretch of what was then known as Carrickfergus Road, his Sunday devotions with the Third Congregation in Rosemary Lane, and his part-time service as a recently-promoted lieutenant in Captain Waddell Cunningham's Company of the Volunteers and as an ascending Junior Warden in Past-Master Amyas Griffith's famous masonic lodge. But business came first; and in the early days the range of his goods seemed wider even than the range of his activities, for in July 1783 he was telling the world through the News Letter that he had just imported a cargo of *"best red Deal"* and also had for sale on his premises in Ann Street: *"Dantzig and Memel Timbers; Dronton Deals; Spring poles, laths; sheets & bar lead; Black soap; Dantzig, Barilla, and Pearl Ashes"* and was *"well supplied with his usual kind of powder blue"*.

In later years, however, the range of Bradshaw's activities widened even more dramatically than the range of his goods. In the space of the year 1785, for example, he became a foundation member of the Harbour Corporation; helped to organise and finance the Discount Office; and became one of thirteen equal partners (at £100 each) in Smylie's glassworks. Five years later the liberalism of his Volunteer politics was expressing itself in his becoming a foundation member of the Northern Whig Club, a forum for moderate liberal thought established by Lord Charlemont, Commander-in-Chief of the Volunteer Army in its heyday. And by 1792 he was culturally involved both in the organisation of the somewhat notorious Harp Festival with its slightly political over-tones and in the duties of the newly-created office of Vice-President of the Belfast Library and Society for Promoting Knowledge (which had been set up in 1788 as the Belfast Reading Society and ultimately became the Linen Hall Library). But in using the library and helping with the administration of the Society he was by no means unusual amongst the businessmen of the day, for many of them were prominently involved in the project from the beginning and remained active in it till the end of their days. For example in a published list of the members of the Society as at 6 December 1798, no less than eleven of the eighty-nine had been foundation members of the Chamber of Commerce in 1783; and a further fifteen became involved in the Chamber after it was reconstituted in 1802. Thus almost a third of the members of the Society ten years after it was formed were affiliated to the Chamber at one time or another.

For Robert Bradshaw as for the whole community in the North of Ireland, the proscription of the Volunteers in March 1793 and the gradual transformation of the United Irishmen from a radical political group into a secret brotherhood that was plotting armed rebellion was a watershed in life. Unlike certain other prominent members of the Chamber, Bradshaw himself "declared for the King" by joining Captain Charles Ranken's Yeoman Cavalry raised by the Sovereign, John Brown of Peter's Hill, in 1797 and by associating himself with a public statement condemning the Rising *("the atrocious insurrection now existing")* after the Battle of Ballynahinch in June 1798. Indeed his stance during that divisive tragedy may have been one of the reasons why he was not immediately restored to his pre-Rebellion eminence when the Chamber was reconstituted in 1802 after the Act of Union; just as a growing disenchantment with the extreme political views of some of his colleagues in the aftermath of the proscription of the Volunteers may have been responsible for his lagging a little in Chamber duties at the end of 1793, causing the Council to resolve in January 1794 *"that the Secretary Mr Bradshaw be requested to attend the next meeting, with a state of the Accounts of the Chamber".*

In due course, however, Bradshaw became totally re-involved in the Chamber of the early 19th Century; and his business too must have flourished during that period, for in 1809 he was able to join with William Tennent, Robert Callwell, and John Cunningham (all Chamber members) together with John Stewart and John Thomson in forming the Commercial Bank, at an initial subscription of £10,000 apiece (about £600,000 in modern money). This particular strand of Irish banking is also woven into the Northern Bank of today; for the Commercial joined with the Belfast Bank of David Gordon and Narcissus Batt to form the Belfast Banking Company in 1827, and that very enduring institution ultimately merged with the Northern in 1970. For Robert Bradshaw, however, the formation of the Commercial Bank in 1809 was the culmination of a progression in financial institutions begun with his involvement in the Discount Office in 1785 and continued through his becoming an original subscriber to the Discount Company in 1793.

This remarkable man remained active in public affairs through the second decade of the 19th Century, for he was named as one of the foundation "managers" of the Academical Institution (later RBAI) in the Act of Incorporation of June 1810; and he was one of the Spring Water Commissioners appointed by an Act of July 1817 to carry on the work of the Charitable Society in the provision and improvement of public water supplies. But his very full life came to an end a few years later; and his passing was marked by a huge funeral which attracted an attendance from all over the country including members of the nobility from near and far. Robert Bradshaw was indeed a "captain of commerce" whose breadth and depth of service to the community and to the Chamber have seldom been equalled in the two-hundred years of our commercial history.

CHARLES BRETT

For people in Northern Ireland the question that arises from the name of Charles Brett in the list of foundation members is whether the well-known Charles E B Brett of today, Chairman of the Northern Ireland Housing Executive and author of the magnificent work on "Buildings of Belfast: 1700-1914", is a descendant of that commercial man of 1783. The answer (in the radio parlance of the Constabulary) is in the affirmative; for the Charles Brett (1752-1829) who joined the Chamber in 1783 was the great-great-great-grandfather of the Charles Brett of today and the grandfather of Sir Charles H Brett (1839-1926) who became President of the Chamber in 1908. The story of these and the other generations of Bretts, stretching back to the William who was granted Letters Patent over some four-hundred acres of land in County Down in

1684, is beautifully told in C E B Brett's "Long Shadows Cast Before" published in 1978; and the Charles Brett of 1783 is also mentioned in the same author's magnum opus on "Buildings of Belfast" published in 1967.

Like so many of the foundation members of the Chamber, the Charles Brett of 1783 was a remarkable man: precocious, enterprising, perhaps even conceited. Son of attorney Charles Brett (1698-1758) of Killough and his wife Mary (née Carr, of Downpatrick), the younger Charles was only six years of age when his father died. The little family then moved to Belfast, largely it would seem to facilitate the development of young Charles as the only surviving child. He thus was endowed with a broad and liberal education in David Manson's famous school in Donegall Street; and on leaving there he opted for commerce rather than for further academic pursuit. Soon he was established as a wholesale wine and spirit merchant with premises in Hercules Lane near Waddell Cunningham's home; and in due course he moved to Hanover Quay to facilitate the growth of the business. By 1783, at the age of thirty-one, he was a man of considerable possessions, able to make a donation of £100 (about £6,000 in modern money) to the fund for the building of the White Linen Hall; and it was entirely natural that he should become a member of the new commercial body that was being formed in the town that year.

In his earlier years Charles Brett seems to have had a single-minded devotion to his own business interests and to have avoided involvement in the town meetings and resultant petitions that characterised the general business scene in the period immediately preceding the formation of the Chamber. Nor did he become deeply involved in representational activities immediately after the Chamber was formed: indeed it was not until nine years later that his name first appeared as a member of Council. But by 1794 he was a member of a "committee of three" (the others being David Tomb and the Chamber's most prominent United Irishman, Robert Simms) who were charged with investigating and reporting upon ". . . the Tolls intended to be taken on the Lagan Navigation". Their report presented to Council at a meeting in the Donegall Arms on Christmas Eve 1794 was meticulous and imaginative; and it showed a fine flash of the social conscience of the latter-day Bretts, with a recommendation for a reduction in the toll on loads of coal ". . . so necessary for the comfort and relief of the Poor . . ."

Apart from looking after his own businesses (which in his middle years ranged from dealing in whalebone to growing flax) Charles Brett was another of the non-executive partners in John Smylie & Co. In the words of the Deed of Partnership this establishment was "making and selling Window Glass, Glass Bottles, and whatever else the said parties may determine"; and when the partnership was first registered in 1785, each of the thirteen partners (who included eight foundation members of the Chamber) had subscribed £100. But when it was re-structured in 1791 to provide total capital of £3,600 some partners opted out and new ones came in; and the twelve who constituted the new partnership (including Charles Brett) each subscribed £300. Nevertheless John Smylie who actually ran the business and brought all the essential expertise to it was to "receive out of the Moneys Profits or Funds of the Partnership a

Yearly Salary of £75 sterling in compensation for his trouble"! But if the business brought small reward to its manager (described in those days as the "active partner"), the same was probably true for the investors, for things did not go as well as they had anticipated. There was disappointment too in another of Brett's investments — in an unsuccessful distillery — but these set-backs were as pinpricks on the totality of his business progress.

Brett did not marry till he was forty-three years of age. His bride, aged thirty, was Matilda Black from Dublin; and they ultimately had seven children, three of whom died young. The survivors were an only son and heir, Wills Hill Brett (1798-1862), and three daughters who each received £1,500 in their father's will when he died in 1829 at the age of seventy-seven. But in the meantime the elder Brett from his home in High Street had tackled one new enterprise after another. He was for a time land-agent for Lord Yelverton's Ballymacarrett estate; he acquired a farm of twenty-six acres in the Castlereagh area on which he built a substantial house that he named Charleyville and used first as a summer residence and later as the main family home; he engaged in a series of "mercantile adventures" around the world, one of which necessitated an extended visit to France that had a significant influence on his later life; and, in 1797, he became barrack-master of Belfast, a demanding public appointment in the context of the intense military activity in the town around the time of the Rebellion of 1798 and during the Napoleonic Wars through to 1815. At the end of the 18th Century his personal property in and around Belfast had been valued at £4,000, almost a quarter of a million today.

In his leisure time Brett the family man played the violin and the guitar; and became deeply involved in the service of the church. In his religious activities he shared with Narcissus Batt and only one or two more of the foundation members of the Chamber the distinction of not being a Presbyterian. Instead his main affiliation was to St George's, the Episcopal church in High Street; and he was clearly an active parishioner, for he and Narcissus Batt were two of the four members of a committee set up about 1815 to raise funds for the building of the present church. Through their efforts finances were provided not only to build a dignified place of worship, but also to make it into one of the most notable buildings in Belfast by the addition of a fine Georgian portico and facade translated from Ballyscullion House, the unfinished Bellaghy home of the deceased Earl Bishop of Derry. No doubt the overall result was deeply pleasing to the Charles Brett of the day when it was accomplished in 1816; and it must be a tribute either to heredity or to the continuity of good taste in matters architectural that the very discerning Charles Brett of the 20th Century was able to write sixteen years ago of St George's as *"this strange, and in parts superb, church"* and to extol its facade as *"a splendidly dignified example of Georgian stonework at its very best"*. In that beautiful place of worship the Charles Brett of the 18th and early 19th Centuries had an *"excellent pew, in the west gallery,...with cushions complete"*. These words come from a newspaper advertisement which Brett placed in 1824. Aged seventy-two he had retired for good to Charleyville and transferred his church allegiance to the ancient parish of Knockbreda; and, commercial to the end, he was inviting financial offers for the use of his erstwhile pew in St George's!

JOHN, THOMAS, AND WILLIAM BROWN

The Brown brothers who joined the Chamber in 1783 are not to be confused with their distant kinsman, the famous John Brown of Peter's Hill who was Sovereign of Belfast on four occasions. Sons of a County Antrim manse, the three Chamber participants of 1783 were then living in Waring Street where they had a large and successful export/import business. Their standing amongst the merchants of the town was indicated by the choice of William and John for the first Council of the Chamber and by the addition of Thomas in the following year, William at the same time becoming Vice-President for a two-year spell. They thus unconsciously created a record which has stood to this day, of three brothers participating in the Council simultaneously. Indeed if S Shannon Millin is right in his claim in "Sidelights" that Samuel Brown (1741-1818) — another Belfast merchant whose joining the Chamber was delayed for a few weeks, probably because of the fatal illness of one of his children — was a fourth brother, then the record was even more notable; for Samuel too was elected to Council in July 1784, giving the Browns four of the fifteen seats.

When John, William, and Thomas first came to Belfast they were apprenticed to their uncle, John Campbell, who had many business interests in the town, some of them in association with Waddell Cunningham. In due course William and John were able to establish their own business in Waring Street; and Thomas (who according to Dr Gamble in his thesis was their half-brother) was taken into the partnership later, though they still traded as William & John Brown & Co. The business developed along the usual lines including the export of provisions and probably linen and the import of grain, tobacco, rum, and requisites for the linen industry. When they joined the Chamber in 1783 the Browns were joint owners with Waddell Cunningham and John Campbell of the Brig SUCCESS; and three years later they had acquired an ocean-going ship of their own appropriately named THE THREE BROTHERS, a vessel of 600 tons. They also engaged in the Irish coastal trade, which resulted in their taking a substantial holding in a merchanting business in Sligo.

William and John Brown also had a long association with the financial institutions of the town. Both had been subscribers to the Discount Office in 1785; and they also became involved in the two banks established later in the decade. John was one of the "Four Johns" in Ewing's Bank; and William became a foundation partner in Cunningham's Bank when it was established shortly afterwards. William continued that association till the partnership was dissolved by mutual consent on 31 December 1793; and John continued to be involved in Ewing's Bank until 1796 when he and John Ewing and John Holmes all withdrew, leaving the bank to be carried on for a further year or so by John Hamilton and Charles Ranken (who had come into the partnership on the dissolution of Cunningham's Bank in 1793). From then until the establishment of the Belfast Bank by David Gordon, Narcissus Batt, and others in 1808, the only financial institution in the town was the Discount Company established in 1793 by a different group of merchants including Samuel Brown and John Brown of Peter's Hill. But as Noel Simpson points out in his history of the Belfast Banking Company, the Discount Company did not issue notes, with the result that over a period of ten or more years all business in the town had to be transacted in coins. This led to an intense shortage of coins and to counterfeiting on an alarming scale.

Thomas Brown, foundation member of the Chamber 1783, in Volunteer uniform.
(From a glass-plate negative in the Ulster Museum)

While his brothers were involved in banking, Thomas had been holding their commercial property in trust and carrying on the business in Waring Street, in order to meet the exclusivity requirement on bankers. That presumably was also the reason why Thomas in 1791 took over the holding that his brother William had had from 1785 in John Smylie & Co, the stake at the same time being increased from £100 to £300 (equivalent to about £18,000 today). A year earlier he had become involved too in a totally new manufacturing venture in the town: this was the Belfast Mustard Works, in which his partners were Richard Callwell and a James Beggs who managed the plant. Although there were occasional claims of export success for their "flour of mustard", the venture was probably always a little shaky; and that may have been one of the factors that contributed to the financial collapse of Thomas Brown in 1798, an unusual occurrence in those days. Certainly the mustard operation was one of those closed down in the aftermath of the bankruptcy, the premises having been sold to the Hyndmans, another business family well-known in the town and in the Chamber. All this was in sharp contrast with Thomas Brown's life-style in 1792/93 when he was Vice-President of the Chamber for twelve months, the third occasion on which a member of the family had held that office.

In the 1790's William and Thomas were still living in Waring Street, on the site of their initial business success. But John had moved out in the middle of the previous decade, for in 1785 he built the most desirable house in the town on a prime site in the fashionable area associated with the White Linen Hall. This was the huge house occupied fifteen years later by the 2nd Marquis of Donegall and subsequently by Narcissus Batt, on the corner of Linenhall Street (now Donegall Place) opposite to the present site of Robinson & Cleaver's store. Its size and siting were measures of the affluence of John Brown at that time, reflected too in the annual rent of £128 (about £7,700 in modern money) which Lord Donegall had to pay when he became the tenant of the property around 1800. In the years when he lived graciously in that prestigious home John Brown must have reflected occasionally on the significant contributions that he had been able to make to the work of the Chamber in its formative years. Notable amongst these were his joint authorship with Robert Thomson of the second petition to Parliament on the Grain Act in March 1784; his joining Robert Bradshaw in February 1785 in making vital representations in Dublin on the improvement of Belfast harbour, after George Black had refused to go for financial reasons; his becoming a Chamber representative on the new Harbour Corporation (together with his brother William); and his co-authorship with Waddell Cunningham and Robert Thomson in May 1785 of one of the most important documents ever produced under the auspices of the Chamber — the reaction of the merchants and people of the North of Ireland to Prime Minister Pitt's notorious Twenty Propositions on the future regulation of trade between Ireland and England.

As Presbyterians in fellowship with the First Congregation in Rosemary Lane, members of the Brown family inevitably also identified with the liberal movement. Thomas was a foundation member of the First Belfast Company of the Volunteers; and twelve years later he was involved too in the inauguration of the Northern Whig Club. William was also involved in the Volunteer movement, for he was a signatory with Waddell Cunningham and two others to an important notice published in the News Letter at the end of April 1783 under the heading "BELFAST MILITARY ASSOCIATION". This invited units throughout Ulster to send delegates to a meeting to be held in Belfast at the beginning of May to plan a great review of the Volunteers in the neighbourhood of the town early in June *"so as not to interfere with the Broughshane Review"*. Meanwhile his name was also appearing increasingly as Chairman of the Belfast Constitution Club, a liberal grouping which sought electoral reform and democratisation of the Parliament. But progress on those fronts was slow, too slow for a large proportion of the population; and the frustration that built up ultimately boiled over into the tragedy of 1798. Change came in later generations; and the Browns contributed also to those generations, for the baptismal records of the First Presbyterian Church for the period April 1756 to July 1790 show a son (John Meredith) for William, a daughter (Isabella Maria) for John, and two sons and five daughters for Thomas all in the space of less than eight years!

THOMAS CAVAN

Thomas Cavan appears to have made few marks on the business records of the period. He was probably a merchant with stores in Ann Street, engaged in the West Indies trade in partnership with a member of the Seed family. This is derived from an advertisement for a sale of rum by auction published in the News Letter in December 1783.

HUGH CRAWFORD

The annals of the Chamber contain many examples of members whose service spanned a period of thirty to forty years. One such was Hugh Crawford (1757-1819) who joined at the beginning; was elected to the Council in 1784; re-joined when the Chamber was reconstituted in 1802; and served as a Council member from then until 1814. In Chamber affairs he was seldom in the limelight; but he was always there to make his quietly effective contribution through small delegations and "working parties" (as the Chamber would call them today). And he was one of the seven Council members who in 1809 quietly took over the Lagan Navigation from the debt-ridden 2nd Marquis of Donegall — and seem never to have reported back to their colleagues on the venture!

But if Hugh Crawford's work for the Chamber over a period of thirty-one years was quietly unspectacular, the same could hardly be said of his own business progress. After coming into Belfast from the Ballymena area, he began with a shop in North Street; moved into the linen trade, probably as a purchaser of brown cloth for bleaching; later began trading in other commodities; and ultimately owned a ship of four-hundred tons built specially for him in 1807 in William Ritchie's yard on the County Antrim side of the Lagan. Meanwhile as his wealth accumulated he had been investing in other businesses as a non-executive partner. First it was £400 (about £24,000 in modern money) in Thomas Ash & Co, manufacturers of cordage and sail-cloth: that partnership was registered in 1790. Next, in May 1792, he was involved in James Mason & Co, another manufacturer of cordage and sail-cloth, to the tune of

£700; and ten years later he increased his stake to £1,500. Sugar refining also attracted his interest; and by September 1792 he and his own partner, Archibald Sinclair, had invested £800 in Francis Jordan & Co, sugar refiners. The total capital in that partnership at the beginning was £5,600; and Francis Jordan himself in addition to being one of seven equal shareholders was to be provided with a *"yearly salary of £50, and also an allowance of £5 per cent upon the annual nett Profits together with the Dwelling-house . . . and a sufficient allowance of Coals and Candles for the same"!* Nevertheless Jordan left Belfast when the first partnership agreement ended in 1799; and the business was carried on as James Kilbee & Co, with Hugh Crawford still involved as a non-executive partner but now to the tune of £1,400 (over £80,000 in modern money). And there was also a substantial involvement in an old flour mill at Crumlin, Crawford's financial participation dating from 1798. He was therefore well prepared to become a foundation partner with David Gordon, Narcissus Batt, and John H Houston in the Belfast Bank in 1808; and to continue in that partnership till his death in 1819.

Despite his intense commitment to business development, Hugh Crawford too found time to become deeply involved — indeed dangerously involved — in the radical movement in the last twenty-five years of the 18th Century. His spiritual home was the "New Erection" in Rosemary Lane, the Third Congregation, where his fellow members included many of the leading Presbyterian radicals in the town. By 1780 that congregation had as its effective minister the Rev Sinclare Kelburn, who had been called from Dublin to assist the ailing Rev William Laird; and the subsequent development of Kelburn's radicalism (and later, republicanism) is proverbial. In that heady environment, heightened in 1789 by the French Revolution, many members of the congregation who like Hugh Crawford had been involved in the Volunteers from 1778 began to espouse more extreme views. And by the early 1790's that movement was finding expression through a growing "greenness" in some companies of the Volunteers — and in the formation of Societies of United Irishmen. In the aftermath of the proclamation of the Volunteers in 1793, the United Irishmen took on an underground military aspect and divided into small secret cells. One such cell was started by John Hughes, a bookseller and stationer in Bridge Street; and Hugh Crawford, a man with much to lose, was recruited into that cell towards the end of 1796 or at the beginning of 1797. In the cell his fellow conspirators included at least three future members of the Chamber (James Luke, Adam McClean, and John Tisdall); and all four were lucky neither to have been brought into the open in the reckless and forlorn rising of June 1798 nor to have been betrayed by Hughes, who was arrested for sedition in October 1797 and subsequently became an informer (so much so that he had to skip the country after the Rebellion, to finish his days in the United States).

Unlike many of the United Irishmen, Hugh Crawford emerged from that tragic period unscathed physically and financially; and his last overt act of radicalism was to join in February 1800 with virtually every other merchant and manufacturer in Belfast in signing a strongly-worded petition against the intended legislative union of Great Britain and Ireland (*"The Petitioners...cannot consent to make an Experiment of so alarming and desperate a measure...").* But the Act of Union became a reality; the flame of Presbyterian radicalism flickered and virtually died; Hugh Crawford and his fellow businessmen began making money again; and the Chamber of Commerce was reconstituted. For Crawford and his wife Elizabeth (1759-1823), business success facilitated the move to a home in the country; for it was probably around this time that they bought Orangefield. There Hugh Crawford finished his days in the company of his wife (whom he predeceased by three-and-a-half years) and a number of children. These included a daughter Elizabeth who (inevitably some might say) married Edward Jones Smith (1780-1859), son of one foundation member of the Chamber (John Galt Smith I) and grandson on his mother's side of yet another (Valentine Jones I). According to George Benn's second book on Belfast there were also many sons, one of whom became the Rev William Crawford, rector of Skerry and Racavan and was still alive in 1880. Hugh Crawford himself died on 15 November 1819 and was interred in the historic cemetery of Knockbreda Parish Church where his tomb is clearly marked by an imposing pillar.

DAVID DINSMORE

David Dinsmore was a merchant with premises at 27 Bridge Street. He seems to have specialised in importing tea; and his customers obviously had discerning tastes when it came to infusions, for in 1783 he was advertising *"a large assortment of new teas, viz Bohea, Green, Congou, Suchong, and Hyfon".* But he also handled tobacco leaf, hops, and the usual range of requisites for the linen bleacher; and he was in partnership for a time with Samuel Jameson and William Auchinleck in the manufacture of finished tobacco products. Besides the Chamber, his public duties centred on the First Belfast Company of the Volunteers which he had joined when the call to arms went out in March 1778. He was also a signatory to several of the famous petitions of the late 18th Century including those that opposed Pitt's Twenty Propositions and the Act of Union.

BENJAMIN EDWARDS

Benjamin Edwards was a manufacturer in what would now be called the Ballymacarrett Industrial Estate, the cluster of little factories located around the County Down end of the Long Bridge in the late 18th and early 19th Centuries. He began in 1781 as a glass manufacturer, with his son making clay pipes in an adjacent unit. Much of the glass was of very high quality and of an ornamental nature, with the result that a few examples have survived to this day. His early success both in home and in export markets soon attracted competition; for the heavily-supported partnership of John Smylie & Co set up nearby in essentially the same business less than four years after the establishment of the Edwards concern. In recognition of their entrepreneurial activity both factories received minor bounties from the Dublin Society over a period of about ten years. Meanwhile Edwards continued to demonstrate his entrepreneurial flair by establishing an iron foundry in 1786. This was complementary to the glass-works both in siting and in product range, the output including bottle moulds, grinding machines, and other pieces of equipment needed for the elaboration of the glassmaking operations. Novel methods of encouraging local sales both of glass and of ironware were also adopted, including the establishment in 1800 of a warehouse in Newry.

JOHN EWING

The name of John Ewing was perpetuated by his emerging in June 1787 as the chief of the "Four Johns" who founded Ewing's Bank. But at the time he joined the Chamber in 1783 John Ewing was a merchant and shipowner, with a particular interest in the tobacco business. For example in August of that year he had for sale a *"large quantity of Fine James's River Leaf Tobacco . . . lately landed from . . . Virginia"* and *"a few hogheads of Maryland which he will sell cheap"*. And two months earlier he had been inviting offers for the Brig SUCCESS, a ship of *"about ninety tuns, seven years old, handsome, strong, and well found"*. Clearly the business community in Belfast found his advertisement convincing for only a few months later the brig was reported to be jointly owned by four of the shrewdest merchants in the town, Waddell Cunningham, John Campbell, and William and John Brown. John Ewing was also for a time one of the agents in Belfast for the Dublin Insurance Company, which was offering cover in the town from about 1780.

Outside his activities as a merchant and shipowner, Ewing shared many interests with one of his banking partners, John Holmes. They had both been original subscribers to the Discount Office; they both belonged to First Presbyterian Church; and Mrs McTier tells us that they made a trip together to Bath about 1795 to take the waters (the two Johns, that is!). *"They are just old enough and rich enough to be panic struck"*, she wrote — and left posterity to wonder exactly what she meant.

ROBERT GETTY

It was William and John Brown that introduced the young Robert Getty to the intricacies of commercial life in Belfast in the second half of the 18th Century, for he was apprenticed to them for some years and they were his advisers and financial backers when he later set up on his own. But the indications are that by the time the Chamber was formed he was making his own decisions. In January he had been advertising the arrival of *"a large parcel of Hyfton, Green, Congou, and Bohea Teas"*; in April it was *"a small parcel of new Dutch Flaxseed"*, *"a large quantity of English Red Clover of an excellent quality"*, and *"a few hogheads of very nice manufactured Roll Tobacco"*; and in June the scene had changed again to *"Malaga raisins, Dutch starch, French barley, Turpentine oil, Prunes, Almonds in the shell, Black rosin in mats, Iron wire, Ombro madder, first and second powder blues, and refined saltpetre"*. Later he became a leading light in the first locally-based insurance company, the Belfast General established in 1791 which provided both fire and marine cover.

But if Robert Getty was well known as a merchant with a wide product range that included insurance, he was equally well known as a radical campaigner with a particular commitment to the cause of Catholic Emancipation. He played a leading part in the great meetings on the subject in 1792, particularly that called by the proclamation of 23 June which included these historic sentiments:

"We anxiously wish to see the day when every Irishman shall be a citizen — when Catholics and Protestants, equally interested in their country's welfare, possessing equal freedom and equal privileges, shall be cordially united, and shall learn to look upon each other as brethren, the children of the same God, the natives of the same land — and when the only strife amongst them shall be, who shall serve their country best."

At that meeting there were "prudent patriots" and "gradual reformers", but the dominant mood expressed by Robert Getty and others (including several fellow-members of the Chamber) was for immediate reform. Predictably, however, Parliament rejected their petitions; and the drift towards rebellion continued unrelentingly.

Despite his intense radicalism, Robert Getty does not appear to have been actively involved in the United Irishmen. Yet he was arrested at the end of May or early in June 1798, and his life was in danger for a time. The reason was that he was unable to produce for surrender to the military authorities two brass fieldpieces that were allegedly under his care from the days of the Volunteers. Eventually through the intervention of the Crown Solicitor it was accepted that the guns had *"been carried away clandestinely long before"* without Getty's knowledge; and he was released. Years later it was revealed that he had been framed and betrayed by James McGucken, the Fountain Street lawyer turned informer, the "Supergrass" of his day.

Unlike many other Protestant radicals of the merchant class, Robert Getty continued his campaign for Catholic Emancipation well into the 19th Century. In this he was associated with men like John Lawless and Dr William Drennan; and he presided at a notable town meeting in the Brown Linen Hall in December 1818 which called for *"an immediate and total repeal of that part of the penal code that still remains in the statute book against our Catholic fellow-subjects"*. He also became immersed in the creation of the Academical Institution as a centre of liberal thought as well as of educational excellence; and he was named in the enabling Act of 1810 as one of the twenty "managers" of the project. He was active too in the Belfast Reading Society from its inception in 1788; and no doubt he was one of the influences that encouraged the Society to adopt a liberal resolution on Catholic Emancipation in the heady days of 1792.

In the Chamber of Commerce his contribution was immense. He was a member of Council from 1783 till 1820, a period of almost four decades broken only by the breaks that occurred in the activities of the Chamber itself. He was Vice-President to Hugh Montgomery in 1802, but did not feature again amongst the office-bearers. He seldom missed a Council meeting and he was often asked to produce documents and schemes for future consideration by his colleagues. The most notable was a plan for the Chamber to provide four lighters on the Lagan Navigation for the Lough Neagh trade: that was in 1802 when he was Vice-President.

Getty's wife was the daughter of Nicholas Grimshaw of Whitehouse, described in his obituary as *"the Father of Cotton manufacture in this country"*. They had a son

Edmund (1799-1857) who was destined to become the famous son of a famous father: Ballast Master at the harbour, first Secretary of the Harbour Commissioners, active in the Chamber, and renowned for his scientific and literary attainments. So between father and son the name Getty was near the centre of the commercial and cultural life of Belfast for more than seventy years.

DAVID GORDON

David Gordon was another of those foundation members of the Chamber who were destined to become leading partners in the new and lasting generation of banks established in Belfast in the first decade of the 19th Century. In his early life he was a lawyer with an office in Belfast; and his church connection was with the First Congregation in Rosemary Lane. For a time he too lived in the Linenhall Street of those days; but he succeeded to the family estate of Florida Manor at Killinchy in County Down on the death of his brother James. When he took the lead in establishing the Belfast Bank as Gordon & Co in 1808, his three partners included Narcissus Batt and Hugh Crawford, who shared with him the distinction of having been founding fathers of the Chamber of Commerce twenty-five years previously. And his third partner, John Holmes Houston (1767-1843), was a full cousin of another foundation member of the Chamber, John Holmes jnr. So David Gordon's business circle gave yet another glimpse of that incredible intermeshing of the main business families that so characterised those days. Sometimes the links were purely commercial; sometimes they were through marriage; often they were both.

THOMAS GREG

The entrepreneurial spirit that pervaded the North of Ireland in the last quarter of the 18th Century was epitomised in the life and work of Thomas Greg (1721-1796) merchant, manufacturer, innovator, landowner, property developer, and philanthropist. So too was that incredible and at times unhealthy interlinking of the main business families to which several references have already been made. For Thomas Greg, son of John Greg (1693-1783), was a son-in-law of fellow foundation member of the Chamber Samuel Hyde of Hydepark, having married Hyde's eldest daughter Elizabeth in 1742; a brother-in-law of Waddell Cunningham, Cunningham having married another of Hyde's daughters; father of Cunningham Greg (1762-1830), a highly successful businessman in his own right, who joined the Chamber with his father in 1783; and uncle and father-in-law of Narcissus Batt, Batt's mother being another sister of Greg's wife, and Batt himself having married Greg's daughter Margaret, his full cousin. And the inbreeding continued in the next generation for Cunningham Greg's son Thomas Richard married **his** full cousin Mary, daughter of Narcissus and Margaret Batt!

But if the Greg connection showed a certain lack of imagination in some of its marriages, there was no lack of imagination or enterprise in the business life and developmental activities of the head of the family, Thomas Greg. Initially he was a merchant with stores and offices in Ann Street at the "Back of the Green". These must have been substantial premises because James Sheridan, proprietor of the Donegall

Arms, was able to use them as a temporary inn when the hotel was being refurbished in 1786. Nearby in an area bounded by the present lines of High Street, Cornmarket, Castle Lane, and Donegall Place Thomas Greg had a fine house with extensive gardens; and under a ninety-nine-year lease of 1767 from Lord Donegall, he also became the developer of an area of dockland between the eastern ends of High Street and Waring Street. There in 1769 he built and paved a very substantial dock which ran due east for more than a hundred yards along the northern side of the Farset. Since the laying of the chief corner-stone on the seaward side coincided with the arrival of news from London of the birth of a son to Lord and Lady Donegall, Greg named the dock Chichester Quay in honour of the infant, the latest Lord Chichester (who was to succeed to the Donegall title thirty years later as George Augustus, 2nd Marquis). This indeed was Thomas Greg's second such gesture to the Donegall family, for four years earlier he had changed the name of a ship that he owned from PROSPERITY to COUNTESS OF DONEGALL after Lord and Lady Donegall and other prominent citizens had been entertained on board in Belfast Lough. It is tempting to speculate that these social contacts and deferential gestures were factors both in Thomas Greg's acquisition of leases from Lord Donegall to farmlands in South Antrim over the heads of the sitting tenants (which led to the "Hearts of Steel" riot in Belfast in December 1770); and in his being offered a baronetcy in 1783, an honour which for reasons that seem to have died with him he decided not to accept.

However there were many more commendable aspects of the business career of Thomas Greg than the land deals in South Antrim; and many more reasons why he should have been honoured than his social contacts with Lord Donegall. Top of the list must come his incredibly diverse and enterprising export activity in co-operation with Waddell Cunningham both while the latter was still in New York and after he returned to Belfast in 1765. But Greg was equally enterprising on the local scene, owning the lighter that made the first commercial trip along the Lagan Navigation to Lisburn in 1765; opening a timber yard in that town about 1767; reviving the Donegal herring fisheries in 1771; and engaging in several unusual industrial ventures. For example in 1766 at a cost of £3,500 (over £200,000 in today's values) he and Waddell Cunningham established the "Vitriol Manufactory" on an island in the Lagan at Lisburn, a remarkable piece of enterprise which enabled sulphuric acid for use in linen bleaching to be produced locally. To facilitate the very large exports of herrings in the 1770s Greg was also responsible for technical innovations in the curing of the fish, a project that attracted a small grant from the Dublin Society which at that time was the only certain source of aid for industrial development. Some years later, around 1787, he established the Downshire Pottery on the County Down side of the Lagan in partnership with Samuel Stephenson and John Ashmore. As outlined in a petition to the Irish Parliament in January 1793 the pottery was from the beginning aimed at the "Manufacture of Queen's Ware and other Kinds of fine Earthen Ware such as are made in Staffordshire"; and the partners had been put to "great Expence in searching for and making Experiments upon Materials for this Purpose . . ." and "in erecting Buildings, in importing Machinery, and in bringing Workmen from foreign Places". Since "Many Materials which have been heretofore overlooked and neglected would be thus rendered useful, and many Workmen and Children would thus find Employ-

ment" the petitioners felt that they should be offered a package of industrial development aids retrospectively. Parliament agreed in principle but delegated further investigation to a Committee — and the good intentions came to nought, again leaving the Dublin Society with a grant of £90 in 1793 and £110 in the following year to be the sole source of aid. This enterprising project continued to occupy Greg's attention till the end of his days; and in 1795, the year before his death, he submitted a successful application for an award offered by the Dublin Society to the first person who erected a successful mill for the grinding of flint for use in making fine china. In co-operation with a wide range of business colleagues Greg had also during his latter years become a non-executive partner in a diversity of enterprises around the town; and he had acquired land in the United States, as well as prospecting for coal and minerals all over Ulster.

Apart from his personal business interests Thomas Greg's services to the community centred on the Charitable Society and the Chamber of Commerce. Like many other businessmen he played a major part over a number of years in the raising of the magnificent sum of £7,592 that was available towards the building of the Poorhouse and Infirmary by the time the foundation stone was finally laid in August 1771. His part in the conception and birth of the Chamber has been recounted in a previous chapter. After that he served as a member of Council in 1783/84 and again in 1785/86; and he frequently presided at Council meetings in the absence both of the President, his brother-in-law and close business colleague Waddell Cunningham, and of the Vice-President (for some unknown reason John Holmes who was Vice-President in 1783/84 did not attend a single Council meeting during his twelve months in office).

There is some confusion about the church affiliations of Thomas Greg, in that his name appears in the records both of the First and of the Second Congregation in Rosemary Lane. With Waddell Cunningham and a George Ferguson he was named in 1767 as a trustee of the Second Congregation in a lease of the church site granted by Lord Donegall; but in the 1791 membership roll of the First Congregation prepared by the minister of the day Thomas Greg and his son Cunningham are both shown as members of that church living at Gaw's Place. It is also known that Thomas Greg's daughter Margaret, wife of Narcissus Batt who was an Episcopalian, continued an association with the First Presbyterian Church long after her marriage. But whatever Thomas Greg's church connections in life, he was in death laid to rest in the historic churchyard of Knockbreda Parish, like many of the merchants of his day; and his burial place is marked by a most ornate mausoleum in which three generations of Gregs were subsequently interred. The inheritance passed mainly to his youngest son Cunningham, his other two sons having previously inherited extensive possessions from uncles on both sides of the family. Samuel who had been working in Manchester with his Uncle Robert Hyde, owner of a cotton mill, received a bequest of £10,000 when the uncle died in 1783; and he came into control of the whole business fourteen years later. Both Samuel and his other brother, Thomas jnr, also inherited sugar plantations in the West Indies from their Uncle John Greg. And so when Thomas Greg snr died on 10 January 1796 he left behind three sons who were already men of substantial possessions and well on their way to the pinnacles of business success that he himself had attained at an early age.

CUNNINGHAM GREG

Third only to Narcissus Batt and Robert Simms in terms of his youth at the time he became a foundation member of the Chamber was Cunningham Greg (1762-1830). Youngest son of Thomas Greg, he was just turned twenty-one at the time. Yet he was already well established as a merchant in his own right with stores in Ann Street; and he had for some time been using the columns of the News Letter both to advertise his incredible range of imported merchandise and to attract offers of potatoes, presumably for export. Public office followed hard on the heels of his precocious business success, for he was named as a foundation member of the Harbour Corporation in 1785, at the age of twenty-three. Eight years later he had a lucky escape when (as Mrs McTier wrote to her brother Dr Drennan) he and an American visitor by the name of Willcocks survived a vicious attack by a gang who had been drinking in the military barracks and poured out on to the street as "royalists" looking for trouble with the Volunteers.

When his father died in 1796 he inherited the family's large house and gardens in the Castle Lane area together with various business interests such as Chichester Quay and the share in the pottery at Ballymacarrett. Meanwhile in his own right he had become a partner in a wine business with Henry Woolsey and in sugar refining with Francis Jordan, these commitments together requiring a total of £2,800 (almost £170,000 in modern money). And he later received a bequest of £2,000 under the will of his uncle, Waddell Cunningham, who died in December 1797. So as the Rebellion of 1798 approached he had become one of the richest and most diversified businessmen in the town. Yet he seems to have come close to a flirtation with the United Irishmen by subscribing to their funds through his business partner Francis Jordan, who was subsequently alleged (perhaps wrongly) to have been Treasurer of the underground movement in County Antrim. In the end Greg "declared for the King" by joining the Yeoman Cavalry in 1797; and he survived the Rebellion unscathed in every sense.

In 1800, at the age of thirty eight, he somehow found opportunity and time to woo and marry a Miss Ellen Gason from Nenagh in County Tipperary. Some time later they moved to a house in Donegall Place, for in 1809 the ancestral home and grounds in the Castle Lane area (occupied at that time by the Earl of Westmeath as a tenant) were advertised as being available for re-renting at £250 a year. Later still the Gregs acquired or built a country house at Ballymenoch near Holywood; and he and his only son, Thomas Richard, were living there when the elder Greg took a shareholding of £10,000 in the Northern Banking Company in 1824 and was elected to the Shareholders' Committee. Greg's wife Ellen had died three years previously at the age of forty-three and was buried at Knockbreda. Greg himself followed in 1830, after one of the most remarkable business careers in our industrial and commercial history.

It can be no surprise that Cunningham Greg did not have much time to devote to matters other than his business interests. Yet he did manage to serve on the Council of the Chamber on three occasions in the early 1800s. He was also an active member of the First Presbyterian Congregation and a generous subscriber to its funds; and he left a unique mark on the history of the Society for Promoting Knowledge, latterly the Linenhall Library. In 1817 he secured from a Mr Magwood of Charleston, South Carolina, as a gift for the Library's collection of scientific curios the stuffed skin of a rattlesnake!

AMYAS GRIFFITH

One of the most colourful of the foundation members was Amyas Griffith (1746-1801). His association with commerce was not as merchant or manufacturer, but as His Majesty's Surveyor of Excise in the town, a post to which he had been appointed in 1780. And in retrospect it may seem odd that a Government official who had the potentially difficult task of keeping an eye on the trading activities of the wily merchants of Belfast should have chosen or should have been invited to join their new representational body. The explanation seems to be that in work and in play, in commerce and in politics, he tended to identify more with the problems and attitudes of the merchants and intelligentsia of the town than with those of the Government machine that employed him. In his mainstream work this was well illustrated by his introduction of the so-called "Lagan duty", a levy on imported beer and porter (and on that from Lisburn!) which so endeared him to the Belfast brewers that they presented him with a handsome silver cup!

Born at Rosscrea in County Tipperary, he came North with a dubious distinction; for seven years earlier a writer in a Dublin magazine had described him as possessed of *"an insatiable love of fame"*. In Belfast he showed that that was an accurate assessment: he was often in the news. But it was his extra-mural rather than his statutory activities that added most to his fame — and ultimately brought about his downfall. For example he was deeply involved in Freemasonry; and within a few months of his arrival in Belfast he was responsible for resurrecting Masonic Lodge No 257 and for setting it on course to a membership of one-hundred-and-fifty by the autumn of 1782. Confusingly the lodge was commonly known as "The Orange Lodge of Belfast", a designation that actually had nothing whatsoever to do with the Orange Order that emerged in County Armagh in the middle of the next decade. But to Griffith, No 257 was *"the first lodge in the Universe"*, *"this never-to-be-forgotten phoenix"*; and his name stood at the head of its membership list as *"Past Master and Captain General"*. Also on that list were the names of another twelve foundation members of the Chamber, who were destined by the end of the century to cover a leftish arc of the political spectrum ranging from constitutional liberalism through "prudent patriotism" to outright republicanism. And much the same could be said of another group of Griffith's friends, the literati of Belfast, who met under the banner of the Adelphi Club, with Amyas the writer near the centre of the stage.

But it was overt involvement in anti-Establishment politics on the issue of Parliamentary reform in association with his leader in the Chamber, Waddell Cunningham, that proved to be the undoing of this remarkable man. He was generally thought to be the real editor of a radical newspaper, the Belfast Mercury or Freeman's Chronicle, which began publication in 1783 with John Tisdall as the front man; but just

Amyas Griffith (fourth from left) and Henry Haslett (fourth from right), foundation members of the Chamber 1783, attending a meeting of the Adelphi Club in the previous year.
(From a painting by Antony WIlliams — Linenhall Library)

about the time that the Chamber began to function Griffith came into the open in the News Letter to nominate Waddell Cunningham to oppose the Establishment candidate in the Carrickfergus election of 1784. He might have got away with that; or even with his publicly announcing that he had seriously considered standing himself; or even with his continuing to support Waddell Cunningham when he had to fight again in 1785. But it was too much for the Establishment to take when it emerged that he had been using a printing press associated with his work to produce election literature in support of Cunningham on both occasions. So he was dismissed from his post in 1785; and he appears to have left Belfast soon afterwards, having cashed both the silver cup given to him by the brewers and his famous painting by Antony Williams of the Adelphi Club "in session" in 1782. He died sixteen years later at the age of fifty-five, but not before he had produced a number of literary works which still give information and pleasure, particularly his "Miscellaneous Tracts by Amyas Griffith".

THOMAS HARDIN

Twelve months after the Chamber was formed, Thomas Hardin was dead. He had been a merchant in the town with an interest in shipping including the emigrant passenger trade from Newry to Pennsylvania. Amidst the patriotic fervour of 1778 he had been a foundation member of the First Belfast Company of the Volunteers. In later life his business associates included George Joy, David Tomb, and Valentine Jones II, all of whom had direct or indirect association with the Chamber.

HENRY HASLETT

Born in Limavady, Henry Haslett (1758-1806) must have become involved in the commercial life of Belfast before he turned twenty, for his name appeared on an early roll of the First Belfast Company of the Volunteers established in March 1778. After it was the note "uncertain attender, mostly abroad", which suggests either that his first job was in the export trade or that he frequently went to England to purchase goods for the woollen drapery in Rosemary Lane with which he was subsequently associated. However by the time the Chamber was established in 1783 he and a William Haslett (probably a brother, though his father was also called William) were advertising their wares in the News Letter: in December of that year they begged leave to inform their friends that they had for sale *"at their warehouse nearly opposite to the new meeting house, Rosemary Lane, a neat assortment of gauzes, shawls, plain, script, spotted, and figured, lawns, lenaws, and catguts white thread etc"* which they would *"sell remarkably cheap by wholesale, for ready money only"*. And business must have been good, for by the early 1790's Henry Haslett's commercial interests in the town had broadened to include shipping, insurance, and the importation of Whitbread's porter. He was at the centre of a shipping syndicate known as the "New Traders", who had broken away from another grouping that subsequently became known as the "Old Traders"; and the new group soon had a number of ships under construction in William Ritchie's yard. Haslett was also by this time Secretary of the local insurance company, the Belfast General, engaging both in fire insurance and in marine cover, under the chairmanship of another foundation member of the Chamber, Alexander Orr.

Both in his shipping activities and in the insurance company there were gentle reflections of the incipient republicanism that was ultimately to lead Henry Haslett to Kilmainham jail. In the insurance company it was the fact that the directors were virtually all involved in, or sympathetic to, the Society of United Irishmen: in the shipping activities it was the fact that the new vessels built in Ritchie's yard emerged with distinctly Irish names like SHAMROCK, HIBERNIA, and SAINT PATRICK. More significantly Henry Haslett himself was one of the original proprietors of the Northern Star, the voice of the United Irishmen; and he was also a captain in a "green" wing of the Volunteers as well as being an original committee member of the First Belfast Society of United Irishmen. After the proscription of the Volunteers in 1793 Haslett became even more deeply involved in the United Irishmen, who were then going underground and taking on a military aspect; and he appears to have become Secretary of the movement for the whole of County Antrim. It was hardly surprising, therefore, that he was amongst a group of eight prominent radicals in Belfast and Lisburn who were arrested on 16 September 1796 on a charge of high treason and taken off to jail in Dublin that evening under heavy escort. The group also included Thomas Russell, Librarian of the Linenhall. Haslett was confined in Kilmainham jail till December 1797; and those fourteen months of incarceration were a period of frightful personal tragedy for him because they saw the deaths not only of two of his own children but also of his twenty-three-year-old sister, who was apparently a very beautiful and accomplished girl. The sister died in Dublin where she had become ill while nursing one of Henry's children who had been visiting him in jail; but her body was brought back in procession to Knockbreda for burial in the historic churchyard, a graveside oration being given by the famous radical minister and leader of the United Irishmen in County Down, the Rev William Steele Dickson of Portaferry.

Although damaged in body and spirit by these experiences Henry Haslett survived to resume a prominent position in the commercial life of Belfast for another ten years or so. In the early years of the Chamber he had been a member of Council on two occasions; and he served in that capacity again in 1802 and in 1804. It was during his spell on Council in 1802 that he was the architect with Robert Getty of an ambitious scheme for the Chamber to provide a number of lighters on the Lagan Navigation; and in the following year he was in the news again when the Chamber was asked to arbitrate in a dispute between himself and two other prominent businessmen about port charges. Three years later, on 4 December 1806, this bright and lively spirit was gone, at the early age of forty-eight. The Rebellion had claimed another victim.

JOHN HENDERSON

There have been Hendersons involved in the Chamber at most times in its history: and there was one there in 1783 as well. He was John Henderson, merchant, with particular interests in insurance and in the European trade. And in the News Letter of 1 July 1783 he was advertising Norwegian train-oil, Swedish bar-iron, blister and German steel, and anonymous liquorice ball, together with the universal panaceas of those days — rum, brandy, and geneva. In addition he was at that time one of the agents in Belfast for the Dublin Insurance Company, the others being his fellow foundation-members of the Chamber John Brown, William Brown, and John Ewing. He was not a forebear of the Hendersons that took over the management of the News Letter in the middle of the next century, since that family was then living in the Newry area.

JAMES AND JOHN HOLMES

One of the distinctions of John Holmes (1745-1825) and his younger brother James when they joined the Chamber in 1783 was that they had for some years been participating in what was known as "the Russian trade", through the White Sea port of Archangel. The main imports from that area were tar and tallow; and the Holmes brothers had been offering these and many other commodities from their warehouse in Donegall Street. In later years they also became the most important of the Belfast participants in the Italian trade, which centred on barilla from Leghorn (now Livorno); and Dr Gamble's researches revealed the existence in 1794 of a related partnership of Webb & Holmes in that port. Around this time Tenerife also became a prolific source of potash for the Belfast merchants, including the Holmes brothers.

However it was not only the import/export business that occupied their attention. John had been a member of the original project committee of the White Linen Hall; and that led him into a financial career, first as an original subscriber to the Discount Office (with his brother James and ten other merchants) and later, in 1787, as a partner in Ewing's Bank. During John's involvement in banking (which continued for about ten years) James carried on the activities that they had previously undertaken jointly, as well as becoming involved in a number of new commercial relationships. Chief amongst these was a partnership with his brother-in-law Robert Davis who had moved to Belfast from Newry in parallel with his sister Jane's becoming Mrs Holmes in 1782. Together Holmes and Davis (who traded as James Holmes & Co) invested in sugar refining and salt manufacture, their total holdings in these ventures amounting by 1799 to £1,900 (equivalent to about £115,000 today); and James Holmes over the same period maintained and indeed increased his own substantial involvement in a milling operation at Inver near Larne, in partnership with Thomas Barklie. Meanwhile another Barklie (Allen) had become the business partner of John Holmes when he retired from banking in the mid-1790s and resumed his mercantile activities.

Perhaps it was whilst he was in banking and detached from the daily grind as a merchant that John Holmes, in contrast to his brother, developed an interest both in public affairs and in having the occasional holiday. Reference has already been made to his "taking the waters" in Bath about 1795 along with his close friend and banking colleague John Ewing; and Dr Gamble in his thesis records that about four years earlier John Holmes had been to Harrogate for a similar break, for he wrote a letter from there to his son-in-law or prospective son-in-law, the younger Henry Joy of the News Letter (Joy married Mary Isabella, eldest of Holmes' seven children). At that time Holmes had a country house at Cliftonville to the north-west of the built-up area; and he had begun his association with the Reading Society which led to his involvement in its accommodation sub-committee, to the Honorary Treasurership, and ultimately (in 1800) to a Vice-Presidency. The affairs of the Charitable Society also commanded his attention; and in the mid-1790s he played a leading part in negotiations to clear the way for the provision of a public water-supply through the agency of the Society.

But it was because of his deep involvement in the burning political issues of the day that John Holmes became even better known, beginning with his proposing the main resolution on Catholic Emancipation at one of the great meetings on that subject in Belfast in the first half of 1792. Together with men like Dr Alexander Haliday, the most eminent physician in Belfast at the time, and Henry Joy of the News Letter, John Holmes was arguing for a gradual approach to Catholic Emancipation; but the mood of the overwhelming majority of the inhabitants of the town, expressed forcibly by men like fellow foundation-member of the Chamber Robert Getty, was for immediate action to dismantle the legal inhibitions on Catholics and any other less-favoured groups in the community. Many who felt that way ultimately became United Irishmen, whereas the moderate liberals in the end "declared for the King" either by joining the Yeomanry or by associating themselves with public statements against armed rebellion. John Holmes therefore joined Charles Ranken's Yeoman Cavalry in 1797; and was one of the signatories to the oft-repeated public condemnation of *"the atrocious insurrection now existing"*.

In contrast with their joint and several contributions to business development and with John's other community involvements (which included membership from 1785 of the

Harbour Corporation), the Holmes brothers left a singularly unimpressive record in the Chamber of Commerce. At the historic first meeting of the Council on 25 October 1783, when Waddell Cunningham was elected President, John Holmes was elected Vice-President; but for some now unrecorded reason he did not attend a single one of the thirty Council meetings that took place between then and the first AGM in June 1784. And worse was to follow: for when brother James was elected President on 7 February 1792 he disappeared from the record about a fortnight later, leaving the historian to ponder why it was that by 23 February the venerable Alexander Orr, Immediate Past-President, was again in the chair and being described simply as "President". Neither James nor John featured again in the records of the Chamber; and it is tempting to speculate that a factor in this was John's overt gradualism in political matters in contrast with the immediacy of the reforming zeal of most of his business colleagues.

In due course John withdrew physically as well as politically from the Belfast scene; for by 1812 he was living in partial retirement in Donaghadee and making occasional Sunday forays up to Belfast to attend both the 11.00 am and the 1.00 pm service at the First Church in Rosemary Street. And at times the devotions as well as the interlude between services must have been chilly, for the church committee (of which John Holmes was a member) talked for thirty years about whether to heat the premises. When a proposition to install a stove was considered in 1803, they settled for curtains; when it was considered again in 1821, it was turned down flat; and it was not until October 1832, seven years after John Holmes had gone to his reward, that the church was closed for six months to permit amongst other renovations, the *"introduction of hot-water apparatus"!*

SAMUEL HYDE

Lancashire-born Samuel Hyde and his wife Peggy (née Hamilton, of Ballymenoch near Holywood) were the centre-pieces of another remarkable mosaic of business families linked by marriage. They had three daughters who all marrried well: Elizabeth to entrepreneurial young businessman Thomas Greg in 1747; Margaret to Waddell Cunningham in 1765, the year that he returned to Belfast from New York with his fortune made; and Hannah, in the same year, to Captain Robert Batt, lately of the 18th Regiment of Foot but since committed to a business career as a condition of the marriage. And so when Samuel Hyde, linen draper and merchant, owner of a substantial property on the northern side of the town which he had named "Hydepark", joined the Chamber in 1783 he could number amongst his fellow foundation members two sons-in-law (Waddell Cunningham and Thomas Greg) and two grandchildren (Cunningham Greg and Narcissus Batt), another record that probably still stands. The Hydes also had two sons, John who was a partner with Robert Legg pre-1777 in the Old Sugar House in Rosemary Lane; and Samuel jnr who went back into the textile industry in Lancashire from which his father had originated.

Samuel snr through his own business activities and through his daughters contributed greatly to the town of his adoption; and he clearly had an early commitment to this, for he was one of the eighteen business and professional men of the town who gathered in "The George", a convivial hostelry in the North Street area, on the evening of Friday 28 August 1752 under the chairmanship of the Sovereign *"to consider of a proper way to raise a sum for building a poor House & Hospital & a new Church in or near the Town of Belfast".* It was that initiative that led to the formation of the Charitable Society and to the provision in 1772 of the Poorhouse and Infirmary. And it was the commitment of merchants such as Samuel Hyde to fund-raising and voluntary service that enabled the dream of 1752 to become a reality twenty years later — a reality that has since served the community well for the whole of its two-hundred-and-eleven years.

HUGH HYNDMAN

The name Hyndman occurs frequently in the commercial annals of Belfast for the late 18th and early 19th Centuries. It is therefore not surprising that there were two Hyndmans, Hugh and James, amongst the fifty-nine foundation members of the Chamber. Little is known of Hugh Hyndman's business connections other than that he became a partner for £300 in John Smylie & Co, glassmakers, when that company was re-structured in 1791. A Robert Hyndman, who became active in the Chamber after 1802 and was Treasurer in 1807, was also a new partner in Smylie's in 1791. Hugh Hyndman served on the Council of the Chamber in 1784/85 and again in the following year; and he was at that time also one of the representatives of the Chamber in the Belfast Marine Charity Society, an organisation that existed to aid widows and orphans of seamen lost in the many shipwrecks of those days.

JAMES HYNDMAN

James Hyndman's business interests centred on wool, for he was a retailer of Irish and English woollen goods in his own right and a partner in one or more wholesale businesses with the Neilsons, the most famous of the Belfast woollen drapers. In contrast with these activities as a merchant, he was also a notary public who acted as Town Clerk for a time. Nevertheless he was another of the Volunteers of 1778 who like Henry Haslett became a captain in the "green" arm that emerged in 1793; and he was active too in the Reading Society, in Masonic Lodge No 257, and in the First Presbyterian Church, in the records of which he is shown as "of High Street" in 1790 and "of Donegall Street" in 1812.

VALENTINE JONES

According to legend, divinity students in their examinations are often asked to distinguish between the major and minor prophets of the Old Testament. For the amateur historian of the commercial life of Belfast as the 18th Century moved towards the 19th, the comparable question is to distinguish between the first, second, third, and fourth Valentine Joneses that co-existed in the town at that time. The younger Joneses were the straight-line descendants (son, grandson, great-grandson) of the Valentine Jones who joined the Chamber in 1783 at the age of seventy-two and presided at the meeting on 23 October to elect the first Council: and he has generally been described since as "Valentine Jones snr" or "Valentine Jones I", even though his Welsh father was yet another Valentine Jones! Exactly what brought the family to Belfast is not known; but what is known is that when Valentine Jones I was just sixteen himself he married a fifteen-year-old Huguenot lass called Rouchet, with the result that Valentine Jones II was around before his father was eighteen or his mother seventeen. And it was this flying start that enabled the family to achieve a unique distinction at a ball in the historic Assembly Room in Waring Street over seventy years later: in a lively quadrille all four of the male partners were Valentine Joneses, ranging from the sprightly great-grandfather aged ninety to the teenage great-grandson making his debut. By then the family connection was huge, for there had been five children of the first marriage of the great-grandparent, several of whom were married and had families of their own; and when his first wife died the bold Valentine I who was then in his fifties had married a young widow, Mrs Ross, who bore him a second family.

In business this venerable and prolific head of the clan was a wine merchant with deep involvement in the West Indies trade, in partnership with Thomas Bateson of Orangefield. From about 1790 his main warehouse was in Winecellar Entry, which ran from Rosemary Lane to High Street. These premises had been provided by rebuilding or renovating the old White's Tavern which was the previous source of attraction on that site. The partnership probably had investments in the sugar fields of the West Indies; and it is likely to have been that that took Valentine Jones II to Barbados, where he spent a major part of his life before returning to Belfast in July of the year in which the Chamber was formed. While overseas he had taken on a number of important roles in the public administration of the colony; and he was the recipient of a warm testimonial from the merchants and principal inhabitants of Bridgetown at the time of his departure for the homeland.

In that homeland Valentine Jones I was also renowned for his contributions to the community. Like Samuel Hyde he had been present at that famous first meeting in August 1752 of the merchants and other prominent inhabitants of the town who were determined to raise funds to provide a home and hospital for the destitute poor: and he continued to be involved in the work of the Charitable Society for at least fifty years. In due course Valentine II on his return from Barbados became equally involved both as an administrator and as a benefactor, providing an unsecured loan of £2,000 in 1797 when the financial resources of the Society had been denuded through its exertions in the provision of a public water-supply. Father and son were also involved in the General Dispensary and in the Reading Society; and they took a moderate liberal stance in the political turmoils of the late 18th Century. The elder Valentine died in March 1805 and his son followed three-and-a-half years later during a visit to Portpatrick. Both were interred in the so-called "New Burying Ground" at the back of the Poorhouse, now known as the Old Clifton Street Graveyard; and their memorials, in so far as they have escaped the attention of the vandals of the late 20th Century, bear striking tributes. In the case of Valentine Jones I (whose tomb was shared by his predeceased son-in-law, fellow foundation-member of the Chamber, John Galt Smith I) it is recorded that he *"lived respected and died lamented by* numerous *Descendants and Friends"*: and in the case of his son, *"If the fulfilment of the Moral and Religious, Relative and Social duties of Life Constitutes a Good Man — THIS WAS ONE".*

HENRY AND GEORGE JOY

"An able and upright Counsellor, an impartial Arbitrator — and an Honest man": such were the recorded words of tribute to the ageing Henry Joy snr from the inhabitants of Belfast when they gathered some five years after the Chamber was formed to present him with a fine silver cup in acknowledgement of his innumerable services to the community over a life-time — a life-time that was destined to end a few months later. That Henry Joy, his brother Robert, and his sister Ann were the children of Francis Joy, founder of the Belfast News Letter, and his first wife Margaret (née Martin); and all three of them made immense contributions to the commercial, industrial, political, and sociological life of Belfast not only by their own efforts but also through their children. Henry was the father of George, a merchant and shipbroker who joined the Chamber with him in 1783; and of another Henry, generally known as Counsellor Joy, who became Chief Baron of the Irish Court of Exchequer. The elder Henry was the father too of Elinor, one of the first pupils of David Manson's famous school, who later married David Tomb, another foundation member of the Chamber. Likewise Robert Joy is remembered not only for his being the amateur architect of the Poorhouse, or for his playing a leading part in the introduction of cotton manufacture to Ulster, or for his being (in the words of his obituary) *"the Venerable Father of the Volunteer Army";* but also for his being the real-life father of the remarkable Henry Joy jnr, historian, writer, successor in the News Letter, and moderate-liberal leader of political and commercial thought in Belfast for several decades. And the third member of old Francis Joy's family, daughter Ann, is known not only for her support for her husband Captain John McCracken in his busy life as seafarer, industrialist, and farmer; but also for her being the mother of seven children five of whom in different ways made indelible impressions on the history of the town. These were the pioneering cotton-manufacturers, Francis, John, and William McCracken; the likeable, socially-conscious, debonair, but impetuous leader of the United Irishmen at the Battle of Antrim on 7 June 1798, Henry Joy McCracken, whose young life ended forty-seven days later on the gallows at the front of the old Market House in High Street; and his devoted sister who reputedly wept by his scaffold, Mary Ann McCracken, arguably the most remarkable woman of her time, who lived as a spinster with her executed brother's illegitimate daughter to the age of ninety-six and worked tirelessly for the relief of poverty, hunger, and suffering in the town for most of that very long life. Such was the fibre and such the future of the Joy/McCracken dynasty represented amongst the foundation members of the Chamber in 1783 by Henry Joy snr and his son George.

Most of Henry's interests whether in business or in community service were shared with his younger brother Robert. When their father left the Belfast scene about 1745 to go into semi-retirement in Randalstown, they jointly took over his two main enterprises in the town. These were the printing business in Bridge Street that included the publication of the News Letter; and the related paper mill in the Cromac district, from which the Joy Street of modern times took its name. Together with their brother-in-law, Captain John McCracken, and Thomas McCabe, the watchmaker, they were associated too in a cotton mill in Francis Street, which evolved from the experimental introduction of cotton manufacture to the Poorhouse some years previously. Henry's son George, on the other hand, appears to have been a merchant, with interests in shipping including the emigrant traffic; and Dr Norman Gamble in his thesis refers to George Joy's having been in partnership up to October 1784 with Thomas Hardin, Valentine Jones II, and David Tomb (all fellow foundation-members of the Chamber) in an agency for sailings of the emigrant ship HOPE from Newry to Pennsylvania. According to Dr Gamble, George Joy indeed became the exclusive owner of that business in October 1784 by buying out the other partners following the death of Thomas Hardin.

But like most members of the Joy family down the ages, the father and son who joined the Chamber in 1783 had as many interests outside business as within. Henry Joy snr and his brother Robert were deeply involved in the Charitable Society from its beginnings till the end of their days. At first their role was in the administration of the great lotteries organised to raise money for the building of the Poorhouse; but later they became leading lights in every aspect of the Society's work. In days when misappropriation and forgeries were everyday occurrences, the trust placed in Henry was shown by his being appointed not only one of the three key-holders of the great triply-locked iron chest that contained the accumulating funds of the Society in the form of Government debentures etc, but also its very custodian. For, as reported by Dr R W M Strain in his fascinating history of the Society, the Committee in 1768 *"Ordered that the said Iron Chest be placed at Henry Joy's in the small closet adjoining his Dining Room"!* At that time Henry had been Deputy Town Clerk for some nine years; and he continued in that office till 1772. Nine years later he was appointed a burgess of the Corporation and town of Belfast, an event which was described subsequently as *"a signal honour for an uncompromising Whig"*. But even if the appointment was a political enigma, it must have been an unqualified success; for many years later the same honour was conferred on his son George. The elder Joys were also enthusiastic supporters of the White Linen Hall project in the 1780's and subscribed generously to the building fund. George Joy of the next generation obviously inherited the tradition of service to his fellow businessmen, for he was elected to the Council of the Chamber on at least six occasions between 1783 and 1808.

For most of their lives the Joys lived next door to the McCrackens in High Street; and the two families were also closely associated in the Third Congregation in Rosemary Lane. But when it came to politics there was a significant difference in emphasis: both were liberal, both sought Parliamentary reform, both wanted to see Catholic Emancipation; but the McCrackens were much more impatient than the Joys. In the end that difference in emphasis became a chasm, with the Joys sticking to the original Volunteers, the Yeomanry, and the King; and the McCrackens gravitating through the "green" Volunteers to the most militant wing of the United Irishmen, resulting in periods in Dublin jails for two members of the family in advance of the Rebellion, and death on the gallows in Belfast for one of them afterwards. For the Joys, on the other hand, there was always a tempering of idealism with realism, a blending of the need for reform with the need for preservation of the constitution. And never was that better illustrated than in the last journey of old Francis Joy, father of Henry and grandfather of George, a few months before his death in 1790 at the age of ninety-three. He had travelled all the way on a dirt-track from Randalstown to Antrim to vote in an important election for the candidates of reform. His grandson from Belfast was amazed to see him. *"What brought you here, sir?"*, he asked. And back came the reply that epitomised the spirit of the Joys then and since. *"The good of my country"*, said the frail old man.

JAMES TRAIL KENNEDY

Sons of the manse played an important part in the commercial and political history of Belfast in the late 18th Century. James Trail Kennedy (1751-1832) who served on the Council of the Chamber on four separate occasions was the son of the Rev Gilbert Kennedy, Minister of the Second Presbyterian Church in Rosemary Lane from 1744 till 1773; and his mother's maiden name was Trail. But the young man's interest in Rosemary Lane was not confined to his Presbyterian heritage or ancestry; for it was there that he first became established as a wine and spirit merchant, a base from which he built up partnerships with other well-known drink and grocery interests over the succeeding years. In the words of George Benn, the 19th Century historian of Belfast, this led to "fame and fortune"; and it led also to a fine country house and spacious riverside grounds at Annadale, a few miles south of the built-up area. Growing prosperity was reflected too in investments in glassmaking and brewing, which by 1791 totalled £1,300, equivalent to about £80,000 in modern money. But there was tragedy as well, for his son James died in 1806 at the age of fourteen and was buried in Drumbeg. Indeed all but one of the Kennedy children died within the life-span of their parents; and that one, a daughter named Elizabeth, survived only by dint of prolonged trips with her mother to a series of health resorts on the Continent. But the substantial investment in her health seems to have paid off; for in the end she outlived her first husband, a Mr Bomford, and went on to finish her days as the wife of the Church of Ireland Primate, Archbishop Beresford of Armagh.

ROBERT KNOX

Robert Knox was a merchant who engaged in the West Indies, Scandinavian, and Baltic trades. In the year in which the Chamber was formed he was therefore advertising in the News Letter a wide range of commodities such as scale sugar, well-cured herrings, and Dantzig ashes. Though he does not appear to have played any part in the 18th Century Chamber other than to pay his membership subscription, he re-joined when the organisation was reconstituted in 1802 after the trauma of 1798; and his second sojourn in membership seems to have been just as quietly inconspicuous as his first!

JOHN LUKE

The John Luke who joined the Chamber in 1783 was probably an older brother of James Luke, who came to prominence in banking and in the Chamber some twenty-five years later. If that is the case, he was the son of James Luke of Islandreagh and

Sarah Thompson of Greenmount; and his main business activity in 1783 would have been as a partner with his brother in a woollen drapery in Bridge Street. Both James and John Luke were clear signatories of the 1785 Parliamentary petition of the merchants and principal inhabitants of Belfast in opposition to Pitt's Twenty Propositions; and five years earlier a John Luke with apparently identical handwriting had signed a petition calling for a "bounty" or export subsidy on linen. There is therefore little doubt that the Lukes were engaged in one or more branches of the textile trade.

THOMAS LYONS

Thomas Lyons was a linen bleacher, with a fine home at "Old Park" built about 1780. Outside his own business interest he became a member in 1783 of the original project committee of the White Linen Hall; and he was also at that time an enthusiastic Volunteer, having joined the First Belfast Company in 1778 and later transferred to Third Belfast as an officer.

HUGH MONTGOMERY

When Hugh Montgomery (1743-1832), the eldest son of Robert and Isabella Montgomery of Glenarm, joined the Chamber in 1783 it was a case of life beginning at forty, for there had been few indications in his first forty years of the fame and fortune that lay ahead. He had a retail business in North Street where he had built up a reputation for fair trading, exemplified in the nickname "Split Fig" (which was unearthed by C Douglas Deane for an article in the News Letter in August 1981). The origin of the nickname was reputed to be that Montgomery was so anxious to be scrupulously fair to himself and his customers that he would even split a fig to get the weight of the order "dead on". This anecdote implies that Montgomery traded in imported provisions; but if that were the case it was not his only line, for in the News Letter of 7 February 1783 he proudly made the following announcement to the fashion-conscious gentlemen of the town:

"Hugh Montgomery has just imported from the best manufacturers an extensive assortment of winter and spring waistcoat patterns, viz. Long and short piled mohair shags of every colour; also a great variety of Rodneys, all silk stripes, lutherines, sattinets, nankeens etc with a general assortment of wollen drapery, which he will sell on reasonable terms for ready money".

And the fashion-conscious gentlemen of the day must have responded well, for Hugh Montgomery in his business in North Street was on a springboard that would take him to a pinnacle of riches and fame before the end of the century.

That commercial success secured for the Montgomery family to the present day an honoured place in Burke's "Irish Family Records"; and the brief account that is given there of the first Hugh's life refers to his return from the American state of Virginia shortly before his purchase in 1798 of the 17th Century home of the Macnaughtens at Benvarden near Dervock in County Antrim. It is therefore tempting to assume that it was a sojourn in the United States that took Montgomery from being a modest fair-trader selling figs and waistcoats in North Street to his end-of-century situation of being

Hugh Montgomery (1743-1832), foundation member of the Chamber 1783, President 1802-1803, and founder in 1809 of Montgomery's Bank, which was the forerunner of the Northern Bank.

(From a portrait by Thompson in the family home at Benvarden)

one of the richest men in the North of Ireland, with property in Belfast valued at £60,000 (equivalent to about three-and-a-half-million today) and a most prestigious seat at Benvarden as well. But there are so many indications of the proliferation of Montgomery's business interests in and around Belfast in the late 1780's and early 1790's that it must be concluded, firstly, that if he did go to Virginia his stay was relatively short; and, secondly, that he was well on the way to his ultimate fortune **before** his reputed flirtation with the New World. For example S Shannon Millin reported in "Sidelights" that in 1787 Montgomery became a £500 partner with Waddell Cunningham and others in John Cranston & Co, maltsters and brewers, and that he maintained the investment when the partnership was restructured in 1791; and Dr Norman Gamble in his thesis reported that Montgomery also invested in a flour mill at Antrim in 1791 and was the senior partner in a firm that was the sole importer of salt from Portugal to the North of Ireland in 1796. Furthermore Douglas Deane in his August 1981 newspaper article referred to Montgomery's living in the fashionable and expensive Linenhall Street in the 1790's, an observation confirmed by an entry in the 1790 membership list of the First Presbyterian Church. Thus the opulence that is usually associated with Montgomery's return from Virginia near the end of the century had in fact begun to appear some ten years earlier; and it is likely to have come mainly from shrewd trading in North Street rather than from his marriage in 1785 at the age of forty-two to Marjorie, daughter of Dr Robert Allen of Ballymena, or from the bequests of his father who died at Glenarm in 1792 at the age of eighty-one and was survived by four or possibly five of his nine children.

Hugh Montgomery's considerable contribution to the work of the Chamber was concentrated into two periods, the first in the ten years after 1783 and the second in the initial five years of the 19th Century. He was elected to Council on five separate occasions between October 1783 and May 1793; and in April 1784 he became a member of a committee established to investigate the feasibility and cost of deepening the seaward channel from the main quay at the end of High Street to the Pool of Garmoyle. That in turn led to his becoming a foundation member of the Harbour Corporation in the following year. Seventeen years later it was the same Hugh Montgomery that presided over one of the most significant events in the history of the Chamber: that was a meeting of twenty-two merchants in the White Linen Hall on 1 March 1802 at which a decision to reconstitute the Chamber after the political and military traumas of the immediately preceding years was confirmed. Two days later at a meeting of the new Council in the Exchange Coffee Room Montgomery was elected President, with Robert Getty as Vice-President and John Tisdall as paid clerk. Under his leadership, the Council was most active on many matters, with meetings being held weekly in the Donegall Arms or at the Exchange; and the keenness and sense of urgency that pervaded the period were such that on one occasion an attempt was even made to have a Council meeting on a Sunday! Montgomery himself turned up but he was joined by only two of his fifteen colleagues; and the meeting had to be adjourned. This notable Presidency came to an end on 15 August 1804, when Montgomery was succeeded by another of the men of 1783, William Sinclaire.

Hugh Montgomery's withdrawal in 1804 from the front line of Chamber activity may have been due to his becoming High Sheriff of County Antrim that year or to his new involvement in the Discount Company, the only survivor of the financial institutions that had been established in Belfast in the late 18th Century. Five years later there were two new commercial banks in the town: "Gordon's" which ultimately became the Belfast Bank; and "Montgomery's" which ultimately became the Northern Bank. Hugh Montgomery was the senior partner in Montgomery's Bank, with James Orr, John Hamilton, and John Sloane as his main associates; and he is therefore rightly regarded as the founder of the Northern Bank, an institution in which he at one time had an investment of £20,000 and an assured salary of £900 a year. With the bank firmly established as the leading financial institution of the town, he retired in 1822 to Benvarden and was succeeded as a director by his second son, Hugh jnr. Ten years later he died at Benvarden and was interred in the graveyard of Bushmills Presbyterian Church.

Though the first Hugh Montgomery died over a hundred-and-fifty years ago, his memory is perpetuated to this day not only by the continued existence of the bank that he founded but also by the achievements of his descendants. His eldest son John succeeded to the family seat at Benvarden; and John's great-great-grandson, Hugh James Montgomery (another High Sheriff of County Antrim), still resides in the house today, though much of the estate now comprises the Causeway Coast Safari Park. Miss Annabel Montgomery of the Belfast public relations consultancy, Inter-City Bureaux, which is advising the Chamber on the bicentenary celebrations of 1983, is that Hugh's sister; which means that she is a great-great-great-grand-daughter of the Hugh Montgomery who joined the Chamber in 1783. Another branch of the family was sustained through that Hugh's second son, Hugh jnr (1793-1867), who was a director of the Northern Bank for forty-three years and who in the year of his father's death (1832) bought the second family seat, Ballydrain at Upper Malone. One-hundred-and-thirty years later that delightful estate and a very solid house built on it in 1835 by the second Hugh Montgomery became the new home of Malone Golf Club.

And so through the Northern Bank, through Malone Golf Club, and through the work of successive generations of the Montgomery family there are many links to the present day from the 18th Century Hugh Montgomery, a man remarkable by many standards and not least by the fact that two of his grandsons fought with the elite of the Cavalry Division in the Crimean War. One was Robert James, eldest son of John of Benvarden and captain in the 5th Dragoon Guards, which were part of the Heavy Brigade; and he survived. The other was Hugh, eldest son of Hugh jnr of Ballydrain and coronet in the 13th Light Dragoons; and he, in the words of his memorial at Drumbeg Parish Church a few hundred yards from his family home, was *"killed in the Memorable Charge of the Light Cavalry at the Battle of Balaclava, 25 October 1854, aged twenty-four years"*. In that appalling blunder of war, the 13th Light Dragoons were in the front line of Lord Cardigan's little force of six-hundred-and-seventy-three mounted men as they charged into the mouths of the Russian cannon and the enfilading fire of several thousand muskets; and the sudden death of the third Hugh in the first few minutes of the battle was as sure and certain as the sudden climb of his remarkable grandfather to the highest pinnacle of commercial success in the last few decades of the previous century.

JOHN NEILSON

John Neilson came from Ballyroney near Rathfriland in County Down. His father Alexander was the minister of the Presbyterian church there from 1751 till his death in May 1782; and there were at least two other sons, Samuel and Thomas. John was probably the first of the family to come to Belfast; and he was apprenticed for a time to a well-known woollen draper in the town. Later, in partnership with James Hyndman, the Neilsons developed their own business at the junction of Bridge Street and Waring Street (which was then called Broad Street); and this became known as the "Irish Woollen Warehouse", the largest and most profitable establishment of its kind in the town. John was denied the opportunity either to enjoy the fruits of their joint labours in the business or to make a major contribution to the Chamber, for he died in 1787 while still in his thirties. But his early death at least saved him the anguish of seeing the profits of the business being whittled away in support of the extreme radical cause espoused by his brother from about 1792. Samuel became the chief proprietor of the Northern Star and a leading member of the Society of United Irishmen; and when the Star was the subject of several prosecutions for sedition in the middle 1790's, it was the woollen business in Bridge Street that had to bear the heavy fines imposed. In the end, Samuel's partners were left to carry on a mortgaged business without his help, for he was arrested in September 1796 and confined in Kilmainham jail in Dublin till February 1798. And there was worse to come, for he broke a promise not to become re-involved in the revolutionary movement; was captured in Dublin in May 1798 after a fight in which he was seriously injured; and was subsequently imprisoned till 1802, mostly in Fort George in the North of Scotland. Afterwards he was deported to Holland, from which he finally emigrated to the United States after one last secret visit to Belfast and Dublin. Thus the Neilsons were an excellent example of the degree to which sons of the manse were involved both in commercial development and in radical politics in 18th Century Belfast.

ALEXANDER ORR

Judging by the newspaper announcements of 1783, Alexander Orr was another of the Belfast merchants with interests in a wide range of imported merchandise including tea from India, cider from Bristol, and wood ashes from Dantzig. In later years he also became involved in insurance; and Dr Norman Gamble reports that Orr was chairman of the first locally-owned insurance company, the Belfast General established in 1791. In this he was associated with three other foundation members of the Chamber: Robert Getty, William Tennent, and Henry Haslett who was Secretary. The company appears to have operated successfully for a number of years; but it was wound up early in 1797. As Dr Gamble points out this could have been due either to the financial consequences of a fire at the Donegall Arms or to the unsettled times and the arrest of Haslett in September 1796 on a charge of high treason. Alexander Orr meanwhile seems to have avoided involvement in the extreme radical movement, his only recorded associations outside his own business interests being with the First Presbyterian Church and with the Chamber. He was an assiduous member of the first Council, often taking the chair at the weekly meetings in the absence of the President and Vice-President; and he was similarly involved in 1787, having presided at a meeting on 20 January to get the Chamber resuscitated after a dull period in 1786. Eventually his reliability was recognised by his being appointed President for 1791/92; and he continued in that role till early in 1794, when the Chamber apparently faded out for about eight years in consequence of the unsettled state of the country. It would seem, however, that Orr first tried to lay down the mantle early in 1792, for James Holmes was elected President on 7 February that year and presided at a Council meeting thirteen days later. However, Alexander Orr was back in the Presidential chair by 23 February; and the student of Chamber affairs is left to speculate on possible reasons for the reversion, for the records of the period give not the slightest clue.

JAMES PARK

Though James Park made no recorded impact on the affairs of the Chamber he must have an honoured place in its history. The reason is that it was he who presided at a meeting of the merchants of Belfast in the Donegall Arms on 22 April 1783 when the idea of establishing a Chamber of Commerce in the town was first mooted. Thereafter he seems to have taken a back seat, for it was Thomas Greg who presided at later exploratory meetings. In 1783 Park was probably involved in the export of provisions to the West Indies; and earlier in life he had lived there for a time. He had a nephew whose name was also James Park; and it was that member of the family who joined the Volunteers in 1778 and later went to the West Indies as agent in Grenada for Waddell Cunningham.

JOHN ROBINSON

Three-and-a-half years before the Chamber was formed the merchants of Belfast had petitioned Parliament to grant export subsidies on linen. Amongst the signatories to that petition were John and Samuel Robinson, who were presumably involved in the linen trade. As was frequently the case around that time the plea of the merchants was successful; and this and other encouragements to increased trade were acknowledged in a Saint Patrick's Day Address to the King, which contained some memorable phrases. The concluding flourish, for example, referred to *"this indisputable truth that Britain and Ireland must rise or fall together"*. Be that as it may, John Robinson had a second commercial interest, for he was an original subscriber to the Belfast Discount Company, the only 18th Century financial institution to survive into the 19th; and he was still involved in the company in 1804, by which time its offices had been moved from Rosemary Lane to Bridge Street.

JOHN RUSSELL

About the same time as he contemplated joining the new Chamber of Commerce, John Russell was casting his eyes across the Lagan to the County Antrim side. The family home and bleaching greens were at Edenderry on the County Down bank of the river about three miles south of Belfast; and it was in 1783 that Russell also acquired Newforge, about a mile downstream on the other side. He and his wife Catherine Helen (who was a daughter of John Holmes, fellow foundation-member of the Chamber) had two sons who in due course became known as "William of

Edenderry" and "John of Newforge", both bleaching linen in the family tradition. The original John must have been amongst the most important linen drapers of the day, for he was one of the four lessees of the site for the White Linen Hall and a member of the original project committee. Bleaching continued at Newforge until well into the 19th Century.

ARCHIBALD SCOTT

Whether Archibald Scott was a relative of the Robert Scott amongst the foundation members is not known. Both were signatories of the famous petition against the Act of Union in 1800; and Archibald Scott was also a signatory to the historic document opposing Pitt's Twenty Propositions in 1785. Two years earlier, at about the same time as he joined the Chamber, Scott was one of almost fifty business and professional people who called a public meeting in Belfast to endorse the resolutions drawn up by the Volunteer delegates at their second historic convention in Dungannon, on 8 September 1783. Thus whatever his main activity in life, his politics were liberal.

ROBERT SCOTT

In partnership with John Scott of Falls, who was presumably either his father or his brother, Robert Scott was a linen draper and general merchant. In June 1783 their names were coupled as signatories to a notice in the News Letter in which over twenty linen drapers expressed their commitment to a monthly market for unbleached linen that had just been established in Kirkcubbin; and seventeen years later, Robert Scott was amongst those who publicly opposed the Act of Union. Apart from his involvement in the linen industry, Scott appears to have been an importer; and the News Letter of 11 November 1783 carried a notice from him about the arrival from London of a consignment of "New Bag Hops" in the sailing-ship SALLY.

WILLIAM SEED

When he joined the Chamber William Seed was a general merchant with premises in Weighhouse Lane, which ran from the dock in High Street towards Ann Street. But 1783 was to be a turning point in his business life for it was then that he acquired an old corn-mill on the eastern side of the Lagan and converted it into a flour mill. Later, with fellow foundation-member of the Chamber Robert Thomson as a partner, this "Beersbridge Mill" of William Seed & Co became one of the most important sources of flour in and around the town. It must have been a major source too of the capital that Seed began to deploy in other businesses from about 1790. And by the second half of the decade he had total investments of about £2,000 in partnerships concerned with the manufacture of muslin, sailcloth, and ropes. By then he must have been even more concerned about robbers than he was in 1783, when he and fourteen other men of substance living mostly to the south-west of the town placed a strongly-worded notice in the News Letter. This offered grants from a rewards fund for information leading to the conviction of the perpetrators of past or future burglaries in the area. And William Seed's contribution to the fund was to be £4:11:6!

ROBERT SIMMS

Second only to Narcissus Batt in terms of his youthfulness when he joined the Chamber, Robert Simms (1763-1845) presumably sprang from the family that had a tanyard and ropewalk on the site that later became Torrens' Market off Garfield Street. If that were indeed his background it is perhaps surprising that neither tanning nor ropemaking featured in the range of business activities in which he engaged in the course of the next forty years in partnership with his younger brother William (1765-1845). To begin with, they were merchants; but by the end of the century they had had quite a lengthy involvement in a flour mill at Crumlin and they were the joint owners of a paper mill at Ballyclare. And they had both been in jail!

The arrest of the Simms brothers in February 1797 on a warrant from Dublin Castle was the inevitable culmination of their increasingly deep attachment to the republican cause. They had been committee members of the First Society of United Irishmen from its establishment in Belfast in October 1791; they were amongst the proprietors of the Northern Star; they had been involved with the Neilsons, the McCrackens, and Thomas Russell in the famous picnic on the Cavehill for the militant patriot Wolfe Tone in May 1795, when he and his family were en route for a period of exile in the United States; they had been there too when Tone and a number of the Belfast radicals took a solemn oath on the ancient site of Mac Art's Fort *"never to desist in our efforts until we have subverted the authority of England over our country and asserted her independence";* and they had been sucked into the preparations for armed conflict as the movement drifted from radicalism to rebellion.

With informers rampant and the Northern Star preaching sedition, the arrest of the Simms brothers in February 1797 can hardly have been a surprise to anyone. But what was a surprise was their release at the end of the year or early in 1798, in company with virtually all the political prisoners of the period; for this enabled them to become re-involved in the republican movement as it sped towards rebellion. For Robert Simms, merchant, flour miller, papermaker, past Secretary of the Linenhall Library, past Council member of the Chamber of Commerce, and joint organiser of the famous Harp Festival of 1792, that involvement with the sword was intended by his brethren to be deep and prominent; for he was selected by the Belfast Directory to be Commander-in-Chief of the rebel forces in County Antrim. But at the eleventh hour, on 1 June 1798, he defected from that unsought role; and Henry Joy McCracken took his place, which led McCracken to the Battle of Antrim on 7 June and to the gallows in High Street on 17 July. The reason for Simms' defection remains a mystery: it could have been on the vital issue of rebellion without the originally intended French aid; or it could have been for purely personal reasons, for he was a family man with a pregnant wife and two little girls at the time. Whatever the reason it attracted a lot of comment then and since: and he was accused of *"playing fast and loose with the cause"*, a sudden fall from grace received by the United Irishmen of County Antrim with *"inexpressible astonishment"*. Nor did his defection save him from the rigours of the law, for he was again arrested and sent this time to the lonely Fort George in the North of Scotland.

After this tragic period the Simms brothers (who were still only in their thirties) resumed their business activities in and around Belfast. And both had clearly had enough of extreme political action, for they did their best to dissuade former Linenhall librarian Thomas Russell, *"the man from God knows where"*, from becoming involved (fatally as it turned out) in Robert Emmet's abortive rising in 1803. Their association with the Chamber in the 19th Century was also minimal, William being listed as a member when the organisation was reconstituted in February 1802 but Robert apparently not bothering to become re-involved. Both did, however, become involved in the new Academical Institution, Robert as one of the three foundation "auditors" and the first stipendiary Secretary, and William as one of the twenty "managers" named in the Act of 1810. In family matters, on the other hand, life was exceedingly hard on both of them, for William and his wife (who lived in a fine house at "The Grove") lost their first and second daughters in infancy and their third at the age of ten; and three of Robert's daughter also died during his lifetime. Peculiarly that similarity of tragic experience, which paralleled their closeness in business, in politics, and in public service throughout their long lives, was to be paralleled again in their departure from the earthly scene. For Robert died in June 1845 at the age of eighty-two and was buried in Clifton Street: and William followed only two months later at the age of eighty and was buried at Knockbreda.

WILLIAM SINCLAIRE

"A well-known figure in his brass-buttoned green hunting coat, while his loud voice echoed the length of the new street". Such was C Douglas Deane's 1981 description of a sporting young linen-bleacher who almost two-hundred years before had by the age of twenty-five become sufficiently prosperous to be building a fine house for himself and his family in the most fashionable and expensive thoroughfare in Belfast. The thoroughfare was "The Flags", which ultimately became Donegall Place; and the prosperous young linen-merchant was Will Sinclaire (1760-1807), foundation member of the Chamber at the age of twenty-three, who had been picked out immediately by his older business colleagues to serve on the first Council and was destined to become its President some twenty years later.

The Sinclaires came from Scotland at the beginning of the 18th Century; and they first resided in the Newtownards area. Will's father, Thomas Sinclaire snr (1719-1798), had been involved in the retail grocery business in Belfast, before succeeding to an extensive linen business on the death of his elder brother John. This included a large home and adjoining business premises in Mill Street, together with three bleaching-greens on the western fringes of the town. Mill Street was the name given at that time to a centre section of the thoroughfare running from "The Parade" (now Castle Place) towards the Falls district; thus it came between the modern Castle Street and the modern Divis Street and included a portion of both. On that thoroughfare the imposing home of the Sinclaires was situated opposite to the end of King Street; and it became one of the most hospitable houses in town under the patronage of Will's father, who was intensely interested in Irish affairs and entertained royally.

Will Sinclaire was the second of four sons in a rich family; and from his father's hearth he inherited not only wealth and a prominent place in the linen industry, but also precocious powers of organisation, leadership, and inventiveness, together with an intense interest in Irish politics and a fanatical love of field sports. In business, he carried on an extensive bleachworks at Ligoniel, which by the early 1790s was reputed to be the largest, the most mechanised, and the most technically advanced in the region. Nevertheless in the last fifteen years of the 18th Century he found time also to become involved in the Discount Office; to be a most diligent Council member of the Chamber for four spells each of about twelve months, in the course of which he seldom missed a meeting; to act as land-agent for David Ker's extensive estates in County Down; to undertake pioneering committee work in the Reading Society; to become a foundation member of the Northern Whig Club in 1790 and its Secretary in 1792; and to join the secret committee whose meeting with Wolfe Tone in Drew's Tavern on Saturday 14 October 1791 led to the establishment of the First Society of United Irishmen, with Sinclaire as Chairman and William Simms as Secretary. Whether he became involved in the paramilitary activities of the republican movement in the last five years of the 18th Century is not known: certainly he was heading that way in 1793 when he was overtly in a position of leadership in the "green" wing of the Volunteers. But his later tracks were well covered, if they were ever made; and he escaped arrest or any ignominy or business disadvantage from his deep association with extreme radicalism.

But Will Sinclaire's smooth rehabilitation in the years immediately after the Rebellion was the result of good judgment as well as good fortune. He had attended the trial of Wolfe Tone in Dublin in November 1798, but less than twelve months later he was entertaining Lord Cornwallis, the Lord Lieutenant, to breakfast in the course of a visit to Belfast by this embodiment of the British connection; and afterwards they went to the bleachworks ("The Green") where the famous visitor was most impressed. In the words of Mary McNeill's enthralling life of the uncompromising Mary Ann McCracken, Sinclaire had *"modified his republicanism in the interests of trade"*. By the same token Mrs McTier wrote to her brother Dr Drennan in October 1799 that: *"WS wishes much to talk with you on the new Union"*. And seven-and-a-half years later Dr Drennan summed it all up, with an uncharacteristically sharp sting in the tail, when he wrote to his sister of Will Sinclaire that: *"His head appeared of the shrewd intelligent kind peculiar to the Belfast merchants, gumption without cultivation"*. And Sinclaire certainly displayed plenty of gumption in his all-too-brief business life after the Rebellion, investing £2,500 in 1801 (equivalent to about £150,000 today) in another linen business in partnership with Alexander Stewart, successfully resisting serious labour troubles in his own business in 1804, and becoming President of the Chamber on 15 August in the same year, in succession to Hugh Montgomery. Unfortunately there is no ready record of his performance in that office, for there is a break in the sequence of the minutes from then until 26 August 1807, by which time Robert Bradshaw had succeeded to the Presidency.

Outside business and politics Will Sinclaire had time for the Linenhall Library, for the First and Third Congregations in Rosemary Lane, and for his field sports. And C Douglas Deane records that at the back of his house in Donegall Place he had a virtual menagerie of hawks, hounds, horses, and fighting cocks. He was also a family man, married to Charlotte Pollock who survived him by over forty years; and they had three daughters who married well, to the Rev Edward May, Vicar and Sovereign of Belfast, to Mr Dobbs of Castle Dobbs, and to Archdeacon Butson of Clonfert. In the last years of the famous head of the family, the Sinclaires also enjoyed the pleasures of a summer house at Fortwilliam, overlooking the Carrickfergus Road and the Pool of Garmoyle. But it was probably in his town house in Donegall Place that on 11 February 1807, at the age of forty-seven, Will Sinclaire died without male issue. And some days later his remains were interred in the plot that he had previously purchased in the New Burying Ground at the back of the Poorhouse. Such was the premature earthly end of this man of many parts, born rich but contributing much in the thirty years of his working life.

JOHN GALT SMITH

Like the Valentine Joneses to whom they were related, the John Galt Smiths of Belfast in the late 18th and early 19th Centuries require careful treatment by the amateur historian, for there were at least five of them within the same family connection. However there is no difficulty in identifying the bearer of that name that joined the Chamber in 1783: he was John Galt Smith I (1731-1802), father of John Galt Smith II (1770-1832) who was at that time in only his fourteenth year. What is less certain is whether it was the old man or the son that became a member of the reconstituted Chamber in February 1802. The son had at that time been in partnership with his father after a spell at sea; and it would have been logical for him to have joined the reconstituted Chamber on account of his father's advanced age. But, on the other hand, the fact that the name John Galt Smith does not appear in the records of the Chamber beyond that entry on the surviving membership list of 1802 suggests that it may have been the father who joined again for old time's sake, despite his rapidly declining powers. George Benn records that John Galt Smith I last signed the minutes of the First Presbyterian Congregation — of which he was a long-serving office-bearer — in October 1801; and it is known from the records of Clifton Street Cemetery that he died on 14 December 1802.

Although the first John Galt Smith made no recorded impact on the affairs of the Chamber, he was deeply involved in the trading and manufacturing activities of the town. The noted solicitor and amateur antiquarian, Francis Joseph Bigger, refers to Smith's being in partnership with a relative, Thomas Barklie, in a woollen drapery at No 47 High Street; and S Shannon Millin records that he had an investment of £1,000 in John Cranston & Co, maltsters and brewers, dating from 1787. But Dr Norman Gamble throws light on Smith's main business activities, recording that about 1778 he had taken over the Old Ropewalk established twenty years previously by Captain John McCracken and had been supplying canvas and cordage not only to the local market but also (in the early 1790s) to the United States. Galt Smith apparently retired from the business in 1794, leaving it to be carried on by Captain McCracken's son Francis who had been involved throughout Smith's ownership. Dr Gamble also provides an interesting commentary on the times as well as on the first John Galt Smith when he records that in 1786, when the community was plagued with under-weight and counterfeit coins, Smith was advertising in the News Letter that he would pay for flax in "good gold". His financial solidarity was also indicated by his contributing £100 (equivalent to about £6,000 in modern money) towards the building of the White Linen Hall.

John Galt Smith also did a prodigious amount of community work, particularly in the Charitable Society and in the First Congregation in Rosemary Lane. In the Society he was one of the trusted "key carriers", with access to the funds and bonds stored in the great triply-locked chest in the home of Henry Joy; and he became Honorary Treasurer in 1781, serving in that capacity for at least two years. In the First Congregation he became a member of Committee in 1760 and was appointed Honorary Treasurer in the following year at the age of thirty. He continued in that office for twenty years, until in 1781 he was asked to concentrate on raising and administering funds for the rebuilding of the church. As Treasurer of the Building Fund he was reported in the congregational history of 1883 to have *watched the laying of each successive course of the masonry* till the building was finished and opened for worship, in the year in which the Chamber was formed. It was therefore fitting that ninety years later one of his grandsons, George Kennedy Smith, provided a beautiful window in the meeting-house commemorating the service not only of the original John Galt Smith but also of his son John Galt Smith II and his grandson John Galt Smith IV, who between them had occupied the same pew for almost a hundred years. (Incidentally John Galt Smith I also contributed well to the congregation in numerical terms, for the church records show ten baptisms under the auspices of him and his wife Jane — daughter of Valentine Jones I — between May 1766 and November 1782!).

Smith was deeply involved too in the liberal movement at the end of the 18th Century. He was a lieutenant in one of the Belfast companies of the Volunteers; and he supported the political involvement of the movement. He was also a foundation member of the Northern Whig Club. Later, however, he became disenchanted with the evolving extremism; and from 1797 onwards he was "declaring for the King" in every way possible. This included signing the public statement of support for the civil power issued in June 1797 by Orange Masonic Lodge No 257, of which Smith was at that time Secretary; and he was associated too with a declaration of loyalty issued by the Belfast Yeoman Cavalry after the Rebellion and in the run-up to the Act of Union. Shortly after the implementation of that Act of Union, John Galt Smith's notable power issued in June 1797 by Orange Masonic Lodge No 257, of which Smith was at in the New Burying Ground (Clifton Street) acquired some years previously by his father-in-law, Valentine Jones I. And only another two years and four months were to elapse before the mortal remains of Jones himself were to be laid to rest in the same plot.

JOHN SMYTH

John Smyth was probably a linen draper who travelled around the country markets buying unbleached linen from the weavers. A person of that name was amongst the twenty-four linen merchants who in June 1783 publicly expressed commitment to a new market in Kirkcubbin. There was commitment too to radical principles, for John Smyth was another of the forty-six signatories to the notice of 17 September 1783 calling a public meeting to endorse the resolutions adopted by the second convention of the Volunteers in Dungannon. It was probably he who leased a tenement in North Street to George Langtry in 1789.

JAMES STEVENSON

As with so many of the wealthiest businessmen of the day, linen was the springboard for James Stevenson. From the simplicity of buying brown linen from household weavers and selling it to bleachers or bleaching it himself he diversified in the course of the last twenty years of the 18th Century into partnership in retail groceries (with Henry McKedy); in importation and distribution of requisites for the linen industry, such as potash and flaxseed (with McKedy's widow); and in the manufacture of glass (with John Smylie & Co), ropes and cordage (with James Mason & Co), and sailcloth (with Thomas Ash & Co). In parallel with his activities as a merchant he also became involved in shipbroking; and he was for a time manager or agent for one of the groups that tried to bring order and planning (and cartel arrangements!) into the shipping services of Belfast in the 1780s. In the Chamber he served faithfully as a Council member in 1783/84 and again in 1784/85. He was also a member of the first Harbour Corporation; and he had answered the call to arms in March 1778, to become a private in the "grenadier division" of the First Belfast Company of the Volunteers in direct support of the Company Commander, the very experienced Captain Stewart Banks, predecessor of Captain Waddell Cunningham in that role.

ROBERT STEWART

The Stewarts were one of the most influential families in 18th Century Belfast. Originally the sole family seat was at Ballydrain, now the site of Malone Golf Club; and the head of the family was Robert snr (1701-1784), who married Jane Legg of Malone (now Barnett's Park). In the next generation, however, the family acquired a second seat that became as much part of the Stewart heritage as the old home at Ballydrain. This was Wilmont, across the road from Ballydrain, now within the Sir Thomas and Lady Dixon Park. The sons of Robert snr who occupied these great houses in the middle and later years of the 18th Century were William and John of Wilmont and Robert jnr of Ballydrain; and it was that Robert (1742-1797) who joined the Chamber in 1783.

Linen was the bedrock of the Stewart family fortune; and Robert and his brother William each subscribed no less than £300 (about £18,000 apiece in modern money) to the fund for the building of the White Linen Hall. Not surprisingly, Robert was subsequently asked to serve on the project committee. Likewise they became involved from the beginning in the Discount Company, the rudimentary financial institution established in 1793 to facilitate the linen trade. They ran a number of bleaching greens, one of which was located close to Wilmont; and that one was operating at least until 1815. Robert having died in 1797 and William in 1808, the proprietor then was John, who had been deploying much of the family fortune in the Commercial Bank. At the beginning John like each of the other four partners put up £10,000; but by 1815 he had withdrawn all his capital and was running an overdraft. Noel Simpson in his history of the Belfast Banking Company speculates that it may have been this that led to a disagreement between John Stewart and his partners and to Stewart's withdrawal early in 1815. Through an Alexander Stewart, the family began an association about this time with Alexander Wallace & Co of Newtownards. Delightfully their business was described in the deed of partnership as *"the Trade or Mystery of Brewers and Maltsters"*!

Personal tragedy loomed large in the life of Robert Stewart of Ballydrain. His wife Mary Isabella, who had been a Miss Mitchell from Dublin, died in 1785 at the age of thirty-five; and their eldest son, another Robert, at the age of eleven. A second son, George Alexander, survived his father by only eight years and died in 1805 at the age of twenty-seven. These and other members of the Stewart family, including Robert Stewart himself, are commemorated by a series of tablets in and around Drumbeg Parish Church. Yet the great estates of Ballydrain and Wilmont nearby, happily now both devoted to recreational purposes, are perhaps more powerful reminders of the enterprise of the Stewarts and of the contribution of linen to wealth creation in 18th Century Belfast. But they are reminders too that that wealth was ill-divided.

JAMES SUFFERN

Of all the foundation members James Suffern unquestionably had the most interesting family history. The Sufferns came originally from the Republic of Lucca in Central Italy; but in the 14th Century they moved to Provence in South-Eastern France. One branch of the family stayed there; and from it there sprang Pierre Andre de Suffern who became Vice-Admiral of France a year after his Ulster kinsman joined the Chamber of Commerce in Belfast. Exactly why a branch of the family had moved to the North-East of Ireland in the late 17th or early 18th Century is not known; though the timing would suggest that it was associated with the revocation of the Edict of Nantes by Louis XIV in 1685, the act that gave rise to the Huguenot migration.

Fifty years later there were at least three families of Sufferns in Ulster, stemming from three brothers who had settled some miles apart on a line from Belfast to Crumlin. Near Antrim there was a William Suffern who had married a Margaret Templeton; and their sons James and John had emigrated to Philadelphia in 1763. They were probably nephews of James Suffern of Belfast; and one of them became the kingpin of a whole community in a strategic area of New York State, so much so that the township later adopted his name. And while his kinsman in Belfast was joining an organisation that saw the ending of the American War of Independence as a stimulus to trade, John Suffern was no doubt reflecting on the war as the most exciting period in his life because General George Washington had for a time used the Suffern home as his headquarters. Nearby there was a fortified area which John Suffern, the owner of half-a-dozen businesses in the district, bought after the war and named New Antrim; so in that township which its historian, Saxby Vouler Penfold, later called "Romantic Suffern" there was a strong Ulster influence in name and in enterprise.

But there was no lack of enterprise back in Ulster either. The antecedents of the 19th and 20th Century farming Sufferns of Crumlin were farming near Nutt's Corner which more than a hundred-and-fifty years later would become an important civil airport; and in Belfast, James Suffern was a respected merchant exemplifying the family motto "Tiens la Veritie", "Hold to the Truth". Linen must have been one of the commodities in which he traded, for in 1780 he had signed a petition to the Irish Parliament calling for export subsidies on Irish linen similar to those paid in Great Britain. Suffern and his colleagues had written of their being *"reduced to very great Wretchedness and want"*; and they had assured Parliament that if the bounties were granted *"it would be a great means of encouraging considerable orders for Linens from foreign parts, as well as induce Merchants here to Export on their own accounts, to the great emolument of this Country and the revival and extension of that staple branch of our Trade"*. Parliament responded quickly and favourably; and exports of linen grew, though not immediately. Meanwhile James Suffern too had followed the path to diversification; and Dr Norman Gamble mentions his involvement in activities as far apart as the manufacture of tobacco products and the distribution of Donegal herrings.

Unlike his kinsman in America (who became a State Senator, a County Judge and the owner of huge tracts of land) the Belfast Suffern was seldom in the news. But in January 1787 he was very much in the news in a way that he would have wished to avoid: there was a serious fire at his home which was prevented from spreading to an adjacent gunpowder store only by the resolute intervention of the army, the task having proved too demanding for the resources and training of the town fire-brigade. And that unfortunately is the last that is so far known of James Suffern of Belfast, for his life still awaits the painstaking research of a Saxby Vouler Penfold!

ALEXANDER SUTHERLAND

Five years before the Chamber was formed Alexander Sutherland, part-time private in David Tomb's "light infantry division" of the First Belfast Volunteers, had become the owner of an import/export business which previously he had managed for Mrs Mary McWaters, widow of James McWaters. The business must have gone reasonably well for a time, because in 1785 Sutherland was named as a member of the prestigious committee of the White Linen Hall and also invested modestly in Smylie's glassworks. But suddenly in that same year he went bankrupt, a rare occurrence in those days; and, unbelievably, in 1789 he did it again. Exactly what happened next is not known; but it is noticeable that when John Smylie & Co was re-structured in 1791, Sutherland disappeared from the list of shareholders. Nevertheless by 1800 he was sufficiently re-established in some line of business to be a prominent signatory of the petition of the merchants, traders, and inhabitants of the town against the proposed legislative union of Great Britain and Ireland. But for him there must surely have been just a twinge of irony in the grandiloquent preamble to the petition, which referred to *"this great and opulent town . . . (which) has flourished in Commerce, Manufactures, Wealth, and Prosperity beyond the Hopes almost of the most sanguine"*.

WILLIAM TENNENT

S Alexander Blair in his authoritative history of First Kilraughts Presbyterian Church in County Antrim tells of the young licentiate of the Presbytery of Edinburgh who was ordained in the neighbouring district of Roseyards near Ballymoney in 1751 and preached for the first twelve Sundays on the same text from the third chapter of Ephesians: *"Unto me, who am less than the least of all saints, is this grace given, that I should preach among the Gentiles the unsearchable riches of Christ"*. The young minister was the Rev John Tennent; and in his fifty-seven years at Roseyards he not only preached "the unsearchable riches of Christ" with great faithfulness, but also raised a substantial family that included at least three sons. And amongst these was William (1759-1832), who was destined to become one of the very brightest stars in the galaxy of business talent that shone on Belfast as the 18th Century merged with the next.

When he joined the Chamber in 1783, William Tennent was only twenty-four years of age; and he was employed as a junior manager in the New Sugar House in Waring Street. Some years later he was admitted to a partnership in the business; and his association with it continued until well after the turn of the century. Meantime he must have developed additional business interests, for it is inconceivable that he generated solely from the small sugar refinery the wealth that he was deploying early in the 19th Century. It is likely that these additional interests included a partnership in a wine business and an involvement in the West Indies trade in parallel with his activities in the New Sugar House. It is known too that he was an active partner in the Belfast Insurance Company, an involvement not entirely appreciated by his father. Dr Gamble reports that in the aftermath of a shipwreck which the insurance company was covering, the cleric from Roseyards wrote to another son, William's brother John, that he hoped that the loss *"will be a profit in the end to engage him (William) henceforward to ensure himself and all he hast in the Insurance Office of Heaven, and also desist from the dangerous station of insuring to others"*. But despite the pitfalls of insurance and because of the success of his other activities, William was able to buy Waddell Cunningham's old home in Hercules Lane from Cunningham's heir, James Douglas, after Cunningham's widow had had her day in the property. It was said at the time that the purpose was to use the building as the offices for a new bank; but instead Tennent proceeded to build a fine new house on the site for himself and his family. However in the following year the financial institution also became a reality, as the Commercial Bank with Tennent as the senior partner in association with Robert Bradshaw, Robert Callwell, John Cunningham, and John Thomson who each like him subscribed £10,000 (some £600,000 in modern money). Though Tennent retained the ownership of property in various parts of the town, banking was the dominant business interest for the rest of his life. Until the merger of the Commercial with the Belfast Bank in 1827 to form the Belfast Banking Company, Tennent was a salaried employee; and thereafter till his death in 1832 he served on the "Board of Superintendence" of the merged institutions.

It is a remarkable tribute to the tenacity of Tennent and to the opportunities of the era that his ascent to these pinnacles of financial success was achieved despite a prime-of-life interruption of almost four years in a Scottish prison. Like other sons of the manse, other successful merchants, and even other members of Orange Masonic Lodge No 257, he had become deeply involved in the extreme radical movement, first as a

William Tennent (1759-1832), foundation member of the Chamber 1783, Vice-President 1821-1827.
(From a portrait — artist unknown — Ulster Museum)

committee member of the initial Society of United Irishmen, then as one of the proprietors of the Northern Star, and finally (according to rumour) as a member of the Belfast Directory of the United Irishmen in the approach to rebellion. In consequence he was arrested soon after the Rebellion and interned at Fort George in Invernesshire till 1802. But the authorities forgave quickly and completely; and William Tennent was subsequently appointed to a number of public bodies such as the Spring Water Commissioners and even the Police Commissioners. Within six years of his release he also became one of the twenty "managers" named in the Act of 1810 establishing the Belfast Academical Institution; and his association with the college was subsequently marked by the annual award of the Tennent Medal, succeeded in modern times by the Tennent Exhibition and financed by the interest from a gift of £100 which he made in 1819. He was also a life-long supporter of the Linenhall Library; and read widely both in the sciences and in the arts.

In the Chamber too his record of service was remarkable. His active membership spanned a period of forty-four years; and he was a member of Council for twenty-five consecutive years in the early 19th Century, including six as Vice-President to John S Ferguson. Finally in a contested ballot just before Christmas in 1827, he was elected President: but he declined the honour, saying graciously that the time had come for him to retire. In the course of his long service on Council, Tennent made many contributions, but none more important than a mission to Dublin in January 1808 with fellow Council-member Robert Davis to confer with representatives of the Cork, Dublin, Limerick, and Waterford Chambers and subsequently to see the Chancellor of the Irish Exchequer on a range of fiscal problems. Despite the weakening of the case by a difference of view with the Dublin Chamber, this was a reasonably successful mission; and the manuscript report by Tennent and Davis, which extended to four tightly-packed large pages, is preserved in the minute book of the period. Davis and Tennent received a payment of £17 for expenses incurred on the trip.

William Tennent and his wife had two lively daughters, Letitia and Isabella, who often gave a hand at the Poorhouse, Letitia being Secretary of the Ladies Committee for a time. This daughter married James Emerson; and he subsequently changed his name to James Emerson Tennent, which causes no end of confusion till the present day, especially since the man in question contested a couple of elections against William Tennent's nephew, Robert James Tennent. In the end both of them became MPs; and Robert James inherited his uncle's fine home in Hercules Lane.

Despite the fears of his ministerial father back in the days of William's involvement with the insurance business, the banker and business tycoon was also very much a man of the church; and he served the First Congregation in Rosemary Street in the office of Honorary Treasurer from 1817 till 1827. He also in his death in 1832 surprised both the First and the Second Congregations by bequeathing to them jointly the title to a block of property in Skipper Street. The congregation with whom he had worshipped for many years therefore acceded readily to the request of his daughter Letitia and his nephew Robert James to be allowed to erect an inscribed tablet to his memory within the sanctuary. And there it was recorded that *"he employed the leisure won from an arduous mercantile career in the cultivation of science and letters";* and also he was *"moderate in times of public excitement and firm when exposed to the reaction of power."*

SAMUEL THOMPSON

Whereas his fellow foundation-member Robert Thomson (also sometimes spelt with a "p") was constantly in the news in 18th Century Belfast, Samuel Thompson seems to have left very few marks on the sands of time. Almost certainly he was a linen merchant with a bleachgreen at Wolf Hill on the old road to Antrim. If that were indeed the case, then he was probably also the father or the grandfather of William Thompson (1805-1852), who became a distinguished naturalist after a period of apprenticeship in the linen industry.

ROBERT THOMSON

"Galloper Thomson rides again!" If that were the headline in the News Letter or the Irish News one of these mornings, the story underneath would be sure to tell that someone had seen a mounted ghost haring along York Road from Jennymount Street towards the city centre and that the trail had gone cold in Rosemary Street. And overnight the enterprising staff of the newspapers would have dug out the background and found that this was by no means the first reported sighting of "Galloper Thomson". The origin of the legendary ghost of Jennymount is appropriately shrouded in mystery; but it is highly probable that the reincarnation at the centre of the affair is that of Robert Thomson (1736-1800), foundation member of the Chamber, owner of the shoreside property that his daughter Jane (also known as "Miss Jenny") named Jennymount, and manager for many years of the Old Sugar House in Rosemary Lane.

Robert Thomson was yet another son of the manse, his father having been the minister for more than thirty years at Carnmoney, one of the oldest centres of Presbyterianism in Ireland. Although deeply involved in the business life of Belfast, Thomson probably maintained many connections with the Carnmoney district, facilitated by the location of his home. His name does not occur in the published records of the three Presbyterian Churches in Rosemary Lane, save for a note that his wife was one of the *"Ladys of Belfast"* who subscribed towards the provision of the pulpit in the First Congregation's new church of 1783. In total that may indicate that the family worshipped at Carnmoney, for many of the ladies who helped to provide the pulpit were not members of the First Congregation. It is also known that as Thomson accumulated wealth from his business activities in Belfast, part of it was deployed in purchases of land in the Carnmoney area.

Although ultimately involved in partnerships concerned with glass-making, muslin manufacture, and flour milling, Thomson was first and foremost a sugar refiner. Whether the sugar refining came with his wife or the wife with his sugar refining is not clear. What is known is that in 1761 he married his cousin Jane, daughter of Benjamin Legg of Malone, one of the partners in the Old Sugar House in Rosemary Lane; and around the same time became manager of that operation. Later when the Leggs and their other partner John Hyde sold their shares to the Stewarts of Wilmont and Ballydrain, Robert Thomson too became a partner; and the refinery was carried on as Stewarts & Thomson from 1777 till Thomson's withdrawal in 1793. During that period Robert Thomson became the chief spokesman of the whole sugar refining industry in Ireland, which was facing economic ruin from the threatened withdrawal of protective duties. Dr Norman Gamble's detailed account of their successful campaign provides glimpses of Thomson's powers as an advocate, particularly in the written word; and these were the powers that were later to be deployed to the signal benefit of the Chamber in its formative years. Peculiarly Thomson was also involved in another sugar refinery that was potentially in competition with his own: this was an ill-fated business started in 1773 next door to the Old Sugar House by Peter Galen and Bartholomew de la Maziere, Dublin Huguenots, with Thomson as a third partner. Within a few years Galen went bankrupt and de la Maziere went back to Dublin, leaving Thomson in complete control. This he exercised till 1781, when the refinery was declared surplus and the doors finally closed.

Immediately before his becoming involved in the Chamber, Robert Thomson was spending a considerable amount of his time on another project that was of great importance to the business community, namely the building of the White Linen Hall. As a member of the steering committee he seems to have had special responsibility for the employment of tradesmen. Hence in February 1783 he was advising masons through the News Letter that he already had more masons than he needed; whereas in December he was looking for slaters. In between he had been elected a member of the first Council of the Chamber; and he continued in that role till 1787, when he was elected Vice-President. From the minutes of the period it is apparent that Thomson's ability and willingness to draft clear and cogent memorials and petitions on the business issues of the day were recognised and appreciated by his colleagues; and within three months of the Council's beginning to function he was called upon to produce a petition to Parliament on the Grain Bill *"now in agitation"*. Though the subject was probably quite new to him at the time, he produced in under a week a most lucid and powerful document extending to three-and-a-half large pages of tightly-packed manuscript; and the Council duly endorsed this for signature by the merchants, traders, and principal inhabitants of the town. But it was in May of the following year that he undertook a more vital task for the Chamber; namely to be the chief architect of its response to William Pitt's notorious Twenty Propositions on the future regulation of trade between Ireland and England. The result was, in the words of S Shannon Millin, *"an historic document of which every Belfastman has reason to feel proud"*. And Millin added: *"It displayed no less heroism than that of the Barons at Runnymede when they compelled their vacillating sovereign to sign what has ever since been regarded as the keystone of English liberty"*. But better than fine words of tribute was the practical result of this momentous endeavour — the abandonment for all time of Mr Pitt's Propositions, overlaid as they were by vested commercial interests in Britain.

Thomson also served on the Harbour Corporation from its establishment in 1785; and in the next decade he was deeply involved in the Discount Company, which was conducted from the premises of the Old Sugar House. His son John succeeded him in that role; and the wealth that the father had accumulated was ultimately deployed in the Commercial Bank, formed in 1809 with John Thomson as one of the five £10,000 shareholders. In politics Robert Thomson was liberally inclined without becoming deeply involved. Yet the superb language of his document on the Twenty Propositions included a number of highly political statements, one of which if it were uttered by "Galloper Thomson" tomorrow night on his ghostly ride from Jennymount to Rosemary Street might be endorsed by occasional "Hear, Hears" en route. It referred to *"the degraded state of an inferior assembly, held only for form's sake, merely to register the edicts of a superior assembly, without the power of altering a single iota"*!

DAVID TOMB

From the top floor of the modern Post Office building in Tomb Street there is a magnificent view of Belfast Harbour: and that is rather appropriate, for David Tomb who joined the Chamber in 1783 and later gave his name to the street contributed substantially to the development of the port. As a business partner of Thomas Bateson of Orangefield, he was an extensive user of the facilities of the harbour in overseas trade; and he also acquired land and property near the main channel, part of which was used for the provision of Donegall Quay. With this background, he was a valuable member of the Chamber, serving almost continuously on the Council from 1783 till 1794. In that capacity he was only a moderate attender; but, by contrast, in the First Belfast Company of the Volunteers (which he joined in March 1778, becoming a lieutenant in charge of "the light infantry division") he had according to George Benn qualified to have the words *"a very good attender"* written firmly after his name on the nominal roll.

On 20 February 1770 in the Parish Church in High Street David Tomb was married by the Rev Matthew Garnet to Elinor, daughter of Henry Joy snr, joint proprietor of the News Letter; and they had at least four children. One son, Henry Joy Tomb, succeeded his father in business and joined the elite of Donegall Place. Another son, George Tomb, became a distinguished lawyer and occupied one of the legal offices of the Crown in County Wicklow. And there were at least two daughters, one of whom became the first wife of Dr W H Drummond, famous educationalist, writer, and minister for many years of the Second Presbyterian Congregation in Rosemary Street. Another daughter was a life-long friend of her remarkable cousin, Mary Ann McCracken; and it was she who joined the intrepid Mary Ann in a search of the hills of South and East Antrim for the McCracken brothers, missing after their involvement in the Battle of Antrim on 7 June 1798.

NATHANIEL WILSON

"I have . . . stretched my fortune and my credit to the last string". These were a few of the words in which Nathaniel Wilson, one of the largest employers in and around Belfast at the time, chose to describe his business state in February 1785, less than two years after he had joined the Chamber. He was writing to the 18th Century equivalent of the Industrial Development Board, seeking further support; and his words may

have been taken with a pinch of salt. But three years later, when Wilson died from overwork and depression, his assessment of February 1785 turned out to be all-too-accurate; for his assets valued at almost £40,000 (getting on for two-and-a-half million in modern money) were insufficient to cover his liabilities, and the estate was technically bankrupt. In that moment of truth it first seemed that the whole Wilson empire of interlinking businesses, involving some three thousand employees, would collapse and that his business partner, Nicholas Grimshaw of Whitehouse, would be dragged down too. But several old colleagues in the Chamber, headed by Waddell Cunningham and James Holmes, came to the rescue by buying off parts of the network on terms that enabled Grimshaw to survive and later to prosper.

Nicholas Grimshaw (whose son Robert made many notable contributions in the service of the Chamber in the next century) was a Lancastrian, knowledgeable about technical developments that were about to revolutionise the textile industry. He had come to Belfast about 1776 and had established a textile printing business at Greencastle, just north of the town. From there he provided a service to linen merchants as far afield as Newry and Magherafelt. Parallel to this he was advising the Charitable Society on the establishment of cotton manufacture in the Poorhouse. That project was in due course brought to fruition by Robert Joy and Thomas McCabe, two members of the committee established by the Society in August 1778 to investigate its feasibility. Nathaniel Wilson, as a well-established manufacturer of fine linen fabrics, was another member of that committee; and it is likely that it was through this association that he became the financial backer of Grimshaw in a series of entrepreneurial developments in cotton manufacture.

Hence by the time the Chamber was formed, Wilson and Grimshaw had two water-powered cotton spinning-mills in operation, one of which was at Whitehouse; and soon they were moving into the manufacture of mixed linen/cotton fibres and other technological advances, with the aid of grants from the Government and the Linen Board and, to a lesser extent, from the Dublin Society. Despite external aid of around £2,000, the financing of these developments put a serious strain on Wilson's resources (as evidenced, for example, by the dissolution in 1783 of a wine and spirit business in which he had been in partnership with Henry Joyce and John Trail Kennedy); and the result was that he had to borrow heavily. He therefore had a crucial interest in Pitt's Twenty Propositions, which included aspects that would have undermined his business aspirations; and he made a journey to London early in 1785 to join directly in the campaign to have the propositions withdrawn. No doubt he was at that time acting partly on behalf of the Chamber, for he had been a member of the first Council in 1783/84 and he re-appeared in 1785/86 and again in 1787.

Outside business, Wilson seems to have had few interests save for the Third Presbyterian Church in Rosemary Street. There he was Honorary Treasurer of the congregation for many years. In the days before his own financial crisis he was also a substantial subscriber to the building fund of the First Congregation as it prepared to be re-housed in 1783. Generous to a fault, entrepreneurial always, Wilson regrettably was one of the very few businessmen of the day who was under severe financial pressure in the final years of his life; and there is a certain poignancy in the words and phrases of that letter of February 1785 to the authorities in Dublin appealing for more aid to enable him to see things through. *"I have struggled as well as I could with these great matters"*, he wrote, *"and both stretched my fortune and my credit to the last string"*. Tragically, in the end, the string broke.

*   *   *   *   *   *

These then were the change merchants of 1783 — a quite remarkable assembly of entrepreneurs who knew no bounds in trade, in industrial development, or in political thought. At other times in history the Chamber would be served by remarkable men and women; and there would be periods, particularly in the late 19th Century, when many industrial and commercial giants would happily co-exist within its ranks. But at no time in its history would the Chamber have a proportionately greater or more powerful or more entrepreneurial wealth of human resources under its flag than when the march to progress and to change began on 25 October 1783. These were the men who would see it through till the end of the beginning.

Chapter 5

TILL THE END OF THE BEGINNING: 1783-1794

In political terms the summer of 1783 in Belfast was long and hot. The issue was Parliamentary Reform; and the Volunteers were extremely active. In the North their campaign reached a crescendo in the second convention of Dungannon at the beginning of September; and the stage was set for a bitter election to the Irish Parliament in the weeks immediately afterwards. Though the spirit of liberalism was abroad in the land, the limited and selective franchise made it impossible to effect political change quickly; and when the new Irish Parliament met in Dublin on 14 October 1783, the balance seemed much the same as before. The Volunteers therefore had to press on with their plans for a great National Convention in Dublin in November, with the objective of pressurising the Parliament in the direction of reform.

It was in the short breathing-space between the election fervour of early October and the build-up to the Volunteer convention in November that the "merchants of change" in Belfast turned aside to get the Chamber of Commerce underway. With Valentine Jones I in the chair, there was a meeting of the subscribers on 23 October to elect a Council of fifteen, in accordance with the plan agreed back in May; and two days later the Council met to appoint the office-bearers. Their choice fell upon Waddell Cunningham as President (though he was up to his eyes in the prevailing political ferment); John Holmes as Vice-President; and Robert Bradshaw of Carrickfergus Road as Honorary Secretary and Treasurer. And the noble task of furthering the interests of the business community in the North of Ireland over the next two-hundred years had begun.

From October 1783 until the first annual meeting in July 1784 the Council met at least once a week. The meetings were usually held in the evening at one of the better hostelries in the town, such as Captain Scott's Crown Tavern or the Donegall Arms; and there were fines for absence and unpunctuality. The meetings were held whether or not there was business to transact; and it would seem that they were attended by a degree of conviviality, probably financed by the fines. Without explanation Robert Bradshaw made occasional little entries like "6s:8d" in the margin of the minute book, which may indicate either the proceeds of the fines or the cost of the hospitality or both! And there is ample proof that it was not all work and no play, for Bradshaw's minutes for almost half the meetings held in the first year read simply: *"No business done"*!

Much of the business that was done in the first year was concerned in one way or another with shipping. Within weeks of its appointment the Council was responsible for organising a petition to the Irish Parliament on the need for a lighthouse on the South Rock off the coast of the Ards Peninsula, an area where more than sixty ships and over two-hundred-and-fifty seamen had perished in the previous fifty years. Next they were protesting to the Revenue Commissioners about the reinstatement of two tidewaiters (sea-going customs officers) who had been guilty of *"the most wicked and bad Action"*. And by April 1784 they had begun an historic campaign for the improvement of Belfast harbour, their first action being to appoint a committee of five (including Hugh Montgomery and Captain John McCracken) to commission a professional survey of the area and to consider the feasibility of deepening the channel from the town docks to the Pool of Garmoyle.

With the help of Lord Kilwarlin, the representations about the lighthouse off the County Down coast were successful, in that Parliament voted a sum of money (very inadequate as it turned out) for that purpose; but there was a convoluted sequel which reflected the political tensions of the period. On Christmas Eve 1783 the Council asked one of its members to prepare a letter to Lord Kilwarlin thanking him for his help; at the next meeting, on 7 January 1784, it was reported that the letter had not yet been drafted; and a week later the Council, by five votes to four, decided not to send a letter at all. Even that was not the end of the affair; for three meetings later the Council resolved:

"That no motion shall be admitted or Resolution taken about thanking Lord Kilwarlin for anything until every member of this Council shall first be served with written Notice of the Time when such motion is intended to be brought forward".

The reason for the tetchiness was that in the election of October 1783 Lord Kilwarlin had played a major part in the defeat of the liberal candidate in County Down; and the feeling was obviously intensified as Waddell Cunningham himself struggled against the "lordly power" of another nobleman in the Carrickfergus by-election of February 1784. But by the summer, passions had cooled; and the Council having resolved to dine in Hillsborough on 6 June, deputed Thomas Greg to call upon Lord Hillsborough and Lord Kilwarlin to invite them both to join in the occasion.

While the minor controversy about writing to Lord Kilwarlin was at its height, the Chamber was much more constructively involved on a major task as well. This was the matter of commenting on a new Grain Bill that was before the Irish Parliament. The measure was intended to stabilise the grain market in Ireland by permitting imports only when average internal prices exceeded certain limits; but the Council was apprehensive about its likely effects in the North. On 28 January 1784 they decided to petition Parliament on the subject; and they deputed the task of preparing the first draft to Robert Thomson of Jennymount. Thomson's skill in marshalling a case was well-known, for some years previously he had been the champion of the sugar-refiners of the whole island; but he excelled himself in his petition on the Grain Bill, the first of many such tasks that he would undertake for the Chamber. Though he probably had to consult with various trade interests in order to familiarise himself with the nuances of the subject, his draft extending to three-and-a-half huge pages of tightly-packed quill-penmanship was available in less than a week; and it was duly endorsed by the Council for signing by the leading inhabitants of the town and submission to Parliament. Parts of it have a familiar ring to the modern ear:

"It is a well-known fact evinced by long experience that in general grain is much dearer in the North than in the South of Ireland, insomuch that in time of Scarcity the Manufacturing and Labouring Poor in several of the Northern Counties would be absolutely perishing with famine before the average price of the whole Kingdom would amount so high as to admit importation from foreign places".

For "Manufacturing and Labouring Poor" substitute "pig and poultry industries" and it could almost have been written in 1983! PLUS ÇA CHANGE . . .

Later in the year the Council prepared a second petition on the Grain Bill, when John Brown joined Robert Thomson in the drafting. And they were concerned too about the need for protective duties against imports of linen; about certain limitations in the tobacco regulations; about Government grants towards the deployment of ships on whale-fishing; and about delays in the post and the urgent need of a "cross post" to Londonderry via "Newton Limavady", and from thence to Sligo to facilitate the herring business (in which Waddell Cunningham and Thomas Greg had a deep personal interest). The shots that were exchanged on postal services in the first year of the Chamber's existence were but a whiff of battles and skirmishes with the postal authorities that would rumble on for almost a hundred-and-fifty years. In an age that had neither telephone nor telegraph, telex nor fast travel, overseas business was entirely dependent upon the reliability and speed of the mails; and there was an unbelievable sense of urgency about receiving and answering letters from customers and suppliers, the objective invariably being to get the replies off on the day that the communications arrived. So the Chamber was determined from the beginning to keep a close eye on the postal services, as well to review the Revenue Laws, to study Irish Statutes generally, and to improve the collection and dissemination of commercial statistics.

Though the Council had done a solid job in the first year there was a disappointment when the time came for the annual meeting of the whole Chamber at the beginning of July: the attendance was so poor that the election of the new Council had to be deferred to a second meeting twelve days later. On that occasion there seems to have been quite keen competition for places on the Council, for six of the original fifteen were replaced. When the new Council met afterwards to appoint office-bearers and draw up its "rules of order", Waddell Cunningham was re-elected President; John Holmes who had not attended a single meeting in his period as Vice-President was replaced in that office by William Brown, though he continued as a Council member; Robert Bradshaw who had not missed a single meeting in his term as Secretary/Treasurer was re-elected to both offices; and it was agreed that the Council would meet in the Crown Tavern on the second Wednesday of each month as the clock struck seven, with fines for absence or unpunctuality remaining unchanged and no excuses accepted save illness or absence from town.

In view of the number of occasions in the first year when there was no business to transact, the change in the frequency of meetings from weekly to monthly was a sensible move. In the second year the Council met sixteen times, four of which were described as "occasional meetings", being additional to the monthly routine; and the phrase "No business done" appeared in the minute book only twice. So the Council worked hard. And it also worked effectively, for the year's achievements included the completion of the harbour survey as the basis for a petition to Parliament; the demolition of William Pitt's Twenty Propositions on Anglo-Irish trade; and the establishment of the Belfast Marine Charity.

To the intense frustration of the Council, it proved difficult to get the professional survey of the harbour carried out. Originally it was to be done by a Mr Barker, who was approached by Robert Bradshaw in August 1784. By mid-September, Bradshaw was reporting that Barker was willing to begin *"as soon as the Gentlemen who were requested to assist in this business will provide him with boats and the necessary assistance";* but by late October the survey had still not been started and the Council asked Hugh Montgomery and Bradshaw to call on Barker to find out the reason for the delay. By 8 December 1784, the Council was becoming impatient; and John and Samuel Brown together with Hugh Montgomery were delegated to tell Barker to start the next day or the job would be given to someone else. In the end the job did have to be given to someone else, a Mr Macoughtry; and John Brown reported to the Council on 12 January 1785 that the job had at last been done. The result was the map reproduced on the front endpaper of the present work.

Meanwhile a strong petition to the Irish Parliament on the need for improvement of the harbour had been drafted, the intention being to submit this with the survey that the Chamber had commissioned. In the preamble to the petition the Council declared *"That the town of Belfast hath long carried on an extensive Foreign and Domestic Trade and been deemed the third Commercial Town in the Kingdom".* Then they narrated the extreme difficulties in sea traffic into and out of this important commercial centre; and asserted the case for digging a "straight cut" from the docks at the end of High Street to the Pool of Garmoyle to replace the meandering course of the River Lagan and permit larger ships to navigate the last stretch in all tides. Finally they noted that improvement of the harbour would *"tend to the increase of His Majesty's Revenue";* and asked for £2,000 which would be *"faithfully expended for this use, and no other, in the most Economical Manner".* The petition was endorsed by a meeting of the full Chamber and other inhabitants on 4 February 1785; and George Black, the Sovereign, having defected for financial reasons, John Brown and Robert Bradshaw were deputed to travel to Dublin with the petition and survey to *"make use of their utmost endeavours to effectuate that great Publick work".*

Another sixty-four years were to elapse before the straight cut from the town docks to the deep waters was completed, in the form of the Victoria Channel engineered by the famous William Dargan. But the immediate response of the Parliament in Dublin to the Chamber petition of 1785 took a very different form: it was an Act to transfer the responsibility for the efficient management and further development of the port from the townhall to a new Harbour Corporation consisting mainly of members of the Chamber headed by its President, Waddell Cunningham. Parliament may have felt that it was being clever in avoiding public expenditure by transferring responsibility to the merchants; and the merchants may have been disappointed by the denial of resources to match their newly-conferred powers. But with the benefit of hindsight it is easy to discern now that that arrangement reached in 1785 by the initiative of the Chamber was the foundation for a system of user-orientated management and development of the harbour that has served the business community well over the ensuing two-hundred years.

The other major project undertaken by the Chamber in its second year had equally long-lasting effects: this was the marshalling and stiffening of parliamentary opposition to William Pitt's Twenty Propositions on future commercial and financial relationships between Great Britain and Ireland. Entering Parliament at the age of nineteen, Pitt had become Prime Minister in December 1783 at the age of twenty-four, after a period as Chancellor of the Exchequer. Initially his posture towards Ireland had been conciliatory, his objective being the establishment of totally free trade between the two islands. But his position in Parliament was at that time insecure; and in May 1785 he yielded to the pressure of English commercial interests to produce an amended set of proposals which, in the words of the Chamber statement on the subject, would serve only *"to secure the commerce and manufactures of Britain at the expense of those of Ireland"*. Industries on the British mainland were to be protected while Irish industries were opened up to competition; colonial produce for Ireland would continue to come through Britain and be taxed there; Irish trade with three-quarters of the world would be inhibited; and the new-found legislative independence of the Irish Parliament would be tightly controlled, certainly when it came to commercial matters in which Britain had an interest.

In Belfast, reaction to the Twenty Propositions came within a fortnight; and it came from the Chamber. At an emergency meeting of the Council on 25 May, the information available from London was reviewed and a decision taken to call a town meeting on the following day, with Waddell Cunningham, John Brown, and Robert Thomson deputed to prepare *"proper materials for said meeting"*. This resulted in the submission to Parliament of a moderate petition signed by over eighty of the principal inhabitants, the main thrust of which was to secure time for the full study of Pitt's proposals. Given that time, the Chamber some four weeks later published a detailed analysis and rebuttal of the proposals, which had been drawn up by Robert Thomson and endorsed by the full Council at a meeting on 15 June 1785. That document received publicity in the newspapers throughout Ireland; and its penetrating analysis undoubtedly influenced the debate in the Irish Parliament where Henry Grattan, the champion of Northern liberalism both in politics and in trade, made a speech which the Viceroy described as *"incredibly eloquent, seditious, and inflammatory"*. The final outcome was the complete withdrawal of Pitt's propositions and a greater degree of freedom and independence in Irish trade.

While working hard for freedom to trade with the world, the Chamber was not unmindful of the human tragedies that that trade sometimes brought, as flimsy sailing ships with incomplete charts and inadequate navigational aids battled against the elements. In the autumn of 1784 the Council therefore decided to join with the Marine Society in the establishment of the Belfast Marine Charity to aid disabled seamen and the wives and families of those who had perished in shipwrecks. By mid-November the rules of the new body had been agreed and a management committee appointed, which included Hugh Montgomery and John Brown for the Chamber and Captains John McCracken and Charles McKenzie for the Marine Society. And by March of the following year the Council had another reminder of the fragility of life at sea as they recorded their thanks to George Hamilton, the Revenue man at Strangford, for the way in which he assisted the salvage of the wreck of the brig ISABELLA *"lately stranded in Dundrum Bay"* on the County Down coast.

After its highly successful second year, the Chamber had a spell in the doldrums. With the White Linen Hall opened (though subscriptions for it were still being sought), the Discount Office established, and Pitt's Twenty Propositions defeated, the merchants either became lethargic or were so busy making money and playing soldiers that they had little time or need for the Chamber. An annual meeting was held on 1 July 1785; and a new Council was elected, the membership again showing six changes from the previous year. A month later Waddell Cunningham, William Brown, and Robert Bradshaw were re-elected President, Vice-President, and Secretary; and the stage was set for another year's work. But all that the official minute book had to show for that year was a decision on 2 January 1786 that *"Mr Bradshaw do publish an advertisement in the News Papers concerning the shameful deficiency in the size of Bricks"*!

In the wake of such an inconsequential year's work, no one can have been surprised by the disastrous attendance at the annual meeting on 1 July 1786. Once again the election of the Council had to be postponed to another day; and the consequence was a minute book that remained blank until after a general meeting on 20 January 1787, with Alexander Orr in the chair. The Council elected was not radically different from those of earlier years; and the office-bearers remained unchanged save for the replacement of William Brown by Robert Thomson as Vice-President. So the hiatus from July 1786 till January 1787 was not due to serious internal dissension or to lack of confidence in the leadership or in the Council. However there was evidence of a determination to restore the vigour of the Chamber's activities, in that they decided to revert to weekly Council meetings and to apply even stricter rules about attendance and punctuality:

"Resolved that this Council do meet on every Thursday evening precisely at 7 o'clock at the Crown Tavern, and that every member who shall not be present within 5 minutes after the clock strikes 7 shall be fined one British shilling; and that every member who does not appear within 20 minutes after the clock strikes 7 shall be fined one British half-crown, the time to be determined by the Secretary's watch".

And there was again an afternote that no excuse would be admitted for non-payment of fines except sickness or absence from town.

Despite the new surge of enthusiasm in January 1787, the Chamber achieved little in the course of the next few months. Enquiries were pursued about duties on foreign linen imported into Ireland and into Great Britain, which ultimately revealed that the tariff barrier was higher in Ireland. That should have been welcome news to those involved in the local linen industry; but it may well be that some of the merchants were already interested in importing foreign linen and re-exporting it as Irish, in which case they would have viewed the protective tariff differently. Nevertheless the subject was not large enough to keep a Council of fifteen occupied once a week; and the words *"No business done"* soon began to re-appear in the minute book. And that in turn led the Council to decide on 19 April that monthly meetings would again be adequate.

Meanwhile the Council had embarked on an ambitious scheme to raise money for the completion of the centre section of the White Linen Hall, one of the most remarkable and mysterious escapades in the history of the Chamber. The main building erected in 1783 under the patronage and direction of many of the men who simultaneously established the Chamber took the form of a plain two-storeyed structure around a large hollow square; and a wide gap was left at the front for the addition later of a more ornamental centre-section. It was this section that was being planned in 1787; and it was this that the Council set out to finance. Their chosen method was one that was used fairly frequently in those days; namely a lottery with substantial stakes and large prizes. But the surprising thing was not the choice of the lottery approach: rather it was the speed with which the whole scheme was worked out. In the course of one Council meeting in the Crown Tavern on 8 March 1787 the budget was drawn up as follows:

One Prize of £400 is	. . . . . .	£400	
2	100	. . . . . .	200
2	50	. . . . . .	100
5	20	. . . . . .	100
10	10	. . . . . .	100
20	5	. . . . . .	100
600	1	. . . . . .	600
First drawn		. . . . . .	50
Last drawn		. . . . . .	100
			£1,750

2000 Tickets at £1:2:9
each is £2,275:0:0
Prizes £1,750:0:0 . . . . . . 1,750:0:0

Remains 525:0:0

And the rules were also laid down. The "remains" would be used preferentially to facilitate the completion of the centre section, with any residue reverting to the Chamber; the financing of the building would be dependent on Council approval of the plans; the arrangements would all be made by a committee consisting of Waddell

The White Linen Hall, built in 1783, but pictured here in the late 19th Century, many years after the addition of the centre section and the tower and cupola.

(From a water-colour by Theo Gracey — Ulster Museum.)

Cunningham, James Ferguson, Will Sinclaire, John Neilson, and Robert Bradshaw; a Mr James Carson (probably a professional man) would be asked to act as Treasurer of the whole scheme; the draw would commence on 5 May, with the prizes being paid ten days after the drawing; and approved bills and notes would be taken for blocks of twenty or more tickets.

The lottery really was an ambitious project, when one takes into account that the cost of a single ticket was over £60 in today's money — and the first prize, the equivalent of over £20,000. Yet it was all organised in one Council meeting; and it was not mentioned again in that forum till 3 May 1787, two days before the draw was due to commence. Ominously the decision then was to postpone the draw till Monday 4 June; and the implication must be that not enough tickets had been sold to provide the anticipated profit. At that point the would-be historian comes up against a blank wall, for there is a gap in the records of the Chamber from that meeting on 3 May 1787 till 5 May 1791. Posterity is therefore for the moment left to ponder whether the draw ever took place; whether it yielded a profit; whether someone absconded with the funds; whether some aspect of the lottery was the cause of the four-year break in the recorded activities of the Chamber; or whether it all went well and it was only the minute-writer Robert Bradshaw that took a rest, or was unwell, or was so immersed in other activities as to be caused to neglect his minutes. What is certain is that the completion of the centre section of the White Linen Hall went ahead with or without the proceeds of the lottery and that a small tower and cupola were added some twenty-eight years later to round-off the still-rather-ordinary building.

It is quite possible that the four-year break in the recorded activities of the Chamber was due to business tension between prominent members. Waddell Cunningham, who was a major subscriber to the Discount Office, objected to the opening of Ewing's Bank ("The Bank of the Four Johns") on 1 June 1787: Mrs McTier wrote to her brother Dr Drennan that Cunningham described it *"as a matter hurtful to the public"*. That must have brought Cunningham into conflict with three prominent members of the Chamber who were partners in the new bank; namely John Ewing, John Holmes, and John Brown. And the situation must have become even more difficult when Cunningham, despite his protests of two years earlier, opened his own bank at the beginning of 1789 (which Mrs McTier found strange). Yet when the records of the Chamber resumed briefly in 1791, Cunningham was still President, though partners in Ewing's Bank were noticeably absent from the single Council meeting recorded.

But if the 1780's finished with tensions in the Chamber there were much greater tensions abroad in the whole community. The French Revolution in 1789 had caught the imagination of radicals in Belfast; and by the summer of 1790 even the moderate Northern Whig Club formed earlier in the year was calling on the townspeople to meet on 14 July, the anniversary of the Storming of the Bastille, *"to celebrate that astonishing event, which constitutes a glorious era in the history of man and of the world"*. The celebration duly took place; and afterwards there was a splendid banquet in the south wing of the White Linen Hall when some three-hundred-and-fifty members of the Volunteers sat down at a single long table and drank twenty-seven toasts. And in the following year, events took another turn with the formation in Belfast of the First Society of United Irishmen, the secret committee of which consisted mainly of members of the Chamber. The next year too was one of intense communal activity, with a succession of meetings on Catholic Emancipation; another celebration of Bastille Day (ending with thirty-three toasts); the conversion of more and more of the Volunteers to the "green cockade"; and the continued growth of secret societies of United Irishmen. Naturally in the midst of all this there must have been stresses and strains within the business community, though the differences at that time were more between degrees of radicalism than between radicalism and support for the Establishment. Hence it proved possible to resume Chamber activities on a reasonable scale for most of the year.

There was a general meeting on 1 February 1792 to elect a Council; and the most notable feature was that Waddell Cunningham, who had by then been a full-blown banker for three years, had withdrawn from the centre of the Chamber stage. Alexander Orr, a foundation member who had been responsible for reviving the Chamber in 1787, had replaced Cunningham as President sometime in 1791; and he again succeeded in breathing new life into the organisation. But he had serious problems to overcome, for James Holmes who was elected President in succession to Orr on 7 February 1792 had disappeared from the Chamber scene sixteen days later; and Orr himself had to resume the Presidency and to continue in that role for several years. Nor was his Vice-President, Thomas Brown, a tower of strength, for he attended less than half the meetings held in 1792. Robert Bradshaw, on the other hand, was as faithful as ever, attending every single meeting till he faded out temporarily at the beginning of 1793, probably for political reasons.

The year 1792 began strongly, with fortnightly meetings of the rejuvenated Council in the Crown Tavern. The fines for absence or lateness were down from half-a-crown to a shilling: but there was a new penalty of 2s:8½d for anyone who left the room during a Council meeting without the permission of the President. The main subjects that occupied the attention of the Council were the state of the docks and quays; the rates charged by "car-men" (carters) for the delivery of goods around the town; the rules governing banking; the propriety of establishing a company to build lighters for use on the Lagan Navigation; and the need to revive the Marine Charity.

The problems at the docks and on the quays were pursued with the Ballast Board and with Thomas Greg (who personally owned the most important quay). The Ballast Board promised to have work done as soon as the season would permit both on the removal of obstructions at the entrance to the Limekiln Dock and on the widening of that entrance. They would also be consulting with the Corporation about cleaning out the docks generally. After representations from the Chamber, Thomas Greg promised to fulfil the requirements of his lease by paving Chichester Quay and by removing various nuisances both from it and from the other quays in the area, one of his obligations being to have the quays swept at least twice a week. But when the work had not been started a fortnight later the Council became very aggressive with their old colleague; and instructed the Secretary to deliver an ultimatum to his home:

"If all nuisances be not removed from off the Quays before the 1st of April and if the quays are not put into proper repair before the 1st of June next we will as far as in us lies by our recommendation and example resist the payment of quayage untill these measures so necessary are complied with".

And Thomas Greg seems to have complied, for the subject is not mentioned again in the minute book.

The involvement of the Chamber in prescribing the rates payable to carters was an interesting development. It was a case of the customers getting together to determine what they would pay, which would hardly be acceptable today. Separate rates were determined for some eighty different articles of merchandise; and these were detailed in the minute book. They are interesting today not only as transport rates, but also as a reminder of the goods that were being transported around Belfast in the last decade of the 19th Century. The rates varied from a half-penny per cask of figs and three farthings per keg of gunpowder to fourpence per tierce of rice and thirteen pence per ton of coal; and a member of Council was deputed to tell the car-men how they would be paid thereafter and to ask each of them in future to fix a number to his cart for ease of identification.

The minutes were not so explicit on the banking laws; but the interest of the Chamber, expressed at a Council meeting in the Exchange Coffee Room on 23 February 1792, led to a town meeting and a petition to Parliament. Nor is the fate recorded of the proposal to examine the building of lighters for use on the Lagan Navigation, though it is interesting to note that this was the first of a series of interactions of the Chamber with the further development of the waterway. Customs regulations and procedures were also under close scrutiny in 1792; and human interest came into the scene with the decision to revive what was described in the minutes as "that useful institution, the Marine Charity". Indeed the funds of the charity may even have been augmented marginally by the fines collected at Council meetings for absence and lateness; for the Chamber under Alexander Orr had decreed that the fines "be spent in the Town of Belfast in such manner as the majority of the Council may direct".

The year 1793 was one of great difficulty and tension in the community, both economically and politically. The radical movement was becoming more extreme; and men of moderation were becoming more worried. Constitutional liberals like Henry Joy jnr, the brilliant proprietor of the News Letter following the deaths of his father and of his uncle in the previous decade, were (in the words of Mary McNeill in her biography of Mary Ann McCracken) beginning to realise with profound sadness that the lead in public affairs in the town they loved had passed from them to more radical opinion. The Volunteers too were split down the middle; and the "green" wing was becoming more militant. By March the Government had acted to proscribe the movement; and the more radical spirits reacted by turning to the Societies of United Irishmen, which now took on a military aspect. Meanwhile the Northern Star, which was owned and directed mainly by members of the Chamber and had first appeared in January 1792, was pumping out news and views in a way that added to the tension, despite its literary refinements.

With the community in such a ferment it is remarkable that Alexander Orr was able to keep the Chamber going through the second half of 1793 and into January 1794. He no longer had the assistance as Secretary of Robert Bradshaw, who as a constitutional liberal probably felt unable to be active in a Council that included at least four leading members of the United Irishmen — Hugh Crawford, Henry Haslett, Robert Simms, and William Tennent. Orr therefore had to resort to writing the minutes himself, as well as chairing the meetings; and by January 1794 the Council was resolving that *"Mr Bradshaw be requested to attend the next meeting with a State of the Accounts of the Chamber"*, a request that Mr Bradshaw seems to have ignored.

But unlike Robert Bradshaw, another of the great figures of earlier years made a brief return to the Chamber scene in 1793: this was Waddell Cunningham. Accompanied by Hugh Montgomery, who was fast becoming one of the richest men in town, Cunningham had gone to Dublin at the beginning of May to tell the Commissioners appointed by the Lord Lieutenant about the very depressed state of business in the North; and to claim for the Province a share in the Government loan of £200,000 which was to be made available through the Bank of Ireland to support stretched credit in industry and commerce in the island generally. Cunningham and Montgomery reported back to the Council on 18 May 1793 and tabled a letter from the Commissioners offering to advance the sum of £30,000 to Belfast against the personal securities of eight of the principal traders in the town. In response the Council decided, firstly, to accept the offer provided that the eight guarantors could be found; secondly, to ask for subscriptions from other businessmen to provide a fund that would at least partially indemnify the guarantors; and, thirdly, to thank Waddell Cunningham and Hugh Montgomery for their exertions and to pay the expenses of their visit to Dublin.

The Chamber having provided the vehicle for the application of Government aid to the troubled economy of the North appears to have become relatively inactive until December 1793, when there was a surge of activity concerned with various aspects of the Lagan Navigation. As narrated in an earlier chapter, this commercial waterway (consisting partly of the River Lagan and partly of parallel stretches of canal) had for almost thirty years been navigable only as far as Sprucefield, just beyond Lisburn. But in a remarkable piece of engineering spearheaded by Richard Owen from Lancashire and financed largely by Lord Donegall, the waterway had in the eleven years from 1783 been pushed right through to Lough Neagh, mainly in the form of a canal from Sprucefield via Aghalee. The completed waterway was then twenty-seven miles in length; and it had no less than twenty-seven sets of locks, most of them on the stretch from Sprucefield to Lough Neagh. The potential of the waterway for opening up the whole hinterland of Lough Neagh including the County Tyrone coalfields was obviously immense; and the Council of the Chamber at its meeting on 21 January 1794 was clearly elated to receive a message from a David McIreavey that he had just arrived at Belfast docks in the sloop SALLY with a load of wheat and turf from the shores of Lough Neagh — so much so that it was decided to send *"Captain McIreavey"* a gratuity of three guineas *"for his exertions"*!

Meanwhile, however, the Council too had been exerting itself, both on the commercial and on the technical aspects of the waterway. Early in December 1793 a committee consisting of Charles Brett, David Tomb, and Robert Simms had been appointed to investigate the tolls that were to be charged on the navigation; and they reported back to a meeting in the Donegall Arms on Christmas Eve. Their first observation was that lighters ideally suited to the new stretch of canal were not yet available, in consequence of which they recommended that tolls should be agreed only for a year. Next they asserted the principle that the toll from Belfast to Lough Neagh should in no circumstances be more than the toll from Newry to Lough Neagh (the Newry Canal had been opened fifty years earlier). On this basis, the business community should be prepared to pay £1:11:0 Irish for a large load from the lake to Belfast, and £1:2:9 for a small one; and lower charges were suggested for intermediate distances. Finally exemptions were agreed for empty vessels and concessions for those loaded with bulky commodities of low value such as stone, sand, brick, and manure; and the committee strongly urged that coal and turf should be added to that list because those commodities were *"so necessary for the comfort and relief of the Poor and so essential to the well-being of so many Valuable Manufactures"*.

But as an aside to its recommendations on tolls, the Council committee of 1793 had noted *"the great impediment this canal sustains"* from low bridges and other technical limitations. This led the Chamber to commission a professional survey of the waterway from the first bridge to Lisburn; and the task was entrusted to William Ritchie, a remarkable Scot who had come to Belfast in March 1791 to begin building boats in the Old Lime Kiln Dock and would ultimately become known as the father of shipbuilding

William Ritchie (1756-1834) who began shipbuilding in Belfast in 1791 and undertook a survey of the Lagan Navigation for the Chamber of Commerce in 1793

(Artist unknown.)

in the town. Ritchie's report was available within ten days; and it showed clearly that there were indeed serious problems not only because of low bridges (inconsistent with rigging for sail in Lough Neagh) but also because of shoals of sand and gravel in the Lagan and of the practice of the linen bleachers in drawing excessively on the flow of water at various points along its natural course.

Armed with William Ritchie's meticulous and disturbing report the Chamber met on 23 January 1794 in Drew's Tavern, the hostelry in which the First Society of United Irishmen had been formed in October 1791. There they approved a lengthy document to the Board of Commissioners of the Lagan Navigation, welcoming what had been done but also highlighting the problems and *"the absolute inutility of any navigation on which proper boats cannot freely pass"*. Both William Ritchie and the Council of the Chamber had great confidence in the ability and zeal of the Board's engineer, Richard Owen; and the Commissioners were assured that all he needed was their orders. Until those orders were given, however, it would be impossible for the business community to proceed with the *"construction of vessels calculated for the navigation, as such property would become not only useless but burthensome to the owners should any of the obstructions complained of be suffered to remain"*. But great as was the confidence of the Chamber about Owen's ability to clear the obstructions it must have been quite a lengthy business, for two of the offending bridges were substantial structures of stone; and another of the bottlenecks was created by a poorly-placed water-wheel.

Such was the peaceful business on which the Chamber was engaged immediately before it effectively ceased to exist for a period of eight years. A strong beginning had been made; and great things had been achieved. The Grain Bills had been modified; Pitt's Propositions routed; control of the harbour secured; the White Linen Hall completed; the private quays improved; Government aid channelled; and the potential of the Lagan Navigation recognised. Though fiercely independent in their business activities and in their politics, the merchants of the town had been fully convinced about the benefits of collective action in dealing with the Government whether in Dublin or in London; and their obvious success both as individuals and as a business pressure-group had taken them to a place of leadership in the whole community. The lessons of Volunteer power in matters political had been applied to matters commercial and matters industrial; and the outlines of the blueprint for the next hundred-and-ninety years had been faintly sketched. But for the first eight of those years nothing would be added to the blueprint, as the whole community was sucked irresistably into political passions that led downwards to hopeless rebellion.

Chapter 6

LIFE AFTER DEATH: 1802-1819

The Chamber died in February 1794 and it rose again in February 1802. In between, the whole community in the North-East of Ireland had passed through a fire and its face was changed. The way to the fire was the long slope of accelerating political dissension, which the people of Ulster followed from 1792 till the spring of 1798; and the final push into the June flames of Rebellion came from a heady mixture of frustration, idealism, and repressive measures by an apprehensive Government. Beyond the fire, the unwanted therapy included the Act of Union; but recovery was remarkably swift, and attitudes were remarkably changed.

For several members of the 18th Century Chamber the fire of 1798 and of the preceding and succeeding years was more physical than metaphoric. Hugh Crawford, a man with many business interests in the town, must have come perilously close to being arrested; Robert Getty, the most eloquent of the merchant champions of Catholic Emancipation, was in custody for a number of days, for mislaying an old Volunteer cannon; Limavady-born Henry Haslett spent fourteen months in Kilmainham jail in Dublin on a charge of high treason; Robert Simms, the most important of the Chamber's United Irishmen, spent eleven or twelve months in another Dublin jail and several years at Fort George in the North of Scotland; the highly-successful Will Sinclaire was deeply involved though he escaped detection; William Tennent, pillar of the Church and one of the most respected businessmen in the area, was another to spend almost four years in Fort George; and Henry Joy McCracken, son of Captain John McCracken, led the United Irishmen at the Battle of Antrim on 7 June 1798 and paid the ultimate price on the gallows at the front of the Old Market House in High Street on 17 July.

While the whole community was being sucked towards the tragedy of 1798, business did not stand totally still though its organisation had disappeared. Henry Joy jnr, disillusioned by the failure of moderation, had sold the News Letter to an Edinburgh consortium including Alexander Mackay who would buy out his partners in 1804 and become sole proprietor. About the same time as the great newspaper passed out of the hands of the family that had started it, the postmaster in Belfast was complaining that *"the Merchants who are in the Habit of sending little Boys for their Letters in the Evening will be pleased in Future to send more proper Persons, as the Confusion occasioned by the very improper Conduct of these Boys causes Mistakes to be committed very prejudicial to the Interests of the Merchants"*. But the postmaster's problems were put into perspective by a fire at the Donegall Arms Hotel in 1797 and the subsequent failure of the Belfast General Insurance Company. There were problems too in the financial sector, for there was no proper bank in Belfast with the result that there was excessive dependence on coins, and they were likely to be counterfeit or "light" through wear or defacement. And the coach service to Dublin was suspended from the eve of the Rebellion till April of the following year.

In the immediate aftermath of the Rebellion, community tension was heightened by arrests, trials, and executions; and informers were rampant. Families and organisations were split physically and politically, for many had "declared for the King" including former stalwarts of the Chamber like Waddell Cunningham and Robert Bradshaw. There was financial depression and emotional depression; and the situation was compounded by unusually wet weather in 1799, with heavy snow in April, which brought starvation and fever in Belfast. Yet in the midst of the depression there were signs of profound change — of people anxious to make a new beginning. One such was Will Sinclaire, foundation member of the Chamber in 1783, United Irishman in 1798; and so when the Lord Lieutenant paid a visit to Belfast in October 1799, Sinclaire and his wife were amongst the first to entertain him. The flirtation of the businessmen with extreme radicalism was nearing its end: and commercial considerations were again becoming paramount. The Irish Parliament was about finished and the Act of Union of Great Britain and Ireland was on its way.

And so as the 19th Century dawned the town of Belfast was undergoing tremendous change. Soon it would take on a new face physically, for one of the last acts of the Irish Parliament was to provide for the establishment of two Police Boards in Belfast which would have responsibility for paving, lighting, and cleaning the town and for providing law-enforcement and fire-fighting services. In the same year the Dispensary and the Fever Hospital would be established; and the public soup-kitchens would be off the streets by October, streets on which name-plates and house-numbers would be appearing for the first time. The better-off were going back to the theatre; and Dr William Drennan, in whose fertile mind was first conceived the idea of the secret brotherhood that became the United Irishmen, was writing to his sister in Belfast of a modest little party where his guests had had to be content with *"ducks, lambs, spinach and eggs, broccoli, cold salmon, cold chicken, ham, scalloped oysters and salad, blamange, custards, oranges, almonds, and apples"* all washed down with *"good Port from Lisbon"*! Earlier in the week he had had a proper party for fifty guests, with a more ambitious menu, dancing and so on — all on a salary of £150 a year!

But the greatest change of all was represented by the flag that was hoisted on the Old Market House in High Street on 1 January 1801. It bore the cross of St Patrick superimposed on the crosses of St George and St Andrew, for the Act of Union passed by the Irish Parliament in the middle of the previous year came into effect that day, and the centre of legislative power and political representation moved back to London. Eleven months earlier when this momentous change was under discussion the merchants of Belfast flocked to sign a petition totally opposing it; and the survivors of the 18th Century Chamber of Commerce, old and young, were there to a man. But their opposition was short-lived and half-hearted; and by the time the measure was implemented, it had ceased to be a live issue in Belfast.

In such an environment was the Belfast Chamber of Commerce reborn, in February 1802. Surprisingly some of those present must have thought it was a birth rather than a re-birth, for the list of members was headed *"Belfast Chamber of Commerce, Instituted in February 1802"*. On that list there were sixty-nine names; and there were certainly fifteen of them who knew that they were re-establishing rather than establishing a Chamber, for they had been through it all before in 1783. The "old hands" were Thomas Andrews, Narcissus Batt, Robert Bradshaw, Hugh Crawford, Robert Getty, Cunningham Greg, Henry Haslett, George Joy, James Trail Kennedy, Robert Knox, Hugh Montgomery, William Seed, William Sinclaire, John Galt Smith, and William Tennent. Noticeably the membership old and new included both those who had espoused the cause of the United Irishmen and those who had declared for the King: so for most of the merchants, the deep divisions of the preceding years were largely gone. It is just possible, however, that a residue of political tension was responsible for Robert Bradshaw's not immediately regaining his pre-Rebellion position of prominence in the Chamber.

Francis McCracken (1762-1842), manufacturer of ropes and sail-cloth, who joined the reconstituted Chamber of Commerce in 1802 and lived to be the last survivor of the Belfast Volunteers of 1788. Henry Joy McCracken, executed leader of the United Irishmen in 1798, was one of his brothers.

(From a glass-plate negative after R Rothwell — Ulster Museum.)

The new blood amongst the membership included several who would become outstanding figures in the commercial life of 19th Century Belfast. There was John S Ferguson who was destined to become the leader of the linen industry and a long-serving President of the Chamber; George Langtry who would become the pioneer of passenger-steamer services across the Irish Sea and serve the Chamber as a Council member for more than thirty years; Adam McClean, one of the four mercantile sons of the inn-keeper at Shane's Castle, who had just begun his activities as a property-developer by buying the Old Market House and would go on to much greater things in other parts of the town; James McCleery, who would play a key part in the development and management of the inland waterways; and Francis McCracken, brother of the executed Henry Joy McCracken, who would carry on his father's old rope-making and sail-cloth business for many years and live to be the last survivor of the Belfast Volunteers of 1778.

However it was to the older members experienced in the activities of the 18th Century Chamber that the reconstituted body turned when they gathered in the White Linen Hall on 3 March 1802 to appoint the office-bearers and Council. Twenty-two of them had met two days earlier in the same venue under the chairmanship of Thomas Andrews; and had decided to call upon the services of John Tisdall as a part-time paid clerk. Tisdall was a well-known figure in the town for he had been at least the nominal editor of the Belfast Mercury in the 1780's and the printer of the early issues of the Northern Star in the 1790's; and he subsequently carried on business as a notary public and auctioneer from an office near the Exchange. His first job with the Chamber was to call the general meeting for 3 March and to publish beforehand a list of all the members so that they would know the full field when they balloted for office-bearers and Council members on the following day. Their choice fell upon Hugh Montgomery for President and Robert Getty for Vice-President; and a strong Council of fifteen including nine more of the men of 1783 headed by Robert Bradshaw.

With a commendable sense of urgency the new Council met two days later at the Exchange; and decided that thereafter they would have weekly meetings on Tuesday mornings at eleven o'clock in John Tisdall's office, with Tisdall "causing summons to be served on each morning of meeting" so that forgetfulness should not become an excuse for absence. They also persuaded the President to act as Treasurer; and they then got down to work immediately by instituting a survey of the charges made by Custom Houses at Londonderry, Cork, Waterford, Greenock, and Liverpool in relation to the scale applied locally. So the show was back on the road!

The problems of the Lagan Navigation provided continuity between the Chamber of 1794 and its reincarnation in 1802. Within a fortnight of taking office the new Council was calling for the widening of various stretches of the waterway; and by April they were again discussing a plan to form a company that would build and operate four lighters suited both to the Navigation and to the Lough Neagh trade. The investment required was estimated to be about £2,000; and it was planned to offer shares not only to Council members but also to merchants and traders in Armagh, the Moy, Coalisland, and "other Places contiguous to the Lake and Navigation". Robert Getty and Henry Haslett were deputed to see the project through. And soon there was a much larger project in the wind when George Augustus, the 2nd Marquis of Donegall, offered to sell his rights in the Navigation to such merchants as were willing to subscribe. The nobleman had come to live amongst his tenants in Belfast just a few months previously, the first of the family to do so for nearly a hundred years; and he was constantly looking for money to service his debts. That was the reason for his offer to the merchants; but if he was looking for quick results he must have been deeply disappointed, for seven years were to elapse before the deal was completed.

THE Post-Master returns his sincere thanks to the Inhabitants of the Town and Vicinity of Belfast, for having so seldom given him the trouble of delivering out Letters at any other time in the Morning than from Ten to Twelve o'Clock on Week days, and from Ten to Eleven on Sundays; and assures them that, although they are in the habit of calling or sending for their Letters at those very convenient times, he does not limit to the above Hours, but, on the contrary, has particularly ordered that Letters shall be delivered out, when called for, at any time before Ten o'Clock at Night, except the time of sorting, making up, and dispatching the Mails, and during the time of Divine Service on Sundays.

The Post-Master also acquaints them that, if possible, the Morning delivery on Sundays shall commence at a quarter before Ten o'Clock; and that when an Express Packet happens to arrive from Donaghadee on Sunday Morning, too late for the Letters to be delivered out before Eleven o'Clock, the Office shall be opened at half past Three for that purpose.

Post-Office, Belfast, April 9th, 1802.

Printed notice displayed in the window of Belfast's only post-office in April 1802, in response to criticism from the Chamber of Commerce.
(Public Records Office, Northern Ireland.)

Meanwhile the Chamber was devoting most of its time and energy to securing improvements in the postal services. Initially the butt of their criticism was the local postmaster in Donegall Street, Thomas Whinnery; and the exchanges were so sharp at times that it is difficult to avoid the conclusion that there were old scores to settle. Leaving his wine and spirit business in Newry, Whinnery had come to Belfast in 1795 to take over the post office; and he was soon under suspicion from the radicals of the town for allegedly intercepting their correspondence and passing information to the authorities. Henry Joy McCracken, for example, referred to him in a letter to Mary Ann McCracken as *"that scoundrel Whinnery"*; and the Drennan Letters also cast doubts on his respect for the integrity of the mail. And so when the Council of the Chamber began a prolonged skirmish with Whinnery in March 1802 about the opening hours of his post office, it is just possible that a few of the old radicals found it difficult to be totally objective about the narrow issues involved. The abrasiveness between the postmaster and successive Councils was to continue unabated for almost twenty years; but there was to be a fairy-tale ending to the saga, for on 23 December 1822 the new members elected to the Chamber by ballot included the venerable postmaster of Belfast, the same Thomas Whinnery!

The issue with Whinnery in 1802 was whether he conducted his office in a way that permitted earliest possible receipt and dispatch of the mails; and, in retrospect, the merchants were quite unreasonable in their demands. Under criticism from the Chamber, Whinnery convincingly explained his routine to the public in a notice displayed in the window of the post office; and the Chamber's response was another blast of criticism:

"The Chamber of Commerce require from Mr Whinnery nothing but what is usual in other great Towns at Post Offices, to wit, constant and regular attendance from a reasonable Hour in the morning to ten o'clock at Night for transacting all kinds of Business relative to his office: and it is requested he will say whether he will accede to this very reasonable proposal. It is not expected that the office can be opened during the Time of sorting Letters and making up the Mail or on Sundays during Divine Service".

Poor Mr Whinnery! His only two hours of respite in the whole week were to be the hours spent in church; and for him, those were profoundly serious hours because he was deeply involved in the work of the church, becoming an elder and the Clerk for many years of the Antiburgher Synod of Irish Presbyterianism.

But Thomas Whinnery was not the only target for the Chamber as it relentlessly pursued its obsession with the speed of the mails. Communication between Belfast and Dublin was dependent on the Northern Mail Coaches of Anderson and Greer; and they too were subject to continuous scrutiny and frequent questioning. Above all there was a nagging discontent with the packet-boat service between Donaghadee and Portpatrick, which was then a vital link in the chain of communication of the merchant in the North of Ireland with his customers around the world. The cause of the discontent was the unreliability of the service in certain conditions of weather and tide;

and by March 1803 the Chamber found that they had an ally in the person of Edward Hull, the man in charge at Donaghadee. In correspondence with the Council, Hull was quite open about the problems which he ascribed to poor siting of the harbours on both sides of the Channel; and he encouraged the Chamber to press for the completion of major alterations at Portpatrick and the relocation of the harbour at Donaghadee. But Council decided that the matter should be *"deferred for the present, on Account of the State of Public Affairs".*

The state of public affairs had indeed deteriorated in various ways in the course of the previous twelve months. In the early summer of 1802 a depression in trade caused a wave of labour unrest and the emergence of what were described as *"illegal combinations"*, groups of workmen banding themselves together to improve their wages or working conditions by threatening to withdraw their labour. This understandable forerunner of trade unionism had been illegal in Ireland from 1780; but a number of instances occurred at the beginning of May 1802. The response from the Chamber was a deputation to the Sovereign consisting of Hugh Montgomery, Robert Getty, and Will Sinclaire; and their remit was to request that the magistrates used *"active and immediate exertions to suppress the present Combinations amongst the working Trade's people"*. Hot on the heels of this controversy came a serious dispute between muslin manufacturers and a group of home weavers; and the Chamber was called upon to arbitrate between the parties, as it did in commercial disputes between several of its own members during much the same period.

In the following year, there was more labour trouble; and a long condemnation of the attempts of workpeople to organise themselves effectively appeared in the News Letter, signed by nearly a hundred-and-fifty employers including many members of the Chamber. But there was trouble of another kind just around the corner; for Robert Emmet's short-lived rising in Dublin was about to begin. The rising was a pitiful affair, but it did have an unsettling effect on a community that had only just recovered from the trauma of 1798, especially when it resulted in the hanging of Thomas Russell, *"the man from God knows where"* who had once been the Librarian of the Reading Society (Linenhall Library). As has been known to happen in more recent times, the Chamber was irritated by some of the precautions taken by the military; and on 30 August 1803, the Council protested to the local commander, General Campbell, *"that the restrictions laid upon persons coming into and out of the Town are highly injurious to the Trade and Manufacturers of this Part of the Kingdom"*.

Following the minor flare-up of community tension in the late summer of 1803 the Chamber went into a low key for a period of about four years, with few meetings held and few issues pursued. At the beginning of 1804 the Council attempted to meet on a Sunday in the Donegall Arms; but this experiment was not repeated, for only three members turned up — Hugh Montgomery, Will Sinclaire, and Robert Hyndman. The objective seems to have been nothing more urgent than to examine a new schedule of customs duties that was before Parliament at the time; and the comments were duly prepared at two meetings held later in the week. However that was not the end of the matter; for by August, the Council was urging solidarity in refusing to pay the increases that resulted from the Parliamentary review. Their line was one that the Chamber has probably never pursued since or would ever have wished to pursue, for it interfered with the freedom of action of the individual member:

"No Member of the Chamber of Commerce (will) pay greater fees in any department of the Customs House than have hitherto been paid there; or if so, such person so paying, shall not be considered a Member of the Belfast Chamber of Commerce, untill such increase shall be agreed on by a General Meeting summoned for that purpose".

And at the same time the Council decided to dispense with the services of John Tisdall, their part-time paid Secretary, which suggests that he as a notary public may well have been against the peremptory action they were proposing to take on the customs question.

A fortnight later the Chamber held an annual general meeting. Tisdall was gone, having been paid £22:15s:0d for printing and other services; and Hugh Montgomery as President had no difficulty in getting endorsement of the resolution on collective action against the increases in customs duties. Montgomery was by that time involved in the Discount Company, and within five years he would be the founder of the Northern Bank; but on 15 August 1804 he was dealing with money on a different scale — he was reporting that the Chamber had a credit balance of £31:2s:0½d at the conclusion of his stewardship! On that note he came to the end of two-and-a-half years as President; and was succeeded by the reformed United Irishman, Will Sinclaire. The new Vice-President was Waddell Cunningham's nephew Narcissus Batt; and the Council again included Robert Bradshaw (who had lost his place for a time) together with other old stalwarts of 1783 like Hugh Crawford, George Joy, Henry Haslett, William Tennent, and Cunningham Greg. So the faces that were bringing about change were themselves changing only very slowly.

Robert Callwell (1764-1836),
Secretary of the Chamber of Commerce 1807-1812,
President 1834.

(From a portrait in the Northern Bank.)

Though Will Sinclaire was a highly successful businessman, the Chamber seems to have achieved very little under his leadership, for the minute-book is blank for the next three years. But by August 1807 there was a marked upturn in activity, for Robert Bradshaw had at last become President, an office that he would grace for over twelve years. As his running mate in the office of Vice-President for the whole of the period he was to have another of the men of 1783, Narcissus Batt; but there were new faces as Secretary and Treasurer, in the persons of Robert Callwell and Robert Hyndman. The new Treasurer was presumably a descendant of one of the Hyndmans of 1783; and the new Secretary was the son of an old Belfast merchant family that had lost a ship in Dundrum Bay in 1786 and the brother-in-law of William Magee, who sold cheese and wine in High Street. Callwell had literary as well as commercial interests; and he was destined to become President of the Chamber some twenty-seven years later.

Almost immediately the new regime faced a major problem, for the authorities in Dublin were proposing to introduce a new system of charges at custom houses which the Belfast Chamber perceived as potentially damaging to trade. Robert Davis and William Tennent were therefore deputed to go to Dublin and join with representatives from the Chambers in Dublin, Cork, Limerick, and Waterford in a deputation to Mr Foster, the Chancellor of the Irish Exchequer. However when they got there they found the Dublin Chamber committed to the Chancellor to such an extent that the best that Dublin could do was to sit on the fence as the provincial chambers pursued their case, a case with which many of the merchants in the metropolis now agreed. Though not hopeful on the major issue, the Belfast delegation convinced their colleagues on the Council that the visit had been helpful in other directions, Mr Foster having listened intently to their representations on a wide range of revenue points; and the Council had no doubt that the £17 required to meet their expenses was money well spent.

But it was not only the revenue laws that were changing in 1808. The industrial scene was being transformed by the growth of the cotton industry, which was already employing over two-thousand people in the Belfast area; the financial scene was about to be transformed by the establishment of stable banks; and communications were being transformed by the increased use of coaches for carrying the mails and for travelling to places like Lurgan, Armagh, and Newry. The first of the new financial institutions was David Gordon's Belfast Bank in which one of the partners was Narcissus Batt, the Vice-President of the Chamber. Its doors at No 1 Donegall Square North were opened on 1 August 1808; and within a year, it was followed by the Commercial Bank with William Tennent as the chief partner and by the Northern with Hugh Montgomery in that role. The President of the Chamber, Robert Bradshaw, and the Secretary, Robert Callwell, were also involved, as partners in the Commercial.

Yet the pace of change was not sufficient for the Chamber, particularly when it came to postal arrangements. The resilient Mr Whinnery was still under attack about his opening hours; and pressure was building up for the transfer of the packet-station from Donaghadee to Bangor, because of occasional delays in getting the boat into and out of the exposed harbour. But Edward Hull, the manager of the packet-station in

Donaghadee, argued strongly that the problem could be solved by spending some money on improvements there. And the provision merchants argued just as strongly against a proposed increase of a half-penny per firkin in the charge for weighing butter in the Belfast market, the Chamber declining *"any interference in this business so long as such objections continued"*. (Butter was at that time made on individual farms from naturally-soured cream and assembled through country markets for bulk packing and weighing in Belfast.)

The Chamber did not, however, decline the opportunity to become involved in a much larger issue — the propriety of taking over the Lagan Navigation from Lord Donegall. The subject had been mooted six years earlier when Hugh Montgomery was President; but it was Robert Davis who opened it up again in March 1808 by indicating that his lordship wanted to talk. The Council decided that Narcissus Batt, Robert Getty, and Davis should see the nobleman and his agent, Edward May, to hear what they had to offer; but it was eighteen months before a detailed proposition emerged from the estate office. This was put forward by James McCleery to a very full meeting of the Council on 16 August 1809, with Robert Bradshaw in the chair. The Navigation was mortgaged for £10,000 at an interest rate of five per cent and had no other debts. Donegall was prepared to sell it for £5,000 with half payable on 1 November 1810 and the remainder a year later. After a prolonged discussion the Council decided to accept the proposition and nominated a committee of seven to put up the money and see it through with the assistance of James McCleery as Secretary. The members of the committee were Robert Bradshaw, Narcissus Batt, Hugh Crawford, Robert Davis, Robert Getty, Cunningham Greg, and William Tennent; and the waterway passed into their hands at the end of 1809.

With their banking activities and the further development of the Lagan Navigation making demands on the time of most of the key figures in the Chamber, the representational activities of the organisation took second place for several years. Nevertheless it was possible to co-operate with the Waterford Chamber in seeking to have the duty on foreign salt imported into Ireland reduced to the level charged in Great Britain; and there was liaison with the Newry Chamber on an aspect of the flax business. The Council also continued to take a close interest in the speed of the mails; and they reacted warmly to Lord O'Neill when he pressed for initiatives to bring more competition into the coach services. They encouraged the Derry Mail Company to enter the business; and they were ardent supporters of John McCoy, the entrepreneurial operator of services to Dublin and Armagh till his tragic death in a coaching accident in 1811 at the age of thirty-two. And in November that year the Chamber made an important submission on commercial grievances to Lord Castlereagh, the former Robert Stewart of Mountstewart, who in four months time would be British Foreign Secretary in the midst of a major war. Paramount amongst the grievances was the effect on the Ulster cotton industry of the economic war with America that had developed as a consequence of the shooting war with Napoleon in Europe.

Belfast in 1810 had grown to a town of 28,000 people, more than twice its size when the Chamber was formed in 1783. Progress had been made in many directions and yet, in the words of the 19th Century historian George Benn, it *"continued, according to present ideas, very much unimproved, badly lighted, badly watched, and rather inefficiently governed, but yet possessing in its inhabitants the elements of the commercial and manufacturing eminence which it has since reached"*. The wages of a skilled workman in the linen industry were about thirty shillings a week; and wages in the cotton industry varied from a miserable twelve to fifteen shillings a week for a weaver to as much as £2:7s:0d for a top-class spinner. Oaten meal was 19s:2d per cwt, wheat 15s:0d, barley 12s:6d, oats 11s:0d, first-grade flour 38s:0d, potatoes 5d per stone, and butter 1s:3d per "pound" of eighteen ounces. Counterfeiting of coins was still commonplace; and Noel Simpson in his superb history of the Belfast Bank recalls that it was in February 1810 that the authorities discovered a huge illicit coin factory near Toomebridge. Meanwhile in Belfast the little sugar refiners in Rosemary Street and Waring Street amalgamated as another step towards the disappearance of that industry from the local scene; but on the other side of the town centre, an event took place that marked the physical beginning of a great venture that would endure — the foundation stone of the Academical Institution was laid on 3 July by Lord Donegall in pouring rain and, in the words of the News Letter, *"amidst the acclamations of a numerous concourse of spectators"*.

For the Chamber, the last few weeks of 1811 saw the beginnings of another controversy with the postal authorities that would rumble on for a couple of years. This concerned the route of the mail coach from Belfast to the packet-station at Donaghadee. Originally the coach had travelled by an inland route through Newtownards; but the postal authorities decided that in future it should go via Bangor and make a pick-up there. This added several miles to the journey; and the Belfast merchants were furious not only about the extra time taken but also about the insensitivity of the authorities in increasing postal charges to pay for the diversion. So they fired off a memorial to the Irish Postmaster General asserting that:

". . . the trifling advantage which going to Bangor can give the Inhabitants of that small town cannot by any means be put in competition with the additional charges of posting imposed on the Merchants, and others of this town and other places in Ireland".

William Ritchie's dock and boat-building yard on the County Antrim side of the Lagan, with the Cavehill in the background.
(From a drawing made about 1810 — Ulster Museum.)

However their representations seem to have fallen on ears that were deaf at the time; for fourteen months later, as the Peninsular War reached crisis point for Napoleon, the controversy about the route of the Donaghadee coach again reached boiling point in Belfast. And the Chamber in its further submission to the Postmaster General was not at all complimentary to Bangor, describing it as a place *"of little importance in population or commerce"!* So the days when Bangor would become the dormitory town of Belfast and a centre of commercial importance in its own right were still far ahead.

Meanwhile the Chamber itself had a new lease of life as a result of a shake-up in March 1812. Robert Bradshaw and Narcissus Batt remained President and Vice-President; but there were seven changes in the Council. The new faces included Narcissus Batt's brother Thomas; James Luke, a partner in the Commercial Bank, who immediately became Secretary of the Chamber; Bob McDowell, a very public-spirited man who would become President over thirty years later; and the most outstanding of the lot, John S Ferguson of Donegall Place, who had a huge bleach-green at Ballysillan and a paper mill at Antrim and who would take up the mantle of Chamber leadership from the men of 1783 some eight years later. With such a dynamic Council and an increased membership, the Chamber was on course for another notable period in its resurrected life — a period when some old issues would become new and yet a period of change.

Immediately, the vista widened from local issues to one of world dimensions; for the Belfast Chamber chose to be in the forefront of a campaign to dissuade Parliament from renewing the Charter of the East India Company — the charter that had for over two centuries given the company the right to be the sole vehicle for British and Irish trade with India and China. The local campaign began at a general meeting of the Chamber on 26 March 1812 when a committee was appointed to draft a memorial to Parliament and a request was sent to the Sovereign, Thomas Verner, to call a town meeting. The meeting of the merchants and other leading inhabitants duly took place on 3 April; and it fully endorsed a superb memorial drafted by the committee and beautifully written in the hand of the President, Robert Bradshaw. Arrangements were made for Lord Donegall to present the memorial in the House of Lords and for Edward May, the MP for the town, to do likewise in the Commons; and John S Ferguson and William Blacker, another of the new Council members, were deputed to go to London to lobby MPs, noblemen, Ministers, and officials according to a carefully defined remit drawn up by Bradshaw.

The thrust of the Belfast case against the monopoly powers of the East India Company was that in a time of economic difficulty — *"the present distressed state of the Commerce and Manufactures of the United Kingdom"* — the exclusion of private interests from British and Irish trade with the East was *"impolitic and unjust"* and was allowing American merchants to move in on the area. Furthermore it was making Irish goods uncompetitive in that part of the world because of the associated requirement that all trade had to be conducted through the Port of London. The case was pressed home with vigour and imagination in the summer and autumn of 1812 (which cost the

Chamber £51:15s:0d for the expenses of John S Ferguson and William Blacker!); and it was still on the go early in 1813 when the Council asked the Sovereign to hold another town meeting to ratify another memorial which urged that:

". . . the trade to India, to China, and to all the islands and Possessions to the Eastward of the Cape of Good Hope be thrown open to the Skill, Industry, and Resources of the Merchants of the United Kingdom".

But the Charter of the East India Company survived this determined attack; and the Chamber was forced to endure the restrictions on trade with the East for many years, though not without periodic complaint.

Nearer home the Chamber had another problem to face: its funds were exhausted — not for the first time and not for the last. The direct cause of the crisis was not difficult to find, for in March 1812 the annual meeting had decided to reduce the membership fee from a pound to ten shillings a year with effect from 1 April 1813. Whether this was a reflection of the economic difficulties of the time or a move to attract more members is not clear; but in the context of the expenditure on the campaign to clip the wings of the East India Company, a minor financial crisis was inevitable. The shortage of funds had begun to bite even before the decision to reduce the subscription was implemented; for in February 1813 the Council decided *"that as soon as there are sufficient funds a complete set of the Irish Statutes be purchased and those of the Imperial Parliament from the Union to the latest period".* As usual the problem was delegated to a committee; and it was probably this group that was responsible for a potential "solution" that emerged from a Saturday meeting in February 1814. George Langtry and Hugh Crawford were *"desired to wait on the Butter Shippers at this port to have their concurrence in making a charge of 1d per firkin on the export of Butter from this place and in applying the same to the support of the Chamber of Commerce".* This really was an unworthy proposition, for the Chamber was not at that time giving any special service to the butter industry; and the thinking seems to have been that if the shippers paid the levy they would recover it from the farmers, who would thus unconsciously have become responsible for financing the activities of the Chamber. Exports of butter at the time were of the order of fifty-thousand firkins (twelve-hundred-and-fifty tons) a year; so the levy would have raised over £200 annually, almost three times the previous annual income of the Chamber. However the proposition seems to have been rejected or withdrawn; and the income of the Chamber continued to come from membership subscriptions, supplemented by special collections such as the £29:5s:0d raised about that time in support of the initiatives on Eastern trade (which involved a second visit to London and cost £109:11s:3d in total).

As the economic war with America on the high seas escalated into a shooting war and as the long and bloody drama in Europe moved towards its dénouement, the Chamber called on the Lords of the Admiralty to provide a warship to protect shipping in Belfast harbour. But the natural hazards of life at sea also still prevailed, as exemplified by the loss of one of George Langtry's ships on Burial Island off Ballyhalbert in February 1813; and a year later the Chamber enthusiastically became involved in raising funds to provide three life-boats between Donaghadee and Strangford, a project which the Marquis of Downshire had offered to support to the tune of fifty guineas.

Postal matters were never long absent from the Chamber programme; and in 1814 the issue was the need for more coaches on the Belfast-Dublin route. At that time the route was carrying not only the mail between the two commercial centres, but also the English mail to and from Belfast, and the Southern mail to and from Scotland. In these circumstances it happened all too frequently that Belfast mail coming into Dublin from Holyhead lay for up to thirteen hours before it could be despatched to the North; and there were similar problems at Belfast with through mail for Dublin and the South and West. The Council therefore studied the whole situation deeply and drew up a detailed operating plan which showed how extra coaches could save hours and help towards the perennial objective of getting replies away on the day that letters were received. If their plan were adopted, said the memorial to the Postmaster General, it would *"give a fresh spring to that spirit of industry and enterprize in which the inhabitants are not far behind any other part of His Majesty's dominions"*. And two years later these industrious and enterprising inhabitants were battling again on questions affecting the speed of the mails, as they sprayed politicians, postmasters, coach companies, and chambers of commerce all over the British Isles with questions about delays and suggestions about change.

The customs regulations continued to have similar attention; and there was scarcely a month that questions did not arise about duties, about drawbacks (export subsidies), and about the behaviour of individual officers. One of the most interesting of the exchanges concerned the remission in Scotland of "transit duties" on foreign linen re-exported to South America. The Belfast Chamber objected to this because it made the foreign linen handled by Scottish merchants more competitive with genuine Irish linen exported by local manufacturers. The Council therefore sent a major document on the subject to the trade ministers of the day, the preamble of which reminded their lordships that *"the greatest proportion of the Inhabitants both rich and poor of the Nine Northern Counties are engaged in the different branches of this manufacture"*. Delightfully the document then demolished the argument that foreign linen needed to be used for the trade with South America: that, said the Council, was an insult to those Irish linen merchants who were preparing and finishing their goods in such a way as *"to suit the prejudices and tastes of the peoples of the Spanish Colonies"*. So the best marketing principles of the late 20th Century were already well established in the Ulster linen industry of a hundred-and-seventy years ago!

The year 1815 may have been a turning point in the history of the world, but it was a quiet one for the Chamber of Commerce in Belfast. As the Congress of Vienna, "The Hundred Days", the Battle of Waterloo, the Treaty of Paris, and the despatch of Napoleon to St Helena followed in majestic succession across the world stage, the only task undertaken by the Chamber was the appointment of William Newsam as the official sampler and inspector of tobacco in the port of Belfast. With the benefit of romantic hindsight it now seems almost as though the Chamber paused in veneration for the two great figures with local connections who were at the centre of the world stage for most of the year. Lord Castlereagh, British Foreign Secretary and chief architect of the Congress of Vienna and the Treaty of Paris, had been born and brought up at Mountstewart; and the Duke of Wellington, Commander-in-Chief of the Allies, had as a boy spent several holidays at Belvoir Park, Newtownbreda, the ancestral home of his mother.

But if the Chamber paused for a while in 1815, it was by no means a static year in the community generally. The cotton industry was still growing though it was about to enter a depression and many of its employees were deeply unhappy with their wages and working conditions; the long-felt need for a crossing of the Lagan between the Long Bridge and Shaw's Bridge some four miles upriver was being met by the building of the Ormeau Bridge; the centre section of the White Linen Hall was crowned with its cupola; the consecration took place of St Patrick's Catholic Church in Donegall Street, followed by a public acknowledgement from the Catholic community of the generous augmentation of the building fund by *"our much esteemed Protestant and Dissenting Brethren of Belfast and its vicinity";* farmers and traders had become accustomed to the improved facilities of May's Market, named after Edward May's son Stephen and opened two years earlier for the sale of meat, eggs, potatoes, vegetables, and butter; and there was a new source of timber in town, for in 1814 farmer John Corry from Newtownards and William Montgomery from the same general area had set up shop in a little wooden hut at the County Down end of the Long Bridge, out of which would grow the great Ulster firm of James P Corry & Co.

And as butter moved to May's market it was also the subject of the major activity undertaken by the Chamber in 1816. In its first initiative on agriculture in over thirty years of service to industry and commerce in Ulster, the Council wrote on 21 February to the Lords of His Majesty's Treasury about post-war problems in the region's largest industry:

"The Memorial of the Chamber of Commerce of Belfast Respectfully Sheweth:

That the peace lately concluded has occasioned a very serious depression in every article of agricultural produce.

That during the continuance of the war large tracts of land in this country were fully occupied in the rearing and feeding of cattle for the supply of His Majesty's Navy and Armies.

That the demand for these purposes having ceased, nothing now remains for the occupiers of such lands but an attention to the dairy in the manufacture of butter.

That this branch of industry will be materially affected if not entirely annihilated unless protected by a prohibitory duty on the importation of Foreign Butter as the Irish Farmer cannot succeed in the manufacture of this article if the rivalship of foreigners more favourably circumstanced is not effectually checked."

There is no record of the Government's reaction to this plea, but it is unlikely to have been favourable for the whole economy was by now into deep recession, with wages in most sections of manufacturing industry dropping viciously.

Narcissus Batt (1767-1840), foundation member of the Chamber 1783, Vice-President 1802-1819, President 1820.

(From an engraving by McInnes after J Freeman — Ulster Museum)

For the Chamber it was a time to take stock and make changes; and those were the themes of the annual meeting on 15 April 1817. Robert Bradshaw and Narcissus Batt continued as President and Vice-President; but there were six new faces on the Council, including James Goddard whose first wife Mary had died exactly twelve months earlier at the age of twenty-six. Goddard was the agent in Belfast of the Westminster Insurance Company; and he immediately succeeded James Luke as Secretary of the Chamber. Later he would marry John S Ferguson's daughter Matilda; work for the Bank of Ireland; and become a foundation director of the Ulster Railway Company. Also joining the Council at that time was a future President of the Chamber, William Boyd of the Belfast Foundry. And the first business decision of the new session was that the Chamber needed twenty shillings from every member, with anyone who refused to contribute being struck off the list. The President himself reported on the current financial situation; and it was far from satisfactory. There was a balance of 12s:6d to hand over to the new Secretary, but there were also unpaid accounts of almost £50. And in these circumstances yet another committee was set up *"to prepare Rules and Regulations for the future government of the Chamber and to suggest some fit and proper mode of raising the permanent fund for its support"*. Again the search was on for a method of funding other than an appropriate level of membership subscription!

At that time there were seventy-five members on the books, but only fifty-one of them paid the new subscription before June. That reduced the membership to its lowest point in the two hundred years of the Chamber's history. Of those fifty-one, only five were survivors from 1783: Narcissus Batt, Robert Bradshaw, Robert Getty, Cunningham Greg, and William Tennent. And only twenty-one were survivors of the sixty-eight involved in the re-birth of the Chamber in 1802. There had therefore been a substantial turn-over in membership with the passage of the years even though the outward face of the organisation remained relatively unchanged.

In retrospect it is difficult to understand why the membership of the Chamber in the first quarter of the 19th Century allowed it to be in constant financial difficulty. The organisation was clearly proving quite effective in bringing about change to the benefit of the business community; and many of those involved in the Chamber were profiting, at least modestly, from the continued growth of industry and commerce. True there was a serious recession in the aftermath of the Napoleonic Wars, which gave rise to wage reductions and industrial unrest; but it is nevertheless an enigma that it was only in 1817 that the Chamber was able to liquidate advertising and printing accounts with the proprietors of the News Letter and the Commercial Chronicle dating back to 1812. And one also detects a tinge of regret that they had to pay two shillings a meeting for the use of the Exchange Coffee Room and the provision of a coal fire! Times had changed from the late 1780s when the fines alone were sufficient to sustain the convivial accompaniment of a relaxed Council meeting in the Crown Tavern or the Donegall Arms!

Times were changing too in the butter trade, which was so important both to the Belfast merchants and to farmers throughout the North of Ireland. In the recession that followed the Napoleonic Wars butter was in surplus supply, and buyers became more demanding in their requirements. It was in these circumstances that the Council in June 1817 set up a committee to review the regulations governing the trade in Belfast; and the committee did a thorough job for it did not report until February 1818. The report particularly criticised the standard of workmanship in the wooden firkins in which the butter was exported. In many cases the firkins were not capable of "holding pickle"; that is, of preventing leakage of the brine solution in which the butter had to be packed if it were intended for distant markets. Belfast butter therefore had to be confined to the market in Great Britain, which was then less attractive financially than some of the foreign and colonial markets. The firkins used in Cork were much superior, with the result that better markets were open to butter from that part of the country. The committee therefore recommended that an Inspector of Casks should be appointed to enforce much stricter standards on the cooperage and use of the firkins; and that certain conventions in the weighing of the butter should be radically changed.

This report resulted in the introduction of new regulations governing the butter trade through Belfast; and the enforcement of those regulations was soon proving beneficial to the reputation of the product. But then a new problem for the butter merchants began to emerge: to avoid the stricter controls applied in Belfast, farmers and middlemen were increasingly selling their butter through other ports such as Newry, and exports through Belfast were declining. In the summer of 1819 the Chamber was therefore leaning heavily on Mr Arthur Chichester MP to get him to press for uniform application of the butter laws throughout Ireland. And that was not the only problem: a close watch had still to be kept on custom and practice around the weighbridge, for there was a resurgence of pilferage by scraping a thin layer off the surface of the butter in the open firkin immediately after it was weighed. But despite tighter controls, there were still occasional complaints from overseas buyers, some of which were referred to the Chamber as arbiters. After being involved in one such case, in which the problem was "staleness", the Secretary of the Chamber recommended in October 1819 that the date of packing and inspection should in future be recorded openly on each firkin. Open date-marking of butter in retail packs became obligatory in Northern Ireland Ireland on 1 April 1983!

Another major exercise undertaken by the Chamber during this period was a survey of the employment conditions of tidewaiters at ports throughout the British Isles. Tidewaiters were customs officials who boarded incoming and outgoing ships to survey the cargo and assess the duties payable; and the tradition in the port of Belfast was that the shipowner had to provide free accommodation and food for them for as long as their duties required them to remain on board. The survey showed that whereas there was a similar tradition at other ports in Ireland, the position in Great Britain was quite different, with the tidewaiters being responsible for providing their own food and accommodation. In the spring of 1818 the Chamber therefore began a vigorous campaign to secure uniform practice throughout the British Isles, complaining that *"the cost of the present practice in Belfast often Amounts to more than the freight of the debenture goods in Charge of which they are placed"*. Nevertheless the campaign does not seem to have been immediately successful because two years later, in May 1820, the Council was in communication with the Chambers in Newry, Cork, Limerick, and Waterford asking them to weigh in on the subject (the Dublin Chamber was temporarily out of action at that time).

Meanwhile the Chamber had been engaged in a long and difficult series of discussions about the introduction of a system of levies on trade to augment the funds available to the town's two Police Boards for the improvement of the environment and the maintenance of crime-prevention and fire-fighting services. This saga began on 10 October 1818 when the Council considered a request from the Police Commissioners for the Chamber to provide a statistical picture of the imports and exports of Belfast and to suggest a schedule of levies on individual commodities that would in total yield from £2,000 to £2,500 a year. In a quite remarkable piece of work for an organisation that had no staff, the Chamber responded with a complete plan within three days. This envisaged the raising of £990 a year from levies on exports (almost half of it from butter, which the Chamber invariably seemed determined to milk) and £1,450 a year on imports, giving a total of £2,440 in accordance with the request of the Commissioners.

The levy plan was submitted to the Police Commissioners on 13 October; but this was only the first of many stages in the project. Within a fortnight the thought had dawned on a number of leading members of the Chamber that if imports and exports were to be taxed in order to provide amenities and services for the whole community it would not be unreasonable that a proportion of the funds should be diverted to provide support for trade-orientated projects such as the construction of the proposed Ulster Canal from Lough Neagh to Lough Erne and — wait for it — the running costs of the Chamber of Commerce. The committee that had been looking into the funding and future regulation of the Chamber therefore chose this moment to present its report; and this recommended that the taxes to be levied under the new Police Act should be increased by twenty per cent (about £490) but with an obligation laid upon the Police Commissioners to provide an annual subvention of £200 to the Chamber and £1,000 a year to service the capital required for the construction of the Ulster Canal (which was estimated at £10,000). And at the same time the report called both for incorporation of the Chamber by Act of Parliament (so that it could receive the subvention) and for new rules and regulations for the organisation including an annual membership fee of one guinea (so that the Chamber was seen to be engaging in self-help as well).

The revised plan for taxing imports and exports was considered by a joint meeting of the Chamber with other merchants and traders on 10 November. The attendance of over seventy was inevitably divided into a number of factions on the basis of self-interest in relation to the proposals for each sector of trade; and the best that could be achieved that day was to establish a committee of seven, independent both of the Chamber and of the Police Commissioners, to study the schedule in more detail and to bring forward new recommendations. The members of the committee included Nicholas Grimshaw's son Robert, who would become deeply involved in the Chamber later; Robert Gamble, a butter merchant in Waring Street; and James Munfoad, the salt manufacturer and long-time Secretary/Treasurer of the Linenhall Library, who was appointed Chairman.

Munfoad's committee too was soon in difficulties, because three of its seven members headed by Robert Grimshaw felt that a tax on provisions leaving the country was simply a tax on farmers and was *"in its principle contrary to the opinion and policy of the best-informed writers in Political Economy"*. This group proposed that the whole of the sum required by the Police Commissioners should be raised by a tax of a shilling a ton on imports of coal, with substantial relief for manufacturing industry; and indicated that they would not be opposed to an additional levy of fivepence a consignment on goods of all kinds going through the port in order to provide a few hundred pounds a year for the Chamber of Commerce. But the majority report from the group favoured a tax of sixpence a ton on coal with the remainder of the budget being met by taxes on exports, particularly of provisions, and no subvention to the Chamber.

The attempt to reach an agreed schedule of taxes through an independent committee having failed, the problem was next referred to a new committee comprising representatives of the various interest groups — the Police Commissioners, the Police Committee, the Chamber, and other prominent citizens. Officially the Chamber was represented by James Goddard (the Secretary), Bob McDowell, and Thomas Vance; but the three representatives of the Police Commissioners were none other than the Chamber worthies Narcissus Batt, John S Ferguson, and William Tennent. So duplication in the membership of business organisations and public bodies must have been at least as common in 1818 as it is in 1983. The independents on the taxes committee of 1818 included John Lawless, the eternal liberal, who was at that time publishing "The Irishman" from 2 Pottinger's Entry.

Surprisingly enough the committee of interest groups managed to reach a reasonable level of agreement on a tax plan; and their report formed the basis of a six-point programme agreed at a large and representative meeting on 5 January 1819, with the President of the Chamber, Robert Bradshaw, in the chair. The revenue was to be raised entirely from imports of coal, which at that time amounted to about sixty-eight-thousand tons a year: the rate of duty would be a shilling a ton, with a refund of sixpence a ton for manufacturing industry. The Chamber of Commerce should be incorporated by Act of Parliament so that the Police Commissioners could be authorised to finance it to the extent of £200 a year; and (as an early example of openness in public administration) the Police Commissioners should be required to publish full accounts annually. Finally, the meeting made detailed recommendations to the authorities on two other aspects of trade that were then of public concern. Regulations controlling the bakery industry should be introduced, so that loaves were of certain prescribed weights and that the weight and name of the baker were clearly indicated to the purchaser. Unbelievably the second peripheral subject covered was the need for a regulatory system to ensure that *"itinerant shopkeepers"* paid their fair share of taxes! PLUS ÇA CHANGE!

Whatever the decisions on other aspects of this ambitious plan for the future regulation of trade, one aspect that was not agreed was the funding of the Chamber from the revenue raised by the Police Commissioners. Nevertheless in these the final years of the Bradshaw era, the Chamber was more active than ever on an incredibly wide range of subjects. The improvement of the mail services remained at the top of the list, but there were new angles such as the need for a bridge to replace a ferry across the Conway River in North Wales; the need for a coach service from Belfast to Sligo via Enniskillen; the need for a new and more direct road from Belfast to Donaghadee; and the need for a more flexible approach to the routing of the packet-boats on the Irish Sea in the light of weather conditions. Also high amongst the priorities was a campaign for the development on either side of the Irish Sea of a well-sheltered and protected port for use in emergencies, *"a Harbour of Refuge where Vessels of Burthen may find Shelter from bad Weather and adverse Winds"*; and the Chamber expressed a willingness to contribute through levies to the development of the harbour at Holyhead for that purpose. They pressed too for the recognition of Belfast as a harbour suitable for ships engaging in the East Indies trade; the provision of a lighthouse on the Maidens rocks off the County Antrim coast; the use of Ardglass as a centre of communications with the Isle of Man; and, incredibly, for the rejection by Parliament of a bill that would have made it illegal for citizens of the United Kingdom to enlist in the forces of *"the South American Patriots"*. And they must have reflected often on their involvement in August 1818 in the bizarre case of Captain Silas S Webb and the American ship LUCY.

Captain Webb, a stranger in a strange land, had been arrested by the authorities in Belfast on a charge brought by an inhabitant of the town, Richard Wolfenden of Trafalgar Street; and the Chamber, considering that there had been a miscarriage of justice, came rapidly to his rescue in response to a requisition signed on 26 August 1818 by thirteen of its members. Wolfenden alleged that as he strolled on the quay one evening he met Webb who was about to take a few potential passengers out to see his ship which was lying at anchor in the Pool of Garmoyle. Webb allegedly invited him to join the party and later to have dinner on board. According to Wolfenden he was plied with drink and ultimately dumped overboard and left to fend for himself, narrowly escaping a watery grave. Captain Webb and his crew, on the other hand, asserted that Wolfenden wheedled his way into the party going out to the ship, with the objective of having a number of empty bottles that he had with him filled with *"spirituous liquor"* duty-free; that he had become intoxicated during dinner through his own intemperance; and that when a steward whom he approached on deck refused to fill up his bottles he had become objectionable, had demanded to be taken to another ship in the bay, and finally had had to be conveyed by rowing boat to the Holywood shore, leaving him to wade through only a few yards of shallow water to the King's highway. In a remarkable intervention, the Chamber took depositions from members of the ship's crew which fill seven tightly-packed pages of the huge minute-book and are written in the almost indecipherable combination of James Goddard's hand and an unstable ink. Though the final outcome is not immediately clear, the sympathies of the Chamber in the light of their investigations were clearly with Captain Webb and his crew; and there is a noticeable coolness in their response to a number of letters that they subsequently received from the allegedly-aggrieved Richard Wolfenden.

Those notes of liberality, of open mind, of independence of action, of concern for the well-being of a commercial visitor are appropriate notes on which to end the record of the Bradshaw era in the history of the Chamber, for Robert Bradshaw himself was an exponent of them all. His last recorded involvement in the organisation was on 1 June 1819 where he signed a number of letters and memorials. After that it was his Vice-President Narcissus Batt that came to the fore, probably because Bradshaw was dead or dying; and a general meeting held in the centre room of the White Linen Hall on 26 July 1819 under the chairmanship of William Tennent and with the intention of electing new office-bearers seems to have ended inconclusively. In the next twelve months Batt as Vice-President seems to have remained the effective leader of the Chamber, as they battled with import duties on foreign timber, a shortage of flour, the behaviour of the porters around the tobacco scale, the excessive cost of the tidewaiters of Belfast that had to be bedded and fed, and the problems of raising £1,000 to loan to the first person who would start a coach service between Belfast and Enniskillen.

Though its young heart may have fluttered dangerously on several occasions, the Chamber in the first twenty years of the 19th Century was truly alive after the death of 1794. And it would never again falter in the two hundred years of its history. It would be an untiring agent of change.

Chapter 7

PLEASING BUT NOT DAZZLING: 1820-1847

When gas-lighting came to the streets of Belfast on the evening 30 August 1823, the News Letter reported that *"the light now used is of the purest kind, shedding on the streets a brilliant lustre — pleasing but not dazzling"*. By coincidence those concluding words can also be aptly used to describe the progress of the Chamber and its members over the period of almost thirty years from the withdrawal of Robert Bradshaw in 1819 till the appointment of Samuel Vance as full-time paid Secretary on 23 December 1847. This was a period which saw enormous developments in communications and in banking; the unexpected demise of the cotton industry; and the parallel growth of a factory-based linen industry. But it was not a dazzling period in the sense that the second half of the 19th Century justified the use of that term. Nor was it in the slightest dazzling or pleasing in terms of the quality of life for the majority of the people; for poverty and disease were rampant and took a dreadful toll. Yet the progress of the Chamber during the period was pleasingly constant; and the base was being laid for the dazzling take-off of the industrial revolution later in the century.

After his long "apprenticeship" of sixteen years with Will Sinclaire and Robert Bradshaw, Narcissus Batt finally became President of the Chamber on 3 August 1820. Despite his protracted Vice-Presidency and his energetic leadership of the organisation during Bradshaw's last illness Batt's progress to the chair was not uncontested; on the contrary he had to fend off serious challenges from two old friends of 1783, Robert Getty and William Tennent, and from the rising star of the 19th Century linen industry, John S Ferguson. In the end Ferguson scraped in as Vice-President; James Goddard was re-elected Secretary, after an easy contest with Robert Grimshaw and a John E Brown; and a good Council of fifteen was selected from a huge field of thirty-five. So democracy was rampant in the Chamber at that time! And amongst the new Council members was John Barnett who would serve quietly and effectively in that role for many years.

Competition was soon rampant too on the rough road from Belfast to Dublin, for John Bellingham's "Fair Trader" coaches began to take business from the pioneering Newry firm, Anderson and Greer's Northern Mail Coaches; and the Chamber, neither for the first time nor for the last, welcomed the competition while at the same time fearing for the commercial survival of both operators. Bellingham first approached the Chamber on the matter in September 1820, when he rashly pledged that if he got sufficient

Donegall Arms Hotel, Castle Place, early to mid-19th Century. This famous hostelry was the starting point for a number of coach services. It was also frequently used by the Chamber of Commerce.
(After an engraving in Young's "Belfast and the Province of Ulster".)

support he would not raise his fares for at least seven years. By March of the following year, the Council was in discussion with both operators, probably in an attempt to see the competition maintained but not destructively. The Chamber tried too to interest the new operator, John Bellingham, in the Belfast — Enniskillen route; and guided him on the rates he should quote to the postal authorities for the carriage of the mails. Next it was back to Anderson and Greer to press them to increase the speed of their coaches from Belfast to Dublin to enable the travelling time to be reduced to fourteen hours, and a proper link-up to be established with the new steamboat service from Howth to Holyhead. And soon there was pressure too for the establishment of a steamboat service from Donaghadee to Portpatrick; and renewed support for the use of Ardglass as a packet-station for the Isle of Man.

Such were the pre-occupations of the Chamber in 1821, as its members still speculated on the identity of the anonymous donor who some months previously had slipped two £500 notes on to the collection plate at a special service in the Third Presbyterian Church in aid of the work of the Charitable Society. Almost certainly that very substantial and much-needed gift came from a member of the business community; and it was the business community too that had provided the help which the Charitable Society had been receiving from the profits of the Ballast Board, culminating in a gift of £1,000 in 1816. That gift had been sent with a covering letter from Narcissus Batt who was at that time, Chairman of the Ballast Board; and it was from the same Narcissus Batt, President of the Chamber from August 1820, that the Council received an unexpected letter when it met without its leader in the recently completed Commercial Buildings in Waring Street on 14 October 1821. The old stalwart of the Chamber from 1783 had just completed the re-building and massive extension of Purdysburn House, and was beginning his withdrawal from public life; so he wrote to his colleagues *"begging to decline the honour of President of the Chamber"*. They acceded to his wishes; and within five days the thrusting John S Ferguson had begun his eleven-year stint as President, with William Tennent as Vice-President and Samuel Bruce as Secretary in replacement of James Goddard. Bruce was a total newcomer to the Chamber scene; and he seems to have been the nominee of the new President, for the minutes simply record his election as "an Honorary Member of the Chamber" followed immediately by the "announcement" that he would be acting as Secretary for the ensuing year.

As the new regime got down to work, there was change in the air. Within a few weeks, twenty-two new members had been signed on, including Hugh Montgomery jnr who was about to succeed his father in Montgomery's Bank, the forerunner of the Northern. There was renewed pressure too for changes in the postal services, the Chamber being grossly dissatisfied both with the location and performance of the Belfast office and with the reluctance of the postal authorities to pay for the wider use of steamboats in the carriage of the mails across the Irish Sea. The Chamber knew a lot about steamers because the pioneer of their use in passenger services to Liverpool, Greenock and Glasgow was long-serving Council member George Langtry; and they also knew a lot about the goings-on at the local post-office, for they had arranged covert surveillance of all outward and inward movements of mail and people for a period of three weeks.

Thomas Whinnery, the butt of the Chamber's criticism twenty years earlier, was still post-master; and the Council pursued a relentless campaign against his conduct of affairs, both by letter and by delegation to the authorities in Dublin and in London. The chief irritant was that Whinnery had moved the post-office on several occasions, *"the entire of all which removals took place without any previous intimation to the Merchants of the town and apparent regard of their accommodation"*. Before that man Whinnery came on the scene, wrote the Chamber, the post office had been sensibly located in High Street; but he had moved it first to Skipper's Lane, then to Donegall Street, now to Rosemary Street where he had recently made external alterations that appeared *"more calculated to expose to the inclemency of the weather that respectable part of the community who call for their letters than to afford any additional accommodation"*. Above all he had offended the Chamber by refusing to take up an office that they were prepared to organise for him in the Exchange, on the grounds that he wanted to live above his work (which was impossible in that location). Exactly what happened as a result of these altercations is not clear; but it can hardly be without significance that less than a year later, on 23 December 1822, Thomas Whinnery was one of four new members accepted into the Chamber by ballot! Yet the hatchet was not buried for all time, for within eighteen months the Chamber was liaising closely with a Mr Cupples who had been appointed *"to investigate the charges against the Post Master of this town prepared in a Memorial signed by the inhabitants, forwarded to the Lords of the Treasury"*. Poor Mr Whinnery was again to be the victim of the obsessive concern with the speed of the mails, even though letters to and from Great Britain were probably travelling faster than they did a hundred and fifty years later. And he had also to cope with the "dodgers" who would send several letters inside one another to evade the proper charges and yet objected strongly to his closing the bag half-an-hour earlier to allow suspect packages to be candled.

Meanwhile, however, the Chamber was not neglecting larger and more constructive issues. Chief amongst these was a prolonged debate on whether the Irish Chambers of Commerce should collectively establish a "commercial office" in London to monitor proceedings of Parliament and to act as a lobbying channel on business issues. In the past two years an exactly similar debate has taken place between today's business organisations about the desirability of establishing a Northern Ireland commercial office in Brussels; and history has again repeated itself in an uncanny way, save that in the 1980's it has taken marginally longer to reach less decisive conclusions! In the 1820's the issue first came before the Council of the Chamber on 14 November 1821 in the form of a letter from the Limerick Chamber putting forward an outline plan. Belfast immediately expressed interest in the idea but explained that they were short of funds. By January 1822, however, the Council was offering to support the Limerick initiative to the extent of £50 a year. A month later there was confirmation from Dublin that the Chamber there would also contribute £50; and the Committee of Merchants in Sligo made a similar commitment. Next the various groups had to clear their lines with the MPs for their respective areas, so that the project was seen to be complementary to Parliamentary activities rather than competitive; and in token of this the business organisations at first expressed a willingness to allow the MPs to select the person to man the office. But soon the Belfast Chamber was writing to the others (including Cork) to put forward their own ideas on the job specification and to nominate a Mr William McQuoid from Belfast for the post!

Whether because of the forwardness of the Belfast Chamber or for some other reason, the subject of the "Parliamentary Agent" (as the post began to be called) went rather cold for about five months. Then there was another spurt of activity at the end of May, with the Belfast subscribers offering £80 a year towards the overall cost and re-stating their support for McQuoid. And again the subject went cold, till early in January 1823 when Cork and Limerick Chambers intimated that they were appointing a Mr James Roche as their agent and would be willing to have Belfast as partners. Belfast responded by enquiring about the position in Dublin; and soon it emerged that the Chamber there was proposing to proceed independently. In the end Dublin and Belfast co-operated in the appointment of Mr McQuoid, the Belfast candidate; and by May of that year he was in post at No. 1 Derby Street near the Palace of Westminster, communicating with the machinery of Government there and reporting back frequently to a committee of the Council in Belfast, presumably with a similar arrangement for Dublin. Regrettably, however, this bold initiative seems to have perished in less than a year, probably because a proportion of the pledged subscribers defaulted on their payments; and by the summer of 1824 the name of the intrepid Mr McQuoid had disappeared without comment from the Chamber records.

Amongst the many other subjects that occupied the attention of the Chamber in the early 1820's, the one that stands out is the campaign for the construction of a commercial waterway from Lough Neagh to Lough Erne, the project that became known as the Ulster Canal. The Chamber had been interested in the concept from about 1815; but it was not until the early summer of 1822 that the Council began an intensive programme of meetings and memorials to whip up public interest in Belfast and Enniskillen, enlist the support of the nobility and Members of Parliament, and persuade the authorities in Dublin to come up with the plans and the funds. James McCleery, the Secretary of the Lagan Navigation Company, played a key part in the campaign for he brought a respected professionalism to the debate; and it is probably to him more than to anyone else that the credit should go for convincing the authorities to introduce the Ulster Canal Bill of 1825, which enabled the work to begin. In their enthusiasm for opening up the West the Belfast merchants pledged themselves to raise the interest payments on the £10,000 that a canal from the Blackwater to the Erne was expected to cost; and in March 1825 they suggested that this should be done by a special duty of a penny a ton on imports of coal. Despite the fact that this would have raised less than £500 a year the Council talked hopefully of a surplus that might be available to the Chamber; and there must have been some head-scratching either for our illustrious forebears in the Chamber or for the members of the Board of Public Works in Dublin when it turned out that the construction of the canal lasted for seventeen years and cost £250,000!

But if the construction of the Ulster Canal was the most ambitious of the improvements in communications sought by the Chamber in the early 1820's, it by no means monopolised their interests in this field. Year after year they pressed for the establishment of a coach service from Belfast to Enniskillen; and the offer of a low-interest loan of £1,000 to the first person to accept that challenge still stood. They pressed too for lighthouses on the Isle of Islay in the Inner Hebrides, on Barra in the Outer Hebrides, on the Maidens Rocks off the County Antrim coast, and at St John's Point in County Down; and they supported the calls from local residents for marker buoys on the rocks off Whitehead, a proper survey of the harbour at Cushendun, and the improvement of the harbour at Bangor. The port of Belfast also commanded their constant attention; and there was a moment of triumph when in March 1824 it was at last approved as a base for the East Indies trade. Across the Irish Sea, they supported the petition for a canal from the Severn Estuary to the English Channel; they called for an enquiry into port charges in Bristol; and they identified strongly with the plans of the Manchester and Liverpool Railroad Company to connect those two cities by the new method of locomotion despite intense opposition to the intended route. Hence when they heard a month or two later that a railroad company (the Leinster and Ulster) had just been formed on their own side of the Irish Sea, they immediately resolved that *"this Chamber do approve of the establishment of Railways in Ireland and...are ready to forward the undertakings...by every means in their power"*. And that prompt and progressive recognition of the potential of the railways was the beginning of a whole new facet of Chamber activity.

The mid-1820's were years of change too in various other facets of commercial life, but particularly in banking. Under an Act of 1824, the Northern Bank became the first

The town dock at the eastern end of High Street, about 1830. In the previous century the River Farset ran open for the full length of the street.

(From a painting by T M Baynes — Ulster Museum.)

joint-stock bank in Ireland; and in the following year the Bank of Ireland opened its first branch in Belfast, followed by branches in Newry and Londonderry. By that time the Provincial Bank had also spread to Belfast; and two years later, the Belfast Banking Company was formed by the amalgamation of the local companies, Gordon's and Tennent's. In the newspaper world, the News Letter still reigned supreme; but the Commercial Chronicle was still in existence, and F D Finlay's Northern Whig had been launched in 1824 as the new voice of Liberalism. In insurance, there should have been quite a competitive situation for there were no less than nine companies operating in the town in the early 1820s: the Albion, Atlas, Belfast, Commercial, Globe, London Union, Norwich Union, Royal Exchange, and Sun. Yet as the decade progressed there was some talk in the Chamber about the need for more insurance companies; though it may be that what they wanted was more locally-owned companies. And in the entertainment world the facilities now included James Ward's Commercial Hotel in Ann Street where the Chamber held its first annual dinner in December 1824, a diversion that was repeated on New Year's Eve 1825 and subsequently became a regular feature of each year's programme.

Maritime matters were to the fore again in 1827. In February a general meeting of the Chamber charged the Council to join with the Ballast Corporation in a study to investigate *"the cause for the delays, inconvenience and expense occasioned to the Trade of this Town by the present state of the Harbour and of Quay accommodation — and to recommend such improvements as they deem best calculated to remove the defects"*. But the Ballast Board spurned the proposed joint approach, saying that the matters mentioned were already well in hand; and the Chamber had to be content to turn its attention to the need for a pier at Cultra and a lighthouse on the Mull of Galloway!

At the end of the year the Chamber came close to a "palace revolution"; for in the annual meeting on 20 December 1827, William Tennent who had been Vice-President to John S Ferguson for six years secured more votes than Ferguson in the election for President. But Tennent averted a difficult situation by announcing that he did not wish to accept either the Presidency or the Vice-Presidency; and that left Ferguson to continue as President, with George Langtry coming in as Vice-President. Ferguson was therefore in the chair at the third annual dinner, on New Year's Eve 1827, when the meal was to be on the tables *"precisely at half-past-five o'clock"*.

The year 1828 began with something of a mystery. A Mr Reid was in touch to say that he had invented *"a machine for conveying the mail to Dublin with greater dispatch"*. That immediately appealed to the Chamber; and a committee was appointed to interview Mr Reid and report on his machine. This they no doubt did; but they failed to submit a written report — and history is left to wonder about Mr Reid and his machine.

As the year ended the Chamber opened its first bank account: it was with the Provincial, and the sum deposited was £70. That was a satisfactory surplus in a situation where the annual membership fee was still only half a guinea; and it would suggest that membership was at the least being well maintained. In the annual meeting just before Christmas William Boyd of the Belfast Foundry in Donegall Street became Vice-President in succession to George Langtry.

Despite the discouraging noises from the Ballast Board, the Council had been continuing to take a close interest in the improvement of the port. To this end James McCleery went to London on behalf of the Chamber to see a Mr Telford who was planning major changes in the harbour; and McCleery reported to the Council in August 1829. This led to a series of meetings large and small in October and November, with the Chamber leaving no doubt that they considered themselves to have a right and a responsibility to comment in detail on the proposed changes.

By December 1829 the Chamber had another Presidential crisis on its hands. John S Ferguson wrote to the Council on the twelfth of the month to say that he did not wish to act as President again; and this was reported to the annual general meeting some days later. But when the vote was taken, Ferguson again came top of the poll. The meeting therefore passed a warm resolution of thanks to their long-serving President and appointed a delegation to call upon him immediately, with a view to expressing the confidence of his colleagues in his leadership and persuading him to continue. The delegation returned just as the meeting was finishing; and there was relief all round when they reported that Mr Ferguson had responded well to the encouragement and would indeed continue.

The Belfast of 1830 in which John S Ferguson would resume the Presidency of the Chamber with renewed vigour had changed in many ways from the Belfast of 1820. For one thing the population had increased by about fifteen thousand and now stood around fifty thousand. In parallel with this there had been substantial property development, stimulated in part by Lord Donegall's decision in 1822 to begin granting long leases for ready money — money that he and his son Lord Belfast badly needed to service the family's huge debts and sustain their expensive life-style. The rapid growth in the population and area of the town together with increased industrial activity had placed a severe strain on the public water supply, which from 1817 had been the responsibility of the Spring Water Commissioners, a body in which several Chamber members played a prominent part; and sectors of industry had been subject to a form of water rationing from March 1829.

The cotton industry had reached its peak in 1825, when it employed up to four thousand people in some twenty mills in and around Belfast; but now it was in rapid decline as the result of the removal of protective duties in 1824 and overcapacity and general recession in the period from 1826 till 1829. A new factory that was about to open in Henry Street would be the watershed between one phase of the industrial revolution and the next: it was Thomas Mulholland's flax-spinning mill that would ultimately become the great York Street Flax Spinning Company. The Mulholland brothers had been in cotton spinning till their main mill was destroyed in a spectacular fire on a Sunday morning in June 1828; and instead of rebuilding for cotton, they decided to provide for wet-spinning of flax by a new process that had been developed in England — a process that they had been studying secretly for several years with the

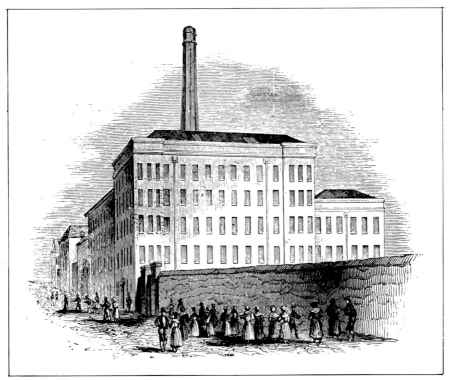

Mulholland's flax-spinning mill in Henry Street, opened 1830.   (From Hall's "Ireland" — Ulster Museum.)

aid of John Hind, an entrepreneurial Englishman who had already contributed much to the textile industry in Ulster. Hind's son, also John, would be President of the Chamber in 1861/62.

But working conditions both in the new mills and in the old were poor; and wages were low. Amongst the house weavers, deprivation was even more intense; and the News Letter in February 1830 was reporting that weavers in Ballymacarrett were reduced to subsisting on Indian meal that was unfit for cattle. Manual workers everywhere were discontent, though there was as yet relatively little tendency to take advantage of the repeal of the Combinations Act in 1824; and there were relatively few who could afford to take advantage either of the facility provided by the Belfast Savings Bank, which had started in 1816 with a deposit table in the House of Industry two evenings a week and graduated in 1829 to a solid building in King's Street, with the music room of the Anacreontic Society on the upper floor. Meanwhile a dreadful pestilence endemic to Asia — a virulent cholera — was creeping towards the eastern frontiers of Russia; and by the autumn of 1830 there were a few people in Belfast wondering how long it would be till it reached their town and what the effects would be.

Strangely enough it was the quarantine arrangements in the port of Belfast that occupied the attention of the Chamber as the new session began. The Government had proposed a revised system in which vessels could be released from quarantine more quickly on payment of an additional fee; and the Chamber not only submitted comments but also put forward the name of a young medical gentleman as a person fitted for the post of Superintendent of Quarantine at the port.

The other two issues of the early weeks of 1830 were old issues resurrected; for the Chamber decided, firstly, to join with other mercantile interests throughout the United Kingdom in again opposing the renewal of the East India Company's Charter and, secondly, to co-operate with the Dublin Chamber in a renewed campaign to rid the country of the iniquitous import duty on coals. Success on the first issue came slowly for the East India Company was to retain its monopoly position for several decades; but on the second issue only two years were to elapse before John S Ferguson was able to report with obvious delight at the annual general meeting of the Chamber on 8 February 1832 that:

"Your Council feel the greatest satisfaction in bringing before you the great benefit which has been conferred upon this part of the Kingdom during the last year by the repeal of the duty on coals". But he remained unable to report complete satisfaction on communications with Enniskillen, for the mail was still travelling by post-boy on horseback, even though there had been a light stagecoach on the road from August 1830! And the post-boy had just been intercepted and robbed!

The Chamber had a very early interest too in a more modern means of communication — the telegraphic cable. In the summer of 1830 the Council was in touch with an expert in Liverpool about the possibility of using the new system to transmit information on shipping movements from point to point along the coast. At first they talked of a cable from Bangor to Belfast; but later the discussions centred on an observation post at Grey Point on the southern shore of Belfast Lough, with a connection to the Commercial Newsroom in Waring Street. And meanwhile there had been an important change in connection with one of the older forms of communication; for the resilient Thomas Whinnery, post-master of Belfast from the mid-1790's and adversary of the Chamber in many a battle, had at last decided to retire. His successor was a Mr Dickey; and he was obviously a man of some shrewdness, for one of his first actions as post-master was to wait upon the Council of the Chamber to enlist their help in securing increased resources from the postal authorities in Dublin.

In the following year, the Chamber played a major part in securing the defeat in Parliament of proposals to increase duties on timber from Canada and to reduce duties on timber from the Baltic region. The Canadian timber was important to the North of Ireland and the contacts were well established. Belfast therefore took the lead in mustering Parliamentary opposition; and the President and Council were rather pleased by the outcome.

But another of the issues of that year was destined to remain unresolved for a very long time: that was the question of whether Donaghadee and Portpatrick could advantageously be replaced by more sheltered ports as the packet stations. Steamers had eventually been introduced for the mail runs; but they frequently had difficulty in clearing the harbours on either side because of strong winds. At first the call was for more powerful steamers; but gradually the emphasis changed to the need for examination of alternative terminals such as the Lough Ryan ports on the Scottish side, and Bangor, Larne, and Belfast on the Ulster side.

But by March 1832 issues such as the speed of the mails, the need to get rid of tea permits, the excessive costs of marine insurance, the limitations of the bankruptcy laws — these and many more — all paled into insignificance as the Council read and re-read a letter from the Board of Health which said simply:

"The Indian Cholera has manifested itself in this town".

So the rumour that had swept the town a few days previously was right; and the long-dreaded moment had come for Belfast, just as it had come five months earlier for Sunderland and ten months earlier for Dantzig and Riga.

The Council's immediate response to the news of the cholera outbreak was to call upon the editors of the newspaper not to sensationalize the story; and, above all, not to publish reports about new cases till they were properly authenticated by the Board of Health. These were sensible moves, as were the precautions taken and the preparations made by the Board of Health and by the Charitable Society in the six months preceding the outbreak. But the pestilence raged throughout the summer; and by the autumn there had been nearly three thousand cases, four hundred of them fatal — and the unmarked Cholera Ground in the new cemetry at the back of the Poorhouse in Clifton Street had received its first cartloads of corpses. Belfast had had a new and dreadful experience; and it would be repeated on many occasions over the next hundred years as cholera recurred, as typhus followed, and as tuberculosis and other diseases of the lung dwarfed them both.

While the cholera of 1832 raged in the town the Chamber continued to meet, but the cases pursued and the projects undertaken were mostly of a minor nature. And so when the pestilence disappeared towards the end of the year there was an obvious need for the Chamber to step-up its activities if it was to retain the interest and support of its members. Directly or indirectly that may have been the reason for the change of office-bearers that took place at the annual general meeting on 12 February 1833. But there is a possibility too that the changes were a reflection of the intense political controversy generated by the elections of December 1832 in the wake of the great and long-awaited Parliamentary Reform Bill which became law in June that year. Anyhow John S Ferguson's long Presidency came to an end; and he was succeeded by his Vice-President, William Boyd of the Belfast Foundry. The new Vice-President was Robert McDowell, who had several business interests in the town, was a member of the Spring Water Commissioners, and had served on the Council of the Chamber for almost twenty years. The Secretaryship too was the subject of change; for Samuel Bruce who had come with John S Ferguson departed with him as well. His replacement was Conway Blizzard Grimshaw, a member of the Whitehouse family that had made notable contributions to the cotton industry in earlier decades. And in the mood of the moment the Chamber decided to change its banker as well; for the

£63:6s:3d that Samuel Bruce handed over to his successor was deposited in the Northern rather than the Provincial.

Though it was a year of "all change" not only in the Chamber but also in the nation, 1833 was remarkably dull in terms of the issues considered. There were the beginnings of a great controversy about the method of measuring the tonnage of ships for purposes of registration; there was a Government inquiry into the state of agriculture, industry, commerce, and shipping; and there were three meetings about the problems of trade with China. But it all lacked sparkle; and the concluding sentence of the minutes of a Council meeting on 23 December 1833 was an apt summary of the year's work:

> "A good deal of conversation but the meeting departed without coming to any conclusions"

Against the background of 1833 it was no surprise that the annual meeting in February of the following year brought another change of President and Vice-President. William Boyd gave way for a year to Robert Callwell, a most accomplished and distinguished septuagenarian who had been secretary many years earlier; and Robert McDowell was succeeded as Vice-President by John Harrison, who thirteen years later became Mayor of the town. But again the year's work was rather mundane save for the opening up of communications with the London Shipowner's Society on legislation and custom governing relationships between maritime employers and their seamen. The Chamber did, however, also join effectively with the Ballast Board in convincing the Commissioners of Irish Lights that the proposed lighthouse on the County Down coast would be much better situated at St John's Point than off Ardglass as was intended.

And so this unspectacular phase in the Chamber's history moved on to the annual meeting in February 1835. Despite the paucity of interesting subjects in the Chamber programme at the time, there was a good attendance of forty-seven members, including a David Henderson and one of the Dunvilles, who had been distilling in Belfast from about 1808. The meeting brought back the old team of William Boyd as President and Bob McDowell as Vice-President, with C B Grimshaw continuing as Secretary; and that team would continue unchanged for eight years.

The first half of that eight-year spell was a further dull period, relieved only by a considerable fuss in November and December 1835 about the activities of a swindler in England who had managed to take advantage of a number of members of the Chamber. But in the broader community interesting things were happening. Following the example of the Mulhollands, the transition from cotton to flax-spinning was continuing; and there were now as many people employed in one as in the other. William Ewart, whose family had been engaged in aspects of the linen business from the latter part of the 18th Century and had apparently not become involved at all in the cotton phase (though there are contrary reports in previous publications), had built the great Crumlin Road Mill in partnership with his son. From that base would ultimately stem no less than six Presidents of the Chamber of Commerce, four of them

Ewarts and the others sons of Ewart mothers. The rumours about groups of entrepreneurs getting together to establish railway companies — rumours that had pervaded the Chamber for over ten years — were at last coming true; and by May 1836 there was Royal Assent for a Bill to establish the Ulster Railway Company, with a foundation board of directors that included six members of the Chamber headed by the former Secretary James Goddard. And in a year that saw the collapse of the Dublin-based Agricultural and Commercial Bank of Mooney and Chambers (with disastrous consequences for many Belfast people who had invested through the local branch), a new and enduring financial institution that would contribute greatly to industrial and commercial development in the future was formed in the town: it was the Ulster Bank.

Amongst those who began to feature in the Chamber around that time were Gustavus H Heyn, Hugh Montgomery jnr, and Andrew Mulholland. Of Dutch extraction but born in Dantzig, Gustavus Heyn settled in Belfast in 1825 at the age of twenty-three. Soon he had a number of business interests in shipping and insurance, which were the beginnings of the company known today as G Heyn & Sons Ltd. Marrying a Pirrie of Conlig, Heyn also became Consul for Prussia and various other European states; and that tradition was maintained by his younger son, Frederick L Heyn, who in a long and busy life of many parts found time to perform consular duties in Belfast for Spain, Turkey, and Greece. Gustavus Heyn served on the Council of the Chamber in the 1830s; and his younger son was one of its most active members fifty years later, becoming President in 1899. Late in life, Gustavus Heyn was appointed to the Order

Cartloads of unbleached linen being taken away to the bleach greens from the Brown Linen Hall in Donegall Street, about 1830.
(From a painting by T M Baynes — Ulster Museum.)

of Leopold; and his name thereafter appeared in various records as "Chevalier Heyn", which some times causes confusion. Hugh Montgomery jnr was the second son of previous President and foundation member, Hugh Montgomery snr, the initiator of the Northern Bank. Not surprisingly he followed his father into the bank and was a director from 1824 till his death in 1867. Some years before his appearance in the Chamber he had become the owner of Ballydrain, now the home of Malone Golf Club; and as he participated in the annual meeting of the Chamber in April 1837 there were two young lads running around the big house at Ballydrain who would both ride into battle with the Cavalry Brigade at Balaclava seventeen-and-a-half years later, one of them never to return. When he became a Council member of the Chamber in 1837, Andrew Mulholland was running the great flax-spinning mill in York Street with his younger brother Sinclair Kelburn, his elder brother Thomas jnr having died in 1830 at the age of forty-four. Later Andrew Mulholland would buy land in the Ards Peninsula and create the magnificent family seat at Ballywalter Park; and he would be remembered too for his service as Mayor of Belfast in 1845 and his provision sixteen years later of the great Mulholland organ in the Ulster Hall, beautifully restored in the period 1976-1982 by his distinguished great-great-grandson, the present Lord Dunleath. The family would also provide a President for the Chamber in 1948/49, in the person of Sir Harry Mulholland immediately following his fourteen years as speaker of the House of Commons at Stormont.

The way to that distant future from the reality of 1836 and the accession of the eighteen-year-old Queen Victoria to the British Throne in June of the following year would lead through a sequence of engineering marvels based on the steam engine, the generation of electricity, and the controlled combustion of paraffin hydrocarbons. For Belfast and its Chamber of Commerce, the first objective in that era of engineering change was the creation of a railway link with Dublin through Armagh; and the Ulster section of that link had been talked about for many years. However it was not until 12 August 1839 that the great and the good were able to assemble at the tiny station in Belfast to make a ceremonial journey by rail to Lisburn, just as their grandparents had done seventy-six years previously to mark the opening of the Lagan Navigation. In reflection of the very different journey times, there was less hospitality on board in 1839 than in 1763; but there was no shortage of drama, for the engine went off the rails a few hundred yards from the starting point! But the men of the day were equal to the moment; and the engine was soon back on the track to symbolise the beginning of another significant phase in Ulster's commercial history. And the face that lay behind that change was that of William Dargan, Carlow-born engineer supreme, who exhibited his genius not only in railroad construction throughout Ireland but also in the Ulster Canal and in Belfast Harbour's Victoria Channel, the long-delayed fulfilment of the Chamber's 1785 demand for a straight cut from the docks to the Pool of Garmoyle.

The Belfast from which that little railway engine left for Lisburn in August 1839 was still showing the effects of an incredible eruption of Nature eight months previously: it was "The Night of the Big Wind", Sunday 6 January. In that horrific gale, which began about about four o'clock on the Sunday afternoon and raged through most of the night, dozens of ships were dashed to pieces around the coasts and many seamen drowned; thousands of homes were destroyed and several families wiped out; hundreds of thousands of trees were uprooted and scarcely a chimney-stack left standing. One of the most spectacular events was the collapse of the towering chimney of Mulholland's mill in York Street; and one of the most tragic, the disordered plunge of a stagecoach from the Long Bridge into the Lagan taking with it to a watery grave its driver, footman, and two passengers who were female visitors from Scotland. In the long aftermath of that dreadful night, there was literal proof of the adage about ill-winds; for it was a boom time for firms such as J P Corry & Co who supplied timber and other building materials. And it was a fortunate time too for the Belfast Botanical and Horticultural Society, the creators ten years previously of the public amenity that later became known as Botanic Gardens; for if their great Palm House had been a reality rather than a subject of intense discussion in January 1839 it too would have become a victim of the "Big Wind".

At that time the paid-up membership of the Chamber had fallen to about fifty; but the organisation was nevertheless very active, particularly in its advocacy of further development of the railways. There was a feeling that the Government was intent on giving priority to extending the network in the South; and the Chamber had to press the Northern case strongly, drawing attention to the relative achievements and needs of Belfast and Dublin in terms of trade. These were the themes of a great public meeting mounted by the Chamber in the Commercial Buildings in March 1839, when John F Ferguson (son of Past-President John S and a future President himself), Sinclair K Mulholland, and Robert Grimshaw condemned the Government for *"the parsimonious and illiberal spirit they had manifested in their treatment of this part of the Kingdom"*; and a Dr Montgomery showed that the combined import and export trade of Belfast now exceeded that of Dublin by about sixteen per cent.

Soon, however, the attention of the Chamber was temporarily diverted from the new method of transportation to the old; for there was a major crisis in relationships with the Lagan Navigation Company, the successors of the consortium of merchants formed by the Chamber some thirty years previously to take over the waterway from Lord Donegall. On the strength of investigations carried out on its behalf over a number of years the Council of the Chamber felt that those who had taken over and operated the waterway nominally as a public-spirited gesture had in fact been doing rather well out of it financially. They had been empowered by Act of Parliament to collect duties on certain goods so as to provide additional funds for the maintenance and improvement of the navigation; and the allegation was that only a small proportion of the revenue had in fact been applied in that way. The Chamber's investigations culminated in the presentation of a sub-committee's report at a tense general meeting on 23 November 1839. The President, William Boyd, was in the chair when the report was presented by Robert Lepper, joint owner of a spinning mill on the Antrim Road; and the attendance included James McCleery, Registrar and Manager of the Lagan Navigation Company, who had survived an attempt to have him ejected from the meeting before the proceedings commenced.

The report alleged that the affairs of the company had been conducted in such a way as to deny the public *"the advantage which they had a right to expect from a canal contracted, in the first instance, with public funds, and for the maintenance and improvement of which very large sums of public money had from time to time been granted"*. James McCleery, the old friend and adviser of the Chamber in many a previous endeavour, strenuously denied the allegations: the report was based, he said, on a *"flagrant error"* which totally invalidated its conclusions. This brought forth penetrating speeches by Robert Grimshaw and by James Bristow, the long-serving director of the Northern Bank who would be President of the Chamber on three separate occasions in the course of the next twenty years. McCleery having again defended himself and his employers in quite a convincing way went on to attack the Chamber for the underhand manner in which its investigations had been conducted.

That was too much for veteran Council member George Ash: *"Mr McCleery has treated us with the reverse of courtesy,"* he exclaimed. And the meeting must have agreed; for when Mr McCleery finally departed, the report of the sub-committee was adopted unanimously and a memorial to the Treasury agreed. The preamble alleged that over a recent period of eleven years the company had spent only £8,325:18s:4d on the waterway out of total receipts of £69,615:19s:9d; and the memorial concluded with a strident call for the transfer of the assets to a public board that would command the confidence of the Government and of the business community. There was therefore considerable satisfaction when the President was able to report at the annual general meeting of the Chamber on 23 March 1841 that the Government had responded to their representations by introducing a bill to vest the management of the Lagan Navigation in the Board of Public Works. And so ended another of the major sagas in the history of the Chamber.

While the controversy about the Lagan Navigation was raging a foundry had been started in Albert Street by James Scrimgeour to make textile machinery; and many years later it would be taken over by its young Scottish manager and ultimately become the great Albert Foundry of James Mackie & Sons Ltd on the Springfield Road. James Mackie himself would advance through the ranks of the Chamber to the office of Senior Vice-President; but in the end would decline the Presidency because of business problems and the death of his nephew. That disappointment for the Chamber did not occur until 1919; but there were disappointments too in 1841. The Authorities still refused to abandon the Donaghadee-Portpatrick route for the movement of the mails to and from Scotland and the North of England; there was intransigence too on the need for change in the Bankruptcy Laws; and only forty-four members of the Chamber had paid their subscriptions on time, which equated to little more than the Secretary's honorarium of £20 a year.

As the Chamber entered the 1841/42 session, the big issue was the need for alteration in the Corn Laws. Following the Napoleonic Wars the importation of foreign corn had been regulated in the interests of domestic agriculture. At first, importation was prohibited until internal prices reached a certain trigger-point. Later a system of duties varying with average internal prices had been introduced. On the whole this was considered by many people to be too restrictive; and a movement for reform gathered momentum in England between 1838 and 1841. By May of the latter year the Chamber was taking the lead on the subject in the North of Ireland; and at a general meeting on the 8th of that month James Steen (who would become President nine years later) proposed a motion condemning the existing system and calling for a flat rate of duty at a lower level. George Ash spoke up for domestic agriculture; but a Mr Workman (probably from the family that later became involved in shipbuilding with the Clarkes) expressed the opinion that *"the agricultural interests can take care of themselves"*. And that must have been the majority view for the Chamber identified with the campaign for repeal, in the hope that that would lead to lower prices for corn and bread.

Three days after the Chamber debate on the Corn Laws the Union Workhouse on the Lisburn Road opened its doors, with spartan provision for a thousand inmates. That seemed adequate in 1841; but things would be different before the end of the decade as the town tried to cope with the dreadful consequences of potato crop failure. It would seem too that Belfast in 1841 still had a drink problem, for a directory of the period recorded seventy-three hotels and inns and over three hundred taverns for a population of just over seventy thousand!

When the Chamber met for its annual general meeting in March 1842 William Boyd, President since 1835, was ill. The meeting recorded its satisfaction at hearing of an improvement in his health and re-elected him to his old post. But he was dead in less than a year, leaving his faithful Vice-President Bob McDowell to succeed to the Presidency at the annual meeting on 21 March 1843. McDowell had already completed over thirty years of service to the Chamber in various capacities; and he would occupy its highest office for almost six years. Throughout that period his Vice-President would be James Bristow, director and later chairman of directors at the Northern Bank, who would himself achieve a unique distinction in the service of the Chamber. Coleraine-born Bristow was the son of Skeffington Gore Bristow of the 75th Regiment. He began his banking career with the Belfast Bank and joined the Northern in 1827. Married to Jane Smith, the sister of one of the John Galt Smiths, he was the father of seven children; and his many other distinctions included playing the double bass in the Anacreontic Society's orchestra. In later life he lived at Wilmont, now part of the Sir Thomas and Lady Dixon Park.

Despite the eminence and ability of its new leaders the Chamber had two more quiet years. The flax spinners were concerned about the possible consequences of a renegotiated commercial treaty with France; and the Chamber advised London of their fears. Tolls on the Lagan Navigation were increased with the acquiescence of the Chamber, save in respect of the rate for coal. The Council continued to take a keen interest in the butter business and in internal communications. There was a welcome for the introduction of a second coach service to Londonderry, but dissatisfaction that it was using exactly the same route as the first. The Council pressed for the second coach to be routed by Glenshane so as to provide postal services to Randalstown, Castledawson, Magherafelt, Maghera, and Dungiven. And the whole Chamber joined

The Waring Street end of Donegall Street mid-1820s, showing the old Exchange and Assembly Room (right of centre) and the new Commercial Buildings (straight ahead). The Chamber of Commerce used both building from time to time; and its offices were located in the Commercial Buildings in the second half of the 19th Century.

(From a painting by W H Maguire — Ulster Museum.)

with the bankers and retailers of the town in support of the efforts of the Ulster, Newry, and Enniskillen Railway Companies to get the go-ahead for a line from Belfast to Enniskillen via Portadown, Armagh, Monaghan, and Clones. James Bristow opened his campaign to have the post office in Belfast re-located; and the Chamber contributed towards a national testimonial to Rowland Hill, the originator in 1840 of the penny post. There was news from England that a railway from Chester to Holywood would cross the Straits of Menai by a new bridge which would be liable to impede navigation; but the Chamber decided to steer clear of the controversy. Instead they took a keen interest in the news from Scotland that the railway from Glasgow to Ayr would be extended to Cairnryan, opening up the possibility of using the Lough Ryan ports as an alternative to Portpatrick in the Irish packet services.

While these matters were developing in a predictable way, an unpredictable disaster was about to befall the people of Ireland — a disaster that directly and indirectly would reduce the eight-and-a-half-million population by nearly a quarter in the course of six years. Rural Ireland was dependent upon the potato; and when fungal blight first struck in September 1845 in areas of the South and West of the country, it spelt the beginning of a disaster of incredible magnitude. By February 1846 it was apparent that three-quarters of the potato crop in the entire island had been affected; and that famine and disease were already taking a dreadful toll in Munster and Connaught. To begin with, the North-Eastern counties were affected only marginally; and Belfast, not at all. But in the aftermath of a second and total crop failure in the summer and autumn of 1846, hundreds of starving people from the country areas began to drift into Belfast seeking shelter and food and carrying disease. By the spring of 1847, dysentry, typhus, and small-pox were raging in the town; every hospital and institution was crammed to the doors and temporary medical accommodation was being provided in tents and other makeshift buildings; the older cemeteries were full, with coffins scarcely being covered; cartloads of corpses were being taken daily to unmarked graves in the Cholera Ground off Clifton Street; and soup kitchens in York Street and Howard Street were feeding fifteen-thousand people a day, with the aid of funds subscribed by the town's business and professional communities. In the course of that one year over thirteen thousand fever victims were admitted to hospital in Belfast; and over a thousand of them finished up in the cemetery in Clifton Street, in addition to hundreds buried elsewhere. In the whole island, at least eight-hundred-thousand died from starvation and pestilence in the five years of famine (1845-49); and a further million-and-a-half left the country for good. In Belfast the typhus of 1847 was followed by the cholera of 1848 which spread along the Lagan Valley in the first weeks of 1849 and brought death to over three hundred people in Lisburn, Lurgan, and Dromore.

While these horrendous events were unfolding in the community the Chamber continued to function, but in a relatively low key; for many of its members were involved in charitable work and in attempting to maintain production despite the ravages of disease amongst their employees. The annual meeting in March 1846 welcomed the appointment of Mr Theodore Bozi as Spanish Consul; and within twelve months he was involved in the work of the Chamber. The site of the post office was an issue again; and opinion was moving towards locating it with the new custom house which was expected to be built in the course of the next few years.

But for the Chamber itself, change would be quicker and it would be more radical. As typhus raged in the town, Robert McDowell sent a letter to the annual meeting on 30 March 1847 indicating that he wished to resign from the Presidency. He may have been ill, or he may have been depressed or overworked, or he may just have wished to clear the way for change as a greater level of democracy came into society generally. But whatever his motivation, the reaction of the Chamber was to appoint a committee to review the rules and procedures of the organisation and to draw up a plan for its rejuvenation and expansion. McDowell himself later took part in this work, presiding at a general meeting on 13 November 1847 at which the reorganisation plan was adopted; and he agreed under pressue to continue as President till 1 January 1848 (subsequently extended). But after that it was all change in the Chamber. Like Ireland itself in the aftermath of famine, the Chamber would be different. The period that was pleasing but not dazzling was over; and a really dazzling period lay ahead. The pace of change was quickening.

Chapter 8

OUR GREAT AND RISING TOWN: 1848-1885

At the annual general meeting of the Chamber on 15 February 1875 Elias H Thompson, the outgoing President, maintained a recently-established custom of giving an hour-long address on the state of the industrial and commercial nation before taking his place on the back benches. In the course of that address, which highlighted the achievements and problems of a linen industry that then employed fifty-five-thousand people, he referred to Belfast as *"our great and rising town";* and that was the backcloth to the history of the Chamber, its faces and changes, over the thirty-seven years from its own reformation in 1848 till the year before the first of the great Home Rule controversies of the late 19th and early 20th Centuries.

Belfast during that period was moving into the front rank of British industrial towns. With machine-spinning of flax well established and the demise of the cotton industry complete, the move to factory-based weaving of linen at last gathered momentum. Truth to tell, the chief reason why that had not happened earlier was that the merchants had been so successful in beating down the wages paid to home weavers that power-loom weaving could not compete. As that situation changed, employment in the industry boomed, especially when the American Civil War of 1861-1865 disrupted cotton supplies and changed the whole balance in textiles internationally. By 1885, the linen industry in Ulster was employing sixty-two-thousand people, approximately two-thirds of the total number employed in all manufacturing industry in Northern Ireland today.

Shipbuilding too was thrusting forward, from the opening in 1853 of Robert Hickson's yard on the Queen's Island which subsequently became the world-renowned Harland & Wolff and had as one of its competitors a second Belfast yard of no mean standing, Workman, Clark, & Co Ltd. The land of Queen's Island itself was a symbol of change for it was in part created by the spoil from the excavation of the Victoria Channel and other improvements in the harbour, resulting in its first being called Dargan's Island after the great engineer who planned it. And traffic through that harbour built up at remarkable rate, from about four-thousand ships and half-a-million tons in 1848 to twice as many ships and three times as many tons thirty-seven years later.

In association with linen and shipbuilding, the engineering industry too was proliferating; and these were the years which saw the emergence of the great names in the business such as Mackie's, Musgrave's, Combe Barbour, and Davidson's Sirocco. Shipbuilding would be the progenitor too of the Belfast Ropeworks, which from small beginnings in 1873 would develop into a world-famous company employing three-and-a-half-thousand people on a forty-acre site. And one of the town's oldest industries, the manufacture of tobacco products, would become more important as demand increased and diversified, and as the long-established Murray & Co were rivalled by Thomas Gallaher following the transfer of his operations from Londonderry to Belfast in 1867. Enterprise was apparent too in the operation started in Bank Street in 1852 by Dr T J Cantrell, a Belfast chemist, and Dublin-born Henry Cochrane: they began the manufacture of aerated waters on a modest-scale, but from their endeavours sprang a whole industry exporting its products to the world.

Industrially and commercially Belfast was indeed a great and rising town in the period 1848-1885; and there was progress too in education, in architecture, and in the improvement of communications. In education, the establishment in 1849 of Queen's College Belfast as a constituent college of the Royal University of Ireland was a massive step forward; and nineteen years later the secondary level would be enhanced by the addition of Methodist College to the Academy (1785), the Academical Institution (1814), and St Malachy's College (1833). In architecture, the scene would be dominated for another fourteen years by the genius of Charles Lanyon, who before he turned to politics would give the town another five buildings of outstanding merit: Queen's College (1849), the Courthouse on the Crumlin Road (1850), the Head Office of the Trustee Savings Bank in Queen's Square (built for the Northern Bank, 1852), Assembly's College (1853), and the Custom House (1857). After that, the young genius of his arch rival, W J Barre from Newry, would add the Allied Irish Bank in Royal Avenue (built for the Provincial Bank, 1867) and the Albert Memorial (1869), the latter posthumously for Barre died in 1867 at the age of thirty-seven. And in communications there would be massive changes in the harbour, with the old docks at the end of High Street and Waring Street being filled in to become Albert Square and Queen's Square; the railways would be extended in many directions; and horse-drawn omnibuses and trams of the same ilk would make their appearance successively on the streets of the town.

All of that was progress; and the Victorian forebears of the businessmen of today were justly proud of it. *"The town of Belfast has made itself"*, said a well-briefed visiting speaker at a business occasion in 1879. But the dazzle of progress in industry, commerce, education, science, technology, architecture, and communications obscured massive social problems of low wages, long hours, unhealthy working conditions, poor housing, lack of sanitation, excessive drinking, low expectation of life, and the absence of even the most basic amenities for the great majority of the people. The industrial revolution had sucked thousands of men, women, and children into Belfast from the country areas; and the population had grown from about eighty-five-thousand in 1848 to almost two-hundred-and-thirty-thousand by 1885. Though some of the housing provided was good, most of it was poor and overcrowded; and disease was rampant. A stroll around any old graveyard in the Belfast area suggests that in the second and third quarters of the 19th Century it was more usual for a child to "die young" than to reach adult life. The reform of the Corporation in 1842 (from which time the first citizen was known as the Mayor rather than the Sovereign) had resulted in a greater general concern for the needs of the people even though the Liberals failed to secure a single seat; and the Corporation tackled many of the problems of the town with courage and vigour under the effective leadership of the unscrupulous John Bates as Town Clerk. But the basic conflict of interest between property-owning rate-payers and the great mass of the people inhibited progress. And underneath it all there were the seeds of a greater conflict; for toleration of religious and political differences had weakened in the wake of a sharp increase in the Catholic proportion of the town's population and as Protestants were induced by fiery prelates to fear the possible political consequences. So there were sectarian riots in 1857, 1864, and 1872.

That look into the future from the standpoint of 1847 is intended to provide a backcloth for the history of the Chamber over a period of thirty-seven years. Immediately it helps to explain why the Chamber in 1847 was concerning itself with drawing up rules, making the organisation more democratic, and attracting more members. For decades the Chamber had spoken for the whole of industry and commerce without having a remit from the whole of industry and commerce through a large and representative membership. A paid-up subscription-list of forty to fifty in the middle of the 19th Century was very much less representative than a membership of fifty-nine when the Chamber was formed in 1783. And the long Presidencies that had characterised the organisation from the beginning were out of accord with the new-found partial democracy of Parliament and the Corporation of the town.

The production of a plan for the reorganisation of the Chamber was entrusted to a committee chaired by Robert Henderson, who in the same year became a member of the new controlling body at the port, the Belfast Harbour Commissioners. This committee came up with a simple set of proposals embodied in six rules, the most important being that the way to the Presidency should be through a year as Junior Vice-President followed by a year as Senior Vice-President; and that the President should hold office for only one year. The plan also provided for the annual election of a Secretary and a Council of fifteen, as in the past; and for a membership fee of a pound a year, which was double the fee of the immediate past but a shilling less in money terms than the fee set by the founding fathers sixty-four years previously. And these proposals were unanimously accepted by a special general meeting on 13 November 1847.

To get the new system underway Robert McDowell who had been President from 1843 agreed to continue till 1 January 1848, which seems later to have been extended till 1 January 1849; James Bristow who had been Vice-President throughout McDowell's Presidency became Senior Vice-President, with James Steen as Junior Vice-President; and a new Council was elected. Later, on 23 December 1847, there was an election for the paid office of Secretary; and Samuel Vance was appointed almost unanimously, at a salary of £50 a year. He was then about thirty-nine years of age; and he was destined to serve as Secretary, subject to annual re-election, from then until his death fifty years later.

Robert Henderson, Chairman of the Committee which re-organised the Chamber in 1847. Henderson became President in 1864.

The first Josias Cunningham who was well-established as a stockbroker by 1847, having opened an office in Donegall Street on 1 November 1843.

(Coey Collection — Ulster Museum.)

In the arrangements relating to the Presidency the 1847 revision of the rules set a pattern that remains virtually unchanged to the present day. In other respects, however, the membership (which more than doubled after the 1847 reorganisation) perceived the need for early change; and a much more elaborate set of rules was adopted in July 1849. The most important changes were the inclusion of a system of balloting for membership (black and white beans and all that) and the stipulation of the method by which the rules could be further changed. But the balloting must have caused problems; for within three years the rules were changed yet again and membership became open to anyone who paid the stipulated subscription. At the same time the size of the Council was increased from fifteen to twenty; the period of service of an individual on Council was increased from one year to four; provision was made for the retiring President to serve a further three years on Council ex-officio; and the office of Honorary Treasurer was introduced, the post being immediately filled by Edward Coey who would hold it for twenty years — years in which his other distinctions would include the Mayoralty of the town (1861), a knighthood (same year), and the Presidency of the Chamber (1868).

The sharp increase in membership in 1848 was the result of a well-organised campaign. James Bristow as Senior Vice-President wrote a strong address to potential members. This was printed over the signature of C B Grimshaw and sent out to all merchants, industrialists, and bankers in the town that were not already in membership.

Arrangements were also made for existing members to call upon potential new members a few days after they had received the circular; and the reports from these visits indicated assent from just over a hundred people. These included two from Whitehouse (Bell), one from Carrickfergus (Stuart), and one from Crumlin (Macauley); and that provided the stimulus for the issue of another four hundred copies of the circular, all to the country districts. Though the results of that exercise are unknown, it was quite a significant move, indicating both the widening of the Chamber's interest and the improvement in transportation within the Province.

Another of the innovations of that period was a half-yearly general meeting to receive and discuss a report from the Council. At the first of these, held on 17 July 1848, there was a lively debate on a motion that the Belfast Harbour Commissioners should be asked to admit the press to their meetings so that the proceedings could be publicised. The motion was carried by eight votes to seven; and a letter was duly despatched to the Ballast Office. This brought forth a long and spirited reply which asserted that *"it would not be conducive to the interest of the Public to adopt a course similar to that suggested in the resolution of the Chamber"*. The Commissioners also pointed out that a summary of the proceedings of their forerunners, the Harbour Corporation, from 1785 till 1845 had been published; that it was now their custom to issue an annual report; and that their accounts were audited by persons publicly appointed by rate-payers. In the circumstances the Chamber had no alternative but to drop the issue; and the historian is left to ponder why it was raised in the first instance when the Chamber had no legal basis for action and when there was almost certainly a substantial overlap in membership between the two bodies. Most probably the flare-up was a reflection either of personality clashes or of the increasing political tension between Whigs and Tories; for Ulster in those days had both, and organisations were tending to become dominated either by one political faction or by the other.

If the members of the Chamber needed any reminder of these political differences it came from the surroundings in which they met; for after a short and unsatisfactory spell in the Commercial Buildings (to which they would return later) they had rented the old premises of the Reform Club which were also in Waring Street. Many of them must have been familiar with those premises for the liberal tradition in the business community was still quite strong; and businessmen had been to the fore when the Reform Society of Belfast was established about 1831 to support the Whig campaign for Parliamentary Reform. In its new accommodation the Chamber was able to exercise its long-intended role in commercial arbitrations; and ultimately to provide a commercial library and map-room, financed by special subscriptions from the banks and other business organisations and public-spirited individuals.

The delay in the establishment of the commercial library was something of an embarrassment to the office-bearers of the Chamber; but it was put into perspective by the saga of the fog-bell on the Copeland Islands in Belfast Lough. At the half-yearly meeting in July 1848 the President, Robert McDowell, announced that in response to their representations a fog-bell was about to be provided. At the annual meeting in January 1849 he said that *"for technical reasons connected with the difficulty of preparing the machinery, the fog-bell on the Copeland Lighthouse has not yet been effected".* And two years and two Presidencies later, John F Ferguson was able to announce on 15 July 1851 that *"the fog-bell on the Copeland Islands has at last been provided and is proving beneficial"!* And there it stood for many years as a warning to mariners and a memorial to the infinite patience of the Belfast Chamber of Commerce!

While the fog-bell was in gestation, James Bristow's first spell as President had come and gone. It was a year in which old issues like the inadequacy of the post office, the need for further extension of the railways, and the limitations of the Bankruptcy Laws were again to the fore. But there were new issues too. The Chamber was concerned about the effects of a Danish naval blockade on trade with parts of Europe; they began a campaign for the adoption of Greenwich Mean Time throughout Great Britain and Ireland in replacement of regional sun times which were becoming inappropriate as communications improved; unbelievably they identified with a plan for extending and improving navigation on the rivers of India; above all, they received the Queen Empress and her Consort with pomp and circumstance.

As soon as the Chamber and the Town Council became aware that Queen Victoria, Prince Albert, and the young Prince of Wales (the future King Edward VII) would probably be visiting Belfast in August 1849 at the conclusion of their visit to Ireland generally, there was a flurry to form committees and draft addresses of welcome. Primary responsibility for the arrangements lay with the Town Council; and the Mayor, William Gilliland Johnson, moved quickly to form a large town-committee, up to half of whom were Chamber members. But the Chamber itself also set up a committee — a ginger-group to see that things were done well — which met under James Bristow's chairmanship almost every day from the moment that the Mayor imparted the news (25 July) until the morning that the Royal Squadron actually sailed up Belfast Lough (Saturday 11 August). Incredible as it may seem today, the first clear indication of the expected date and time of arrival of the Royal party was received from the Lord Mayor of Dublin only on Wednesday 8 August, that is just three days in advance.

Some of the representations made by the Chamber committee to other bodies during the preparatory phase were glorious:
—to the Town Council, *"no processions with insignia, banners, or music"* (reflecting concern that the Orangemen might want to parade);
—to the traders of the town, *"all persons having bills falling due on the day of the Queen's visit should have them paid on the day before";*
—to the Harbour Commissioners, *"kindly see that the quays are cleaned up";*
—to the Town Council, *"kindly consider the propriety of making arrangements for the exhibition of suitable fireworks";*
—to the Mayor of Carrickfergus, *"kindly arrange a bonfire on a suitable hill at 8 pm on Saturday evening";* and
—to the Town Council, four days before the visitors were due, *"We wish to draw your attention to the necessity of having the streets through which Her Majesty will pass properly repaired!"*

But as they probed and prodded other organisations, they also devoted a lot of thought to their own part in the proceedings. This consisted of the preparation and presentation of elaborate addresses of welcome and loyalty to the Queen and the Prince Consort individually; and co-operation with the Flax Society in mounting and manning an elaborate display of the finest Irish linen in the centre block of the White Linen Hall. And on the day it all went well save for the misspelling of the traditional Irish greeting "céad míle fáilte" on a floral arch near the docks and the disappointment of eight members of the hard-working Chamber committee at their exclusion from the further assembly of the great and the good in the specially-erected welcoming pavilion at the harbour. The notorious Town Clerk John Bates, who could fix everything, had not in the end come up with enough tickets; and so on the eve of the visit, the Chamber worthies had to meet in solemn conclave in an office in Waring Street to draw the names of the lucky four from a hat! Perhaps Bates was just getting his own back for all that he had had to endure from the Chamber in the course of the fifteen hectic days that had gone before!

As the Royal party sailed out of Belfast that evening there were fireworks in the streets and bonfires on the hills and a great celebratory banquet in the Donegall Arms. For a while everything else was forgotten and the town was united. But the euphoria was short-lived, for there were underlying social and political tensions that would soon come to the surface again. Through the machinations of John Bates and the political ineptitude of the Liberals the Corporation was totally dominated by Conservatives. The Chamber, on the other hand, tended to be a haven for disillusioned Liberals: so the seeds of an uneasy relationship were in place. And the results were apparent in 1850 when the Corporation brought forward the latest in a succession of Town Improvement Bills, proposing further expenditure on the Blackstaff River and on the extension of Oxford and East Bridge Streets. With Robert Grimshaw and William Dunville in the lead, the Chamber mounted vigorous opposition; and the Corporation was forced to drop the Bill. Instead, however, they sought a massive extension of the town boundary, with the objective of regulating the suburbs and bringing in rates from a much larger area; and in this they were successful after an independent investigation had recommended in their favour.

Though the extension of the area under their jurisdiction from one-and-a-half to ten acres was a master-stroke on the part of the Corporation it proved to be their undoing, to the obvious delight of the more extreme Liberals in the Chamber. The introduction of the legislation on the revision of the boundary provided an opportunity for an unsettled solicitor John Rea to file a suit against the Corporation alleging a whole series of irregularities in the conduct of their affairs and pointing the finger particularly at the Town Clerk John Bates. After an eight-day hearing in June 1855 before the Lord Chancellor of Ireland, the court found the defendants guilty on all the main counts; and the town was in crisis, as the Town Clerk resigned to go to an early grave and several long-serving members of the Corporation were held personally responsible for £273,000 allegedly raised illegally or used inappropriately over the previous ten years.

Inevitably these events were discussed in the Council of the Chamber on a number of occasions in the summer and autumn of 1855; and they could have wrecked the organisation but for cool heads on both sides of the controversy and the experienced leadership of James Bristow of the Northern Bank, now in his second spell as President. Although the membership of the Chamber was weighted towards the Liberal viewpoint, the organisation also had its Conservatives; and one of them was not only Senior Vice-President of the Chamber but also Borough Treasurer of the Corporation, up to his neck in trouble in the light of the court's decision. That person was John Thomson jnr (1798-1874), son of John Thomson snr (1766-1824) of Lowwood, and grandson of Robert Thomson (1736-1800) of Jennymount, foundation member of the Chamber; and his dual role in 1855 obviously made the discussion of Corporation issues in the Chamber rather difficult. Thomson was a long-serving, hard-working, and well-paid director of the Belfast Banking Company; and one of the court's findings was that about £36,000 of the Corporation's unauthorised borrowings for infrastructure improvement had been made available through an overdraft account in Thomson's personal account in his own bank. With this unusual situation exposed, Thomson resigned from his position as Borough Treasurer but continued as Senior Vice-President of the Chamber, taking over as President from James Bristow on 15 January 1856.

Though the Chamber collectively had relatively little sympathy for the Corporation in its disarray, many members wanted to see the matter cleared up as soon as possible, because of the damage that was being done both to internal and to external confidence in the town. At an extraordinary general meeting in November 1855, attended by ninety-four members, the Chamber therefore accepted a

Sir Thomas McClure
President 1858

John Thomson
President 1856

Sir James Hamilton
President 1870

(Coey collection — Ulster Museum.)

recommendation from its special committee on the subject that a delegation should wait on the Attorney-General and ask him to go easy on the whole affair till a bill to absolve the nominated members of the Corporation from personal financial responsibility had been submitted to him. But when the matter was discussed again at the annual general meeting in January 1856, with John Thomson in the chair in the absence of James Bristow, there were some rather sharp exchanges on the propriety of the Chamber's having become involved at all. Meanwhile the Liberal element in the Chamber had been at work in other ways as well; for it can hardly have been a coincidence that John Thomson's two running mates in his year as President were both prominent Liberals, Robert Grimshaw and Thomas McClure. Nor was it in these circumstances surprising that the Council did not accede to a request from a Corporation delegation for three Chamber representatives to join a committee that was preparing a bill to effect *"an equitable settlement of the municipal difficulties and put a stop to the serious expense attending the present proceedings"*. But at the end of the day a way out of the morass had still to be found; and that was provided by a Royal Commission, which was very much less critical of the Corporation's conduct of affairs and narrowed the possible financial responsibility of the nominated members to the cost of the court action, thought to be of the order of £50,000. The final decision that the unfortunate members of the Corporation had to pay costs was taken by an arbitrator and embodied in the Belfast Awards Act of 1860.

For the Chamber as an organisation that was the end of this protracted affair. But for several of the Liberal activists in the organisation it was something quite different: it was the beginning of an opportunity to become meaningfully involved in local government. Thomas Sinclaire jnr, the nephew of Will Sinclaire of the 18th Century Chamber and proprietor of a provisions business in Tomb Street, secured a place on the Corporation immediately. So too did William Dunville, the distiller, and one of the Grimshaws of Whitehouse. There they joined their Chamber colleague Bernard Hughes, the baker, who had been returned with five other Liberals at a municipal election in 1855. And in 1861 the Liberals on the Corporation were sufficiently strong to capture the Mayoralty, Edward Coey the Honorary Treasurer of the Chamber from 1852 taking over from Conservative William Ewart, the flax-spinner, and being knighted in the course of the year. Thus a strong interaction between the Chamber and the Corporation in terms of shared personalities had begun; and this would henceforth be a notable feature of Chamber history, illustrated by the fact that ten Presidents between 1863 and 1983 also attained the office of Mayor or Lord Mayor before, during, or after their terms of office in the Chamber. The earliest was William Ewart, President in 1863/64 after being Mayor in 1859-60; and the latest Sir Myles Humphreys, President in 1982/83 after being Lord Mayor in 1975-77.

Though the Chamber spent a lot of time in the 1850s on municipal affairs, it would be quite wrong to leave the impression that the more usual interests of a mercantile body were neglected during that period. On the contrary, the Chamber tackled a bewildering array of topics at home and abroad. The achievement of a railway link between Belfast and Dublin was a major preoccupation, not fulfilled until 1853 with the completion of the great viaduct over the Boyne at Drogheda; and the Chamber

James Bristow (1796-1866)
President 1849, 1855, 1859

Sir William Ewart MP
President 1863

(Coey collection — Ulster Museum.)

had co-operated with the Belfast and Dublin Junction, the Ulster, the Ballymena, and the County Down Railway Companies in securing a Government loan to finance the project. They had co-operated too with the Corporation and the Harbour Commissioners in a great struggle to have the Custom House erected on the spot where it stands today as one of Belfast's finest buildings and arguably Charles Lanyon's peak of architectural achievement. That struggle began in 1847 and it ended ten years later with the opening of the new building housing all the departments of custom, but not the post office as had been vigorously advocated by the Chamber. However there was a Chamber triumph in connection with the location of the building, for the authorities originally had other plans; and it was with considerable satisfaction that John F Ferguson, son of former President John S Ferguson and now President himself, was able to announce at the annual general meeting on 15 January 1852 that the joint representations of the Chamber and the Harbour Commissioners not only on the need for the new facility, but also on its location had eventually been successful.

In the same year the British Association for the Advancement of Science, formed twenty-one years earlier, met in Belfast for the first time, with the full encouragement of the Chamber; and the Chamber also became enthusiastically involved in correspondence and discussions with other chambers about the framing of a "National Code of Commerce for the United Kingdom", a concept advanced by a Mr Leoni Levi, Professor of Commercial Law at King's College London. This would eventually be one of the stimuli for the formation in 1860 of a formal Association of Chambers of Commerce in the United Kingdom, the forerunner of today's Association of British Chambers of Commerce. And the Belfast Chamber had been enthusiastically involved too in another of the stimuli to greater recognition of the role of industry and commerce in national and international affairs — the "Great Exhibition of the Works of Industry of all Nations" held in London's Hyde Park in 1851 and visited by more than six million people. The planning of the Belfast involvement took place during the Presidency of James Steen; and the implementation during the Presidency of James F Ferguson, successor to his father in the linen industry as well as in the Chamber and prominent too in the Liberal movement.

The increasing importance of the linen industry was fully reflected not only in Chamber personalities but also in Chamber affairs. In January 1852, for example, John F Ferguson as President announced the formation of a Linen Trade Committee of the Chamber aimed primarily at the collection and assessment of commercial intelligence and the production of a weekly market report. Similarly in October 1853, during the Presidency of William Valentine, the Chamber organised a conference of linen interests to protest about the imposition of increased duties on linen by the Government of the United States; and the speakers included many of the great figures in the industry at that time — William Ewart, J J Richardson, John Hind, James Shaw, John Charters, Joshua Pim, and N G Andrews. And a year earlier the Chamber had had a long debate on the liberalising of trade with France, which was really aimed too at making things easier for the sale of Irish linen. That was perhaps not immediately apparent as the Chamber articulated the pure doctrine of Free Trade — *"trades artificially supported are invariably carried on with less economy and skill than when exposed to healthful competition"* — and called for a reduction in the UK import duty on French wines so that *"the mass of the people would be enabled to use the wholesome beverage in place of the stimulants to the use of which they are now restricted"!* But the "hard sell" came at the end with a call for a parallel reduction in French duties on imported linen!

Regrettably the real needs of "the mass of the people" were accorded a lower priority than the pursuit of industrial growth and concomitant wealth. The Chamber therefore opposed legislation seeking to improve working conditions at the expense of manufacturing and shipping costs; and no industrialist of today can be proud of some of the attitudes that were prevalent then. In 1850, for example, the Council in its half-yearly statement reported that: *"The Bill for preventing the working of Young Persons by relays in factories appearing to your Council to involve a principle of interference with adult labour, likely to be seriously prejudicial to the interests of Commerce, a memorial was presented against such interference".* Nor was it purely for reasons of supply that the Chamber took a keen interest in the possibilities of growing flax in India and in New Zealand over the period from 1857 till 1861.

By 1861, however, the members of the Chamber, having honoured James Bristow with a remarkable third term as President (1859), could reflect with some satisfaction on the part they had played in many developments in communications inside and outside the Province. They had vigorously supported the extension of the railways from Randalstown to Cookstown, from Ballymena to Portrush, from Castledawson to Coleraine; they had campaigned for at least one train a day to Dublin that would do the journey in four hours and for lines from Armagh to Cavan, Fintona, and Newry, from Downpatrick to Lisburn and Comber, from Banbridge to Lurgan; they had enthusiastically supported the steady improvement in cross-channel steamer services including the formation of the Belfast Steamship Company in 1853 and the abandonment at last of the unsatisfactory Donaghadee — Portpatrick route for the mails; and they had even memorialised the appropriate authorities in the aftermath of the Crimean War (1854-55) *"to remove the obstruction to the free navigation of the Danube which would afford great relief to Ireland by allowing the importation of large quantities of Indian Corn and Wheat, much wanted here in the present state of prices"!* Supply and demand were their constant concern; and their unstated and unchanging objective was to achieve excess supply in relation to demand save in the case of Belfast linen and Belfast ships!

No subject was too large and none too small — from the need for the construction of a canal across the Isthmus of Suez (which they were advocating in 1857 though the project was not completed till 1869) to the scandal of the mail from Ballymena to Londonderry still being carried by a "one-horse car" despite the availability of a rail link (which they exposed in 1856). The provision of a telegraphic cable across the Atlantic also fired their imagination, as did the possible establishment of a packet-station on the West Coast of Ireland for the American mails. And they had the self-confidence too to press a shipping company that ran services from Liverpool to Canada to arrange for its ships to call at Belfast or Donaghadee to pick up and unload passengers and mail, in much the same way as businessmen today press rather more mutely for cross-Atlantic air services to touch-down at Aldergrove.

This period also saw the beginnings of the Chamber interest in commercial education. Within a few years of the establishment of Queen's College Belfast in 1849, the Chamber had invited the Professor of Law and the Professor of Political Economy and Jurisprudence to become honorary members of the Chamber and of the Council. Though the motive may have been partly to obtain free legal advice on difficult issues, liaison between town and gown was also in mind. The way was therefore open for the College to bring forward its first scheme of commercial education; and that was done in January 1860 when the Chamber in the Presidency of John Herdman received a delegation from the College led by its President and Vice-President, Dr P S Henry and Professor Thomas Andrews. The College, which then had a student population of around three-hundred-and-fifty, proposed a kind of sandwich course as it would be called today, through which young men *"intended for general pursuits or for mercantile life"* could acquire a "College certificate of proficiency" by attending lectures and taking examinations over a period of two years in four subjects including obligatory science and engineering. Though the Chamber commended the proposals to its members and suggested that in-house apprenticeships should be shortened to enable young men to undertake the course, the scheme seems to have failed totally; for Moody and Beckett in their excellent history of Queen's record that there is no evidence that anyone was ever awarded a certificate! But there would be other more fruitful contacts between the Chamber and the College in future years.

In the 1850s the linen industry had been the great growth area in the economy of the Province; but as the scene shifted to the 1860s, shipbuilding too was taking off. From the pioneering days of William Ritchie in the last decade of the 18th Century, Belfast had had a shipbuilding industry. Through the middle of the 19th Century, the industry was continued on a modest scale by several small companies building wooden vessels. But it was only as the building of iron ships on the newly-created Queen's Island began in the 1850s that the potential for the 1860s and far beyond began to appear. As with all great ventures, success depended upon the foresight, the acumen, and the leadership of a few outstanding men: in this case, the engineering genius and the general charisma of Edward J Harland and the financial prowess and business contacts of Gustav W Wolff. Yorkshire-born Harland came to Belfast in 1854 at the age of twenty-three to manage Robert Hickson's yard on the Queen's Island. Four years later he bought the yard from Hickson, with the financial backing of the Liverpool uncle of his personal assistant, a young man by the name of Wolff. And that was the beginning of one of the most remarkable stories in the history of human endeavour.

Great as was the ability of Edward Harland to organise the building of ships, the key to the success of his remarkable venture lay in the market, just as the problems of Harland & Wolff in more recent times have stemmed from competition and changed market requirements. The breakthrough therefore came in the form of the first order from the Bibby Line, facilitated by the personal contacts of G W Wolff and his uncle in Liverpool. That was received towards the end of the 1850s and it was for three ships. And soon the yard was also building great clippers for the Star Line, the very significant shipping company developed in the second half of the 19th Century by J P Corry & Co, the old Belfast timber merchants. A succession of fine ships therefore sailed and steamed away from the Harland & Wolff yard in the course of the 1860s; and by the beginning of the next decade the stage was set for a development that ultimately would take the yard to the foremost position in world shipbuilding. That was the signing of the first contract with the White Star Line for the building of the OCEANIC, the forerunner of a whole fleet of modern liners and the stimulus for the rapid growth of the workforce to its first peak of around five thousand by the end of the 1870s.

The activities of the Chamber in the 1860s showed little reflection of this rapid growth in shipbuilding, though it was noticeable that Edward Harland began to attend Chamber meetings by the middle of the decade and was elected to the Council in 1870. Through most of the decade the more significant influence was the boom in the linen industry as a result of the interruption of cotton supplies by the American Civil War. This led the Chamber to take a close interest in sources of supply of flax and to encourage Ulster farmers to grow more, despite advice that had been given from elsewhere to the effect that the boom would be short-lived. At the annual general meeting of the Chamber in January 1864 the Council reported that the 1863 flax crop

John Hind
President 1861

Sir John Preston
President 1873

John Herdman
President 1860

in Ulster had reached an unprecedented level: over six-hundred-thousand tons from two-hundred-and-fourteen-thousand acres, giving a gross return to farmers of nearly four million pounds. But the linen industry wanted more, for the UK was still importing almost seventy per cent of its total flax requirements.

The buoyancy of confidence in the linen industry was apparent too in the ready involvement of the Chamber in two great events in France in the course of the 1860s. The first was at the beginning of the decade when a strong delegation led by Andrew Mulholland and including William Ewart and John Herdman went to Paris for discussions with the French Government about the easing of tariff barriers against Irish linen, the discussions being (in the words of their report) *"conducted in the French language"*. And the moguls of the linen industry had another opportunity to use their French or their interpreters seven years later when the Chamber mounted a major display of Irish linen in the great Paris Exhibition of 1867, plans having been discussed in the Council from time to time over the previous two years. Furthermore this particular event had a sequel which leads on to one of the unsolved mysteries in the history of the Chamber: that is the current whereabouts of a gold medal awarded to the Chamber for the design and workmanship of the "Irish Linen Trophy" displayed on the Chamber stand in Paris. At the subsequent annual meeting of the Chamber, the President John Lytle proposed and James P Corry seconded that the medal should become the badge of office of succeeding Presidents, a suitable chain for its display having been provided by the Chamber at a cost not exceeding £20; and that was agreed. But there the story ends — till the subject is further researched in more leisurely times!

In accord with its forward position in linen, shipbuilding, and engineering Belfast was in those days well to the fore in any general discussions about the interests of industry and commerce in the United Kingdom as a whole. This had been apparent during the exchanges in the previous decade about a "National Code of Commerce" and the harmonisation of commercial law between the different regions of the United Kingdom; and that led naturally to the involvement of the Belfast Chamber in the historic two-day conference in Radley's Hotel, New Bridge Street, Blackfriars, London on 1 and 2 February 1860 to mark the formal establishment of the Association of Chambers of Commerce in the United Kingdom. Belfast was represented by its Immediate Past-President, Thomas McClure; and because of the position of the town in the alphabetical sequence, his name and that of his Chamber stand proudly at the top of the list of members of the new body as recorded on the first page of its first minute book. Thereafter the Belfast Chamber played a full part in the work of the Association which provided a new dimension that was of the utmost importance, particularly in the years preceding the establishment of the Government of Northern Ireland in 1921.

But if the formation of the Association of Chambers was the main entry in the Chamber year-book for 1860, it was pushed into the background in the following year — a year in which the Chamber met specially to mark the death of Prince Albert — by a huge controversy that has a familiar ring to the Ulster businessman of 1983 if motor vehicles and public liability be substituted for fire. It was about a proposal of the insurance companies to increase the premiums for cover against fire by fifty per cent because of *"the frequency of fires in Belfast, the unsatisfactory state of the arrangements for extinguishing them, the want of harmony between the Water Commissioners, the Town Council, and the Fire Brigade, and the objectionable nature of the construction of new buildings"*. The Chamber immediately called a special meeting to discuss the situation; and the general thrust of the occasion was to mount pressure on the Water Commissioners to lay more pipes, the Fire Brigade to improve its equipment and training, and the Town Council to tighten and enforce its building standards. The meeting also passed a resolution that: *"The interests of the Insurance Companies and of the town would be much promoted if the rate of premium on each building was based more on the merit of the risk and less on the class as hitherto, so giving parties an additional inducement to build their premises in a substantial and safe manner and take every possible precaution against the occurrence and spread of fire therein"*. This fine statement having been duly recorded for transmission to the insurance companies, the meeting adjourned for eight days to await replies from the various authorities and to enable a specially-appointed committee to give further consideration to the situation.

When the meeting re-convened on 20 June 1861, the first item on the agenda was to read a long letter that the father-figure of the Chamber and three-times President, James Bristow, had written to the current President John Hind jnr, son of John Hind who had played a major role in the establishment of the cotton industry and in the conversion to power-spinning of flax. James Bristow was not at the meeting, nor had he been able to attend the previous meeting; but he had read the minutes of that

George Reilly, Chief of Belfast Fire Brigade in 1877, with the first of a group of steam fire-engines purchased by the Corportion at that time.
(Ulster Folk and Transport Museum.)

meeting and felt very disappointed by the attitudes expressed. *"There seems"*, he wrote, *"to be a great anxiety to cast blame everywhere but at home and to discover and regulate the duties of the several public bodies"*. And he went on: *"There appears to me to have been a sad overlooking of our duties and of the practical remedies for the existing state of things"*. In short, James Bristow had a lot of sympathy with the insurance companies and felt that property owners should engage in more self-help. The Town Clerk, James Guthrie, wrote in similar vein about the responsibility of owners in the building of property and in the maintenance of fire precautions; and he also defended the Fire Brigade strongly. The Water Commissioners, on the other hand, wrote to say that there could be a case for extending the pipework around the town; and that they had asked a distinguished civil engineer to look into the matter. Against that background, the final decision of the meeting was that a deputation should be sent to London to tell the insurance companies about the action that was being taken and to urge them to delay the implementation of their threat to increase the premiums so sharply. Whether the delegation was successful in that endeavour is not clear from the records of the Chamber.

It was about this time that the Chamber itself again changed home. After several years of searching, suitable accommodation became available in the Commercial Buildings as a result of a move by the Flax Society. Though the Chamber's earlier experience in the Commercial Buildings had been unsatisfactory, they had no hesitation in going back since the accommodation now available was much superior — so much so that there was a sharp rise in membership. At the same time the rules were amended to reduce the quorum at general meetings from twenty to fifteen so as to improve attendances! The rationale of that particular piece of Irish logic was that some members objected so strongly to having to wait for the arrival of a sufficient number to form a quorum that they stayed away! But there was one member that over the next forty years seldom stayed away from a Chamber occasion, whatever the group that was meeting, whatever the subject, and whatever the location: that member was Robert Lloyd Patterson, the most prodigious part-time contributor that the Chamber has produced in the two-hundred years of its history.

Second son of prosperous ironmonger and distinguished naturalist, Robert Patterson FRS, the younger Patterson first came to prominence at a general meeting of the Chamber on 15 July 1863 when he proposed resolutions welcoming the establishment of a Meteorological Department of the Board of Trade and calling for the Chamber to acquire from the Harbour Commissioners the publications issued regularly by the Patent Office. These resolutions reflected his inherited interest in matters scientific (which resulted in his acquiring later in life the unusual distinction of FLS, the Fellowship of the Linnaean Society); and they were the first of hundreds that he would bring forward over the next forty years at Council meetings, general meetings, and the annual meeting of the Association of Chambers of Commerce in the United Kingdom, where he became the constant ambassador of the Belfast Chamber. In a busy life in which he would form his own flax and yarn business, sail regularly both with the Royal Ulster at Bangor and the Royal North of Ireland at Cultra, and become an expert on the fauna of Belfast Lough, he would find time to be President of the Chamber twice, in 1880 and 1895; he would be the chief organiser of two highly-successful visits of the Association of Chambers to Belfast, in 1879 and 1899; he would be Honorary Secretary, Honorary Treasurer, and Honorary Auditor at different times between his retirement from business in 1886 and his death early in 1906; he would be appointed an Honorary Life Member in 1897; and he would be knighted in 1902, specifically for his services to the Chamber — a quite remarkable record that will never be approached let alone equalled.

As Sir Robert Lloyd Patterson in the last three years of his life reflected on his days in the Chamber he must have thought of many instances where incredible change had taken place over the years; and yet of others where the same subject recurred periodically in almost identical form. In 1863, the year in which he burst on to the Chamber scene, two subjects came up for the first time that have probably recurred at intervals of about ten years ever since and are still current in 1983. At the annual general meeting in January 1863 the Council reported on the difficulty of obtaining accurate statistics about exports, in the following terms:

"The exports from Belfast to Foreign Countries being chiefly made by way of Liverpool or London, do not appear in the Government Returns as Exports from Belfast, but from the Port in which they are shipped for their final destination. Your Council have made enquiries as to how far it might be practicable to remedy this evil, which places Belfast so far below the position it ought to hold among the Seaports of

the United Kingdom. Your Council regret to say that so great a change would be necessary in the Custom House arrangement of the Country to effect a more correct return in this respect that they see no prospect of succeeding in such an object". That was said in 1863, not 1983! And at a general meeting on 15 July 1863 with William Ewart in the Presidential chair, Robert Henderson proposed and Charles Duffin seconded that:

"It is the opinion of this Chamber that a junction of all the railways having termini in Belfast, a central railway station, and tramway from the junction to the quays and markets would greatly promote the welfare of the town of Belfast and the many important interests connected therewith". And in 1983 one link in the chain is still missing. PLUS CA CHANGE!

The suggested need in 1863 for a central station was but a tiny part of a much larger problem; for the railways had developed so rapidly over the twenty years from 1839 and there were so many companies involved that the need for rationalisation and reform was already beginning to be apparent. This would become a major issue in the Chamber in the next decade, but it was adumbrated in 1866. And as the Chamber began to wonder whether the country had too many railway companies, they also came to the conclusion that there were too few cross-channel steamer services; so they welcomed the suggestion that the Donaghadee-Portpatrick route could usefully be re-opened now that there was a suitable railway connection on the Scottish side. By this means it was hoped to have the London mail from the previous evening in Belfast by 10 am; and the Belfast mail in London by 9.45 am though not dispatched till 6 pm on the previous evening. William Ewart as President went to London to present a memorial on the subject; and he must have been successful in general terms — for in later years when he was a Member of Parliament and had to spend a lot of time in London, it was said that he was able to run the great business in Ulster from a suite on the top floor of Brown's Hotel in Mayfair only because of the incredible speed and reliability of the mails to and from Belfast!

And as the decade closed the Chamber itself underwent an important change in style and standing, becoming incorporated at minimum cost under a provision of the 1867 Companies Amendment Act. This clause enabled bodies such as the Chamber to be registered with the Board of Trade as limited companies without using the word "Limited" in their title. The certificate of incorporation was dated 24 August 1869, the Articles of Association having been agreed in July and confirmed in January of the following year. This was the fulfilment of a long-felt and oft-discussed desire to have the Chamber established in a more formal way than a mere gathering of individuals with common interests; and it was unfortunate that James Bristow, the Past-President with the unique distinction of three separate periods in office, did not live to see this formality completed. He died on 12 April 1866 at the age of seventy; and the members of the Chamber recorded their deep sorrow at the passing of their *"upright, intelligent, and highly-esteemed fellow-citizen, the purity of whose conduct in private life formed the best exemplification of the principles by which his public career was guided".*

Though the Chamber had progressed to incorporation, to a profound interest in the potentiality of the electric telegraph, to a renewed interest in technical education inspired by Dr Wyville Thomson of Queen's College, and so on, it was still capable of being incredibly staid and reactionary. An amusing example of this was its opposition in the 1860s to the introduction of envelopes, as an alternative to the traditional arrangement of applying seals to the folded letter. Because the new system would not provide proof of posting on the document itself, the Council strongly recommended that it should be given up *"as one likely to lead to great inconvenience and danger"!* But a much grimmer example of the reactionary spirit of the period was the instinctive and blinkered opposition to any attempts to improve the wages and working conditions of employees, particularly those in the linen industry. For an average weekly wage of about eleven shillings, men, women, and children had been working from five or six o'clock in the morning to seven or eight o'clock in the evening six days a week save for a few hours on Saturday afternoons. And each attempt that the Government made to ease the situation was vigorously opposed; though in February 1871 a committee of the Chamber considering the latest Factory and Workshops Act condescendingly concluded that *"legislation favourable to the protection of women and children from the opposition of cruel employers should in general be countenanced".*

By 1871 the normal working day had been shortened to about twelve hours; but there was consternation in the Chamber in the course of the next two years when a Mr Mundella introduced a Bill in the House of Commons at Westminster to reduce it to nine hours. The Chamber organised a public meeting on the subject which concluded that it would be *"inexpedient to enter upon any changes of the laws affecting the hours of labour in factories, without a previous inquiry as to the probable effect of such a measure on the industrial interest of the country".* The representations were continued during the Presidency of John Preston, himself a prominent figure in the linen industry; and at a meeting early in 1874, he reported that Belfast had been represented in a deputation from Chambers throughout the United Kingdom which had waited upon the Home Secretary to draw his attention to the dire consequences of accepting Mr Mundella's Bill. The deputation had been pleased to find that the Government was not favourably disposed towards the Bill, though accepting that some reduction in working hours was necessary. This came later in the year in the form of an Act which limited the working weekday to ten hours plus two breaks for meals and also stipulated that children under the age of ten could not be employed in factories. True to form, the Chamber memorialised the House of Commons against the Act on the grounds that it would be *"prejudicial to the best interests of the industry of this country".*

But as it fought a rearguard action on working hours, the Chamber had other subjects on the agenda. One of the most difficult was the rationalisation and rejuvenation of the whole Irish railway system, the need for which had been recognised from the mid-1860s. And by February 1871 the debate had been sharpened by the publication of a Government Bill providing for state purchase of the entire system at around £28 million and the vesting of future policies with twelve appointed trustees and three

A reminder of the frailties of the early railways: crash at Ballymacarrett Junction, 13 May 1871, in which two people were killed and fifty-five injured.

"commissioners of management". In a major report extending to four tightly-packed pages of small print, the Chamber put forward some very cogent arguments against aspects of the Bill while broadly supporting the concept of state purchase; and arranged for its views to be conveyed to the Lord Lieutenant in Dublin by a powerful delegation including the Mayor of Belfast and the two MPs for the town, William Johnston of Ballykilbeg and the Chamber's own Thomas McClure, President in 1858/59. This determined campaign undoubtedly had some influence on the final shape of the Government's proposals, though the Chamber remained unhappy about the method of financing and the system of control. *"The Trustees will be practically irresponsible"*, said the Council, *"and they will be entrusted with powers that cannot be safely lodged in any body of men inferior to Parliament itself"*. And the debate rumbled on into 1873, the Chamber at its annual general meeting on 15 February noting that *"this project still continues to occupy public attention everywhere in Ireland"*.

The President in the later stages of the railway saga was Alexander Johns, one of the most accomplished men ever to occupy the chair. Son of a bank manager in Carrickfergus, he had been educated at Trinity College Dublin and had served as a solicitor with the Belfast municipality in the days of the notorious Town Clerk, John Bates, whose daughter he had married. Having joined the Belfast Banking Company, he had become a director in 1860; and would ultimately succeed to the top management post. With the Chamber, he became President in 1872; and he was one of only four people who in the post-1849 history of the organisation would hold that office on more than one occasion (three others had spells of two successive years for special reasons). Alexander Johns' second term was in 1878/79; and he occupied many other posts in public life, not least a seat on the Grand Jury (or council) of his native Carrickfergus for all of thirty years. Furthermore it was of him that Sir James Hamilton (President himself in 1870/71 as James Hamilton) spoke in 1873 when he coined what could be said to be the specification for Presidents of the Chamber. *"He possesses the qualities which make a model President"*, said Sir James, *"— acuteness of mind, accuracy of knowledge, perspicuity of language, and facility of expression!"*

And Alexander Johns used that acuteness of mind and facility of expression to make a memorable and quotable speech at the end of his first term as President. He began by apologising for not launching into a review of the state of trade. *"I do not feel competent"*, he said, *"to deal with the usual subject in any interesting or serviceable way — indeed I have never met with any banker whose knowledge of trade was sufficiently accurate and precise to entitle him to inform mercantile men upon their own peculiar affairs".* Instead he would put forward some ideas for improving the conduct of the business of the Chamber; and he began by suggesting that the Chamber should *"endeavour to knit more closely our bonds of union with the numerous Chambers of Commerce in England".* Success in influencing the House of Commons would not be achieved by independent action for *"nobody who has not had frequent opportunity of hearing the frank expression of English opinion can be aware how humble a position everything Irish occupies in the minds of our neighbours across the Channel".* Matters Irish were received *"with a good-natured indulgence or with pleased surprise".* In Johns' opinion the Prime Minister, William Gladstone, had judged the mood of his English audience correctly when he had said some months previously *"that the principal manufacture in Ireland was the manufacture of false news".* Next Johns argued for the conduct of a greater proportion of the Chamber business by the preparation and consideration of papers rather than lengthy off-the-cuff speeches. *"The facility with which Irishmen, for the most part, can speak in public is a snare to them, and a hindrance to industry",* he said. And he added that a speech of ten minutes might not represent more than ten minutes of thought, whereas a paper of ten minutes would probably represent as many hours of reading and consideration. But memorable as were the phrases that Johns used and the arguments that he put forward, there is little evidence that the Chamber began immediately afterwards to use papers on a larger scale.

Alexander Johns
President 1872, 1878

Thomas Valentine
President 1875

(From portraits in the Northern Bank.)

Meanwhile, in 1870, the Belfast Evening Telegraph, which was destined to have such a vital and lasting role in the communication of news and views to all creeds and classes in Ulster, had begun publication, as Ireland's first half-penny newspaper; and two years later, the town's first horse-drawn trams began to ply between Castle Place and Botanic Gardens. But at the same time the germ of a nefarious idea was probably beginning to ply between Belfast and Cookstown — an idea for a gigantic fraud that would almost wreck the Belfast Banking Company, where the Chamber's articulate President Alex Johns was a senior official. As beautifully narrated by Noel Simpson in his history of the Belfast Bank, the fraud came to light on 4 December 1873. It involved the Chief Accountant of the Bank and a Branch Manager in Cookstown. Between them they had a system for drawing funds fraudulently from the reserves of the Bank to enable them to play the London stockmarket; and they had lost over £135,000 in the course of a few months, thus depleting about half the total reserves of the Bank. Alex Johns was given the task of confronting the manager in Cookstown, which must have stretched his renowned "facility of expression" to the limit; and the two conspirators were ultimately imprisoned for spells of fifteen and twenty-two months, after a sensational trial in Belfast in January 1874. And that was not the only sensation in Belfast that year, for there was a massive breakdown in industrial relations in which employees in some forty textile mills went on strike for seven weeks; and then in August, Belfast moved to the centre of a wider stage when Professor John Tyndall, at the second annual meeting of the British Association in the town, delivered his famous address on the interaction of science and religion and caused a vast furore.

Intense as was the discussion about Tyndall's address, it was nothing to the rumours and speculation that swept the town around this time about the financial stability of the linen industry. With the resumption of cotton manufacture in England, the Ulster textile industry had drifted into a difficult situation which in the opinion of the mill owners necessitated a reduction in wages. That in turn led to widespread strikes, which exacerbated the situation; and it was not long till several firms were seen to be in serious financial difficulty. Chief amongst these was the family business of William Spotten & Co, whose principal had been President of the Chamber a few years previously; and the outgoing President of 1874/75, Elias H Thompson, went to some trouble in his terminal address to attempt to restore confidence in the financial stability of the industry and to advise a more tolerant approach to labour problems in the future. *"I venture to express the hope"*, he said, *"that with the exercise of moderation on both sides for the future we shall not soon again have to resort to such suicidal, or to say the least of it, doubtful policy. It is much better to have compromise at the commencement than at the end of a struggle"*. That is as good advice in 1983 as it was in 1875. And the word used by a certain James Alexander Henderson JP in thanking the outgoing President for his address were words that his great-grandsons, Captain O W J Henderson and Dr R B Henderson CBE, would be just as liable to use in 1983: it was, said the Henderson forebear, *"a most exhaustive and admirable speech"*!

From the valedictory remarks of the next President, Thomas Valentine, it would seem that Elias Thompson's confidence in the future of the linen industry was soon justified. Speaking in February 1876, only a few months after the last of the bankruptcies, he said: *"I venture to say that the linen trade of Ulster never was in a sounder or more healthy state than it is at the present moment"*. However he was concerned about *"the physique of our working classes"* and the increase in the death rate amongst them. The Government was trying to do something about this by legislation but he ventured to suggest that *"until the working classes feel the necessity for spending more of their earnings in procuring good, nourishing food, a better class of houses to live in, more comfortable clothing (especially for the young), and spending less on spirituous liquors, that neither their physique nor their social conditions will be much improved"*. Obviously the thought of sharing a little more of the restored prosperity of the linen industry with the employees on whom it depended had not occurred to Mr Valentine; but he did introduce one novel note in the remainder of his speech. This was a reference to the exports of iron ore from County Antrim through Belfast which had become very important around that time, amounting to over fifty-five-thousand tons in 1875. That very substantial trade, together with the growth in imports of coal to around two-thousand tons a day, had made Belfast into a much busier port than ever before.

In the succeeding year the President was Thomas Sinclair, the first graduate of Queen's College Belfast to occupy the office. He was a grandson of Will Sinclaire, foundation member in 1783 and President in 1804-1806, and a nephew of the Thomas Sinclair who was President in 1862; and his main occupation in life was the conduct of the family's provisions business in Tomb Street. In later years he would become one of the best-known and most-influential figures in public life in Ulster; and he would be honoured with a second term as President of the Chamber twenty-six years after his first. In the family tradition he was a Liberal, till the Home Rule controversies began later in the century. Thereafter he became an outstanding leader of Liberal-Unionism. But in his first session in office in the Chamber he had a relatively quiet year.

James Musgrave, on the other hand, had quite a busy year, for as he came into office at the beginning of 1877 it emerged that the Chamber had a financial crisis, owing its Honorary Treasurer Elias Thompson a substantial sum. In the parsimonious tradition of Chamber subscriptions, these men of substance who were running great enterprises agreed, first, to subscribe an additional ten shillings each in 1878 to help clear the debt and, second, to increase the annual subscription from one pound to thirty shillings as from January 1879. And they also turned their attention to getting a little back from the income-tax authorities by joining with the Glasgow and Aberdeen Chambers in pressing for the introduction of what would now be described as depreciation allowances. Above all, they took the important decision to invite the Association of Chambers of Commerce in the United Kingdom to hold its annual meeting in Belfast in the autumn of 1879: and that would cost them a lot more than would have cleared their indebtedness to the Honorary Treasurer!

James Musgrave, the President in 1877/78, was one of five batchelor brothers who lived at Drumglass House on the Lisburn Road. Co-founder of the great engineering works that bore his name, he would become another of the outstanding figures in the public life of 19th Century Belfast. Chairman of the Harbour Commissioners for seventeen years from 1887, he would be honoured with a baronetcy in 1897 and become one of the most generous benefactors of Belfast and its University College. But as he concluded his year as President of the Chamber, on 15 February 1878, that generosity was apparent verbally in a speech that was most liberal and progressive for its time. His thoughts ranged widely, but the references to trade unionism (which was then growing in strength and influence) were particularly interesting:

"I think it is a misfortune that employers should look with so much suspicion upon trade unions; for insofar as they have been sanctioned by Parliament, they are, I believe, capable of promoting the good of the working man, without injury to any other class of the community. Good trade is like good weather: we do not know when it will come nor how long it will remain. It is neither produced by the efforts of those who employ, nor of those who are employed, and its benefits should be enjoyed by both. Yet it is possible to conceive a set of circumstances in which but for trade unions, trade might come and go, having added but little to the wages of the men, where it had unreasonably swelled the fortunes of the masters. So long, therefore, as trade unions are used to obtain a fair share of the benefits of good trade, for and to protect the interests of the men in a legitimate way, I think you will admit they have a public good; but the danger is — and we see this now in operation in England and Scotland — that when wages have once been raised, and demand has again fallen away, those who control the trade unions are unwilling to accept the inevitable reduction of wages, but by the expedient of strikes and other ways, endeavour to compel the employers either to submit to a reduction of their capital by working at a loss, or to close their works in the hope of saving the money they have realised". For such a fair-minded statement to be made in the atmosphere of 1878 was a remarkable thing and a partial counter to some of the more reactionary attitudes that had prevailed previously.

James Musgrave also had interesting views on technical education. *"Some persons go so far",* he said, *"as to recommend that pupils should have practical training in such things as weaving, carpentry, construction of engines, the forgeing of iron, and the use of the file. In this I cannot concur because much of the short time which the sons of working men can spare to education would be wasted in learning imperfectly what would come naturally and almost intuitively in any well-ordered factory or workshop. What the young men require are a thorough grounding in the elements and general principles at least of mechanics, physics, and, above all, practical geometry and chemistry, applied to the arts, because I have known workmen of great natural ability and with a desire for self-improvement, who by their ignorance of scientific symbols, which are easily learnt at school, have been shut out from all scientific knowledge and confined to what is vulgarly known as 'the rule of thumb' ".* These too were progressive thoughts; and they must have rung in the ears of Alexander Johns as he began his second period as President in the wake of James Musgrave's remarkable speech.

The 1878 annual meeting was notable not only for James Musgrave's valedictory speech, but also for its election results. As Alex Johns took over the leadership he was accompanied by John Young of Calgorm Castle Ballymena as Senior Vice-President, the first instance of a country member moving towards the Presidential chair. And his Junior Vice-President was the remarkable Robert Lloyd Patterson, now forty-one years of age and building upon the position of Honorary Auditor which he had held for a number of years. Furthermore the new members elected to Council included no less than three who would attain the Presidency later in their service: Edward Porter Cowan, Adam Duffin, and William Quartus Ewart, eldest son of William Ewart of the Crumlin Road Mill. And they assumed office at a time of mixed fortunes, for there had been problems in the linen industry and disasters in the grain trade, though the municipality was continuing to develop rapidly in terms of population, housing, and improved sanitation and amenities.

Despite the charisma of its leaders, the Chamber had a difficult year in 1878. Membership had been falling for some time and income was not meeting expenditure. The special subscription to clear the debt owed to the Honorary Treasurer, Elias Thompson, was not going all that well; and a few were grumbling about the increase in the basic subscription that was due to take place in January 1879. The long-standing campaign for the establishment of a local Bankruptcy Court to remove dependence on the Dublin courts was stepped up by sending a very powerful delegation to see the Chief Secretary and the Attorney General in Dublin; but there was not the slightest sign of progress, the feeling being that court officials in the Southern city were determined to keep things as they were in their own vested interest. There was disappointment too on the Factory and Workshops Act, where the Chamber had fought an unsuccessful campaign for the removal of a clause requiring employers to make St Patrick's Day a holiday in lieu of any two half-holidays. The Chamber argument was that *"The provision of keeping a festival of St Patrick as a legal holiday might lead to undesirable demonstrations by public meetings and processions";* but the Home Secretary was unimpressed and the Chamber had to settle for issuing an appeal to employers to make *"every exertion possible . . . to prevent the occurrence of the apprehended dangers, more especially in the earlier years of the operation of this Act".*

Nevertheless Alex Johns in his "end of term" address in February 1879 dared to take as his subject *"co-operative participation by workers in the business".* In another remarkable speech that in many ways was more than a hundred years in advance of its time he spoke of the attractions for both sides of industry of a system in which employees truly participated in the business. Employees could be encouraged and rewarded by the issue of special shares; and yet by their involvement they would have a greater appreciation of the problems of the employer and hopefully would keep their wages claims in accord with the ability of the business to pay! He envisaged, however, that trade unions would not be keen on the idea because in his opinion they thrived on the continuation of conflict between capital and labour. And he finished with a flourish of confidence in the future of the linen industry, especially if a reconciliation between capital and labour could be effected in some such way as he suggested. But his audience must have been stunned into silence, for not a word of comment on his address was recorded; and the captains of the linen industry hurried off to their offices to see if they could really afford to go on paying the current average wage of ten shillings a week, the figure that Johns himself had mentioned in the course of his address.

As the new President from Ballymena, John Young, took up office his vision lifted from the problems of the linen industry to the great event that was to take place in Belfast that autumn — the first visit to the town of the Association of Chambers of Commerce in the United Kingdom. He himself issued the formal invitation at a meeting of the Association in London in March; and detailed planning was soon in progress under the sharpshooter's eye of Robert Lloyd Patterson, who was appointed Honorary Secretary of the organising committee. A subscription list was opened; and forty-two people guaranteed £10 each towards the expenses. Amongst them was James Craig of Dunville's Distillery, father of another James who would have a momentous role in the land of his birth in the first half of the next century. Not a detail was missed, as Patterson led them meticulously through a series of meetings in August, continuing almost to the eve of the great event.

The visit began on the morning of Tuesday 26 August with a reception by the Mayor and the President of the Belfast Chamber in the magnificent offices of the Harbour Commissioners in Corporation Square. Almost one-hundred-and-thirty delegates from forty-seven Chambers throughout the United Kingdom were present; and only five Chambers in membership of the Association were not represented. Afterwards the delegates got down to work on an agenda that included the Partnership Bill, Bankruptcy Law, Bills of Sale, Depreciation of Silver, and Uniformity in Wire and Metal Gauges; and they must have been ready for the light lunch served in the Harbour Office at a cost of a shilling a head to the Chamber, *"including tea, coffee, and meats but not wine or beer"*! In the afternoon they ploughed on through the Australian Mails, the Merchant Shipping Act, and Customs Overtime. And they all survived to join with a great concourse of local notabilities in a splendid dinner given by the Mayor in the Townhall at six o'clock. (The brick building facing Victoria Square and known in this century as the Old Townhall was then in use for municipal purposes.) After six substantial courses provided by Charles Thompson of Donegall Place to the accompaniment of fine wines from William Guthrie of Howard Street, the diners were sufficiently relaxed to endure no less than twelve toasts and sixteen speeches which ranged from the Zulu War to hours of work in the linen industry, a sore point with the local barons who felt that Government interference on this was in danger of making them uncompetitive with Continental manufacturers. In terms that have a parallel today, the future King Edward was described by one speaker as *"the most popular prince in Europe"*; and his Alexandra, Princess of Wales, as *"charming . . . admired for her loveliness and grace . . . universally beloved for her rare goodness and worth"*. And the leader of the visiting delegates, John Whitwell MP, Vice-President of the Association, was equally apposite when he acknowledged that Belfast had no centuries-old industrial tradition but had grown *"by its muscle, its sinew, and its brains"*.

Next day it was back to the Harbour Office for a heavy agenda of Trade with Spain, Parliamentary Inquiries, and the Suez Canal, leavened only by another light lunch for a shilling a head; and then it was on to another dinner table, of eight courses, ten toasts, and fifteen speeches. This time the hosts were the Belfast Chamber; and the venue was the Music Hall in May Street, later known as the Victoria Memorial Hall and demolished only very recently. For a cost to the Chamber of not more than four-and-sixpence a head (excluding wines and spirits which were provided separately) the delegates enjoyed Clear Turtle Soup; followed by Turbot and Lobster Sauce or Fillets of Sole; followed by Vol-au-vent à la Financiere or Mutton Cutlets à la Jardiniere; followed by Roast Sirloin of Beef, or Roast Haunch of Venison, or Corned Rump of Beef, or Boiled Turkey and Ham; followed by Grouse or Lobster Salad; followed by Apple or Plum Tart, or Wine Jelly, or Trifle, or Cheesecakes; followed by Strawberry Cream Ice or Lemon Water Ice; and concluded by "Dessert"! Thus fortified they then listened to much the same speeches as on the previous evening, but with the President of the Chamber, John Young, rather than the Mayor in the chair. Robert Lloyd Patterson, the chief architect of the whole occasion, proposed the toast to the guests; William Ewart, now an MP but not yet a baronet, replied to the toast to the Houses of Parliament (J P Corry also now an MP and also not yet a baronet having performed that duty on the previous evening); and Edward Harland, who had responded to the toast of the Harbour Commissioners the previous evening, this time responded to "The Town and Trade of Belfast". And he did so in a memorable way, concluding: *"It is a new town without a history, but we are writing history; and in time I have no doubt we will possess a reputation for commerce and industry that will assign us an important place in the history of the United Kingdom".*

Thursday 28 August was the day for relaxation from the cares of office, long agendas, pressing business; and the delegates and the few ladies who had come with them from Great Britain to remain quietly in the background till this moment, together with the local worthies and their ladies, made an early start for Portrush by the Northern Counties train. After *"a slight luncheon"* in the Antrim Arms Hotel they were on their way by noon for *"the far-famed Causeway"* in long, open, horse-drawn cars. The sun had been shining brilliantly as they left Portrush; but before they were half-way to the Causeway the heavens opened with a fierce storm and heavy rain. Umbrellas were blown inside out; and became so useless that, in the incredible words of a reporter from one of the Belfast papers, *"in some instances their owners, rather than carry them, gave evidence of their generosity by presenting them to the ragged urchins who thronged the road in the neighbourhood of the Causeway".* Yet they pushed on to the Causeway, in a remarkable feat of endurance; and never was hospitality more enjoyed than the hot whiskies and substantial meal that were awaiting the bedraggled party when they finally arrived back in the Antrim Arms Hotel in Portrush at four o'clock. After a convivial occasion which included a toast to the ladies, they steamed back to Belfast, dropping John Young in Ballymena where he left his carriage *"to enthusiastic cheers from the great body of excursionists".* Though it was half-past-nine in the evening before the train reached Belfast, a few intrepid travellers decided to finish the day by accepting the invitation of the Countess of Dufferin to go down to Clandeboye to witness the shooting of the Ulster Rifle Association. Robert Lloyd Patterson probably had a hand in that, for rifle shooting was another of his many interests.

Next day there were optional visits to the Harland & Wolff shipyard, to the Dunville distillery, and to some of the great linen houses; and then it was all over, but only for twenty years — for Belfast would again host the Association in 1899, with Lloyd Patterson still the guiding star. But the 1879 occasion had cost a lot less than expected, for the Chamber was able to return £5:9s:0d out of every £10 that the sponsors had provided. The hire of the special train to Portrush cost £50; a Mr Fisher had £3:13s:0d for the hire of the Music Hall; and the enormous correspondence undertaken by Lloyd Patterson cost only £4:1s:7d in postage. And soon the glitter of the occasion would be forgotten as the businessmen of Belfast gazed on the demolition of Hercules Street to make way for Royal Avenue; lamented the loss of the Belfast-built, fully-rigged, iron ship E J HARLAND in a mid-Atlantic collision; and wondered whether they should try the strange new communication system being offered locally by Scottish Telephone Exchange Ltd for £20 a year including all calls.

Unlike the financial side of the visit of the Association of Chambers, the funds of the Belfast Chamber itself were in a sorry state. The Honorary Treasurer, E H Thompson, had quietly put up with a highly unsatisfactory situation, in which he had had to fund much of the Chamber activity from his personal account; and when he died in the course of the 1879/80 session, it emerged that the Chamber owed his estate £118 and had other debts of £97. Furthermore the increase of the membership subscription to thirty shillings a year at the beginning of 1879 had had a negative effect, because a number of members had resigned in protest. Unbelievably, the annual meeting in February 1880 therefore saddled the new Honorary Treasurer, Sir John Preston, with a reduction in the membership subscription (to a pound a year) in the hope of attracting new members. In mitigation, however, it has also to be noted that a group of Chamber stalwarts had contributed behind the scenes to a special fund to liquidate the debt; and as he handed over the reigns of leadership to R L Patterson, John Young was therefore quite cheerful both about the Chamber and about the state of trade and the prospects for improvement.

Lloyd Patterson's first term as President (he would occupy the office again in 1895/96) did not see the recovery in the linen industry that John Young had forecast. But it did see a remarkable change in the membership of the Chamber, with the attraction of sixty-five new subscribers. It is hard to believe that this was solely the reflection of a membership fee that was less in money terms and very much less in real terms than when the Chamber was formed nearly a hundred years earlier. More likely it was the keen subscription combined with Patterson's well-organised canvas that produced the results. But Patterson in his valedictory address repeated for industry generally the marketing theory that he had applied to Chamber membership when he said: *"I hold producing cheaply to be the true road to permanent improvement to retain old customers and to open new markets"*. Some of his listeners, however, must have felt that it was easier to pursue that doctrine as a middle-man than as a primary producer; and this great and gentle man was being less than consistent and fair when he concluded by castigating pig producers in Ulster for not fattening more pigs on imported cereals when the local market for hams, bacon, and lard was already undermined by cheap American imports running at over eleven thousand tons per annum, a worrying development of the previous ten years.

As the Chamber moved into a new decade, Patterson was succeeded as President by Robert Henry Sturrock Reade, another of that select band who would be elected for two separate spells of office (his second was twenty-five years later, in 1906). In the 1880s he was one of the key figures in the linen industry. Prominent in the trade associations, he ultimately became Chairman of Mulholland's York Street Flax Spinning Company; and in the latter years of his life he resided at Wilmont, as other great figures in the Chamber over the years had done. But he was a rather severe and distant man, invariably known even to his closest friends and the members of his own family as "Mr Reade". During his first spell of office in the Chamber, the chief topics of discussion were the need for a new central post-office (ultimately provided in Royal Avenue five years later); the new Harbour Bill proposing changes in the system of charges and concomitant improvements, in the interests of increased trade; and the desirability of having a stock exchange in Belfast even if only to monitor and seek to prevent the practice of *"employees speculating in stocks without the consent of their employers"*, as the News Letter put it.

History was made again in 1882 when James Porter Corry, the head of the great Belfast timber and shipping firm, became the first person to be President of the Chamber and a Member of Parliament simultaneously. That combination would recur eight times in the second hundred years of the Chamber's history; but J P Corry's "first" was nevertheless significant. His year in the top office was marked by a resurgence of interest in the inland waterways, with the Chamber calling for the Ulster Canal to be put in order and used in competition with the railways. There was also a new recognition of the importance to Belfast of international trade, with the Chamber following the lead of its President in seeking protection where domestic industries were being unfairly undermined. And there was a "facelift" too for the premises occupied by the Chamber in the Commercial Buildings, including the provision of double glazing to minimise street noise. But the renovation stretched the delicate finances; and the Honorary Treasurer, Sir John Preston, reported at the annual meeting in February 1883 that *"the balance being to the credit of the Chamber amounted to £5:7s:1d, and he hoped it would never be less"*; and that, according to the News Letter, was greeted with laughter.

In the succeeding three years the finances of the Chamber became even more laughable. Sir John Preston's flippant hope that the balance would never fall lower

Sir James P Corry MP
President 1882

(Coey collection — Ulster Museum.)

Sir James Musgrave
President 1877

(R M Young collection — Linenhall Library.)

191

than in 1882/83 was not fulfilled; for they were in the red by £6:0s:2d in 1883/84, £2:6s:8d in 1884/85, and £10:4s:6d in 1885/86. And it verged on the farcical for those "captains of commerce" each handling thousands of pounds daily in his own business to talk gravely each February about such trivial balances and deficits in the Chamber account; have the financial plight of the organisation fully revealed in every newspaper on the following day; and do nothing about it till it all came up again twelve months hence. But it was not only the financial problem that dragged on from year to year; for this was a period when policy issues also moved at a snail's pace whatever the Chamber tried to do. The Presidents who had to endure this frustrating experience were John Jaffé of the old German-Jewish family who are still in business as furriers in Belfast today; Sir Edward Cowan who had been Mayor in the years immediately preceding his election to the Chamber hierarchy; and Robert Megaw who had had a financial interest in shipbuilding on the Queen's Island in the days before Harland and Wolff arrived on the scene. All three had to contend with the intransigence of the Government in London and the legal system in Dublin on the question of common Bankruptcy Laws for the whole of the United Kingdom, with a Bankruptcy Court in Belfast; and all three were variously involved on details of the new General Post Office that was being erected in Royal Avenue. It was John Jaffé, for example, who led the fight to have letters accepted in Royal Avenue rather than only in Garfield Street as was originally intended. And it was also John Jaffé whose farewell occasion was marked by sharp debates first on the merits of Larne-Stranraer as a packet and passenger route; and then on "free trade versus protectionism", with Edward Harland making major contributions on both issues.

Harland on that occasion expressed himself in favour of a measure of protectionism in the interests of "fair trade"; for his great yard was obviously feeling the effects of recession at the time, exacerbated by instances of hidden subsidies and protectionism in various countries around the world. And he spoke from a background in which he and his colleagues had been facing industrial action as they sought to reduce wages to help them enliven the market and cope with competition. The yard continued to have its troubles in the two succeeding years; and the workforce was reduced from five-thousand to three-thousand-five-hundred. Linen too was having quite a difficult time; so the end-of-term addresses of Sir Edward Cowan and Robert Megaw in February 1885 and 1886 were very much less flamboyant than those of their counterparts in the early and middle years of the "great and rising town" era.

And yet as this wonderful era in the history of Belfast and of the Chamber came to an end rather flatly, it was not all gloom and doom. The town had been stirred by the visit of the Prince and Princess of Wales in April 1885 when Robert Megaw had presented an address of welcome on behalf of the Chamber, and the Linenhall Library had contributed £10 towards the illumination of the White Linen Hall; the main shipyard was poised on the brink of the greatest period in its history; the huge five-hundred-pound weight from the clock in the tower of the White Linen Hall had smashed its way through the floors of the building in the dead of night, so injuring no-one; and the prices in the downstairs bar of the Alhambra Theatre were two-pence a "half-un" for whiskey and gin and three-pence for brandy!

Chapter 9

APPROACH TO POLITICAL CHANGE 1886 — 1920

The thirty-four years from the publication of the first Home Rule Bill early in 1886 till the final ratification of the Government of Ireland Act a few days before Christmas in 1920 arguably comprise the most interesting period in the history of Ulster. In the early part of the period the emphasis was on the phenomenal growth of the shipbuilding, engineering, ropemaking, and tobacco industries of Belfast, paralleled by a huge expansion in the housing stock and general infrastructure of the town and by the appearance of the motor car. Later the emphasis moved to politics, as a majority in the Southern part of Ireland raised the old cry of legislative independence, and a majority in the North prepared to resist it by force of arms if need be. And in the middle of it all came the trauma of a World War of horrifying dimensions, which left an everlasting scar on the people of Ulster.

As a non-political body, the Chamber might have been expected to steer clear of the intense political controversies of the age; but it is a fact of history that the Chamber construed such a detachment to be unwise even if it were possible. In its view Ireland was economically incapable of independence; and its members feared for the future of their industry and commerce in a detached state governed by a Parliament in which the agricultural vote of the South and West would predominate. In accordance with the wishes of all but two or three of its members, the Chamber therefore became involved in 1886, 1893, 1912, and 1917 in arguing against Home Rule for Ireland, on commercial and economic grounds. And when the decision was ultimately taken to partition the country, creating a Parliament in Dublin and another in Belfast, the Chamber played a major part in shaping the new Government of Northern Ireland, even though its members like most people in the North had no great enthusiasm for it.

Following a Westminster election in 1885 on a wider franchise, the Liberals came into power with the support of the Irish Nationalists; and William Ewart Gladstone, on his restoration to the office of Prime Minister, soon indicated that he was prepared to pay the price of that support — the introduction of a Bill to give Ireland Home Rule, with a Parliament in Dublin. That sparked off a period of intense political controversy in the North and resulted in the division of the substantial Liberal interest there into Home Rulers and Anti-Home Rulers, with the strong Liberal grouping in the Chamber headed by men like Thomas Sinclair joining the "Anti" faction and becoming Liberal-Unionists. And the tension was heightened by the publication of the Bill early in 1886

Robert H S Reade, Chairman York Street Flax Spinning Company, President of the Chamber 1881 and 1906, and Hon Treasurer 1891-1913.

Thomas Gallaher, founder of Gallaher Ltd, tobacco manufacturers. Began manufacture in Londonderry 1857: moved to Belfast 1867.

Sir James Henderson, proprietor of the Belfast News Letter, Lord Mayor of Belfast 1898, active in the Chamber.

(From R M Young's Collection — Linenhall Library.)

and the famous visit to Belfast in February that year of Lord Randolph Churchill, when prominent Chamber-member, James Henderson of the News Letter, was one of those who accompanied him into the Ulster Hall to deliver his historic speech.

It was against that background that the Chamber now led by James Theodore Richardson, who had interests in linen and artificial fertilisers (or "chemical manures" as they were then called), held a special meeting on 22 April 1886 *"to consider the proposals now placed before Parliament by Mr Gladstone"*. After a prolonged debate on the possible commercial and economic consequences of the proposed measure, the fifty-eight members present voted unanimously for a resolution proposed by R H S Reade and seconded by W J Hurst, a linen spinner from Ballynahinch, which completely rejected any dilution of the union with Great Britain. Later at the suggestion of Lloyd Patterson, supported by Sir James Corry MP and David Lytle (who became President in 1892), the meeting agreed to incorporate its decisions into a document that would be presented to both Houses of Parliament and copied to every Chamber of Commerce in Great Britain, as well as to appropriate public representatives. The Chamber therefore played a part in the build-up of the political opposition to the Bill which resulted in its defeat in the House of Commons in June 1886; and the precedent was set for the involvement of the Chamber in succeeding phases of the constitutional drama, in 1893, in 1912, and in 1917.

The six years between the first and second Home Rule crises were one of the most dynamic periods in the history of the Chamber. Under the leadership of William Quartus Ewart, the membership of the Council was broadened by the co-option of the Mayor of Belfast; the Members of Parliament for the town as well as those for Counties Antrim and Down; and the chairmen of various public bodies and trade associations. At the same time Lloyd Patterson, who had retired early from business, volunteered to become almost full-time Honorary Secretary, coming into the office daily to help his old friend Samuel Vance, who had been Secretary since Christmas 1847 and was now about eighty years of age. In addition Vance's son Robert was employed part-time to collect membership subscriptions on a commission basis and generally to help the Honorary Treasurer. And the process of change continued in the following year under the leadership of Charles C Connor, the first of only two men in history to be Mayor or Lord Mayor of Belfast and President of the Chamber simultaneously (the other was the 9th Earl of Shaftesbury in 1907). During Connor's Presidency, which ended in February 1890, a committee structure was established that would continue unchanged for many years. It comprised six committees covering Trade and Tariffs; Parliamentary and Legal Affairs; Traffic Matters; Postal and Telegraphic Services; Commercial Arbitration; and General Purposes. Several "trade sections" were also established in which members involved in a particular industry met alone from time to time. And all of this was reflected in a rapid growth in membership, from a low of one-hundred-and-sixty-three in 1888 to a record of almost two-hundred-and-fifty by 1892, bringing with it a long overdue uplift for the finances of the Chamber (which Lloyd Patterson, in the euphemistic verbiage of the Victorians, had described some years previously as *"the reverse of favourable"*).

Concurrent with the restructuring and expansion of the Chamber there was a noticeable increase in its impact on public and commercial affairs. For example it was the Chamber under the leadership of F D Ward, head of the famous Marcus Ward printing and publishing house, that initiated the campaign which led to Belfast's being granted the dignity of a city in 1888; and it was the Chamber too that could justly claim most of the credit for the establishment in 1889 of a local Bankruptcy Court, after many years of agitation. Likewise its long campaign for the institution of a fast packet-steamer service between Larne and Stranraer in the interests of speeding the mails was ultimately successful in 1891; and the strong support given by the Chamber to local bodies in County Down was a factor in the decision to extend the railway network to Ardglass and Killough to serve the needs of the fishing industry. The start of construction work on that project was announced at the annual meeting of the Chamber on 12 February 1891 by the outgoing President, Adam Duffin, who was destined to become one of the most influential figures in the Chamber and in the public life of the Province generally over the next thirty-three years.

It was Adam Duffin too who referred in his valedictory remarks early in 1891 to the *"very full and general employment for labour of every description"*, a situation which he used to illustrate his philosophy that low wages and full employment were better than high wages for a proportion of the population and unemployment for the rest. Duffin also referred to a downturn in shipbuilding; but it must have been slight or short-lived because his successor, W C Mitchell (who is commemorated today by the Mitchell organ in the Whitla Hall at Queen's University), proudly announced at the annual meeting of the Chamber in February 1892 that on the basis of tonnage finished in the previous year the Harland & Wolff yard was now the most productive in the United Kingdom. And Mitchell and his colleagues were obviously proud too of the continued growth in shipping movements through the port of Belfast, reflecting annual exports of sixty-five-thousand tons of iron ore, thirty-five-thousand tons of linen, twenty-four-thousand tons of whiskey, eleven-thousand tons of grass-seed, almost

Gustav W Wolff MP
President 1898

Francis D Ward
President 1887

John Greenhill
President 1893

Sir William Q Ewart
President 1888

Frederick L Heyn
President 1899

Dr R Kyle Knox
President 1897

Rt Hon Robert Thompson MP
President 1901

Sir Charles Brett
President 1908

R Ernest Herdman
President 1914

Sir John Milne Barbour
President 1911

Sir Samuel C Davidson
President 1915

John Rogers
President 1910

(Mostly from R M Young's Collection — Linenhall Library.)

nine-thousand tons of mineral waters, and some sixty-five-thousand head of cattle; as well as imports of nearly half-a-million tons of coal, over one-hundred-and-sixty-thousand tons of wheat and Indian corn (maize), and some eighty-six-thousand tons of iron and castings.

Meanwhile in 1887 Queen Victoria had celebrated her Jubilee; and the Chamber had been represented at a vast memorial service in Westminster Abbey by the then President, F D Ward, who described it as *"an event written in letters of gold"*. In the same year the oldest secondary school in the town, the Academy, which had moved seven years previously from Donegall Street to the Cliftonville Road, was permitted to add the royal epithet to its name; and on the other side of town, in Gloucester Street, Ayrshire-born veterinary surgeon John Boyd Dunlop was fabricating the world's first pneumatic tyre, for his son's tricycle. Two years later the President of the Chamber was doubly amongst those who welcomed a royal visitor to the town — 'doubly' because he was Mayor as well. The visitor was the ill-fated eldest son of the Prince of Wales, Prince Albert Victor, Duke of Clarence, who would die less than three years later at the age of twenty-eight. The cold hand of death was apparent too in the Chamber as six of its Past Presidents died within a short time of each other, between 1889 and 1891: they were Sir William Ewart, Alexander Johns, Sir Edward Cowan, Finlay McCance, Sir James Corry, and Sir John Preston (who was succeeded as Honorary Treasurer by R H S Reade). Whether the world-wide epidemics of influenza, which were a feature of that period, contributed to any of their deaths is not immediately apparent; though the outbreaks were sufficiently serious to be mentioned by Charles Connor in his "state of the nation" address in February 1890 as a factor depressing international trade.

On a more topical note, one of Belfast's most prominent landmarks — the Robinson and Cleaver store at the corner of Donegal Place and Donegall Square North — was completed in 1888; and as this great emporium opened for business, the builders were hard at work re-constructing the Albert Bridge (which had collapsed dramatically in 1886) and putting the finishing touches to the Tropical Ravine in Botanic Gardens. Three years later the Irish News would begin publication as a popular daily, in succession to the much older Morning News; and within a year from that, the Mayors of Belfast would for ever after be known as Lord Mayors, the first person to be endowed with the title being Sir Daniel Dixon, the head of the building supplies firm of Thomas S Dixon & Co whose partners contributed much to the Chamber over the years. And in the meantime the Chamber itself had been displaying a certain forwardness, for it was beginning to be interested in an Irish Channel Tunnel from Donaghadee to Portpatrick and had joined the Imperial Decimal Association, a body set up to promote decimalisation of weights, measures, and money throughout the British Empire.

Meanwhile, at the centre of political life in London, thoughts were turning again to the promotion of a much more controversial cause — Home Rule for Ireland, on essentially the same lines as the House of Commons and the electorate had rejected in

Sir Thomas Dixon Bart, director of Thomas S Dixon & Co Ltd, builders merchants. Active Chamber member early 20th Century.

Sir Otto Jaffé, linen manufacturer and furrier, Lord Mayor of Belfast 1899, active Chamber member.

Edward Robinson, joint founder of Robinson & Cleaver Ltd. Both he and John Cleaver were Chamber members.

(From R M Young's Collection — Linenhall Library.)

1886. Despite the weakening of the Irish Nationalist party by the controversy in 1890 about the private life of its then leader, Charles Stewart Parnell, the feeling was growing that the Gladstonian Liberals and their potential allies in Ireland could muster sufficient support in the country to oust Lord Salisbury's Conservative administration and bring the Home Rule issue back to the centre of the political stage. Anticipating this, many of Ulster's best-known businessmen again became deeply involved in organising resistance and in publicising the commercial and economic arguments against Home Rule, climaxing in the vast Ulster Unionist Convention of 17 June 1892 in a specially-erected building near Botanic Gardens. It was a Chamber member, Robert MacGeagh, that called the assembly of almost twelve thousand delegates to order and introduced the Duke of Abercorn as chairman; and it was two of the Chamber's most distinguished members — Sir William Quartus Ewart and Thomas Sinclair — that proposed and seconded the main resolution.

The fears of the Unionists were justified, for within eleven days Parliament was prorogued; and, in the aftermath of the subsequent election, William Gladstone at the age of eighty-three became Prime Minister for the fourth time, again with the conditional support of the Irish Nationalists. Parliament then adjourned till February 1893, when one of Gladstone's first acts in the new House of Commons was to introduce his second Home Rule Bill. The Bill had its first reading on the 16th of the month; and there were reverberations in Belfast five days later when the Chamber met in the Commercial Buildings for its annual general meeting.

There was tension in the air as the outgoing President, David B Lytle, ploughed his way through the usual long report from the Council followed by his own valedictory comments. Council was concerned about the state of things on the land, about freight charges on the railways, and about *"the utter insufficiency of the siren on Mew Island"*. With the support of the Cork, Dublin, and Londonderry Chambers, Sir Edward

Harland had been appointed to the committee of Lloyd's Register of Shipping; the city fire-brigade had been reorganised and re-equipped and there were three steam engines, eight horses, and forty men *"ready for instant service"*; exports of powdered soup were up and of iron ore down. But not a reference to the one subject that was uppermost in everyone's mind — the second Home Rule Bill!

As soon as the President resumed his seat, Robert MacGeagh who had called the Ulster Unionist Convention to order the previous June was on his feet. While recognising that the Chamber normally steered clear of party politics, he deplored the studied absence of any reference to the Home Rule Bill in that day's proceedings; and he argued that the Chamber would be failing in its duty to the commercial interests of the Province if it did not immediately declare its total opposition to the proposed measure. But while MacGeagh was still in full flight he was courteously interrupted by John Burke, a respected member of the Chamber who had his own shipping business in the Corporation Street area. Burke contended that MacGeagh was out of order because the subject was party-political and had been raised without notice. But the President thought that MacGeagh had been sticking quite closely to the commercial and economic aspects of the proposed Bill and ruled that he could continue. Thus vindicated, MacGeagh continued at some length, until Lloyd Patterson brought the meeting back to earth by asking a series of detailed questions about through bookings on the railways and the transport of the American mails from Queenstown to Cork, Dublin, and Belfast!

But MacGeagh's intervention turned out to be only the beginning of the subject for the day; for the debate continued immediately after the new President, John Greenhill, was installed. At that stage the main proponent of action by the Chamber was the very able and eloquent ex-Liberal, Thomas Sinclair, whose speech eight months earlier at the Ulster Unionist Convention had been generally regarded as the most cogent and convincing of the day. In the Chamber, Sinclair was equally convincing, as he examined the possible consequences of Home Rule for the industrial and commercial interests of the Province; and he even succeeded in securing the gracious acquiescence of John Burke with many of his points. Nevertheless Mr Burke, after further skirmishes with Robert MacGeagh, stood out against Chamber involvement in the controversy; and was the sole dissentient to a resolution proposed by Sinclair and seconded by his fellow Past-President, Francis D Ward, which instructed the Council of the Chamber *"to consider the relation of the Irish Government Bill to the financial, manufacturing, and commercial interests of Ulster, and to report to an early Special Meeting of the Chamber"*.

The Council delegated the detailed study of the Bill and its possible consequences to a small committee headed by Thomas Sinclair; and the report of that group was considered by a special meeting of Council on 9 March 1893. That in turn led to an Extraordinary General Meeting attended by some eighty members on St Patrick's Day at one o'clock, when the committee's report was endorsed for submission to Parliament, to Chambers of Commerce throughout the British Isles, to public representatives, and to the newspapers. As in 1886, the essence of this comprehensive and lengthy document was that Ireland was economically incapable of independence and that the industrial and commercial prosperity of Ulster would be destroyed by the severance of the union with Great Britain. *"All our progress has been made under the Union"*, wrote the committee. *"We were a small insignificant town at the end of the last century, deeply disaffected and hostile to the British Empire. But since the Union, and under equal laws, we have been welded to the Empire, and have made a progress second to none"*. And in a further reference to earlier times, the document concluded that if the Home Rule Bill were to become law *"the result would be a blow as deadly to Irish Commercial Interests as were the measures framed centuries ago intentionally to ruin Irish trade"*. The Belfast Chamber of Commerce had changed a lot from its heady radicalism in the 18th Century!

Though there must surely have been a few streaks of Liberalism, if not Nationalism, left in the Chamber in 1893, the report of the committee condemning the Home Rule Bill was adopted unanimously. However there was just a moment in the meeting when it seemed that events might take an unexpected turn: that was when Samuel Davidson, founder of the Sirocco Works, proposed an amendment expressing a willingness to discuss a measure of Home Rule in the interests of avoiding civil war. But in the words of the historic minute, his amendment *"not having found a seconder fell to the ground"*; and the meeting instead enthusiastically accepted a suggestion from the pugnacious Mr MacGeagh that the Prime Minister should be asked to receive a deputation from the Chamber and other public bodies in the town.

In response to a request made through Members of Parliament, Mr Gladstone agreed to receive a deputation from the Chamber led by the President, John Greenhill, and accompanied by representatives of the Harbour Commissioners and the Linen Merchants' Association; and the historic meeting took place in London on Tuesday 28 March 1893. There were no less than twenty-one members in the delegation; and they comprised a remarkable assembly of talent and influence. The Chamber representatives in addition to the President were the Rt Hon John Young, George S Clark, Adam Duffin, Robert MacGeagh, Lloyd Patterson, Thomas Richardson, and Thomas Sinclair. The group from the Harbour Commissioners included Thomas Dixon, Herbert Lanyon (son of Sir Charles), Samuel Lawther, and Robert Thompson; and the representatives of the Linen Merchants' Association included Sir William Q Ewart and William Crawford. Furthermore the Chamber was strongly represented amongst the four Members of Parliament present, for they included Charles Connor (President in 1889/90), Sir Edward Harland, and Gustav Wolff. Thus the delegation of twenty-one members included no less than twelve who had been or would be Presidents of the Chamber.

The Prime Minister listened carefully to what this formidable group had to say in support of the Chamber's printed submission; and he did his best to allay their fears without showing signs of deviating from his intended course. But the group remained adamant that the industrial and commercial future of Ulster was in peril; and they produced a further pamphlet to refute the arguments put forward by the Prime Minister in a statement issued shortly after their meeting with him. In mid-April, as that

Horse-trams in Castle Place about 1900, Ulster Club on the left, with historic first-floor balcony from which Sir Edward Carson spoke in 1912. (Photo by J Valentine — Ulster Folk & Transport Museum.)

pamphlet went into circulation, the Bill had its second reading in Westminster; and there was rioting in Belfast when the news came through. After a summer of discontent, the Bill passed from the committee stage to a third reading on 3 September. Surviving that hurdle by a margin of thirty-four votes, it faced the final obstacle of the House of Lords five days later; and it crashed by a majority of more than ten to one. Mr Gladstone was dispirited and the Chamber of Commerce in Belfast was relieved. The second Home Rule crisis had ended; and there would be a respite of nineteen years till the next.

By the time of the annual meeting in February 1894 when H O Lanyon took over the Presidency from John Greenhill, the Home Rule controversy was almost forgotten; and the Chamber was busying itself with less controversial subjects like fire-insurance rates, commercial education for boys, wrecks and derelicts in international shipping lanes, and breaches of the Merchandise Marks Act. And there were little touches that reminded of changing times: a welcome for the installation of electric lighting at the docks to facilitate nightwork; congratulations to the Water Commissioners for moving towards *"an inexhaustible supply of good water from the Mourne Mountains"*; a proud announcement that the Chamber had equipped itself with a handsome seal for the authentication of certificates of origin and other official documents; and there might even have been congratulations for the Irish rugby team who won the Triple Crown that year by beating Wales on a water-logged pitch at Ormeau.

Herbert Owen Lanyon was one of the more colourful Presidents of the Chamber, the artistry of his great architectural father being often apparent in his language if not in his works. His terminal review of the state of trade in February 1895 was therefore liberally laced with literary allusions. *"Sweet are the uses of adversity"* was his way of saying that there were lessons to be learned from a deep recession that had affected most sectors of trade; and he measured Ulster's linen exports in the previous twelve months not in tons, but as a girdle for the world three yards wide. The new-fangled church bazaars were *"the connecting link between commerce and charity"*; and as farming went through a rough time of over-supply and low prices he wondered whether the community was *"paying too dearly for the cheap loaf"*. Thomas Sinclair was the man to appreciate Lanyon's creativity of phrase; and in his vote of thanks to the outgoing President he referred warmly to his *"literary charm not usually associated with such dry-as-dust business"*. But not all the business was dry as dust, for the Chamber was pressing for the introduction of mechanical trams to take the place of the Tramway Company's eight hundred horses which tended to leave their marks on the street: their replacement would take about twelve years. And the hoary subject of uniform time for the whole of the United Kingdom was back in vogue; and the remarkable Robert Lloyd Patterson was about to begin his second spell as President.

In the fifteen years between Patterson's first and second terms of office Belfast had changed dramatically. The population had increased from a hundred-and-eighty-thousand to over three-hundred-thousand; and that was a reflection mainly of the growth in the industry and commerce of the town. Nowhere was that growth more apparent than in shipbuilding, as Harland & Wolff became the trusted suppliers of more and more of the great shipping lines of the world; and the "wee yard" of Workman, Clark & Company also grew in importance. With the distinguished founders more and more attracted to public life, the real power in the Harland & Wolff yard had long since passed into the hands of William Pirrie; and he in turn was now about to begin making his own mark on municipal affairs. In time, Pirrie and his wife would make many contributions to the improvement of social conditions in the city; but the entertainment scene had already improved with the opening of the Empire Theatre in Victoria Square in 1894 and the Grand Opera House in Great Victoria Street in the following year. The educational scene too had been improved around this time by the opening of Campbell College.

Lloyd Patterson made his money in business and he was skilful with the pen and as a sportsman; but at heart he was a scientist, with an insatiable thirst for knowledge of Nature and all her secrets. He was therefore delighted that one of the ceremonial duties of his year as President was to inaugurate the telephone service between Belfast and London by conducting a brief conversation "down the wire" with one of Ulster's greatest sons, Lord Kelvin, the pioneer of submarine cables and many other innovations in pure and applied physics. And Patterson's scientific and technological interest also shone through his farewell speech, which spoke of typewriters and sewing machines, of sanitation and printing, and of the great bridges across the Forth and the Thames.

Sir Edward Harland MP (right), whose engineering genius was the basis of the Harland & Wolff Shipyard: seen here with his effective successor at the Yard, William James (later Lord) Pirrie.
(Photo from Harland & Wolff.)

But when it came to history, Patterson's touch was less sure. Unbelievably, he and the aged Secretary, Samuel Vance, somehow came to the conclusion that the Chamber had been established in 1796 — so they called a centenary for 1896, just thirteen years late! At the annual meeting in February that year, Patterson explained that the available records went back only to the beginning of Vance's marathon Secretaryship in 1847; but he nevertheless asserted unequivocally that 1796 was the foundation year. That being so, Dr Robert Kyle Knox of the Northern Bank who was to have become President in 1896 had kindly given way to the Marquis of Londonderry, his lordship having graciously consented to honour the Chamber by accepting the Presidency in its "centenary year". Lord Londonderry duly took the chair and delivered a lengthy "centenary" address, his most significant contribution to the Chamber in the course of his year in office; and at the conclusion of the meeting a distinguished member thanked all concerned, but particularly Lloyd Patterson. *"His facts were well mustered"*, said the speaker, *"and his observations to the point"!* And that was effectively the end of the "centenary" celebrations, though the myth of 1796 as the foundation year was perpetuated for several decades on the Chamber seal and in its letter-heading, as will be apparent from one of the illustrations in the present work.

But on the very day on which the Chamber enacted the farce of the false centenary, there was another event in the city which related back to the true origin of the organisation in 1783. The White Linen Hall, built in the year that the Chamber was established, had outlived its usefulness as a centre of commerce; and the Townhall in Victoria Street, though in use for only twenty-five years, seemed to the Corporation to be an inadequate reflection of the industrial and commercial glory that Belfast had attained. So a plan was agreed for the Corporation to acquire the White Linen Hall and its site for a sum of £26,000; demolish the old building, which in a very real way commemorated the work and wealth of the founding fathers of the Chamber of Commerce; and put in its place a magnificent new City Hall that future generations would admire and cherish. The demolition had begun a few weeks before the annual meeting of the Chamber on 4 February 1896; and as Lloyd Patterson and Lord Londonderry delivered their addresses in the Commercial Buildings in Waring Street, a certain Frank Byers, clerk of works to the Corporation, was keeping an eagle eye on the accumulating rubble in Donegall Square. In the midst of the noise and the dust he was looking for the foundation stone laid by John Brown and the brethren of Masonic Lodge No 257 on 28 April 1783: and he found it just below ground level in the north-east corner, almost exactly where an antiquarian had predicted. Cautiously the upper half of the layered stone was levered off to reveal a brass plate; and underneath the brass plate there was a cavity; and in the cavity there was the glass tube of documents which Robert Bradshaw and John McClean had placed there one-hundred-and-thirteen years earlier, six months before the historic first Council meeting of the Chamber of Commerce on 25 October 1783. So by a quite incredible coincidence the false centenary of the Chamber and the true link to the men of 1783 were both reported in the same issue of the News Letter, on 5 February 1896!

This was a period when organised labour was also building up its links — links that were designed to bring greater co-ordination and strength to its dealings with employers. The Belfast and District United Trades' Council had been formed as early as 1881; and had affiliated with the Trades Unions Congress in Britain in the following year. In 1893 the TUC had held its annual conference in Belfast; and in the course of the next year the Belfast Trades' Council had affiliated with the Irish Congress of Trades Unions as well. By then the trade union movement in and around the city had a membership of about thirteen-thousand; and that was the state of play when the Chamber in October 1895 completed negotiations with the Belfast and District United Trades' and Labour Council (as the central organisation had then become) to form a Conciliation Board *"for the purpose of promoting amicable methods of settling labour disputes"*. The new body was to have twelve members nominated by the Council of the Chamber and twelve by the Trades' Council; and its role was to be very similar to that of the Labour Relations Agency today. Unfortunately however there is no evidence in the Chamber records that it ever operated as intended; and eight years later, in the Presidency of James Wilson, the Chamber had a letter from the Trades' Council seeking the return of any residue of the £5 that that body had contributed towards the funds of the board when it was first established. Obviously by that time this early attempt at organising to anticipate and solve industrial disputes had petered out.

To the immense satisfaction of the Chamber, there was a happier outcome to another of the great projects of those years: that was the campaign for new policies and new structures to provide technical education and advisory services in industry and agriculture. The story began with the publication in the second half of 1896 of a very remarkable document known as "The Report of the Recess Committee". This report of over four-hundred pages was the work of a group of twenty-two talented people from all over Ireland; and the group was known as the Recess Committee because most of the deliberations had to take place during Parliamentary recesses in order to accommodate its six MPs. The Chairman was Horace Plunkett MP, the visionary founder of agricultural co-operation in Ireland; and the Northern representatives included prominent Chamber-member, Thomas Sinclair, who in the course of his service on the committee became a member of the Irish Privy Council. James Musgrave also became involved, as chairman of a special consultative committee for Ulster; and his colleagues in that group included James Dempsey, Sir Daniel Dixon, Sir William Q Ewart, and Robert MacGeagh, who were all active in the Chamber.

Guided in part by an exhaustive study of structures and policies in nine countries of Continental Europe, the Recess Committee put forward an imaginative plan to improve agriculture and industry in Ireland. *"We have in Ireland"*, said the opening paragraph of the Report, *"a poor country, practically without manufactures — except for the linen and ship-building of the North and the brewing and distilling of Dublin — dependent upon agriculture, with its soil imperfectly tilled, its area under cultivation decreasing, and a diminishing population without industrial habits or technical skill".* Having analysed that situation in greater depth and reviewed the faltering steps taken over the years in attempts to improve it, the Committee put forward a detailed plan centring on the establishment of a Department of Agriculture and Industries in Dublin, controlled not only by Ministers and civil servants but also by representatives of industry and agriculture from all over the country.

The Council of the Chamber discussed the Report at length on 3 December 1896; and a press statement was issued that evening:

"The Report of the Recess Committee is a most valuable contribution towards the amelioration of the economic conditions of Ireland. It represents in most readable and accessible form a large amount of important information as to the state of agriculture and manufacture in our own country, and shows with great clearness how effectively Continental nations have outstripped Ireland in the markets of Great Britain, largely through the wise and judicious application of State aid to their agricultural and industrial interests. The recommendations of the Recess Committee have the special merit that they condition Government Aid in Ireland upon local effort and self help, and thus avoid the demoralising effects that are likely to accompany indiscriminate State assistance. They have also the important advantage of proposing, by means of a consultative council, to enlist local experience and knowledge in the administration of public aid. While, therefore, the Council reserves to itself liberty of judgement as to details of the Recess Committee's Report, it cordially recommends its proposals for the establishment of a Department of Agriculture and Industry to the favourable consideration of Her Majesty's Government, with the view of making them the basis of legislation in the coming session of Parliament. And specially representing, as the Council of the Belfast Chamber does, a manufacturing community which keenly feels the pressures of Continental competition in its staple industries, it earnestly urges the Government to lose no time in inaugurating a much-needed system of efficient technical education in Ireland". Thus the Chamber recognised the merit of the proposals in economic and commercial terms; and did not for a moment waste time and energy searching for political overtones, despite its intense opposition in 1886 and 1893 to the proposed devolution of powers in other matters of state to an all-Ireland Dublin-based institution.

Matters arising from the Report of the Recess Committee occupied the attention of the Chamber on many occasions over the next five years. Before that, however, the Chamber had also to deal with another set of proposals that impinged on the unity of the United Kingdom. These were contained in the Report of the Financial Relations Commission, which in effect suggested the separation of the British and Irish fiscal systems, and gave rise to the prospect of a different taxation regime in Ireland. The response of the Chamber came in January 1897 in the form of a public statement issued after analysis of the proposals by the appropriate standing committee, the Council, and a general meeting of over sixty members. Despite some internal opposition from two members sympathetic to Irish political independence and therefore receptive to prior financial separation, the Chamber condemned the proposals as a clear breach of the Act of Union; and elected for the continuation of uniform taxation and common funds, with the special problems of Ireland being dealt with by special measures on the expenditure side. *"We would suggest"*, said the Chamber statement, *"that an effective channel for judicious help may be found in the relief of local burdens, in the establishment on broad and general lines of an Agricultural Department, in the extension of technical education, in the development of the means of inland communication, and in the carrying out of such public works and undertakings as can be shown to be productive of permanent advantage to the people of Ireland"*. That too has a familiar ring!

And there is an equally familiar ring to the reaction made by the Chamber in March 1897 to a Bill that was then before Parliament to amend the provisions of the Companies Act of 1862. After commenting briefly on new proposals about the liability of directors and the contents of the prospectus, the Chamber came quickly to the crux of the matter, which was a proposed requirement for the publication of financial results annually. The Chamber argued cogently that that might be appropriate for large public companies whose shares were quoted on the Stock Exchange, but that it was inappropriate both for companies engaged largely in highly-competitive foreign trade and for *"Family and other Companies sometimes called 'private Companies'"*. The Chamber solution was that publication should be at the discretion of shareholders; and the specific proposal was that companies that had decided against publication would officially inform the Registrar and be empowered by him to add a distinguishing term (additional to "Limited") to the name of the company. Though a history of the subsequent developments on the detail of Company Law is outside the scope of the present work, it is appropriate to note, firstly, that from that beginning in 1897 the Chamber has been in the forefront of the subject ever since; and, secondly, that the publication provisions of the 1897 Bill are only now being implemented in the case of private companies! But there have been very good reasons for the delay, as the Chamber has maintained vigorously over the years: and some of these reasons are still valid today.

There was a delay too in the Government's reaction to the report of the Recess Committee, where the Chamber was at one with public bodies throughout Ireland in seeking action through a new Department of Agriculture and Industry. But the delay, though frustrating at the time, was measured in months rather than years or decades; and the cause was not one of principle, but simply the Government's desire to give precedence to a Bill to reform Local Government in Ireland by disbanding the Grand Juries and creating the County Councils etc. The Chamber was not convinced, however, that the passage of one Bill justified the temporary withdrawal of the other; and the organisation was therefore strongly represented in a huge delegation from all over Ireland that waited upon the Chief Secretary in Dublin Castle on 30 November 1897. They were assured that the Agriculture and Industries (Ireland) Bill would be reintroduced at the first opportunity; and the Belfast Chamber felt sufficiently confident about this to decline a subsequent invitation from the Dublin Chamber to join a joint deputation to the Prime Minister, Lord Salisbury.

In due course the Government more or less kept its promise, though the measure brought before Parliament in May 1899 was decisively narrower than originally intended: it was about Agricultural and Technical Instruction, rather than about Agriculture and Industries. And it resulted in the establishment of a Department of Agriculture and Technical Instruction in Dublin which served agriculture and its related industries well over the next thirty years, but offered little to other sectors of industry. Horace Plunkett, the chairman of the Recess Committee of 1896, became the effective head of the new department as Vice-President; and the Council duly invited him to come to Belfast to address a joint meeting of the Chamber and the North-East Agricultural Society (the forerunner of the Royal Ulster Agricultural Society) on his aspirations for the further development of agriculture and its related industries. The Chamber was also quick to urge upon the Government the necessity of appointing to the new Board of Agriculture a person *"having a practical knowledge of the cultivation and treatment of flax in the North of Ireland and at the same time conversant with the best Continental methods to promote in Ireland the cultivation of this crop which might be very profitable to farmers and is of great importance to flax spinners"*. And in the best traditions of the pursuit of vested interests, the Chamber was able to add casually that a person with the necessary qualifications was available and would be willing to serve!

Though pre-occupied over several years with matters arising directly from reports of the Financial Relations Commissions and the Recess Committee and with the revision of Company Law, the Chamber had not neglected other initiatives in the field of technical and commercial education. Indeed it may well have been an increasing realisation that the Bill ultimately emerging from the work of the Recess Committee would major on agriculture that led the Chamber to decide as early as December 1897 *"to appoint a deputation to wait on the Belfast Corporation to press for the establishment of a Technical School"* — a move that found its fulfilment almost ten years later in the opening of the Technical Institute (later the College of Technology) in the grounds of the Academical Institution. The initiators of that movement within the Chamber were Sir James Musgrave, the Rt Hon Thomas Sinclair, and R H S Reade; but the factor more than any other that gave assurance of progress was that James Henderson was then Lord Mayor and was strongly in favour of the project. The Chamber therefore found an open door when the President, Dr R Kyle Knox, led a deputation to the Corporation, in which the Chamber was joined by representatives of the Flax Spinners' Association, the Power-Loom Manufacturers' Association, the Technical Schools, the Working Men's Institute, the Linen Merchants' Association, the United Trades' and Labour Council, the Bleachers' Association, and the School of Art. Five years later the erection of the great building modelled on the War Office in London would commence; and Belfast would for ever after have to endure the piece of planning vandalism and financial expediency that allowed it to foul the gracious lines of the now partially-obscured Academical Institution.

Though the location of the new Technical Institute offended many an eye, the facilities that it provided were to be a boon to Ulster industry and commerce for many generations. The same would be true of another educational project first advocated by the Chamber at around the same time: this was the establishment of a School of Commerce at Queen's College Belfast. To pursue this the Chamber set up a Commercial Education Committee; and that Committee reported early in 1902. It strongly recommended the establishment of a Faculty of Commerce in the Royal University of Ireland on the model of developments elsewhere and with the objective of awarding degrees in Commercial Science. On the local scene it was recommended that a School of Commerce should be established at Queen's College Belfast, under the control of a council nominated jointly by the College and the Chamber of Commerce. The report also included suggestions for the curriculum of the course; and discussed financing in a preliminary way. The Committee did not envisage that the costs could be met by the fees levied on the students; and a minor degree of funding by industry was not ruled out. However the final conclusion was that *"if any systematic commercial teaching is to be attempted in Ireland with the hope of success, the Governmental assistance which has been given to Agriculture and Technical teaching must also be extended to this nascent but equally important movement"*. But this nascent movement regrettably did not see its fulfilment in the establishment of a School of Commerce at Queen's for another eight years, by which time the College had become an independent University with a representative of the Chamber (Sir Charles Brett) on its Senate and generous grants from Sir James Musgrave, Harland & Wolff, Sir Otto Jaffé, and other business interests in its development fund.

The Municipal Technical Institute, later Belfast College of Technology, provided by the Corporation 1902-1907, in response to Chamber of Commerce pressure.   (From R M Young — Linenhall Library.)

But as the debate on technical and commercial education wended its way from 1896 till 1910, there had been many triumphs and many traumatic experiences for the nation, the Province, and the Chamber. Queen Victoria had celebrated her Diamond Jubilee in June 1897; and the Chamber was amongst the thousands of organisations who "addressed" her on that occasion. Two-and-a-half years later the nation was involved in a bitter war with the Boers in South Africa; and the octagenerian Queen and most of her people found it hard to accept that British military might was not invincible. James Craig, son of the Dunville distillery magnate, stock-broker in his own right, part-time officer in the 3rd (Militia) Battalion of the Royal Irish Rifles, and future Prime Minister of Northern Ireland, had turned the key in his Rosemary Street office for the last time and headed for the action, on secondment to the 46th (Hunt) Company of the Imperial Yeomanry. And as Craig and his colleagues sailed for the Cape in the CYMRIC, the President of the Chamber, William Crawford of the York Street Flax Spinning Company, and his Senior Vice-President, Robert Thompson of Prospect Mills, were heading for the Viceregal Lodge in Dublin by the GNR train to present yet another address to the Queen. That was in May 1900; but there was no reply from the Queen till October — and three months later she was dead. The Chamber met on the following day and passed a resolution of tribute and respect which referred to the late Queen's *"splendid qualities of heart and mind, the exercise of which rendered Her Majesty's rule illustrious and beneficient, and Her example a blessing to mankind"*. But soon the Chamber was equally solicitous about the well-being of her son, King Edward VII and his Queen Alexandra; and appropriate resolutions were dispatched to Buckingham Palace on the occasion of the Coronation in June and the serious illness of the new King in the following month. Within a year the war in South Africa would at last be finished; but not before it had claimed many more victims, amongst them Lieutenant R E Reade DSO of the 60th Rifles, second son of R H S Reade of Wilmont, Honorary Treasurer of the Chamber.

The Chamber itself had undergone dramatic changes in the succession as the centuries changed. When the Council met on 13 January 1898 its first duty was to record a tribute to the work and worth of its long-standing Secretary Samuel Vance, who had just passed to his eternal reward at the age of eighty-nine without laying down the reins of office. Vance had been Secretary for fifty years; and the Chamber was so devoted to him that it had put up with an unsatisfactory situation in the last ten years of his life when he had had to have the assistance first of a part-time Honorary Secretary and latterly of a full-time Assistant Secretary. The Assistant Secretary appointed for one year in January 1897 at a salary of £75 a year was a Mr B W Caughey; and he duly succeeded to the Secretaryship when Vance died within the year. His salary was fixed at £120 a year; and he retained the part-time assistance of his predecessor's son Robert as Sub-Treasurer at £10 a year plus five percent on subscriptions collected.

But before another twelve months had elapsed, Caughey had disappeared from the scene without explanation in the minutes; and the Chamber was involved in a most elaborate process to appoint his replacement. There were eighty-seven applications for the post; and these were eventually narrowed to six by a committee of the Council. Then on 12 January 1899, with Gustav Wolff in the Presidential chair and over seventy members present, the matter was decided by a series of ballots but only after an altercation with William Johnston of Ballykilbeg, the MP for South Belfast, who thought that he should have a vote even though he was present only in an ex-officio capacity. The result was a clear-cut victory for a Mr W J P Wilson who would serve the Chamber in an outstanding manner for the next twenty-eight years.

As the staff scene in the Chamber underwent its successive changes in the two years from January 1897, there was no shortage of new subjects in the monthly meetings of the Council. In April 1897 a Mr McConnell gave notice of his intention to raise the question of communication with Great Britain by an Irish Channel Tunnel from Donaghadee to Portpatrick; a month later the very lively James Dempsey fired the first shots in his campaign to have two tunnels constructed under the Lagan in the area of Queen's Square and Pilot Street, so as to replace a ferry service that was proving inadequate; and these two subjects rumbled on for years — without result, other than extensive paper-work! Over much the same period of time the Chamber continued its exchanges with the National Telephone Company on what were seen as unsatisfactory aspects of its services; and there was even heady talk of getting the Corporation to take over the running of the telephone service. And in the real world of industry the Harland & Wolff yard at Queen's Island was turning out a steady stream of bigger and better ships culminating in the second OCEANIC, a vessel of seventeen-thousand tons with a length of almost seven-hundred feet and a speed of twenty-one knots and described at her launching on 14 January 1899 as *"the finest vessel ever produced, and the crowning success of the Century in naval architecture and marine engineering"*.

The OCEANIC slipped graciously into the sea two days after the new Secretary of the Chamber emerged less graciously from the succession of semi-public ballots that gave him his post. And soon he was confronted with a major task: for Lloyd Patterson felt it

Samuel Vance, Secretary of the Chamber from December 1847 till his death fifty years later at the age of eighty-nine.

(Coey Collection — Ulster Museum.)

Belfast Harbour from the Liverpool Boat, about 1890.
(From the Welch Collection — Ulster Museum)

in his bones that the time had come again to invite the Association of Chambers of Commerce in the United Kingdom to have its annual conference in Belfast. Starting from the modest blue-print of the first visit twenty years earlier, Patterson and his colleagues therefore organised and carried through one of the most glittering and meticulously-planned series of events that has ever taken place in the city. And from the beginning it was apparent that the arrangements were to reflect the new and more confident Belfast, the great commercial city, the great centre of shipbuilding, linen manufacture, ropemaking, tobacco processing, whiskey distilling, and water aeration. The documentation was to be much more elaborate and the subscription list longer and fatter; the menus were to be in French and the evening functions formal; there would be alternative destinations for the scenic visits, with the launching of another great ship at the Queen's Island as a third choice; there would be flowers and champagne, cigars and string music, theatre and opera; a garden party at Belfast Castle; Belfast would put its best foot forward. And Lloyd Patterson would lead and cajole and get through a quite incredible amount of work himself in the course of the preparatory period.

In another field, Louis Magee of Bective Rangers would also lead and cajole and work hard that year, for he was the captain of the Irish rugby team. And in February, as Magee and his colleagues prepared for the last hurdle in Cardiff that stood between them and their second Triple Crown, Lloyd Patterson and his colleagues in the Chamber were facing the first hurdle that they had to clear if they were to have a second glittering conference in Belfast that autumn for the English, the Scots, the Welsh, and the Irish — they needed to raise at least £1,000 to fund the social events. So a subscription list was opened; and the new President, Frederick L Heyn, gave it a magnificent start with a donation of £100. Gustav Wolff followed with £25; and the show was on the road, as member after member responded generously. In the end the list had one-hundred-and-thirty entries, pledging a total sum of £1,700, which having regard to the cost of food and drink then and now was the equivalent of at least twenty times that amount in today's money. So there was no need for parsimony in the planning and none was shown.

Most of the delegates arrived in Belfast on Monday 4 September and settled into their hotels, which included the Grand Central and the Avenue in Royal Avenue; the Northern Counties at York Road; the Imperial in Donegall Place; the Eglinton in High Street; the Commercial in Waring Street; the Grand Metropole in York Street; the

Prince of Wales in Victoria Street; Robinson's Temperance in Donegall Street; Balmoral Temperance in College Square East; and the Whiteabbey Hydro at Whiteabbey. Next morning the proceedings began with a reception at the Harbour Office where the delegates were received by the President of the Chamber, Frederick L Heyn; the Lord Mayor, Councillor Otto Jaffé; and the Chairman of the Harbour Commissioners, Sir James Musgrave. Afterwards the formal business ran throughout the day, broken only by a light lunch in the Harbour Office. And while this was going on, the ladies were being entertained by the wife of the Belfast President, Mrs F L Heyn, at the Prince's Restaurant in Fountain Street followed by a run to Bangor by horse-drawn coach. But the climax of the day was a civic reception for the delegates and their ladies, given by the Lord Mayor and Lady Mayoress in the Exhibition Hall at Botanic Gardens. Evening dress was the order of the day!

Next morning it was back to business for the delegates, as they plodded their way through the remainder of the long agenda. Then in the evening there was another magnificent function in the Exhibition Hall at Botanic Gardens. This was the dinner given by the President of the Belfast Chamber for the delegates, with the ladies left to fend for themselves. The organisation was superb and the hospitality unbelievable. On arrival at Belfast every delegate had been provided with several items of documentation, crowned by a magnificent "pocket card" printed by Marcus Ward in the manner of an illuminated address. This contained details of the programme for the week; and it was accompanied by a little card showing the individual delegate's place in the great table plan for the Chamber banquet. Then or later each delegate also received a little book of coloured tickets to enable the drinks at the banquet to be fairly allocated and smoothly served. For each person there were two pink tickets for sherry; two yellow ones for hock; six slightly greenish ones for champagne; two pink ones for claret; one red one for brandy; and two grey ones for whiskey! And there was a clear instruction that any unused tickets were to be returned at the end of the evening to W J P Wilson, the new Secretary of the Belfast Chamber. One suspects that not too many were returned!

As the string band of the 2nd Battalion of the Royal Irish Rifles made its way through a programme that began with the Whistling March "Hunyadi Indulo" by Erkel and concluded with a Caprice "Echo des Bastions" by Kling, the delegates and the great and the good from Belfast and district ate their way through eight courses from "Aspic à la Mirabeau" to "Oeufs à la Chimay", followed by "Dessert" and "Café". And to match the ten courses there were ten speakers proposing and responding to six toasts! Naturally these included a toast to the Association of Chambers of Commerce, which was proposed by Lloyd Patterson and acknowledged by the President of the Association, the Hon Sir H Stafford Northcote Bart CB MP.

Next morning about half the delegates and their ladies together with local members of the movement left York Road Station by the Northern Counties Railway for Portrush at 9.40 am; and the remainder left fifty minutes later from the terminus of the County Down Railway for Newcastle. As in 1879, the Portrush party dined early before setting out for the Giant's Causeway; but this time the journey was by the little electric tramway (established in 1883) and the weather was fine. For those who remembered

ROBINSON & CLEAVER,

By Special Appointment

| To HER MAJESTY QUEEN VICTORIA. | | To The EMPRESS FREDERICK OF GERMANY. |

MANUFACTURERS OF

Irish Damask Table Linen.	Irish Linen Collars, Cuffs, & Shirts.
Irish Towels & Household Linens.	Irish Poplins, Tweeds and Cloths.
Irish Cambric Pocket Handker-	Irish Knitted Wool & Balbriggan
chiefs,	Hosiery.
Plain, Printed and Embroidered.	Irish Hand and Machine-made
Irish Lace and Embroidery.	Underclothing.

N.B.—Crests, Coats of Arms, &c., Woven in Table Linen at a moderate cost. Initials, Names, Monograms, &c., Embroidered in the richest manner, on Handkerchiefs, Household Linens, &c., &c.

SYSTEM OF BUSINESS.

ALL GOODS sold at lowest Wholesale Prices for Prompt Cash direct to the Public, thus saving all intermediate profits.

BELFAST, Ireland.

R. MORTIMER,

The Only Practical Umbrella Maker in Belfast.

UMBRELLAS & WALKING STICKS

Of every description kept in Stock and made to Order.

Real Irish Blackthorns from 1s. to 15s.

UMBRELLAS RE-COVERED IN HALF-AN-HOUR IN ANY MATERIAL.

REPAIRS DONE AT ONCE.

PLEASE OBSERVE—

Mortimer's Umbrella Manufactory and Travelling Goods EMPORIUM,

5a, HIGH STREET, BELFAST.

THE

"ULSTER" OVERCOAT

THE ORIGINAL IRISH FRIEZE

DRIVING AND TRAVELLING WRAP.

Patterns of Materials, and all Instructions for Self-Measurement, with Illustrated Catalogue, forwarded on application.

M'GEE & CO., BELFAST, IRELAND.

Nineteenth Century advertisements for products made in and around Belfast.
(From "What I saw in my rambles", H T Higginson, 1890 — Linenhall Library)

the dreadful journey twenty years previously through a fierce rain storm in open horse-drawn coaches, the contrast was unbelievable. And meanwhile, the Newcastle party having dined lightly in the Slieve Donard Hotel was taken for a drive through the Mournes by Norton & Company's Car Service from Kilkeel. No doubt their journey included a visit to the Silent Valley area where the great water schemes of the Belfast Water Commissioners were beginning to take shape; and the Chamber certainly got value for money, for the transportation for one-hundred-and-fourteen people around the Mournes for three hours cost only £11:8s:0d. Fares were also keen on the Giant's Causeway and Portrush Tramway Company's system, for the Chamber had a bill for only £9:13s:9d for the transport of one-hundred-and-fifty-five people there and back.

When the delegates had all gone home the administration had to be tidied up and the bills paid; and interesting reading those bills make today. For four-hundred-and-fifty lunches at the Harbour Office on the two days of the business sessions the Chamber paid £56:2s:6d. And at these lunches the delegates got through thirty-six bottles of whiskey at 4s:5d each and forty-four bottles of claret at 2s:0d each. The staff of the Harbour Office also had to be looked after; and amongst the papers preserved to this day is a note to Mr Vance, the Sub-Treasurer of the Chamber, from Lloyd Patterson explaining that each of the porters had been given 5s:0d; the three cleaners 6s:0d each; and Mrs Young, the office-keeper, 12s:0d; and that *"they all appeared well satisfied"*! There can be no doubt either that the diners at the Chamber banquet were well satisfied, for they got through almost two-hundred bottles of champagne at 7s:0d a bottle; eighty-four siphons of soda water at 5d each; forty-seven bottles of hock at 3s:9d a bottle; twenty-six bottles of sherry at 2s:6d a bottle; and five-hundred-and-fifty cigars at a total cost of under £13. The drink was supplied by Lyle & Kinahan, whose total bill was £89:15s:3d; and the smoking materials by E & W Pim of the Antrim Road, whose bill was £13:3s:5d, including the Swan Vestas! William H Drennan, Electrical Engineer and Contractor of 22 Wellington Place, who had installed electric lighting in the Chamber offices a few months previously, was responsible for the temporary lighting at the Exhibition Hall; and his bill was £2:10s:0d. The string band of the Royal Irish Rifles had £6:10s:0d and the Corps of Commissionaires 3s:6d! But the most incredible account of all was that for the ten-course dinner in the Exhibition Hall: for the three-hundred-and-forty dinners, the Chamber paid £178:10s:0d or 10s:6d a head!

Undoubtedly the chief architect of this prestigious occasion for Belfast and its Chamber of Commerce was the remarkable Robert Lloyd Patterson. This was the culmination of almost forty years of continuous service to the Chamber, a unique contribution recognised in a unique way three years later when Patterson was knighted specifically for his conspicuous services to the Chamber. The honour was conferred by the Earl of Cadogan during a farewell visit to Belfast in August 1902 as he laid down the seals of the Lord Lieutenancy of Ireland. The new knight continued to work for the Chamber for the remainder of his life; and his first action following his award was to present the Chamber with an engraving of Luke Field's portrait of King Edward VII. Five years earlier his colleagues in the Chamber had conferred on him the highest honour that was at their own command — the Honorary Life Membership instituted in November

The Giant's Causeway Tramway opened in 1883 and used by delegates to the Associated Chambers of Commerce conference in Belfast in 1899. (From the Welch Collection — Ulster Museum.)

1896 on the proposition of Henry Incledon Johns, nephew of Alexander Johns, seconded by John Burke, the man who was unhappy about the Chamber's having become involved in the Home Rule controversies in 1886 and 1893. Patterson was the second person to be honoured in that way, the first being the 1st Marquis of Dufferin & Ava who returned to Ulster in 1896 after a most distinguished career in the diplomatic service and is commemorated to this day by a statue in the grounds of Belfast City Hall. The Chamber's highest award was also conferred on its Past-President, the 6th Marquis of Londonderry when he became Postmaster General in 1900. To mark its award to Lloyd Patterson, the Chamber commissioned and gave him a magnificent life-size portrait in oils by J Haynes Williams, which now hangs in the Ulster Museum as part of the Patterson Collection. The other works in that collection had been acquired over the years by Patterson and possibly by his father; and they comprised some one-hundred-and-thirty paintings, prints, drawings, and bronzes. After the expiry of Mrs Patterson's life interest in the mid-1920's, this collection together with an endowment of £6,000 became the property of the Ulster Museum, which was then still housed in 7 College Square North — a fitting reminder that business people such as Lloyd Patterson and his father had from the establishment of the Belfast Natural History Society in 1821 been a major influence in the exploration of Nature, the stimulation of the arts, and the preservation of the past.

Lloyd Patterson was in the news again in 1903 when the Chamber decided that a paper on the linen industry which he had read at annual meetings of the British Association in Belfast in the previous year should be reproduced and circulated to Chamber members as an appendix to the annual report. James Wilson, who had qualified as a mining engineer early in life, was then in the Presidential chair of the Chamber; and it was he who had to deal with a delicate situation in March 1903 when the Chamber was threatening to censure Past-President John Young of Ballymena, Chairman of the Northern Counties Railway, for selling the company to the Midland Railway. In the end, however, Young was able to convince the Chamber that this was a sensible move for the Province as well as for him and his shareholders. And as this delicate matter was resolved there was another reminder of the importance of the mineral-water industry in Ulster as Patrick Dempsey of the Belfast Mineral Water Company and Joseph McGinley of McKenna & McGinley were admitted, to join the representatives of Cantrell & Cochrane and several other manufacturers in the

Two the the greatest figures in the history of the Chamber.

Sir Robert Lloyd Patterson FLS (1836-1906), President 1880 and 1895, Hon Secretary 1889-1896, Hon Auditor 1875-1889 and 1900-1906, organiser of annual meetings of Associated Chambers of Commerce in the United Kingdom in Belfast 1879 and 1899. Business interest: linen.

(From a portrait by J Haynes Williams — Ulster Museum.)

Rt Hon Sir Thomas Sinclair MA (1836-1906), President 1876 and 1902, first Chairman of Convocation of Queen's University Belfast, guiding hand on politico-commercial matters in the Chamber 1883, 1893, and 1912. Business interest: bacon curing and provisions, Tomb Street.

(From a portrait by Frank McKelvey — Ulster Museum.)

Chamber. And there was a reminder too that public facilities for commercial education were still grossly inadequate, which was the reason for the Chamber's entering into the business of encouraging home study and staging examinations in its offices under the Commercial Education Scheme of the London Chamber.

This instance of co-operation with the London Chamber was mirrored by many instances of continued co-operation with the Chambers in the South of Ireland as well as in Newry and Londonderry. In May 1904, for example, the Chamber agreed to support the Newry Chamber in its campaign to have a railway line laid from that town to Tynan in County Armagh; and in the previous month the Belfast delegation gave strong support to the Duke of Abercorn when at a meeting of the Associated Chambers in London he argued on behalf of the Londonderry Chamber for the continued use of Lough Foyle as a port of call for steamers in the Canadian trade. Shortly afterwards, the Belfast Chamber had its own very personal problem, when the President of the time, Walter H Wilson, William Pirrie's very able lieutenant at the Queen's Island died in office; and was replaced by the Senior Vice-President Alex Cooke. Earlier that year the Chamber's third Honorary Life Member, Sir James Musgrave, had also died — eleven days after receiving his award.

It was during Alex Cooke's Presidency that a determined effort was made to amalgamate the Chamber and the Commercial Newsroom. Though there was some overlap in membership many members of the Chamber were not members of the Newsroom; and the proposition was that if there were sufficient support the benefits of both could be made available for a joint membership subscription of £2:2s:0d a year, as opposed to the current £2:5s:0d for the Newsroom alone and £1 for the Chamber. But the scheme perished through lack of support amongst Chamber members, who at that time numbered almost three-hundred. Soon, however, they would have two important additions to their number in the persons of the Duke of Abercorn from Baronscourt and E C Herdman from Sion Mills.

By November 1905 the Chamber was echoing the first expressions of concern about national defence; and Adam Duffin proposed that the members *"express their gratitude to Field Marshall Earl Roberts for the timely and weighty warning as to the condition of the Army which by his recent speech before the London Chamber of Commerce he has addressed to the nation. The Chamber ardently desirous of the preservation of peace and convinced that this end can be obtained only by adequate preparation for war, represents to His Majesty's Government the urgent necessity for providing the country with an army sufficiently powerful to defend these islands against invasion and to repel aggression on the distant frontiers of the Empire".* Inevitably the resolution was seconded by Captain Fred H Crawford, who would become famous or notorious nine years later as the organiser of the gun-running for the original Ulster Volunteer Force. Crawford had a sure sense of the patriotic occasion; and in a quite incredible way turned up at Chamber meetings only when issues of patriotism, loyalty, and politics were in the air.

The year 1906 was notable for the death of Sir Robert Lloyd Patterson, which occurred at the end of January. In the middle of the previous year, the other surviving member of the old office team of the 1880s and the 1890s — Samuel Vance's son Robert, the Sub-Treasurer — had also passed on; and the Chamber had decided to amalgamate the offices of Secretary and Sub-Treasurer, giving W J P Wilson a minor increase in salary in token of the change. But as the faithful servants of the past withdrew behind the veil, a new face was moving towards the "engine-room" of the Chamber: he was David McKee, a director of the Belfast Banking Company, who first came to prominence in 1804 during the negotiations with the proprietors of the Commercial Buildings Ltd about a possible basis of amalgamating the Chamber and the Newsroom. Succeeding Lloyd Patterson as Honorary Auditor in 1905, he would in due course become Honorary Treasurer and Financial Adviser for fourteen years and Chairman of the Commercial Education Committee for nineteen years, thus making one of the most significant contributions in the entire history of the Chamber. He would not, however, serve the Chamber in the office of President; and that almost certainly was his own choice, for he was deeply respected by his colleagues.

In the year that David McKee took over the chairmanship of the Commercial Education Committee, the Chamber had an outstanding President in the person of the 9th Earl of Shaftesbury. This hard working nobleman who lived in Belfast Castle on the lower reaches of the Cavehill was a son of Harriet, the daughter of the 3rd Marquis of Donegall; and it was his father's marriage that had united the Donegall and Shaftesbury estates, since Lord Donegall's sole male heir had died at the age of twenty-five. In his year as President of the Chamber, Shaftesbury was most attentive to the business of the organisation and seldom missed a meeting, even though he was

Lord Mayor of Belfast in the same year. In the following year he became the first Chancellor of Queen's University; and his public service continued through to the 1930's when he donated Belfast Castle and its grounds — the last ancestral seat of the Donegalls and the Shaftesburys in the North of Ireland — to the Corporation and people of Belfast. Built in 1870, the Castle had been another of the venues visited by many of the delegates to the 1899 meeting of the Association of Chambers in Belfast, when the Earl and Countess of Shaftesbury had given a garden party on the Friday afternoon for those who were able to stay beyond the official programme, which ended on the Thursday.

Shaftesbury's year in office in the Chamber coincided with a recurrence of serious labour troubles in the city, which led to the establishment of the Belfast Employers Protection Association with W J P Wilson, the Secretary of the Chamber, taking on the secretarial role. Matters came to a head at the end of July when the Chamber discussed a major strike that was then taking place amongst dockers and carters in the city, with the fiery labour leader, Jim Larkin, addressing meetings of up to twenty-thousand men from the Custom House steps. A member of the Chamber referred in a letter to *"the prevalence of mob law throughout the city"*; and called upon the Chamber *"to take action to urge upon the authorities the necessity for promptly bringing back the city to a state of order"*. The Secretary of the Chamber read a draft memorial that the Employers Protection Association was proposing to send to the Lord Lieutenant, protesting about the prevalence of illegal picketing, the destruction of property, and the widespread use of threats and violence by the dockers and carters. The Chamber was divided on whether to be associated with this memorial; and the discussion was adjourned for two days to allow tempers to cool. Nevertheless the Irish News on the day following the first discussion in the Chamber carried a story that the employers' organisation was advocating the introduction of Martial Law. This was strongly repudiated when the Chamber met again on 31 July 1907; and there was also an unsuccessful witch-hunt aimed at establishing the identity of the person who had talked to the newspapers. In the end, however, the tension subsided; and the only carry-over was that the Belfast Chamber tabled a motion at that year's meeting of the Associated Chambers, calling for a re-definition of "peaceful picketing" under the Trades Disputes Act.

When Sir Charles Brett, grandson of the Charles Brett of 1783, took up the Presidency of the Chamber in the spring of 1908, he was only the third person in history to have been knighted before he attained the office. Yet the offical record of the Presidency, inscribed in letters of gold on two large boards in the offices of the Chamber would indicate that Brett had ten predecessors entitled to use the epithet "Sir" at the time that they were President of the Chamber. The explanation is that the first of the two boards — or "tablets" as they were called at the time — was not presented to the Chamber until 1898, though it was to be used for the names of Presidents going back to 1849. The second board would not be presented to the Chamber until 1926, when H O Lanyon's old friend, Frederick L Heyn, noticed that the original board was filled; and offered to provide an identical one to take the names from 1925 onwards. This all means that after 1898 someone had to dig out the names of the Presidents stretching back to 1849 and have them inscribed on Lanyon's "tablet"; and that that someone was responsible, accidentally or deliberately, for recording the names in the style which the people concerned ultimately attained, whether in respect of knighthoods or other public honours. To sort out the matter in 1983 was not an easy task; but the result is shown in an Appendix to the present work which records the names of the Presidents of the Chamber over the two hundred years of its history in the style and title which they possessed and used at the time that they respectively occupied the office. A notable absentee from the list is Sir James Henderson of the News Letter, who worked closely with the Chamber during his year as Lord Mayor of the city and made many other contributions over the years, but never seemed to become involved with sufficient intensity to take him to the top office in that particular field.

Sir Charles Brett's year as President was a busy one. The new projects included a campaign spearheaded by a Mr Hartford Montgomery for the introduction of depreciation allowances into the taxation system; the establishment of a Scholarship Fund in support of commercial education; and the renewal of discussions with Queen's about the establishment of a Faculty of Commerce. The discussions on commercial education took place in the context of the upgrading of Queen's from the status of a College of the Royal University of Ireland to that of an Independent University; and the Chamber felt that progress was being made with the commissioners responsible for drafting the statutes of the new institution. However there was deep disappointment when it emerged in June 1909 that the statutes made no provision for commercial education; and the Chamber, under its new President George S Clark of the ship building family, registered a strong protest with the University authorities. Aided no doubt by the involvement of Past-President Sir Charles Brett in the Senate, the Chamber's persistence was eventually rewarded in June 1910 by a favourable decision on the part of the University authorities.

Meanwhile the President for 1909/10, George S Clark, had to deal with national as well as local issues; for there were doubts throughout the Chamber of Commerce movement about the adequacy of the defence policy of Herbert H Asquith's Liberal Government which had come into power in April 1908. These doubts were apparent in a Chamber discussion on 3 March 1909, which led to the submission of a resolution to the Prime Minister and the First Lord of the Admiralty: *"The Council of Belfast Chamber of Commerce recognising that safety of the Empire is the paramount question for the consideration of the nation pledges itself to support His Majesty's Government in any arrangements that they may make for the protection of the Empire's trade and commerce by the maintenance undisputed and indisputable of Great Britain's supremacy on the seas against any foreign combination"*. And the subject was on the agenda again at the April meeting of the Council when the angle discussed was whether the Chamber should ask the Lord Mayor to organise a public meeting *"to impress on Her Majesty's Government the importance of maintaining the Naval supremacy of the Empire"*. George S Clark was in favour of this; and he had support from Lord Londonderry and R H S Reade. But there was strong opposition from Adam Duffin, H M Pollock, Sir Charles Brett, and David McKee, who thought that *"such intervention might be regarded as inspired by political motives and so prejudiciously affect the Chamber's interest"*. In the end the Chamber decided to take no further action on the matter in the meantime; and the same was their reaction when they were pressed to attend a meeting in London *"to consider the advisability of bringing together in conference the principal Chambers of Commerce of the United Kingdom and Germany in the discussion of the increasing expenditure in both countries on armaments with a view to its reduction"*.

But soon the Chamber had a subject nearer home to occupy its attention: This was the Irish Land Bill, which was discussed at length in a series of meetings in May and June 1909. Yet by the autumn, they were back to defence; for the London Chamber of Commerce was encouraging Chambers throughout the United Kingdom to make representations to the Government on the strength of the Navy. The clouds of war were gathering for the nation: but Ulster first had its own crisis to endure.

As the world crunched forward to a disaster of incredible magnitude, King Edward VII died; and the Chamber in Belfast, under the Presidency of John Rogers, Chairman of the Brookfield Linen Company, met to record its thankfulness for *"the commanding qualities of heart and mind which so abundantly and advantageously characterised his illustrious rule"*. The Chamber's letter of sympathy to Queen Alexandra and to the new King George was acknowledged by Winston S Churchill, who had just become Home Secretary.

Meanwhile the Chamber was attending to routine business in the interests of its members. There was support for Murray & Sons Ltd, the tobacco manufacturers, when they vigorously opposed a new duty which they described as *"oppressive and unworkable"*. And there was support too for Messrs Cullen Allen & Co when they fought against an embargo on the importation of straw from France. But there was less interest in free trade when the Chamber adopted a motion in favour of Imperial Preference by the establishment of an Empire Trade Mark, Fred Crawford (who had then become a major) being strategically on hand to second the resolution!

In the midst of his other duties in the Chamber, David McKee had at this time become the new champion of the campaign for the establishment of uniform time throughout the United Kingdom. He was the exponent too of daylight saving by changing the clock; and he would ultimately be successful on both issues, after many disappointments and much frustration. It was his committee too that brought forward a resolution in 1909 recording *"profound dissatisfaction with the present administration of the intermediate education system in Ireland, more especially with its entire failure to provide a scheme of commercial education suited for boys intent for a commercial career"*.

But it was R Kyle Knox who in July 1910 succeeded in interesting the Chamber in the then current debate about Agricultural Organisation. In consequence, the Chamber issued a statement which contained a number of memorable thoughts: *"Recognising that an improvement in the business methods of Irish farmers must increase their consuming powers and so benefit not only agriculture but also all other interests in the country, and having regard to the fact that agricultural co-operation is the form of combination more suitable for farmers and is widely adopted by the Continental competitors with Irish farmers in the British markets, the Council are of the opinion that a portion of the funds provided by Government for the purposes of developing the farming industry in Ireland may properly be devoted to the instruction of farmers in the principles and details of agricultural co-operative organisations. The Council conceives it to be altogether proper and legitimate that public monies so provided should be applied through any voluntary association not trading for profit which is prepared to do the special work, and in this connection they heartily commend the good work done by the Irish Agricultural Organisation Society".* And the Chamber was equally forthright in a campaign to have a proper balance maintained in public expenditure as between the railways and the canals.

Coincidentally there was a strong link between agricultural co-operation and the next President of the Chamber, John Milne Barbour: his brother Harold had been a generous supporter of the co-operative movement from its earliest days and would ultimately become the first President of UAOS, the post-1922 organisation of farmer co-operatives in the new state of Northern Ireland. And as John Milne Barbour came to the Presidential chair of the Chamber, its links with the organisations of the linen industry were more securely forged as a result of an agreement that the Secretary of the Chamber would also take up the secretaryships of the Flax Supply Association, the Flax Spinners' Association, the Linen Merchants' Association, and the Power-Loom Manufacturers' Association. That in turn gave rise to the necessity for a larger suite of offices that would serve the needs both of the Chamber and of the trade associations; and the problem was remitted to a small committee headed by David McKee. The answer that emerged was that the Chamber should move from its longtime home in the Commercial Buildings in Waring Street to an upper floor of the imposing Scottish Provident Building in Donegall Sqare West, overlooking the magnificent new City Hall which had been opened just five years earlier by the Lord Lieutenant, the Earl of Aberdeen. The Scottish Provident Building itself had been built in sections over much the same period as the shell of the City Hall and was finished four years earlier, in 1902.

The move to the new offices took place at the beginning of November 1911; and it was a godsend for the hard-working Secretary, W J P Wilson, who had for some months been operating out of two separate centres. Writing to a publisher in Manchester in January 1912 he expressed himself freely about the impossible life he had been living prior to the move; and of the way in which the whole situation had been eased by the new central office. Unfortunately, however, the pressure that he had been under must have narrowed Wilson's judgement on the important question of historical records; for meticulous as he was about proper recording of current work, he seems to have regarded the vast piles of disordered papers that his predecessors had left behind in the old offices in Waring Street as just so much rubbish. That may be a temptation to anyone moving house or moving office; and Wilson, in a letter of 19 October 1911 to a Mr H Perkin in York — probably a relative of Samuel Vance, the

Scottish Provident Building, Donegall Square West, opened 1902, home of the Chamber of Commerce from 1912-1966. (From R M Young — Linenhall Library.)

long-serving Secretary of the second-half of the 19th Century, and his son Robert, the Sub-Treasurer — showed that he had succumbed:

"There is a pile of old letter and account books here which belong to Mr Vance and his father. What is to be done with them? So far as I know they are absolutely useless, and this is the opinion of Mr MacIlwaine of Carson & McDowell, to whom I spoke on the subject today. Shall I give them to the flames or the Sexton, or shall I send them on to you? Please let me know at once as we move on Tuesday next, and I cannot take them with me!"

Let it not happen again! There is a Public Records Office in Balmoral Avenue!

But if W J P Wilson was insensitive to the historic value of the old accounts and letter-books of his predecessors in October 1911 he must surely have changed his ground in the course of the next twelve months as he found himself at the very centre of history-making. Even before political drama returned to the Chamber scene in the Spring of 1912, there were great issues in the air; and the Chamber was fortunate to be led at that time by a President of such ability as John Milne Barbour, whose career would fully blossom ten years later. A strike by railwaymen in September 1911 resulted in violence, intimidation, and secondary picketing; and the Chamber called on the

Government to appoint a commission to review the workings of the Trade Disputes Act of 1906, which in their opinion had *"by authorising peaceful picketing and relieving trade unions from responsibility for their acts, made possible such intimidation, violence, and interference"*. The Chamber also engaged in strong Parliamentary lobbying in connection with a National Insurance Bill, culminating in a trip to London by four prominent members accompanied by the Secretary; and there they had meetings both with Sir Edward Carson, leader of the Irish Unionists since February 1910, and with John Redmond, leader of the Irish Nationalists. Next it was back to the uniform-time issue, with the help of the Earl of Shaftesbury prompted by David McKee. Now, however, that subject had taken on an Irish political dimension; for there were public representatives in the South of Ireland who felt that the elimination of the time difference with Britain would strengthen the ties with the larger island at a time when they would have preferred to see them loosened. The Dublin Chamber of Commerce, however, continued to be strongly in favour of uniform time, judging the issue purely in terms of commercial convenience and commonsense.

No doubt the vast majority of members of the Belfast Chamber would have argued that it was these same two considerations — commerce and commonsense — that caused them to become involved to the hilt in the Ulster Crisis of 1912, just as they had become involved in 1886 and 1893. The origin of the crisis was exactly the same as before: a Liberal Government able to remain in office only with the support of the Irish Nationalists was prepared to pay the price of its power — by introducing a third Home Rule Bill, giving a substantial degree of legislative independence to an all-Ireland Parliament in Dublin. But there were two important differences in relation to the earlier crises: the first was that the power of the House of Lords to block leglislation indefinitely had been removed; and the second was that the Unionists in the North were much more organised and determined to resist. Therein lay the tinder of conflagration.

The issue first came before the Council on 19 April 1912, four days after the most swingeing disaster in Belfast's maritime history. As the Council met that day to receive a preliminary report from the Parliamentary and Legal Committee on its examination of the third Home Rule Bill, there was a deep sadness in every heart; for it was only two days earlier that the unbelievable news had reached the city that the greatest ship yet built at the Queen's Island — the TITANIC — had on its maiden voyage from Southampton to New York struck a huge iceberg in mid-Atlantic and sunk in less than three hours, with the loss of almost fifteen-hundred lives. But life had to go on; and the Council's decision on the Home Rule Bill was that it should be remitted to a small group that would subject it to detailed analysis and draft a comprehensive response. This was the course of action which the Secretary had previously planned, in consultation with Thomas Sinclair who was now the most experienced campaigner in the Chamber, being a veteran of 1886 and 1893. Nevertheless it was Adam Duffin rather than Sinclair who prepared the first draft of the Chamber response; and that provided a basis for intense discussion in committee throughout the month of May. Then on 3 June there was a special meeting of the Council to consider the committee's report, with the President of the time, Robert A Mitchell LL B, in the chair. As anticipated by Wilson and Sinclair, the Council was divided on the matter because its membership included three moderate Home Rulers — John Burke, Samuel Gibson, and Archibald Savage, the representative of the Chemists' Association. The debate was therefore rather tense as Burke argued, first, for consideration of the report to be deferred for a month; and, later, for it to be declared *ultra vires*. In the end the President conceded that more time should be given; and the meeting was adjourned for three days.

When the Council re-assembled on 6 June, it did not take long to complete the business. The President moved the adoption of the report and R E Herdman seconded. John Burke again held that the report was *ultra vires;* and the President ruled against him, a decision which Burke accepted. Burke then moved an amendment that a large part of the report be deleted; and Samuel Gibson seconded. The amendment was put to the meeting and was defeated by eighteen votes to two. The report was therefore adopted for submission to a meeting of the entire Chamber in the Ulster Minor Hall on Tuesday 11 June 1912.

This historic occasion attracted *"a numerous attendance"*. In the absence of the President through illness, the chair was taken by the Senior Vice-President, George Herbert Ewart, brother of Sir William Quartus Ewart; and he was supported on the platform by a bevy of eleven Past-Presidents marshalled by Wilson, the Secretary. It was Wilson too who began the proceedings by reading the notice convening the meeting, and laying on the table the report of the Council on the Government of Ireland Bill. After some sharp exchanges about the permitted length of speeches and about whether the report could be taken as read, G H Ewart moved and J Milne Barbour seconded: *"That the Report of the Council on the Government of Ireland Bill now submitted be received and adopted; that it be embodied in a petition to be submitted to the House of Commons; that copies of it be sent to the Chambers of Commerce, Members of Parliament, and the Press; and that the Council be and are hereby authorised to take such other steps as they deem advisable regarding it"*. John Burke then moved an amendment: *"that as the report presented by the Council is a political and religious pronouncement, and not a report...dealing with the advancement of the commerce and manufacture of Belfast and its neighbourhood, it be sent back to the Council for amendment"*. The Chairman ruled that that was unacceptable as an amendment since it was a direct negative; and John Burke then moved that the first three pages of the report be deleted. This was seconded by Archibald Savage and supported by Martin Burke. The amendment was defeated by one-hundred-and-forty-six votes to three; but Archibald Savage nevertheless moved a further amendment proposing the deletion of a particular paragraph of the report. This was seconded by Martin Burke; but again, it attracted only three votes. Next Martin Burke moved that a full page of the report be deleted and John Burke seconded; but this too was defeated by essentially the same majority. At that moment the bold Major Fred H Crawford stepped forward and proposed *"that the question be now put";* and he was supported by a Mr W R A Jefferson. Accordingly the question was then put; and the report was adopted by one-hundred-and-thirty-seven votes to three.

As the members of the Chamber filed out of the hall Wilson was dispatching telegrams to the editors of newspapers in every corner of the British Isles, having previously supplied them with embargoed copies of the Council's report and indicated his intention to communicate the result of the meeting as soon as it was known. The consequence was that the Chamber's decision featured on the front page of many newspapers on the following day; and the great publicity campaign had begun. Next Wilson sent a parcel of at least fifty copies of the report to every Chamber of Commerce in the British Isles; and asked them to note its contents and lend their support, on account of *"the commercial and financial aspects of the measure, and its probable effects, if passed, on our trading and manufacturing interests"*. And the letter-book for 1912 bulges with the vast correspondence that ensued, as Members of Parliament and members of Chambers from every corner of the British Isles raised questions or expressed their support. W J P Wilson was now at the centre of history; and he really must have burned the midnight oil.

But there was more to come; for within days the idea had crystallised that as in 1893 the Chamber should seek the opportunity of putting its views direct to the Prime Minister by way of a delegation. That decision was ratified by the Council on the same day as Walter F Clokey of W F Clokey & Co and S Hall Thompson of Lindsay Thompson & Co were admitted to membership — 24 June 1912 — and W J P Wilson was immediately involved in a welter of communication, both by letter and by telegram. There was no certainty that Asquith would agree to a meeting; but as Wilson remarked in a letter to Past-President Robert Thompson MP who was advising on procedure: *"Our objective in seeking an interview with the Prime Minister is to secure additional publicity for the Chamber's report on the Home Rule Bill; and either his willingness or his refusal to receive a deputation would serve that purpose"*. In the event there was no need for publicity for a rebuff; for Asquith did agree to see them, on the strength of a personal approach from three of the Belfast MPs — Robert Thompson, James Chambers, and Robert McMordie (who was also Lord Mayor at the time). To fit in with other London business of one of the key members of the Ulster delegation, Thomas Sinclair, the meeting was arranged for Wednesday 10 July at 4.30 pm in the Prime Minister's room at the House of Commons; and Robert Thompson invited the group to join him for a working lunch at the Constitutional Club in Northumberland Avenue immediately beforehand.

The arrangements in London were finalised only four days before the meeting was due to take place; and a subsequent telegram from Robert Thompson to the Chamber offices in Belfast signalled the beginning of a most stressful period for the Secretary, who was already beleaguered by the volume of correspondence arising from the earlier circulation of the Chamber report. He had the task of contacting fifteen or sixteen potential members of the delegation, mostly Past-Presidents, to get them to attend a briefing meeting in Belfast on 9 July if possible; and then to help them get to London by the following forenoon for a rendezvous with Robert Thompson over lunch and the meeting with Asquith in the late afternoon. Even with communications as they are today that would be quite a formidable task; but Wilson had to be content with letters and telegrams, overnight boats and trains. The telephone that was now

The coming of the motor car: De Dion 6hp Phaeton, 1901/2.
(Photo from Ulster Folk & Transport Museum.)

installed in his office seems to have been of limited use both because of very restricted telephone ownership and of technical faults. For example it was only a fortnight earlier that the Chamber had complained to the Head Postmaster about the telephone service between Belfast and Dublin: *"Not only is it with great difficulty that connection between the cities is obtained, but owing presumably to the state of the wires, communications are frequently inaudible"*!

But apart altogether from the limitations of the means of communications available to him, Wilson's task was complicated by the dispersal of his forces. John Milne Barbour was on the Continent on business; and there were frantic telegrams to a hotel in Paris, before he was finally tracked down at Courtrai in Belgium — on the day before the historic meeting in London. Yorkshire-born John Greenhill, President in 1893/94, was now living in Londonderry as managing director of the Ulster Chemical Manure Company; and he had to be contacted there. Gustav Wolff and Dr R Kyle Knox were already in London. So too were Lord Londonderry and Lord Shaftesbury; and they were both slow to respond to Wilson's telegrams. And then there were last-minute approaches to be made to three members who were not Past-Presidents but were brought in because they had particular points to make and also because the size of the delegation was in danger of falling below the eighteen to twenty that were considered necessary for maximum publicity. The three were R Garrett Campbell of Henry Campbell & Co Ltd; W J Hurst from Ballynahinch, who had been involved in 1893; and Bangor-born Hugh MacDowell Pollock, who was living at Balloo House at

Killinchy and would later become a key figure in the Chamber and in public life generally. And finally Wilson had to get invitations off to the editors of the Daily Mail, the Morning Post, and the Daily Telegraph, who would be permitted to send representatives to accompany the Ulster delegation into the Prime Minister's room.

On the day, it all went well despite the strains placed on Wilson during the brief preparatory period. And the delegation which lawyer Robert Mitchell, the President, led into the Prime Minister's room that day was again a formidable one: in addition to those already mentioned it almost certainly included R H S Reade, F L Heyn, Alex Cooke, John Young from Ballymena, John Rogers, George S Clark, and Sir William Crawford, together with the three MPs who had made the initial approach. Again the economic and commercial case against Home Rule was put to a Liberal Prime Minister; and again he listened carefully. Afterwards the delegation had a meeting with Conservative leaders including Bonar Law and Lord Landsdowne; and that provided another opportunity for publicity. So too did the Prime Minister's decision to issue a statement — a statement which the Chamber, as in 1893, attempted to refute point by point in another printed document which also contained edited versions of their submissions to Mr Asquith and his response. This in turn was circulated by the thousand to Chambers of Commerce, public representatives, and interested individuals in every corner of the British Isles, including the editors of the Times, the Daily Telegraph, the Scotsman, and the Glasgow Herald.

But as these events unfolded they were superceded by an outburst of political and sectarian bitterness in Belfast. As a foolish consequence of a particularly reprehensible fracas at Castledawson involving an attack on a party of Sunday-school children from Whitehouse, there were wholesale ejections of Catholic workers from Harland & Wolff — and the Chamber appealed for calm:

"The Council of the Belfast Chamber of Commerce, while recognising the serious aggravation which has brought about the recent unfortunate industrial unrest in one district of our city, view with sincere regret the molestation to which certain employees in local industries have been subjected. The Council would earnestly appeal to the good sense which has always characterised the working people of Belfast, and urge that in the interests of the common wellbeing of the community all persons, irrespective of their creed or political opinions, who are willing to work should be allowed to do so without interference".

And the Chamber itself had to exercise calm when Wilson had a letter from Mr Dunwoody, the Secretary of the Association of Chambers, saying that the President of the Association felt that it would not be in accordance with their rules for his executive to take any action on the report of the Belfast Chamber on the Government of Ireland Bill. Nevertheless individual Chambers both in England and in Scotland continued to express their support.

In the latter part of the year, as the recently-formed Chamber of Trade in Belfast under its first President, Mr McAlery, sought the assistance of the Chamber of Commerce in securing "early closing" of retail outlets (10.30 pm on Saturdays and 8 pm on weekdays!), the Home Rule Bill made its way through the House of Commons, with the combined support of the Liberals and the Irish Nationalists; but when it came to the House of Lords in January 1913 it was defeated by a majority of almost five to one. However in the light of an earlier constitutional change, the power of the Lords to block the Bill could be sustained only for a limited period, which meant that it could become law in the autumn of 1914. In the meantime there were dramatic events in Ulster that are outside the scope of the present work, save to note that it was the Chamber's most accomplished draughtsman, Thomas Sinclair, that wrote the Ulster Covenant; and the Chamber's most Imperial martinet, Fred Crawford, that effected the gun-running. And then, on the brink of disaster and after the failure of attempts to negotiate an exclusion for the North-Eastern counties, Ulster was saved from a strange kind of civil war by the onset of a conflict of world dimensions. A chain reaction that began with the assassination of a Central European archduke in Sarajevo on 28 June led to a German invasion of Belgium on 3 August; and on the following day the British Empire was sucked into the great conflagration that had long been feared. The "war to end wars" had begun; the world would be changed; and many thousands of Ulster's brightest and best and of their fellow countrymen from the South of Ireland would be sacrificed in the mud and the blood of France and Flanders.

As the world went over the brink, the Chamber was led by Robert Ernest Herdman, managing director of Henry Matier & Co Ltd of Belfast and cousin of the Herdmans of Sion Mills, where the family's main interest in linen was based then as now. It was R E Herdman too who as Senior Vice-President had chaired an important meeting in April 1913 when the Chamber had intervened publicly in a dispute between the Belfast Corporation and the Harbour Commissioners about a site for the erection of "an electric light and power station" — the Harbour Power Station as it became. In a statement couched in the most diplomatic terms, the Chamber urged the Corporation and the Commissioners to sink their differences in the interest of securing this much-needed development quickly.

But by the third week in August 1914 Herdman was presiding at meetings where the sole item on the agenda was "The situation created by the European War"; and in the succeeding years till the Armistice on 11 November 1918, the Chamber under the leadership of S C Davidson of the Sirocco Works, J H Stirling who was in linen, and H M Pollock whose stature in public affairs was constantly growing, did its best both to further the war effort and to protect the interests of its members. Shipbuilding in Belfast moved into top gear under the control of Lord Pirrie (he had been made a baron in 1906), who was appointed Controller-General of Merchant Shipbuilding for the whole of the United Kingdom. Extensive new facilities were added at the Queen's Island; and the workforce increased from fifteen to twenty thousand. The linen industry too had a major part to play as its output was required in increasing amounts not only to replace other fabrics that were less available but also for use in the construction of the light aircraft that grew in strategic and tactical importance as the armies were deadlocked in the mud of Northern France. "The war in the air was won on Belfast wings", said Earl French years afterwards. And for the Chamber itself, it was a constant round of discussions about shipping rates and the coverage of war risks; about the controls which the Government found it necessary to impose on overseas trade; about the possibilities of manufacturing goods that were formerly supplied by Germany and Austria, including aniline dyes (they wondered if they could be made from Irish potato spirit!); and, as the struggle appeared to be moving towards its climax, about the likely problems of the post-war years and the adjustment of industry and commerce to ensure their survival. It was a busy time for the Chamber; and there were disappointments and triumphs.

There was also personal tragedy for individual members of the Chamber, as fathers, sons, and brothers were killed on and above the battlefields of France and Belgium, Gallipoli, Palestine and Mesopotamia, or drowned in the world-wide war at sea. Typical of that personal tragedy and mirrored in many thousands of Ulster homes was the loss of S C Davidson's son James Samuel, who had been active in the Chamber before the war and must have been much in his father's mind as the elder Davidson occupied the Presidential chair in 1915 and in the early months of the following year. In the Battle of the Somme in the first few days of July 1916, the Davidson son and heir — a captain in the Machine-Gun Company of the 13th Battalion of the Royal Irish Rifles in the 36th (Ulster) Division — made the supreme sacrifice with five-thousand-five-hundred of his fellow Ulstermen. And the severity of that scar would never quite be erased from the face of Ulster. When the news reached Belfast and the telegram boys had finished bringing their dreaded messages to those thousands of Ulster homes, the Lord Mayor called a day of mourning; and the business life of the city stood still for five brief minutes of deep pathos.

But the Chamber pressed on, with scarcely a reference to the tragedy though it must have been deeply felt. And within six weeks there was a triumph to record, for the Government had at last acceded to the long-standing campaign of Chambers of Commerce throughout Ireland for the introduction of uniform time — Greenwich Mean Time as it became known — and David McKee, who had taken up the baton early in the century, had a deep satisfaction as the President (James Stirling), proposed and he himself seconded a resolution of thanks to Sir Edward Carson who had helped to ease the Time (Ireland) Bill through the House of Commons: *"We commend the sagacity and resolute courage with which Sir Edward successfully confronted the unreasoning opposition of a parliamentary coterie, which, in defiance of the express wish of the non-political community in Ireland, deliberately sought to defeat the enactment of a reform, admittedly advantageous to the whole United Kingdom, and consistently advocated by this Chamber for upwards of 60 years"*. At last the absurdity of a twenty-five minute difference in time between Britain and Ireland had been removed; and no longer would vessels plying across the Irish Sea have to be equipped with clocks that had two minute-hands.

Throughout the war, the Chamber had maintained its link with the Association of Chambers of Commerce in the United Kingdom; and Robert Thompson MP had taken up a place on the Council of the Association as a representative of the Belfast Chamber. Later that place would be taken by David Douglas Reid, who when he was appointed to the Executive of the Association in 1916 was living at 1 New Square, Lincoln's Inn, London. Reid was educated at Queen's College Belfast and the University of Oxford; and he would become the Westminster MP for East Down, serving from December 1918 till his death in 1939. He would become President of the Chamber in 1932/33; and be knighted in 1936. But as he became involved in the Association of Chambers in 1916, the organisation was discussing the possibilities of raising an investment fund of £30,000 to provide future income. In January 1917, David McKee as Honorary Treasurer would recommend that the Belfast Chamber should subscribe a hundred guineas towards that fund; and this would be agreed.

By that time David McKee had yet another role in the Chamber: he was the chief proponent of the introduction of Summer Time in the interests of daylight saving. On every occasion when it seemed that there might be an opportunity of discussing this in the Council of the Chamber, he would walk round from the head office of the Belfast Banking Company in the Old Exchange Building to the offices of the Chamber in the Scottish Provident Building with a carefully typed resolution in his pocket; and he would get the President to propose it, with the author taking the less conspicuous role of seconder. That was the route by which the Council came out strongly on the subject on 22 November 1916: *"The Council of Belfast Chamber of Commerce having carefully inquired into the effect generally of the Summer Time Act 1916 are satisfied that, from every commercial point of view, it cannot but be regarded as satisfactory. The additional hour of natural light in the evening provided thereby has resulted in material curtailment of the use of artificial luminants and consequent reduced expenditure; it has enabled clerical staffs, shop assistants, and industrial workers to enjoy a longer evening period in the open air, presumably with advantage to health; while the commencement of work at the same clock time although not in consonance with the real sun time has in no way interfered with the conduct of industry. Speaking on behalf of the important industrial community the Council are convinced that the continuance of the Summer Time experiment so successfully inaugurated will increasingly contribute to the public welfare".* But the going was not easy and McKee had to become embroiled again in March 1917 when there was strong agitation to prevent the extension of the Summer Time Act to Ireland that year.

By then the Chamber had been plunged again into a greater controversy — the renewal of the Home Rule debate. David Lloyd George as war-time Prime Minister of a National Government acceded to American pressure to make another attempt to settle the Irish question. His thoughts were either that the pre-war Home Rule Act should be applied to twenty-six of the thirty-two Irish counties or that a Convention should be established to enable Irishmen of all political persuasions to hammer out their own solution. Again the Chamber became deeply involved in the debate; and it was noticeable that because of the searing experiences of Thiepval Wood and the Somme and the intensity of feeling about the 1916 Easter Rising in Dublin, opinions in the Chamber had hardened, to the point where public pronouncements were liable to go beyond the economic and commercial aspects which, it had been argued in the past, were properly the concern of the Chamber.

The President asked his Senior Vice-President, H L Garrett, together with J Milne Barbour, George S Clark (who became a baronet later in the year), Adam Duffin, F L Heyn, H I Johns, R Kyle Knox, James Mackie, and J H Stirling to constitute a committee to examine any proposals in detail from an economic and commercial point of view and to bring forward recommendations to the Chamber. One looks in vain for the name of the celebrated Chamber draughtsman of former years, the Rt Hon Thomas Sinclair, in the list of members of the committee; and the explanation is simply that that great scholar and gentleman had died in the year that the war began. The committee, though missing his services, reported to the Council on 15 May 1917; and it was agreed that their view should be adopted for wide circulation throughout the British Isles. Again, therefore, the Chamber was in the business of distributing a document to kindred organisations in Great Britain and to public representatives; and it was, in places, a very forthright document: *"We are firm in our belief that the best service Ulster can render to Ireland is to save her, misled by false national sentiment and ill-considered views of true Irish interests, from losing, either in whole or in part, the full communion of interest and economic life with Great Britain which is secure to her under the Union"*. And it went on to examine the possible economic consequences in some detail and to pass comment on the policy of partition which was then being canvassed: *"The policy of a partition of Ireland would never have been suggested by Unionist Ulster or found support from such a body as this Chamber except as a last resort from a greater calamity...We therefore reiterate our claim to remain in the security of the Union with Great Britain, in reliance on which we have built up our industries, and under which alone Ireland can attain to peace and prosperity"*. Again there was a remarkable contrast with the spirit of the Chamber of Commerce of 1783 and with the attitude of the merchants of Belfast who signed the petition against the Act of Union on 5 February 1800!

Belfast Custom House in the early 1900s. Opened in 1857, this was arguably the best of Sir Charles Lanyon's many architectural contributions to the City. The Chamber of Commerce was involved in a long controversy about the location and purpose of the building.
(From R M Young — Linenhall Library.)

A month after the issue of the latest Chamber document on the Home Rule question, the Council, with H M Pollock in the chair, met to honour three of its oldest and most distinguished members — Sir William Quartus Ewart, Adam Duffin, and Dr R Kyle Knox — by electing them to Honorary Life Membership. At the same time it was decided, on the proposition of David McKee, to extend the Honorary Life Membership to Sir John Newell Jordan, an Ulsterman who had been British Ambassador in Peking and *"whose brilliant diplomatic career had reflected lustre on his native Province"*. But his native Province in June 1917 was again bubbling with turmoil about the likely course of events in Ireland after the war. The latest topic of conversation was the establishment of the Irish Convention, where Irishmen were to be charged with working out their own solution. The President of the Chamber, H M Pollock, reported that he had received a letter from the Prime Minister inviting him to participate in the Convention; and it was unanimously agreed that he should accept.

In that ill-fated forum, Pollock was joined by his Belfast Chamber colleagues, Sir George Clark and the new Lord Londonderry (the 6th Marquis had died in February 1915) and also by the President of the Dublin Chamber. Sir Horace Plunkett, with whom the Belfast Chamber had had extensive dealings in his days as Vice-President of the Department of Agriculture and Technical Instruction, was appointed Chairman of the Convention; and that was no easy task. The discussions rumbled on through the summer, autumn, and winter of 1917; and there was still no sign of a consensus by the time that the Chamber was due to hold its annual meeting in February 1918. It was therefore decided to postpone the meeting indefinitely in order to permit the President, H M Pollock, to continue his work in the Convention. Two months later, when the end of the Convention was still not in sight, the Chamber decided that its Articles of Association should be amended to allow Mr Pollock to continue in office for another full year. But the reality was that the Convention could not reach a consensus whether it continued its discussion for one year, two years, or ten!

Meanwhile on the business front the Chamber had been addressing itself to such diverse subjects as the decimalisation of the coinage (for the umpteenth time); the need for the establishment of a training college for primary teachers in association with Queen's University; the particular problems of the grain and flour trades in the context of war-time restrictions; and the rehabilitation of wounded army officers in civilian employment. The Dublin and Cork Chambers were also thinking about post-war problems; and there was an invitation to the Belfast Chamber to attend a conference of Irish Chambers *"for the purpose of reviewing the position of Irish trade after the war and taking such action as might be thought desirable in the interests of the country"* But it was a sign of the deepening political divisions that Belfast replied *"to the effect that no useful purpose could be served by such a conference at present"*. Shortly afterwards, in August 1918, the Chamber had to note with deep regret the passing of the Rt Hon Robert Thompson DL MP, President in 1901, who had made an immense contribution not only to public life but also to the linen industry through his chairmanship of Lindsay Thompson & Co Ltd.

David McKee continued to be a major influence in the Chamber, though he never accepted its highest office. As Honorary Treasurer he succeeded in getting the annual subscription increased from a pound a head to two guineas from 1 January 1918; and as Chairman of the Commercial Education Committee, he played the major part in having a Bill for the Imporvement of Primary Education in Belfast piloted through the House of Commons, with the support of the Belfast Corporation and the Ulster MP's at Westminster. He was also on hand to congratulate the President of the Chamber, H M Pollock, on his election to the Chairmanship of the Harbour Commissioners in August 1918. He had a positive approach too towards the Association of Chambers; and in the Presidency of H L Garrett, he welcomed the change in the name of the organisation to "The Association of British Chambers of Commerce" — the name by which it is still known. More importantly he did not balk when the subscription to the Association was increased by a factor of two-and-a-half in April 1919, as the organisation raised its activity profile in response to the formation of the Federation of British Industry (later the Confederation) in 1916.

The end of the great world conflict on 11 November 1918 was scarcely noticed in the Chamber, so pre-occupied were its members with postwar adjustment in the economy and the achievement of generally-acceptable political structures in Ireland. But the leadership of the Chamber did turn aside from those issues, in April 1919, to enter into discussions with the Lord Mayor and Corporation about the organisation of a reception for the remnants of the Ulster Division on its belated return from the war. They had time too to talk later that year about the Government's Irish Labour Policy, about which there were alarming rumours; and about the submission of evidence to a Royal Commission that was considering the nationalisation of the coal mines. On a more personal level, James Mackie who was due to become President in February 1920 wrote in June of the preceding year to say that he wished to be relieved because of the death of his nephew and the burden of work arising from the involvement of his company in huge re-construction projects in France and Belgium. And John Milne Barbour who had represented the Chamber on the Senate of Queen's University since 1914 felt that he should give way to Adam Duffin. Duffin would serve in this capacity for the next five years, till his death in 1924 at the age of eighty-three.

For those who don't believe that history repeats itself, it will come as a shock that on 16 October 1919 the Council of the Belfast Chamber, with H L Garrett in the chair, discussed the need for strike ballots in industrial disputes. In consequence they decided to put forward a resolution to the autumn meeting of the Association of British Chamber of Commerce:

"That in the opinion of this Association an amendment of the Law is urgently required such as, while preserving to industrial workers the ultimate right to strike, will render a stoppage of work illegal until, under Government regulations, a ballot has been taken of the Trade's Society or District Branch of the Trade's Society afflicted on the direct issue for or against a strike, and by a majority of the membership of the Society or Branch a vote is given in favour of a strike".

The Secretary reported that this resolution, which had been drawn up by the Parliamentary and Legal Committee of the Chamber, had at first seemed somewhat too strong to the Executive of the Association in London; but that the President of the

Belfast Chamber had corresponded with the President of ABCC and had ultimately secured the inclusion of the item on the agenda.

At the next meeting of the Council, the President reported that he and his junior Vice-President, William McMullan, had attended the quarterly meeting of ABCC in London and had put forward the resolution on strike ballots, with the support of the London Chamber. However there had been moves behind the scene which suggested that the time for pursuing the resolution was inappropriate; and the Belfast delegation had ultimately withdrawn it. Instead they were advised that they should press for a direct amendment of the Trade Disputes Act; and this would be done at the next quarterly meeting.

But by the time that meeting came around, Belfast was pressing not only for the amendment of the Trade Disputes Act, but also for the improvement of the trunk telephone service between Great Britain and Ireland and the withdrawal of all Government controls on industry. *"This Association"*, said one of the Belfast resolutions, *"deprecates the continued interference of the Government in many industries, and strongly urges that all Government control be immediately discontinued, in order that those industries may be reorganised and reconstructed, so as to deal successfully with present conditions"*. And these themes were evident too in successive meetings in Belfast about that time, as the Chamber pressed not only for reduced Government interference but also for reduced Government expenditure and for better management of the expenditure that was undertaken. The serious financial situation of the country was due, said H L Garrett at a meeting on 4 February 1920, to Government failings and, specifically, *"to their utter neglect not only during the war but since its termination to take care to see that they got even reasonable value for their lavish expenditure"*. But there was some disagreement with the general line, as the Lord Mayor was anxious that nothing should be said that would interfere with much needed public expenditure on housing in the city; and the flax-spinners wanted Government control to continue to ensure a fair distribution of limited supplies of raw material. Again some of these points have a familiar ring in the context of the 1980s!

By May 1920, the climax of the Home Rule saga begun in 1886 and continued in 1893, 1912, and 1917 was at hand. Like public bodies and politicians throughout Ireland, the Chamber was confronted with another Government of Ireland Bill which proposed the establishment of two Parliaments in the island and dealt with the financial relationships between them and the Mother Parliament in London. And in the midst of these great events Belfast was for a time denied of its tea because of the absence from the docks of an official tea taster and the consequent inability (or unwillingness) of the Custom and Excise authorities to release stocks. But as soon as that problem was sorted out, it was back to the Government of Ireland Bill! And prominent members of the Chamber played a vital part in the resolution of some of the very complex issues on the financial side. For example Past-Presidents H M Pollock and H L Garrett and Council member S B Quin had a meeting on the subject with Bonar Law, the Conservative leader who would be Prime Minister in October 1922; and Pollock and Quin, together with former Lord Mayor Sir James Johnston, were constituted as a committee to discuss the financial provisions with Treasury officials. However the intimacy of these discussions did not inhibit the Chamber from issuing another forceful and deeply analytical statement in the summer of 1920:

"We are as strong as ever in the conviction, constantly reiterated, that in the maintenance of the Union and the full communion of interest and economic life with Great Britain which it ensures, lies the best hope for the future of Ireland; but if we are faced with the position that Great Britain, tired of the long conflict, and despairing of the ability of Parliament — influenced as it is by party issues — to restore peace and order to the Irish people, has resolved to yield to the frenzied demand for self-determination in one shape or another, we have to consider whether the proposals of the present Bill are such as to minimise the evils which we anticipate".

And on the whole, they felt that the Government of Ireland Bill did minimise what they saw as evils; and they decided to make the best of it even though they had no great enthusiasm for the structures that were being discussed.

Those were the thoughts that lay behind a great meeting held in Belfast, under the auspices of the Chamber, on 25 November 1920. There was an attendance of more than one-hundred-and-fifty business leaders from all over the Province. There were apologies from Lord Londonderry, Lord Pirrie, Sir James Craig, John Milne Barbour, and Harry Ferguson, the restless genius from Dromore whose engineering skills were about to blossom. But the attendance included J M Andrews, a future Prime Minister of Northern Ireland and a future President of the Chamber; John Milne Barbour's brother Harold who was deeply involved in linen and agricultural co-operation; and H M Pollock who with H L Garrett, had done more than anyone to understand the financial implications of the proposals and secure the best possible deal for Northern Ireland. That experience would not be lost on Pollock; and no one could have asked for better training for the job that he was destined to occupy later in life. The bold Fred Crawford, now a colonel, was also on hand to bring military order and precision into the proceedings by proposing that speeches apart from those of Pollock and Garrett should be confined to five minutes each.

Hugh Pollock and Hugh Garrett then made detailed statements on the provisions of the Bill and the possible effects of its financial arrangements on the industrial and commercial life of the Province. Many questions were asked and much discussion ensued; and then, a Mr Malcolm Gordon proposed and a Mr R J McKeown seconded the historic resolution that represented the culmination of thirty-four years of approach to political change:

"That in the opinion of this meeting the proposals of the Government of Ireland Bill before Parliament should be accepted as the best possible method for conferring enlarged powers of self-government upon Ireland under present conditions, especially as it maintains a common fiscal system for the whole of the United Kingdom, any departure from which would be detrimental to the economic interests of the country. The meeting accordingly authorises the Council of the Chamber to take such action as may be necessary in support of this Bill".

William McMullan, who in the absence of the President Lord Londonderry had the honour of presiding at this memorable meeting, put the resolution; and there was a sea of raised hands in support. He then asked if there were any in opposition; and a single hand was raised. It was the hand of a man who was consistent for he had opposed the Chamber action on the Home Rule Bill in 1912: it was the hand of Archibald Savage, the representative of the Chemists' Association on the Council of the Chamber

The pace of change was quickening again: but Ireland would still not be at peace.

Chapter 10

THE DEVOLUTION OF CHANGE: 1921-1965

To a degree that will surprise many people today the Government of Northern Ireland was the child of a reluctant Belfast Chamber of Commerce; and, not surprisingly, the child ultimately took over many of the functions of the parent. Whereas from 1783 till 1920 the Chamber had taken the leading role on a wide range of local issues and pursued them with remote authorities in Dublin or London, the Irish settlement of 1920 transferred power of decision in most of those matters to the Parliament and Government of Northern Ireland, elected by the people of Northern Ireland, responsible to the people of Northern Ireland, and consisting mainly of opinion-formers who before devolution would have found their vent for public service through the Chambers of Commerce and Trade, local government, or one of the utility boards. There is therefore nothing peculiar about the fact that many prominent members of the pre-1921 Chamber of Commerce became local MPs or aspired to ministerial office. And equally there is no point in evading the corollary that the Chamber in a self-governing state with a population of less than one-and-a-half million, its own civil service, and short lines of communication to the decision-makers was bound to have a different role than the Chamber of the 18th, 19th, and early 20th Centuries which dealt directly with remote decision-makers in Dublin and London. Inevitably the balance between the representational role and the provision of services to individual members had to tilt in the latter direction; and the Chamber would become able to dissociate itself from the prejudices and passions of local politics, for there was now another local forum.

But first, there was a very political period when the Chamber was involved in attempting to persuade Sir Edward Carson to head the new Government that was to be formed in the new state of Northern Ireland in the summer of 1921. This was discussed at a meeting in the Chamber on 17 January 1921, with William McMullan, Senior Vice-President, in the chair and Harry Ferguson making one of his rare appearances. A Chamber deputation that included Lord Londonderry, William McMullan, W H Webb, H M Pollock, D D Reid, E W Andrews, S B Quinn, H L McCready, and the Secretary was appointed to wait on Sir Edward in London *"with a view to securing his services and Parliamentary experience in connection with the formation of the Government of Northern Ireland"*. That meeting took place on 25 January 1921; and William McMullan reported on it three weeks later. Sir Edward had been unable to meet their wishes but he had assured them that his services would still be at the disposal of Northern Ireland in the Imperial Parliament.

Meanwhile the Chamber had appointed a standing committee of thirty-three distinguished members *"with the objective of advising on all matters in relation to the establishment of the Government of Northern Ireland, and to exercise their influence in the constitution of the necessary Departments with a view to economy and efficiency of administration"*. Those involved included Lord Londonderry, J M Andrews, J M Barbour, J R Bristow, Sir George Clark, Adam Duffin, H L Garrett, F L Heyn, R E Herdman, H I Johns, Sir James Johnston, James Mackie, Thomas Somerset, and W H Webb. And this committee was also charged with *"getting competent businessmen elected to the Ulster Parliament"*.

Exactly a month after it was appointed the committee tabled its recommendations. These envisaged that there would be eight ministries including a Ministry of the Prime Minister. The others would be designated as Treasury, Labour, Civil Government, Law and Justice, Agriculture, Commerce, and Education. And for each ministry the committee listed the subjects that would have to be covered. For example in the case of Commerce these were Industrial Research, Board of Trade, Transport (railways, roads, canals, harbours), Bankruptcy, Company and Partnership Registration, and Trade Statistics. Thus it was a comprehensive blueprint for devolved government; and it found a large measure of acceptance in Dublin Castle where the details were being finalised. Five of the seven ministries ultimately established were in full accord in name and content with the Chamber proposals. But the proposed Treasury became the Ministry of Finance; the proposed Ministry of Law and Justice became the Ministry of Home Affairs; and the role of the proposed Ministry of Civil Government was re-allocated, mainly to Home Affairs.

Before elections had been held and the new Government set up, the Chamber became deeply involved in another task that would soon be outside its remit: this was the organisation of a major conference on the state of education in the area. Hugh Pollock played a leading role; and it was he who reported back to the Council of the Chamber in March 1921. The conference had a clear message for the new Government:

"As the present inadequate and unsatisfactory system calls for immediate investigation and reform, it is resolved that upon the formation of a Government of Northern Ireland the Premier be urgently requested to constitute a commission, including representatives of those engaged upon and interested in educational work of all grades and departments in the Ulster area, to examine and report on the questions involved with a view to early legislation".

Already it was clear that the new Government would not have to look far for its problems, either in education or in other fields. In world recession and the aftermath of war, there was stagnation and depression in Ulster's staple industries; and unemployment would run at distressing levels for the next twenty years, peaking at a hundred thousand just before the Second World War. And in the first few years the Government would also have to cope with civil unrest and street disorders, stirred up by the activities of "flying columns" of republican terrorists from the South — another period of Irish madness that had cost the lives of four-hundred-and-fifty people by July 1922.

Meanwhile, in June 1921, the Chamber was congratulating eight of its members who had been elected to the new Ulster Parliament and especially three of its Past-Presidents who were to become Ministers. The three selected by Prime Minister Sir James Craig were H M Pollock as Minister of Finance; Lord Londonderry as Minister of Education; and J M Barbour as Parliamentary and Financial Secretary in the Ministry of Finance. Four years later, Barbour would be appointed the first Minister of Commerce, the responsibility previously having been shared with that for Agriculture by E M Archdale. Later still, E M Archdale and J M Andrews (who was to be the first Minister of Labour) would become Presidents of the Chamber while still Ministers. So five of the seven men who comprised Sir James Craig's cabinet in 1925 either had been or would become Presidents of the Chamber.

King George and Queen Mary came to Belfast in June 1921 to open the new Parliament in Belfast City Hall. A fortnight earlier there was a visit from the Lord Lieutenant; and the Chamber presented an historic address of welcome in terms that demonstrated the determination to make the new system work if at all possible:

"Your Excellency's visit officially marks the opening of a new era in Northern Ireland, and a momentous change in that system of Government under which we have lived and prospered. While holding ourselves free from any responsibility for the creation of the conditions which have been brought into being, it is our fixed resolve to utilise them in earnest endeavour to promote the social and economic well-being of the entire community. It is our hope that the Northern Parliament just inaugurated may provide the means for more rapid and efficient legislation on local affairs than has hitherto been possible, and that its conduct in all things may be so influential and regulated so as to command general approval. We fully recognise that the maintenance of order is essential to the well-being of this great industrial district, and we confidently look to the Northern Parliament for such firm impartial enforcement of the law as will ensure peace and protection to well-disposed citizens of every class and creed. We sincerely pray that your Excellency's regime may be speedily signalised by the restoration of law and order throughout the whole of Ireland, and that Irishmen, North and South, will take prompt and full advantage of the opportunities now afforded to them for the regulation of their own affairs, and devote their best energies and talents to the advancement of the welfare of our beloved country".

But if the Chamber was in a way the progenitor of the Northern legislature, that did not mean that it was not prepared to differ with its offspring. The earliest example was the controversy that began in August 1921 and continued till October 1922 about the location of Government offices and other public facilities. At a Council meeting on 25 August 1921 it was rumoured that the Government was proposing to purchase Stormont Castle as a site for Parliament, Ministerial offices, and the new Courts of Justice. The Chamber resolved to investigate and to have a special meeting on the subject five days later. From that meeting there was a missive for Sir James Craig:

"The Council do not feel called upon to express any opinion on the location of the meeting-place for the Parliament for deliberative purposes, but they are convinced that economic and expeditious administration of affairs necessitate the establishment

of the Courts of Justice and the several Departmental offices in an easily accessible position, and that the site suggested would prove unnecessarily inconvenient to the more important general interests affected, and render the prompt discharge of administrative and legal business very difficult".

Craig's reply was that no decisions had been taken and that the observations made by the Chamber would be fully assessed before any decision was taken.

The subject then went quiet until July 1922, when the Secretary of the Cabinet wrote to draw attention to resolutions passed unanimously by both Houses of Parliament on the question of a Stormont location. This infuriated the Chamber; and they blazed off a fierce reply which urged *"the immediate abandonment of the Stormont Castle Scheme so far as it concerns the Administrative Office, as one eminently calculated to impede the progress of its administrative machinery and create dissatisfaction throughout the whole of Northern Ireland".* The response from the Prime Minister's office was an assurance that an attempt would be made to find locations in the centre of Belfast for all those departments which required extensive public use; but there was also an admonition that the Chamber should have raised its objection earlier, when the subject had been under consideration by both Houses of Parliament in September 1921. This was a serious error in the Prime Minister's office because the Chamber had made its views known to Sir James Craig as early as August 1921.

Towards the end of September 1922, the Premier agreed to receive a deputation from the Chamber; and the meeting took place on the 29th of the month. The deputation was led by W Hubert Webb, who was now the President. Webb was a son of the founder of the Old Bleach Linen Company at Randalstown; and he had twice been Open Amateur Golf Champion of Ireland in the last decade of the 19th Century. But he had a big match on his hands on 29 September 1922; for Sir James Craig was determined to talk the delegation out without changing his plans any further. *"The next generation will call me 'blessed' for having gone to Stormont",* said Sir James. But J H Stirling, a member of the delegation, was not convinced and said afterwards that *"he had never heard a weaker or poorer argument put forward in connection with any case by any person than that put forward by the Prime Minister in favour of Stormont as the headquarters of the Government".* Others, however, felt that Sir James had made a reasonable case; and that he had responded adequately by agreeing to locate many sections of the Government machine in the centre of Belfast. And to convince the Chamber about that, the wily Sir James arranged for their old friend and Past-President, John Milne Barbour, to forward the details — and smooth the waters.

As the controversy about the location of Government offices raged, there were important developments in the Chamber itself. First a decision was taken to begin a monthly journal in co-operation with a Mr Edmund Parker who was able to convince the Council that the publication could be financed entirely by the sale of advertising space. And he was right; for the first issue which appeared in April 1923 contained sixty pages of advertising to eighteen of text, a remunerative ratio that was consistently maintained for many years. Amongst the advertisers in that first issue were at least fourteen companies or organisations that are still in membership of the Chamber in 1983. For a number of them and for many other advertisers the great appeal of the journal was that Parker contrived to give it an international circulation, which by 1930 extended to no less than sixty-five countries. The quality of the features and routine commercial information was also high; and in the early years there were many favourable comments both from Chamber members and from overseas. Dunville's whiskey frequently featured on the front cover; and the advertising copy included a glorious quote from "The Lancet", the leading medical journal. Concerning Dunville's whiskey, readers were assured: *"Deleterious qualities practically non-existent"*!

A business lunch in the Ulster Hall on 22 February 1923, when the chief guest was Henry B Thompson, Canadian Food Controller during the 1914-18 War, who spoke about the potential for further development of agriculture in Northern Ireland.
(Photo from Chamber of Commerce Journal)

The second significant development of that time was the initiation of a series of business luncheons addressed by prominent politicians, diplomats, and civil servants — not unlike the luncheons which are still part of the Chamber programme today. The first was held on 5 December 1922 in the Ulster Hall, when the speaker was Sir James Craig; and one of the most notable visitors of the early years was Winston Churchill as Chancellor of the Exchequer in March 1926. In introducing his guest, the President of the time, Robert B Henry, referred to *"his broad capacity and unresting energy"*; and the ebullient Churchill delighted an audience that included all but one of the seven members of the Northern Ireland Cabinet with a reference to his being diverted from the Ulster Hall to Celtic Park during the Home Rule controversy in 1912. *"It's a very fine hall"*, he said, *"but it always seems to be fully booked"*! Other speakers in the first ten years included two Prime Ministers of New Zealand — Limavady-born W F Massey in 1923 and G W Forbes in 1930 — and other venues included the Grand Central Hotel in Royal Avenue, where a single room in 1930 was 7s:6d a night and lunch 3s:0d.

The third significant development during Hubert Webb's Presidency was a decision to form an Association of Northern Ireland Chambers of Commerce. This was confirmed at a conference in Belfast on 22 February 1923 when representatives of the local Chamber were joined by delegates from Ballymena, Ballymoney, Coleraine, Londonderry, Newry, and Portadown. The Newry Chamber had existed informally from early in the 19th Century when the trade of the town was comparable to that of Belfast; but it was not until February 1892 that the Chamber was formalised by incorporation. There had been an early start in Londonderry too, the first Chamber there having been formed in 1824. However that organisation had lasted only for nine years; and a revival had not occurred until 1885, when the Londonderry Chamber of today was established and incorporated. The Portadown Chamber had been formed in May 1920, with the Rt Hon Thomas Shillington as first President. Later that year — in November — the Ballymoney Chamber had been formed as a result of a meeting of thirty businessmen in the townhall under the chairmanship of John McMaster, Chairman of the Urban District Council. The President of that Chamber from October 1921 had been W V McCleery, who twenty-eight years later would become Minister of Commerce for Northern Ireland after a few months as Minister of Labour. The presence of delegates from Ballymena and Coleraine at the inaugural meeting of the Association of Chambers is interesting, because it confirms that business organisations existed in both towns in the 1920s whereas the dates of formation ascribed to the present-day Chambers in those towns are in the 1960s.

Hubert Webb, who was nearing the end of his outstanding Presidency of the Belfast Chamber, became the first President of the new Association; and the Secretary of the Belfast Chamber, W J P Wilson, became Honorary Secretary of the new body. Its second President was F D Russell of Newry; and by the time he took office in 1924, the Association had become an effective mechanism for bringing a cohesive

W Hubert Webb DL, President 1922 and Foundation President of the Association of Northern Ireland Chambers of Commerce 1923.
(Photo from Chamber of Commerce Journal).

countrywide dimension to the Chamber of Commerce movement in the North of Ireland. This it continued to do until, in the Presidency of James A Rodgers in 1966, it merged with the Belfast Chamber to form the Northern Ireland Chamber of Commerce and Industry. James Rodgers was at that time also President of the Newtownabbey Chamber; and so when he became the fifth President of the extended Northern Ireland Chamber in 1970, he achieved the unique distinction of having been President in the movement at three different levels. A partial list of Presidents of the Association is provided as an appendix to the present work.

The Belfast Chamber in the 1920s again displayed a progressive face when its Education Committee under the chairmanship of David McKee reported on the new Education Bill that was being brought forward by the Government of Northern Ireland as a result partly of earlier initiatives by the Chamber. Their comments on the sensitive subject of religious education were particularly notable:

"The vexed question of providing for religious education in State-supported schools is rather outside the province of the Chamber of Commerce, and we do not propose to discuss it further than to say that we are conscious that the segregation of children in National Schools on the basis of religious denominations, which has grown up as a result of the provisions in National education and of the Management of the schools having been largely left in the hands of the various churches, has engendered a sectarian spirit often associated with jealousy and animosity and has had a mischievous effect in preventing friendly relations in the civil life of the community. It has also involved the multiplication of small and often inefficient schools and wastefully swelled the cost of National Education in this country. We recognise that it will only be by slow degrees that this separatist element can be eliminated, but we hope that in the new system now being inaugurated nothing will be done to perpetuate or encourage it".

That was written in 1923 and not in 1983; and it exuded the spirit of the men who founded the Chamber one-hundred-and-forty years earlier.

Hubert Webb, whose son William is well-known in the business life of Belfast today, was succeeded as President by Sir William F Coates, stockbroker and member of the Northern Ireland Senate. Early in his term of office Sir William became involved in a subject that was to recur from time to time over the next twenty years: that was the possibility of establishing air services between Belfast and various centres in Great Britain. And as the Chamber in co-operation with the Corporation was examining the first of a number of proposals in the spring of 1924, the business community lost several of its most distinguished figures in quick succession. In May it was to the late Adam Duffin and the late G H Ewart that the tributes were paid; and H L McCready was appointed to succeed Adam Duffin as the Chamber representative on the Senate of Queen's University. Then in June, in the Presidency of Sir Samuel Kelly (who was at that time operating a substantial coal-mine in County Tyrone), the Council recorded the death of Lord Pirrie, who had declined the Presidency some months previously and set out on a long cruise. Though Pirrie had differed with his colleagues politically for most of his life, continuing to hold strongly to the Liberal viewpoint rather than espousing the new cult of Liberal-Unionism, he was deeply respected; and the Chamber wrote a warm letter to Lady Pirrie who herself had made many contributions to social progress in the city. In her own modest and loving way, her response was probably the most eloquent tribute paid to this "captain of industry" in Belfast:

"The high tribute paid to my dear husband by the Council brings solace to my lonely and sad heart and I value it more than I can say. My husband's life was one of 'deeds not words' and I am proud to think that the world has been enriched by his work and by his example".

Lord Pirrie's body was embalmed in South America and brought back to Belfast for burial in the City Cemetery amidst what S Shannon Millin described as *"universal signs of unmistakable grief"*.

By November 1924 it looked as though Belfast, which in the days of Lord Pirrie and his predecessors had often been first in the changing technology of shipbuilding, would also be the first city in the Empire to be served by a commercial air service. That was the claim of Captain Greig, an intrepid aviator, whose plans seemed sufficiently convincing to encourage many shrewd investors, corporate and individual, to contribute £2,500 for shares in his company, Northern Airlines Ltd. There was talk of "air dromes" being constructed at Carlisle, Stranraer, and in the Malone district of Belfast; and in May 1925 (as the Council was noting the appointment of John Milne Barbour to the new post of Minister of Commerce) F L Heyn reported that between 17 and 30 April there had been no less than seventy-four test flights across the Irish Sea. By then Robert B Henry had taken over the Presidency, having moved rapidly up the ladder because of the death of both Vice-Presidents (Lord Pirrie and E A Boas) in the same year; and in late May he referred to a letter from the Ministry of Commerce which said that the payment of a grant of £1,000 to Northern Airlines Ltd by Parliament was conditional upon the company's undertaking to carry passengers and goods on conditions to be approved by the Chamber. Mr Heyn referred to some disappointment about delays in getting started; but there were re-assuring noises from the Chairman of Northern Airlines — a Mr W Scott Scott — who was present at the meeting by invitation. And that, so far as the Belfast Chamber was concerned, was the last that was heard of Mr Scott, Captain Greig, or Northern Airlines Ltd save for a brief note in the July 1925 minutes to the effect that the Secretary reported that the projected airmail service had failed to materialise.

Alleged failure was also at the centre of the next great controversy in which the Chamber became involved. Unemployment had been running at a frightful rate throughout the United Kingdom; and in Northern Ireland, the rate continued to exceed twenty per cent. At national level there had been political reaction which brought the first Labour Government to power, with Ramsey McDonald as Prime Minister. And in Belfast, as elsewhere in the United Kingdom, the Corporation was encouraged to press on with a direct-labour housing scheme which they had initiated some years previously. This gave rise to a furious row in the Chamber, which began in August 1925 when the Secretary read a letter from Messrs McCue, Dick & Co to the Treasurer enclosing their annual subscription but intimating that they expected the Chamber to pay attention to information that they had supplied on the squandering of public money by the use of defective timber in the houses being erected by the Corporation. Fiery debates on this continued within the Chamber through August and most of September; and in the end the Chamber decided not to become involved but to suggest that any action that was taken should be initiated by a committee of rate-payers. Needless-to-say, that was not the end of the story!

In a less controversial area, the Chamber had no hesitation about being involved again with the Ministry of Commerce in stimulating the participation of a large number of local firms in the Ulster Pavilion at the Palace of Industry Exhibition at Wembley in 1925. The local exhibitors included Murray Sons & Co Ltd who had then been making tobacco products in Belfast for a hundred-and-fifteen years; Belleek Pottery and the Belfast Ropeworks as examples of very different crafts; half-a-dozen Ulster distillers; no less than sixty linen firms; and the Department of Agriculture with a display of buttermaking. Involvement in the British Empire Exhibition in the previous year had paved the way for this massive display of Ulster products.

By then the Chamber had a very broad base, for no less than fifteen other trade associations including the Belfast Chamber of Trade were affiliated to it through representation on the Council. The coal merchants, the commercial travellers, the millers, the chemists, the insurers, the wholesale merchants, the distillers, the sawmillers, the motor car trade now all had their places, alongside the various organisations of the linen industry which had been closely associated with the Chamber for several decades. By 1928 they would be joined by the stockbrokers, the auctioneers, and the printers. Noticeably, however, Ulster's largest industry — agriculture — was still not directly involved, though the Royal Ulster Agricultural Society used the Chamber offices for many of its meetings. Later the Ulster Farmers' Union, formed in 1918, would become a full member of the Chamber and take its place alongside the representatives of commerce and manufacturing industry.

Meanwhile in May 1926, as R B Henry handed over to his successor as President — John E Wellwood, Managing Director of Thomas Dixon & Sons Ltd — the whole country had just about survived a General Strike which Henry described as *"an organised outrage upon the State, a reckless challenge to established authority"*. But

Three of the four Honorary Life Members elected November 1926. The other was Frederick L Heyn (photo page 196). (Photos from Chamber of Commerce Journal)

Rt Hon Hugh M Pollock DL, President 1917, 1918; Chairman Belfast Harbour Commissioners 1918-1921; first Minister of Finance in the Government of Northern Ireland 1921-1935.

Viscountess Margaret M Pirrie, widow of Viscount Pirrie of Harland & Wolff, and Lady President and benefactor of the Royal Victoria Hospital, Belfast.

David McKee, Honorary Auditor 1905-1913; Chairman of the Commercial Education Committee 1907-1932; Honorary Treasurer 1913-1927; served for sixty-nine years with the Belfast Banking Company.

Wellwood's Presidency was marked more by recognition of services rendered than by confrontation. The Chamber honoured Viscountess Pirrie, F L Heyn, H M Pollock (Minister of Finance), and David McKee with the Honorary Life Membership. This was marked by a function in the Grand Central early in 1927 when three of the four new Honorary Members were presented with their beautiful illuminated scrolls, an example of which was included in the "Captains of Commerce" exhibition at the Ulster Museum in the last part of 1983. Viscountess Pirrie was unable to be present but she sent a delightful letter. F L Heyn and H M Pollock then followed with lengthy speeches; and when David McKee, who had done so much in the engine-room of the Chamber for so many years, stood up to speak he simply referred briefly to what the others had said and added: *"Mr President, them's my sentiments"!*

A few weeks later the Chamber too recorded its sentiments — sentiments relating to W J P Wilson, their faithful Secretary for twenty-eight years, when he decided to retire through ill-health, at the end of March 1927:

"His literary attainments and wide knowledge of men and affairs made his services invaluable. The present high standing of the Belfast Chamber of Commerce amongst the Chambers of the British Isles is a tribute to his outstanding personality and unwearying zeal at all times in furthering the interests of our Chamber. His record will remain as an inspiring example and incentive to those who succeed to his duties".

And in more tangible form, his colleagues marked his departure with a gift of three-hundred guineas.

Wilson was succeeded by Miles R Whitham, who also took over the Secretaryships of several associations in the linen industry. At the same time David McKee gave up the Honorary Treasurership and was succeeded by his co-director from the Belfast Banking Company, Samuel Johnston. Shortly afterwards Wellwood was succeeded as President by Hugh Latimer McCready, nephew of the late Sir William Quartus Ewart and chairman of Ewart's. The departing President left one unfinished item of business for his successor: it was the initiation of a Chamber golf competition which Wellwood himself had suggested some months previously.

McCready's year began quietly; but within a few months he was in the midst of another furious row about the alleged misdemeanours of the Corporation, which had again spilled over into the Chamber. The administrative competence of the Corporation was at that time under scrutiny by various assessors; and the argument in the Chamber was fundamentally about whether the Chamber should become involved by giving evidence and making accusations or should stand clear of the whole affair. McCready and others argued strongly for disengagement; but W H Alexander was a powerful advocate for involvement in the interest of reform. In the end, in January 1928, the Council felt that it had no alternative but to appoint a committee to co-operate with other representative bodies in seeking to effect reforms in municipal administration by any means in its power.

Meanwhile in July of the previous year there had been a development at Lisnafillan near Ballymena — now the home of Gallaher's modern tobacco factory — which signalled the beginning of a new phase in the history of Ulster industry, a phase which has been painfully in the news in the 1980s. This was the official opening by Hugh Pollock as Minister of Finance of the artificial-silk factory of Sunsheen Ltd — the very first move into man-made fibres, which would become so important in the Ulster economy some thirty-five years later. Soon the new company was advertising its products in the Chamber journal; and the world was reading about artificial silk made in Ulster.

The following year also saw notable developments, many of them during the Presidency of Frank Anderson which began in May. Representatives of the Export Credit Guarantee Department of the Board of Trade made their first visit to the Chamber. There was an Ulster Industries Exhibition in the Ulster Hall. There were suggestions from E M Archdale, Minister of Agriculture, about the formation of a Chamber in Enniskillen. The Irish Linen Guild was formed, to promote and advertise Irish linen generically. And Ulster at last got its first regular air service, as Imperial Airways began operating Calcutta flying boats from Belfast Harbour to Liverpool. The service was inaugurated with an exchange of messages between the Belfast and Liverpool Chambers of Commerce; and Frank Anderson travelled over by the new service to deliver his personally. The seaplane had accommodation for fifteen passengers; and an early announcement referred to its roominess, to the comfort of the seats — headrests, folding tables, and all that; to the decor — including felt on the roof to prevent the metal from "drumming"; and to the food. *A steward has charge of a fully-equipped buffet"*, wrote the Chamber journal, *"and provision has been made to install oil-cookers and serve hot meals en route"*.

But the main mode of travel between Belfast and Liverpool remained the overnight steamer service; and a new vessel for the route was launched from the Harland & Wolff yard in January 1929 for the Belfast Steamship Company Ltd. That was the

Promoting locally-made products over the years.

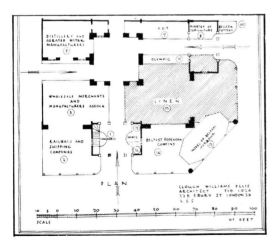

The lay-out for the Ulster Pavilion at the British Empire Exhibition at Wembley in 1924, in which the Chamber co-operated with the Ministry of Commerce.

John M Gray, President of the Irish Linen Guild and joint Managing Director of Wm Ewart & Son Ltd, taking part in a British Week promotion in Copenhagen September 1964.
(Photos from Chamber of Commerce Journal)

ULSTER MONARCH; and she would be joined weeks later by the ULSTER QUEEN and the ULSTER PRINCE to form a noble trio that would give sterling service not only on the Irish Sea over the next ten years, but also in many theatres of war between 1939 and 1945. One of that trio — the ULSTER PRINCE — would not indeed survive the conflagration, for she was destined to have a deadly appointment with German dive-bombers off the coast of Greece in April 1941.

As the ULSTER MONARCH first took to the water in January 1929 the Ministry of Commerce in co-operation both with the Belfast Chamber and with the Association of Chambers was launching a new industrial development and trade support programme. The Ulster Industries Development Association was formed *"to push Ulster goods"*, as Lord Craigavon put it (he had been created a Viscount in the New Year's Honours in 1926). The BRITANNIC was launched for the White Star Line; London and Birmingham saw and tasted Ulster hams, eggs, butter, oatmeal, aerated waters, and whiskey in the British Industries Fairs; Belfast tram-conductors refused to accept "Free State" money from Southern Irish supporters attending a rugby international between Ireland and Wales in Belfast (the match was drawn, five points all); the Chamber, now under the leadership of Minister of Agriculture, Sir Edward Archdale, endorsed a plan to build an airport at Sydenham; there were six-thousand-seven-hundred telephone subscribers in the Belfast area as the service prepared for its 1930 Jubilee; and on 17 August 1929 half-a-million people watched R Carraciola in a Mercedes-Benz win the second Ulster Tourist Trophy Race on the famous Ards circuit at a speed of 72.82 mph.

Quieter days in Donegall Square East, probably about 1930. The well-known building in the left background was then the offices and warehouse of one of the greatest of the old linen companies, Richardson Sons & Owden. The hipped roof was a victim of the air-raids in 1941.
(Photo from Ulster Folk and Transport Museum).

Thus did Northern Ireland enter the Hungry Thirties — a period that brought change but not employment. As the decade began the League of Nations in Geneva was talking about a European Economic Union; and John Miller Andrews, still Minister of Labour in Lord Craigavon's Government, was writing in the London Chamber of Commerce Journal about "Northern Ireland: An Ideal Centre for New Industries". But there was little connection between the two, for Europe was taking only a tiny proportion of Northern Ireland's exports — just over two per cent in the case of linen; and Ulster industrialists still looked to the Dominions and to the United States for economic survival. Almost half the total exports of linen at that time were going to the British mainland or to the Dominions; and nearly thirty per cent to the United States. In the business capital of that great country, which was still reeling from the Wall Street Crash of 1929, polio-victim Franklin Delano Roosevelt was State Governor. Three years later he would be President of the United States; and two years after that, in May 1935, A C Marshall, then President of the Belfast Chamber of Commerce, would in his valedictory address to his business colleagues quote from a recent Roosevelt speech expressing hope for the future:

"Never since my inauguration have I felt so unmistakably the atmosphere of recovery," Roosevelt had said. *"Fear is vanishing and confidence is returning".*

But recovery was slow to come: in fact, for Northern Ireland things got worse, for serious rioting in Belfast in 1935 compounded already intense economic problems.

Meanwhile in February 1930 Belfast's forty-five-thousand unemployed had had their spirits lifted for a while by the news that Joe Bambrick of Linfield and Chelsea had "stuck in six" for Ireland versus Wales at Celtic Park. There had been a few "own goals" at the City Hall; and a Corporation Reform Bill was occupying the attention of the Chamber. In the country areas, and increasingly in business circles as well, there was deep concern about the state of agriculture, a feeling heightened by the fact that the local Minister of Agriculture was President of the Chamber that year. There was concern too about the problems of cross-Border trade with the Irish Free State; and the Association of Northern Ireland Chambers, with W M Irons of Londonderry now in the chair, suggested discussion with the comparable body in the South on *"Restrictions of trade caused by Customs examination of goods at the Border".* And within a couple of years there would be further problems, arising from Eamon de Valera's economic war with Britain.

Business interests were concerned too about the organisation of electricity supplies in Northern Ireland and about the extension of the service. In 1930, the Chamber under the Presidency of Malcolm Gordon, director of Wm Barbour & Sons Ltd of Hilden, had a number of discussions with the Government about this; and the outcome was the establishment in May 1931 of the first Electricity Board for Northern Ireland, with Gordon as Chairman. Earlier in the year the Ministry of Commerce, in the face of a continued decline in traditional industries and with grass beginning to grow on the slipways of the Queen's Island, had put forward a New Industries (Development) Bill. This offered annual grants to developing industries for twenty years at rates equivalent to rental costs on the buildings; and empowered local councils to waive rates on industrial premises. The Chamber welcomed the Bill and continued to co-operate in every way possible both with the Ulster Industries Development Association and with the Ulster Tourist Development Association. Miles Whitham, the Secretary of the Chamber, and his staff also continued to do an excellent job on the monthly journal, which not only advertised Ulster goods to the world, but also fed out a steady stream of information and professional advice to the Ulster businessman. But unemployment continued to rise, as it did in other parts of the United Kingdom — with Scotland presenting a particularly depressing picture of more than thirty per cent of the insured population out of work by the late 1930s.

Not surprisingly unemployment also featured strongly in the very first day's debate in the new Parliament Building at Stormont opened by the Prince of Wales, the future King Edward VIII, on 16 November 1932. The Chamber was represented that day by its President since May, David D Reid, lawyer and Westminster MP, who had for many years been the chief link between Belfast and the Association of British Chambers in London. But the linen industry too had created an interesting link at that time — a link based on flax grown on the Royal farms at Sandringham. The flax was brought to Northern Ireland for processing; the fibres were spun by Ewart's; and the yarns were woven into domestic linens of every type by the group of long-established companies that financed the Linen Industry Research Association at Lambeg. Then, with Christmas just six days away, the linen barons headed by Past-President of the Chamber and Chairman of Ewart's, H L McCready, made their way to London to hand over their wares personally to the King and Queen. Amongst those who travelled that day was a future President of the Chamber, J Graham Larmor, of the Ulster Weaving Company, which made the pillow-cases. And the Old Bleach at Randalstown was represented by N F Webb, who handed over the furnishing linen.

The year 1933 was an important one for the Chamber, for the organisation was a hundred-and-fifty years old in the autumn. That milestone was celebrated in April by a lunch in the Grand Central Hotel which was attended by the Governor of Northern Ireland, the Duke of Abercorn; the Prime Minister, Lord Craigavon, and three members of his Cabinet; the President and Secretary of the Association of British Chambers, Sir Alan G Anderson and Mr R B Dunwoody; and some two-hundred members and guests from all over Northern Ireland. The President in his rounding off of a long occasion referred warmly to the Federation of British Industries — the organisation of larger manufacturers formed nationally in 1916 and destined decades later to become the Confederation of British Industry. In particular he welcomed County Down man, Sir Roland Nugent, whose management of the FBI, said D D Reid, had taken it *"to its present eminence"*. And he was tolerant about the length of the proceedings on such an auspicious occasion:

"Our proceedings lasted just a little longer than some of our members would have wished on a business day . . . but I have been somewhat oblivious of the passing of time".

Andrew Marshall's year as President — 1934/35 — was aviation year for the Chamber. Work on the Harbour Airport was proceeding, but the pace seemed slow. At Newtownards, on the other hand, things happened quickly after Lord

Londonderry had made a suitable site available on the edge of the town. Londonderry had quit Ulster politics in 1926 and was now Secretary of State for Air in Ramsey McDonald's Coalition Government in London; and he must have been pleased to have been so closely associated with Northern Ireland's first civil airport. And the military airport at Aldergrove, which many years later would become Ulster's main gateway to the world, was also pressed into service: its role was to be the Belfast terminal of a daily civilian flight from London via Birmingham, Manchester, and the Isle of Man. This would be operated by a four-engined De Havilland, with capacity for ten passengers together with mail and freight; and the first flight arrived at Aldergrove on 20 August 1934 to be met by the Lord Mayor of Belfast, the President of the Chamber, and other dignatories.

The next President was a descendant of a former one: he was R P C ("Bertie") Gotto, grandson of Sir James P Corry, and director of the family timber-business. He had a difficult role, for the city was in a state of unrest from mid-July 1935 till the end of August; and he had to play his part with other community leaders in seeking to get violence off the streets. But he had been in tight spots before, for he had served with distinction in the Great War, returning as a captain; and, in November 1906 at the age of twenty-six, he had played rugby for Ireland against South Africa in his home town (the Springboks won a magnificent match by fifteen points to twelve).

Despite the problems of 1935, it was a year when Harland & Wolff launched nine vessels including the twenty-five-thousand-ton STIRLING CASTLE for Union Castle. It was Jubilee Year for the King and Queen, and compensation year for owners of buses and lorries as the Government "nationalised" road transport and set up the Northern Ireland Road Transport Board. The perceived need for this radical development was the damage that had been done to the Government-owned railway system by the unfettered and unco-ordinated growth of bus companies and haulage contractors, competing against each other so fiercely as to threaten the very stability of the services. The Chamber as a custodian of free enterprise was not easily convinced,

The changing face of transportation: McClements' Holywood bus on the Sand Quay in Belfast in the early 1920s.

(Photo from Ulster Folk and Transport Museum).

251

though it recognised that some changes were necessary as fifty bus companies owning seven-hundred buses vied with each other and with the railways for a limited amount of business — business that was going to decline as car ownership increased. In the end the Chamber accepted the Government's proposals, in much the same way as they seemed to line up with the Corporation rather than the new Ulster Radio Traders' Association when that body sought their help in opposing a plan by the City Fathers to enter the radio-relay business — a plan that does not seem to have been implemented.

Bertie Gotto continued as President till June 1936. He therefore presided at the special meeting called by the Chamber on 23 January to mark the death of King George V and the succession of his eldest son, the Prince of Wales. That marked the beginning of one of the most extraordinary periods in British constitutional history — a period that ended with the abdication of the new King Edward VIII on 10 December, followed immediately by the succession of his brother, the Duke of York, as King George VI. Meanwhile the clouds of war were gathering, as Adolf Hitler's Germany began the remilitarisation of the Rhineland, Benito Mussolini's Italy pursued its unequal struggle in Abyssinia, and armed conflict between Left and Right broke out in Spain. This was the environment in which one of Ulster's greatest and most modest sons, John Miller Andrews of Comber, Minister of Labour, took up the Presidency of the Chamber on 26 June 1936, in the presence of a large gathering which included Captain D Euan Wallace MC, Parliamentary Secretary in the Department of Overseas Trade in London. Afterwards Wallace gave a business address, in the course of which he welcomed the conclusion of an agreement between Harland & Wolff and Short Brothers of Rochester to establish an aircraft factory beside the projected Harbour Airport in Belfast; and that was to be the beginning of another facet of Ulster's industrial history — a facet that happily shines as brightly in 1983 as at any time in its history.

Despite the other heavy demands on his time, J M Andrews' Presidency was no sinecure, for he regularly attended meetings in the Chamber and generally played as full a part as his Ministerial duties would permit. However his involvement must have been a nightmare for civil servants, just as that of Sir Edward Archdale seven years earlier must have been for his staff in the Ministry of Agriculture. Both situations must have required constant monitoring in order to avoid clashes of interest, the unconscious use of privileged information, and a blurred public image. All of that must have been done well; for there is no evidence that any such problems occurred while either man was President. And in the spring of 1937, as his period of office in the Chamber came towards an end, Andrews was dealing with such neutral subjects as the organisation's subscription to the Ulster Tourist Development Association; the projected visit of the British Medical Association to Belfast in 1938 for its conference (which was expected to bring two thousand visitors); and the slow progress of the construction work at Belfast Harbour Airport.

Soon, however, the pace was to quicken as the aircraft factory took shape and the need for test-flight facilities loomed large. By the end of 1937 no less than six-thousand workers had been taken on for aircraft construction; and the finishing touches were being applied to the loughside runway. Three months later, as Hitler's annexation of Austria brought the world closer to the brink of total war, Prime Minister Neville Chamberlain's wife travelled to Belfast to open the Harbour Airport; and the attendance that day included President of the Chamber, Sir Joseph McConnell, Belfast estate-agent and Westminster MP for County Antrim since 1929. Over the next eighteen months, with McConnell giving way to Captain D C Lindsay, Belfast prepared for war, but hoped for peace. The aircraft factory was working feverishly; the shipyard was designing new naval craft; the engineering factories were converting to munitions; the textile industry was taking on huge military contracts; and the Territorials were perfecting their gun-drill at Orangefield. Neville Chamberlain made three trips to Germany to parley with Hitler and play for time. But time ran out on 1 September 1939 as Germany launched a lightning attack on Poland, in the face of British and French guarantees to that country; and two days later, on a Sunday morning at 11.15 am, the disillusioned Neville Chamberlain who had worked so hard for peace had to tell the world that Britain was at war.

The next six years were testing years for the Chamber as for the nation. Soon the staff were largely occupied in helping member companies to cope with the intricacies of war-time controls on flax supplies, cotton, timber, tea, sugar, and clothing, and with a stream of enquiries both for strategic items like aircraft linen and for the impedimenta of war from canvas webbing for the infantry to serviettes for the officers' mess. Within days of the outbreak of hostilities a Government Flax Control Centre was established in the Chamber offices; and factories became dependent upon that group for the allocation of supplies. Similar arrangements for cotton were introduced later; and in that case, the Chamber itself had a major role. By September 1940, the Government staff had moved out of the Chamber offices again; and a bitter altercation with the Works Division of the Ministry of Finance had begun, as the Chamber submitted what the Ministry held to be an exorbitant account for rent, lighting, heating, and the use of telephones and other office services. That particular exchange lasted for over six months.

Meanwhile Cecil Lindsay had been persuaded to do a second year as President in view of the abnormal conditions and the difficulties in organising meetings. And as he came towards the end of that second year — in the early months of 1940 — he moved rapidly through the military rank structure from captain to colonel, presumably in the Territorial or Reserve Forces, for he was still operating from an address in Donegall Place. It was during those same months that the Chamber became emotionally associated with the strange conflict between Russia and Finland by subscribing £320 to the Finland Fund through the Finnish Consul in Belfast. But as the next President, Frank N Cooke, settled into office in the spring and summer of 1940 the inexplicable war in the snow was soon forgotten; and the British nation was stunned by the ferocity and skill of the German war-machine that smashed its way through Norway, Denmark, Holland, Belgium, and France in under three months.

Next the Battle of Britain would begin; and Belfast and its business community would increasingly feel the pressure of shipping losses, of shortages of materials, of restrictions on international trade, of other Government controls on industry, of censorship of parcels and letters, of petrol rationing, of the blackout, of fire-watching — the nightly vigil for the incendiaries that were beginning to rain on industrial and commercial centres in Great Britain. The Territorials had long since gone to war; and there were gaps in management and in factories and offices both from that cause and in consequence of a steady stream of young men and women volunteering for the forces. But it was a war where the home front also needed resources; and businessmen were not slow to come forward for Air Raid Precaution duties, for the Auxiliary Fire Service, and for the great citizen army — the Local Defence Volunteers, later known regionally as the Ulster Home Guard — formed in the summer of 1940 for defence against possible invasion, particularly by airborne forces. "Dad's Army" may be fun in the 1980s, but it was deadly serious in the 1940s!

In such an environment the representational role of the Chamber was minimal, for Government departments had neither the time nor the inclination to be knocked off course by extensive consultation. There were points to register on compensation for war damage, on the introduction of purchase tax, on the effects of censorship on trade with neutral countries, on a serious credit problem in Madeira for the linen industry; and such points were pursued either with Government offices in Belfast or through the Association of British Chambers of Commerce in London. But the greater thrust was in the direction of helping the war effort, by encouraging the better use of Ulster industry including its agriculture; by facilitating service in the armed forces; by helping with the organisation of the Ulster Savings Campaign; by supporting the Belfast Telegraph's "Spitfire Fund"; by contributing towards forces' welfare; and by providing business representation on a host of committees concerned with everything from timber control to the establishment of the Air Training Corps, a pre-service organisation for teenage boys.

Reminders of inventiveness

Harry Ferguson, the inventor of the Ferguson tractor which transformed agriculture in Ulster and much further afield. Born near Dromore in County Down, Ferguson was moderately active in the Chamber in the 1920s.

The old Horse Bazaar, on the corner of Montgomery Street Belfast, where John Boyd Dunlop, the Ayrshire-born veterinary surgeon, invented the pneumatic tyre in the late 1880s and started a major world industry. The Horse Bazaar was demolished in the mid-1960s.

Sir James Martin, a native of Crossgar, County Down, inventor of the Martin-Baker aircraft ejector-seats, the first model of which saved the lives of a thousand pilots between 1948 and 1965.

(Photos by courtesy of Government Information Service and Chamber Journal).

It was in this environment of Ulster's bracing itself for total war that Lord Craigavon, the veteran of many a previous battle, both physical and political, died suddenly and peacefully in his home at Craigavad on Sunday 24 November 1940. For the Chamber, the event had a double significance; for they mourned the passing not only of Northern Ireland's first Prime Minister, but also of one of their own members of thirty-four years' standing. The Chamber was represented at the funeral by the President Frank Cooke, the Senior Vice-President John G Michaels, Past-President Andrew C Marshall, and the Honorary Treasurer Richard de B Chamberlain. And shortly afterwards the Chamber had reason to rejoice when the news emerged that another of its old members, its Past-President John Miller Andrews of Comber, was to succeed Lord Craigavon as Prime Minister of Northern Ireland.

That winter saw the assault of the German Luftwaffe on the morale and productive capacity of the great cities of the British mainland; and Belfast's deadly turn came in the spring of 1941. It began with a small raid by half-a-dozen aircraft early in April, which destroyed McCue, Dick's timber yard in Corporation Street; but eight days later, the city was subjected to one of the most concentrated attacks launched by the German airforce in the course of the whole campaign. The defences were totally inadequate for the strength and ferocity of the attack, which involved some two-hundred bombers with fighter escort. And Belfast paid an appalling price; for as daylight came more than seven-hundred of its citizens were dead, twice as many injured, thousands of its homes and commercial premises destroyed or severely

High Street and the Albert Clock on the morning of 16 April 1941, after the heaviest of the German air-raids.
(Photo from the Belfast Telegraph).

damaged, fires still raging in many parts of the city, and a substantial part of its population trekking out into the countryside. As always human tragedy was tinged by countless deeds of heroism and self-sacrifice, none more noble than the dash Northwards by the firemen of Dublin, Drogheda, Dundalk, and Dun Laoghaire, notwithstanding the neutrality of their state. And the Belfast Chamber was also deeply touched by an immediate message of sympathy and support from the Dublin Chamber.

Though the big raid had devastated a number of residential areas and severely damaged the commercial centre of the city, the strategic productive capacity of the area was largely unaffected. That was all too apparent to German reconnaissance aircraft that surveyed the scene in the course of the next week; and, inevitably, the bombers came again in force — on the night of 4/5 May. This time they were on target and caused immense damage both in the shipyard and in the aircraft factory. Nevertheless another hundred-and-fifty citizens died from stray bombs and the fires caused by incendiaries; and the authorities were faced with hundreds broken and bruised, thousands homeless, and tens of thousands understandably frightened to continue living in the city. The Chamber under the leadership of Frank Cooke concerned itself with some of these problems as well as with the restoration of commerce and industry; and Cooke was greatly encouraged by a visit paid to Belfast by the President and Vice-President of the Dublin Chamber on 12/13 May when they saw for themselves how the city had suffered, and offered assistance with the emergency-feeding and refugee problems — offers which were subsequently referred to Food Control and the Ministry of Public Security.

Another of the victims of the blitz was the Chamber journal, which had been published monthly from April 1923. As the Secretary, Miles Whitham, wrote to dozens of enquirers in the succeeding years: *"the printing house in which our journal was produced was destroyed by enemy action in May 1941"*. For that reason and also because of a gap of over twenty years in the sequence of the available minute books, information about the problems and activities of the Chamber for the remainder of the war period and in the five years immediately afterwards is most scanty. The early Presidents of that era included Charles S Neill, who is more remembered today as the devotee and benefactor of Collegian's Rugby Football Club and former President of the Irish Rugby Football Union (1932-33); Sir Thomas W McMullan, head of the wholesale grocery business and Stormont MP for the Iveagh constituency of County Down from 1921 till 1929; and Sir Walter Smiles, distinguished soldier and businessman, who as Conservative MP for Blackburn from 1931 till 1945 had maintained a close connection with the Belfast Chamber and with the Association of British Chambers in London and would become Unionist MP for North Down in the course of his year in office.

Meanwhile, in April 1943, J M Andrews had been succeeded as Prime Minister of Northern Ireland by his Minister of Commerce, Sir Basil Brooke, MP for Lisnaskea. Shortly afterwards, Brooke addressed the annual meeting of the Chamber, which was the right way to cultivate the kind of relationship that his predecessors as Prime

Minister had enjoyed with the organisation. Sir Basil also developed a warm relationship with the British Prime Minister, Winston Churchill, whose recognition of the strategic importance of Northern Ireland in the Battle of the Atlantic was often forthrightly expressed. And there would be generous recognition too for the huge contribution that Ulster's generals and field marshals as well as its shipbuilding, aircraft, engineering, and agricultural industries had made to final victory — victory which came in Europe in May 1945 and in the Far East three months later.

As the war approached its end the Secretary of the Chamber was conducting a prolific correspondence with potential customers and suppliers around the world. On the home front there were issues of compensation for war damage, changes in personal taxation arrangements, delays in the release of requisitioned premises, imperfections in the telephone service, and pilferage of goods during transit. And as politicians recognised Northern Ireland's contribution to the war effort, the Chamber itself made a tiny gesture of the same nature towards another complex country: in November 1944 the Council asked the Secretary to send two books to a library in Capetown *"as a thanks offering for what South African soldiers have done in the war"*. And then there was the commercially-minded young lieutenant in the 2nd Belgian Infantry Brigade, stationed at Ballycraigy near Muckamore in County Antrim, who within days of the ending of the conflict in Europe called at the Chamber offices to see whether during the remainder of his military sojourn in Northern Ireland he could be put in touch with potential importers of "artificial manures" in the post-war years! He had an eye to the future: and so too had the Chamber when its Secretary wrote to the Harbour Commissioners a fortnight later to ensure that the Commissioners would be pressing strongly for the use of the Harbour Airport for civil aviation in the post-war years.

The President in 1946/47 was Archibald Scott, Chairman of the New Northern Spinning & Weaving Company. Almost certainly he holds the record for being the oldest President, for he was seventy-six years of age when he took up the post. He may hold the record too for length of service in one firm, for he had completed seventy-two years with New Northern when he retired in 1956. During his year in Chamber office, strong attempts were made to get the Government to return a number of downtown offices to the private sector; and the Chamber made its first recorded and fully comprehensive submission to the Chancellor of the Exchequer on the national budget. Amongst other demands, they urged that the untaxed allowance for a single person be increased from £110 to £120 per annum!

It may be that this concentration of interest on financial affairs reflected the influence of the Senior Vice-President and sometime Honorary Treasurer, Richard de Bohun Chamberlain, senior director in the Belfast Bank and Past-President of the Institute of Bankers in Ireland. He took up the Presidency of the Chamber in the summer of 1947; and he was succeeded by Rt Hon Sir Harry Mulholland, second son of Lord Dunleath and former Speaker of the Northern Ireland House of Commons (1929-45). Sir Harry's year of office was marked by the retirement of Miles Whitham, Secretary of the Chamber from 1927, and his replacement by Frank Coop, the former Secretary of the Halifax Chamber. Coop took up post on 1 January 1949; and he was soon doing a splendid job, though he did once address a letter to *"Cullybackey, Co Tyrone"!* With admirable brevity and total clarity, he dealt each day with six to ten commercial enquiries from around the world, ranging from novelty delph dogs to washed hogs' bristle, from Christmas cake candles to waste hens' feathers, from fishing lines to extractor fans, from side drums to textile machinery. And with his outstanding President, Sir Harry Mulholland, he also played a significant part in the establishment of Belfast Junior Chamber of Commerce some four months after his arrival in the city.

There had been talk of forming a Junior Chamber as far back as 1938; but at that time the outcome was simply the formation of a "junior associate section", in which younger members of the Senior Chamber could meet on their own from time to time. This lapsed during the war years because several of the most enthusiastic members had volunteered for war service. But it was revived in 1949. Hence when Frank Coop took up the Secretaryship of the Senior Chamber in January 1949 he indicated to an enquirer that he thought there were likely to be more urgent problems than the formation of a full-blown and separate Junior Chamber. Yet by 1 April he was inviting Neville Martin, J F Clifton, and T Farrell to come to his office to draft rules for the proposed new body, on the model of the Liverpool Junior Chamber; and the draft was duly adopted at a meeting of prospective members on Monday 9 May 1949, after consultation with the General Purposes Committee of the Senior Chamber. Neville Martin was appointed Foundation President, with Morton McClure as his Vice-President and Jack Clifton as Honorary Secretary. Application for affiliation was then made to the National Council of British Junior Chambers of Commerce; and this was granted in London on 7 July 1949.

Over the thirty-four years since its formation there has been no more enterprising or community-conscious organisation of business and professional people in Northern Ireland than the Belfast Junior Chamber of Commerce. The organisation has been a training ground for business leadership and community service; and it has long been one of the brightest jewels in the crown of the British Junior Chamber movement. It has achieved many successes in regional, national, and international competitions; and it has carried through a large number of ambitious and useful projects in the local community. Amongst these, pride of place must go to the Lord Mayor's Show, the annual pageant of commerce and social progress which has long been one of the most colourful events in the Ulster calendar. The Junior Chamber has played an important part too in the Senior Chamber, since the constitution of the older body provides for representation of the junior organisation in its policy-making and executive committees. Three Presidents of the Junior Chamber have subsequently become Presidents of the Senior Chamber — R D Rolston, J A Gray, and R E M Humphreys (now Sir Miles) — and the Belfast Junior Chamber has also (in 1982) provided a President of British Junior Chamber in the person of Robert T Ferris. The late Lord Brian Faulkner of Downpatrick was a foundation member of Belfast Junior Chamber; and W A McNeill CBE, Chairman of the Board of Governors and Council of the Ulster Polytechnic throughout its history, was its fourth President. Only R D Rolston has been President of the "Jaycees" on more than one occasion; and that was a fitting

The 1967 President of Belfast Junior Chamber of Commerce with most of the Past-Presidents of the previous eighteen years. Front row, from left: J McK Boyle (1959), Wm McCaughey (1958), W A McNeill (1952), R R Dunbar (1967), R D Rolston (1953, 1955), J A Gray (1954), Col H J Porter (1956). Back row, from left: H A Hadden (1966), S H Boyle (1965), T C Dickey (1961), D W Anderson (1962), R E M (later Sir Myles) Humphreys (1964), G S O'Neill (1960), W S Hill (1963).

(Photo by R Clements Lyttle — from R D Rolston's scrapbook).

reflection of the part he played in the early years. A complete list of the Presidents from 1949 till 1983 is provided as an appendix to the present work.

Shortly after the formation of the Junior Chamber in 1949, Sir Harry Mulholland was succeeded as President of the Senior Chamber by Sir Frederick Rebbeck, Chairman and Managing Director of Harland & Wolff, whose shipyard was continuing to employ over twenty-thousand men, as Britain re-armed and companies replaced wartime losses. This was a time too of rapid social progress as the National Health Service introduced in 1948 began to make full impact and as education at every level was re-structured and re-invigorated in the aftermath of the 1947 Stormont Act. But there was post-war depression in other industries; and the total labour force was continuing to grow — so Northern Ireland again had an acute unemployment problem.

Against that background, the year 1950 was a turning point in the history of the Chamber and of the Province: it was the beginning of the second industrial revolution, which by the mid-1960s would have taken employment in Northern Ireland to new record levels and reduced unemployment to around twenty-eight-thousand, representing well under six per cent of the insured population. In that transformation the Chamber played a proud part in support of the efforts of successive Ministers of

Commerce and their departments; and its members were encouraged not only to intensify their efforts in the market-places of the world, but also to play a major part in the attraction to Northern Ireland and habilitation within its industrial scene of new technologies, new industries, new firms, and new faces. Chamber members from the old established firms of the Province entered enthusiastically into that largely altruistic work, as they do today; but just occasionally (then as now) the balance between the attraction of internationally-mobile investment and the further development of indigenous industry became an issue. It was that no doubt that caused Lord Glentoran, son of Sir Herbert Dixon and Stormont Minister of Commerce from 1953 till 1961, to say at the annual dinner of the Belfast Junior Chamber on 9 December 1953:

"Opportunities are the same under the Aids and Industry Acts whether industrialists are born in Ulster or in America."

But there were many in the Chamber that really did not believe that in 1953 — and there could even be some who still do not believe it thirty years later!

For the Chamber itself the beginning of the new era in 1950 was marked by the re-introduction of its monthly journal, as "Northern Ireland Progress". The first issue, in September that year, carried a message from W V McCleery, formerly a stalwart of the Ballymoney Chamber and of the Association of Northern Ireland Chambers, but latterly MP for North Antrim and Minister of Commerce in the Government of Northern Ireland. And it was another great County Antrim man that at that moment was re-invigorating the Belfast Chamber and reminding its members of their responsibilities to the wider community: he was Colonel Samuel Gillmor Haughton, Managing Director of the old Ulster textile firm of Frazer & Haughton Ltd of Cullybackey and former Westminster MP for County Antrim. Colonel "Sam" had become President of the Chamber in July 1950; and in the spring of the following year he and his wife undertook an arduous and personally-funded American and Canadian tour of three months duration, which did much to mobilise the friends of Northern Ireland in both countries and to prepare the way for the "harder sell" of subsequent years by Northern Ireland Ministers and their promotional officers.

When he returned to Northern Ireland at the end of March 1951 and subsequently addressed various meetings, Colonel Haughton (who was also at that time a member of the Grand Council of the Federation of British Industry, the forerunner of the CBI) consistently made two points that are fascinating in the context of public discussion on industrial development in 1983. Firstly, he emphasised the potential of Canada as a source of investment; and, secondly, he urged the Chambers of Commerce in Northern Ireland and the Government to capitalise on the goodwill and the influence of Northern Ireland people overseas and other friends of Northern Ireland around the world. And to aid the second concept — which was the clear forerunner of the Industrial Development Board's Northern Ireland Partnership of 1983 — he started a "Northern Ireland Industries Fund" to enable greater use to be made of the British Trade Promotion Centres in New York and Toronto. That in turn led to the establishment early in 1952 of a Northern Ireland Industries' Council, under the auspices of the Association of Northern Ireland Chambers of Commerce.

Having served on the Northern Ireland Road Transport Board before and after the Second World War, Colonel Haughton also had a deep interest in the other subject that vied with industrial development for the time and attention of the Chamber in the 1950s and well into the 1960s: that was the organisation and financing of road and rail transport in the Province. The basic problem was that the position of the railways had been eroded by the rapid growth and greater flexibility of road transport; and the Government was continuously looking for a solution that would, firstly, enable the losses of the railway companies to be funded by the profits of publicly-owned road transport and, secondly, force a greater degree of rationalisation between the two transport systems. The NIRTB solution had not worked because the Board had found it impossible to make a profit on its road transport operations, let alone counterbalancing the mounting losses of the railway companies through a pooling system. It was this situation that had given rise to the 1948 Transport Act which established the Ulster Transport Authority and charged it with the responsibility for providing an integrated road and rail system, incorporating the operations both of the Road Transport Board and ultimately of the railway companies as well, beginning with the Belfast & County Down Railway which was in the most serious difficulty.

Through the 1950s a succession of able Presidents and Chairmen of Chamber Committees made their distinctive contributions to these twin objectives of economic improvement by industrial development and of rationalisation of transportation by fiscal pressure. But of course each year also brought shorter-term problems and opportunities.

Colonel Sydney Henshall, Chairman of Henry Campbell & Co Ltd of Mossley Mill Carnmoney, was President in 1951/52; so he was deeply involved in the Northern Ireland contribution to the 1951 Festival of Britain, the national promotion organised to mark the centenary of the Great Exhibition of 1851 in Hyde Park. It was also during Colonel Henshall's year that R de B Chamberlain retired from banking and from the Honorary Treasurership of the Chamber, being replaced in the latter role by his colleague S K Neill. A few weeks later Colonel Henshall led the business community in tribute to the "great and good" King George VI who died on 6 February at the age of fifty-six.

Senator Herbert Quin — barrister, accountant, and Chairman of the Royal Victoria Hospital — led the Chamber in the first two years of the new Elizabethan era and was involved in the celebrations surrounding the Coronation of the new Queen. Quin was elected to an unusual second term of office because the Association of British Chambers of Commerce was going to hold its annual conference in Belfast in October 1953. Before that he had the melancholy task of leading the business community in tribute to the victims of two appalling travel accidents in January 1953. First there was an air crash at Nutt's Corner on the night of the 5th in which twenty-seven people lost their lives, including the only son of Past-President Colonel S G Haughton; and then, on the last day of the month, the motor vessel PRINCESS VICTORIA en route from Stranraer to Larne perished in deadful conditions a mere four miles from the Copelands as rescue services searched hazardously and in vain much further North.

The car-ferry PRINCESS VICTORIA which sank off the Copeland Islands on 31 January 1953 with the loss of one-hundred-and-twenty-eight lives including that of Sir Walter Smiles, President of the Chamber in 1945.
(Photo by courtesy of the Government Information Service).

That disaster claimed the lives of a hundred-and-twenty-eight people, amongst them Minister of Finance Major Maynard Sinclair and Past-President of the Chamber, Sir Walter Smiles MP.

That year that began so tragically for families caught up in the travel disasters was one of the best in memory in industrial terms. Harland & Wolff launched fourteen vessels and were fitting out four aircraft-carriers simultaneously. Shorts had orders for two-hundred Canberra bombers and fifteen Comet air-liners. The shipyard and the aircraft factory combined were providing stable employment for thirty-thousand people. And a famous Ulster building firm was celebrating its centenary, for it was in 1853 that a foreman mason and a foreman carpenter both called William had decided to become employers rather than employees — and had formed McLaughlin & Harvey Ltd. Their successors in 1953 were busy with great public works; for roads, hospitals, and schools were still being improved and advance factories built. And it was in this environment of reasonable economic buoyancy that the Association of British Chambers of Commerce held its autumn conference in Belfast for the third time. The proceedings centred on the Whitla Hall at Queen's University; and there were social functions in Thompson's Restaurant, the Ulster Hall, and the City Hall, together with the now traditional visits to Newcastle and Portrush. But it was all only a pale shadow of Lloyd Patterson's extravaganzas in the 19th Century!

By the middle of the following year, as Sir Robert McConnell of the real-estate family settled into office, there were shadows too over shipbuilding, aircraft production, linen manufacture, and agriculture — the main industries of the Province. Unemployment at just over twenty-seven-thousand was at its lowest level for three years. But Harland & Wolff were concerned about future orders; Short's were concerned about the high-altitude safety of the Comet air-liner in the light of several mysterious crashes; the linen industry was concerned about competition from synthetics; and farmers were concerned about the effects of Government decontrol. Amongst the options emerging from the relaxation of Government controls on agriculture and food was the establishment in Northern Ireland of a producer-controlled marketing board for milk, similar to the boards that had existed for milk in Great Britain from the early 1930s and for pigs in Northern Ireland from about the same time. Farmers chose this option; and the Milk Marketing Board for Northern Ireland was established on 1 April 1955.

William McMullan
President 1921

Sir Samuel Kelly
President 1924

Robert B Henry
President 1925

Col S G Haughton DL
President 1950

Irene Calvert BA
President 1965

Col L S Henshall DSO
President 1951

Senator H Quin CBE
President 1952, 1953

Victor F Clarendon CBE MA
President 1955

Rt Hon Sir Edward Archdale MP
President 1929

(Photos from Chamber Journal
and R M Young's Collection —
Linenhall Library).

263

By that time Ewart's had provided their fifth President of the Chamber in the person of their chairman, Victor F Clarendon, nephew of Hubert and Sir William Q Ewart. His first concerns were about a claim by the Ulster Transport Authority for a fifteen per cent increase in fares and freight rates and about an eighteen per cent increase in the price of coal. *"Two trends seem desirable"*, wrote the Chamber journal. *"First an acceleration of the atomic energy programme; and, second, a sharp increase in oil consumption."* And it added: *"Fortunately oil will be available in increasing quantity"*. Twenty years later it would be a different story!

It was also during Victor Clarendon's Presidency that the Northern Ireland Government succeeded in persuading Lord Chandos, Chairman of Associated Electrical Industries Ltd and President of the Institute of Directors, to take on the task of leading a new Northern Ireland Development Council charged both with attracting investment and with stimulating trade. Shortly afterwards the names of a further seven members of the Council were announced; and they included the indefatigable Colonel S G Haughton. However the membership included only one other person living in the Province — H J Curlis, an official of the National Union of General and Municipal Workers. This gave rise to some criticism in the Chamber, as did the inclusion of three trade unionists amongst the eight members. But on the day in February 1956 that Robert H Murphy, latterly manager of British European Airways in Belfast and formerly superintendent of the Belfast-Heysham steamer service, took up the Presidency of the Chamber, Lord Chandos came to the city and addressed the annual meeting of the Chamber in a very convincing way. The first Secretary of the new Development Council was Arthur C Brooke, who later became Permanent Secretary of the Ministry of Commerce and in his retirement gave valuable service to the Chamber in the area of industry/schools liaison. And the Assistant Secretary of the Council was W E Bell, now Sir Ewart Bell and Head of the Northern Ireland Civil Service.

As Sir Graham Larmor, Chairman of the Ulster Weaving Company (who would become President of the Chamber in the following year) thanked Lord Chandos for his address to the annual meeting in February 1956, his audience of over two-hundred included the Prime Minister, Lord Brookeborough; the Minister of Finance, Brian Maginess; the Minister of Labour, Ivan Neill; and the Minister of Commerce, Lord Glentoran. Sir Graham was characteristically generous and forthright in his comments referring to Lord Chandos as *"an industrialist of immense stature who does not suffer fools gladly."* Playing on the visitor's Chairmanship of a large electrical company, Sir Graham concluded: *"He has most generously harnessed his power to the economic problems of Northern Ireland: and we thank him for it."*

That power produced some results in the first year, for the Development Council was able to announce by December 1956 that six new firms had decided to invest in Northern Ireland, bringing twelve-hundred jobs. But that success was put in perspective by some calculations undertaken by a Dr William Black (now Professor Black) and a Professor C F Carter of Queen's University (now Sir Charles Carter, Chairman of the Northern Ireland Economic Council). These calculations showed that to check migration and to reduce unemployment to the Great Britain level over a period of ten years would require the creation of at least fourteen thousand jobs a year. And Professor Carter was in the news again when he made an interesting comment in Londonderry some weeks later:

"The way she trains and uses the brains of her people is far more important in determining the future prosperity of Ireland, North and South, than such incidental things as the Border or the price of coal!"

So Charles Carter's 1983 ability to stimulate the Irish by forthright comment and to run the gauntlet of local politics is not new-found!

Sir Graham Larmor's own year in office saw another notable contribution from university economists: this was the publication of the six-hundred-and-fifty-page survey of the Northern Ireland economy by Professor K S Isles and Norman Cuthbert. The work had been in progress for ten years and the Government had allegedly tried to suppress publication because of the gloomy picture that it presented. Perhaps it was this that led Professor Carter to liken Ulster's quest for prosperity to that of a man running up a descending escalator. And the employment statistics for the twelve months to November 1957 certainly exemplified that feature, for eleven-thousand job losses from traditional industries had swamped six-thousand-five-hundred job creations in new industries. The situation in the linen industry was particularly critical, for employment had fallen by ten thousand (to forty-five thousand) in the course of the previous five years and a number of well-known firms had gone.

But it was the chairman of one of the many new firms that had invested in Northern Ireland — Sir Cecil Weir of the British Tabulating Machine Company — who spoke at the annual meeting of the Chamber in February 1958. And the President installed that day was Sir James Norritt, director of Cantrell & Cochrane and former Lord Mayor of the city. Two years earlier, the new President's own firm had moved from its old location in Victoria Square to a fine new factory on the Castlereagh Road, a development typical of the growth in the local food and drink industry around that

Sir Graham Larmor (left), President 1957, and Sir James Norritt (right), President 1958, with Sir Cecil Weir, Chairman of the British Tabulating Machine Company, at a Chamber business lunch March 1958.
(Photo from Chamber of Commerce Journal).

time. In his new role, the very experienced Sir James presided over a Chamber that now had eight-hundred members and had been in existence for one-hundred-and-seventy-five years, an anniversary marked by a telegram from Sir David Eccles, President of the Board of Trade.

Meanwhile the Ulster Transport Authority, under the Chairmanship since 1953 of George B Howden who would be President of the Chamber in 1964/65, had at last been making progress financially; but it was now to be saddled with taking over the loss-making Northern section of the GNR network. However if there were problems ahead for Ulster's rail-served towns and villages, there was better news for gas consumers; for Belfast Gasworks had made a profit of £86,000 in 1957 even though its customers were paying less for their gas than consumers in most comparable towns and cities in Great Britain. But there was a minor recession in man-made fibres in which Ulster now had a huge stake through Courtauld's, Chemstrand, and Du Pont; and Minister of Education, Morris May, warned that *"Northern Ireland has produced too few of its own industries: too great a reliance has been placed on the work of outside firms"*. And that sounds familiar.

But as J Elliott Forde, Chairman of the Northern Bank, took over the Presidency in 1959, the horizons were widened again, for the talk was of joining the European Economic Community. But in the end it was the "Outer Seven" — the European Free Trade Area — that became a reality for Britain; and the Chamber noted the relevant agreement in November 1959. But the subject was on the agenda again at the annual meeting on Saint Patrick's Day 1960, when the speaker was W H McFadzean, President of the Federation of British Industry, forerunner of the CBI. The new President of the Belfast Chamber was the noted scientist, Dr E Mayne Reid, Chairman of Richardson's (Ulster) Ltd, a company formed the previous autumn to sell the output of Ulster's two long-established chemical manure companies. On the day before Dr Reid launched into his imaginative programme for the Chamber during his year in office, Dame Pattie Menzies, wife of the Prime Minister of Australia, launched *"the*

The CANBERRA, the last and the greatest of a huge fleet of world-famous liners built by Harland & Wolff over a period of nearly a hundred years. The CANBERRA was launched on 16 March 1960.

ship of the century" at the Queen's Island: that was the graceful and revolutionary CANBERRA, a forty-five-thousand-ton liner that cost P & O £20 million. Dr Mayne Reid's year was marked too by his promotion of exports; his timely correspondence with Reginald Maudling, President of the Board of Trade, on agricultural aspects of a supplementary trade agreement with the Republic of Ireland; and his competent handling of the situation arising from the decision of the Secretary, Frank Coop, to retire. The faithful Coop's replacement was W G Buchan, formerly the Deputy Secretary of the Glasgow Chamber; and he took up post in September 1960.

By then Ulster had been enjoying commercial television for nearly a year; and there was plenty of news on the industrial front, for scarcely a month went past without an announcement of another major investment. Cyril Lord, Hughes Tools, Bridgeport Brass, ICI Kilroot, British Enkalon at Antrim, the BP refinery at Sydenham, Tilley Lamps — all these and many more were in the news as established ventures expanding, or units about to open, or firms with a strong intent. The year 1960 indeed was a record one for industrial development and industrial output; for sixteen new firms had opened up to provide four-thousand-five-hundred jobs, and industrial output had increased by seven per cent. But when the President of the Board of Trade, Reginald Maudling, accepted Mayne Reid's invitation and attended lawyer R McD Coulter's installation as President on 28 March 1961 he struck warning notes as well as notes of hope:

"Shipbuilding is the pre-eminent problem here in Belfast and I would be foolish to pretend that the outlook for shipbuilding is anything but difficult."

But Bob Coulter was the recipient of many better pieces of news about industrial development in the course of his year; and he made a positive contribution himself by undertaking a strenuous American tour. Other non-routine subjects that occupied his attention included the impact of transport costs on Ulster industry; the preparation of Aldergrove as a civil airport; and the over-crowding of Queen's University.

As Bob Coulter prepared to hand over the reins of office to A T Robinson, Chairman of Coca-Cola Bottlers Ltd and long-time representative of the Chamber of Trade on the Council, the Ministry of Commerce announced six new projects in the course of a week; and Paul Chambers, Chairman of Imperial Chemical Industries Ltd, spoke at a Chamber lunch of the hope that unemployment in Northern Ireland would ultimately be reduced to one or one-and-a-half per cent. *"If Northern Ireland chooses the right industries and maintains its present progress, its future is assured"*, he said. And he implied that the manufacture of man-made fibres was one of the right industries: *"We have every confidence in the future of Terylene"*, he asserted, as he referred proudly to the company's new fibres factory at Kilroot between Belfast and Carrickfergus. But neither Paul Chambers nor anyone else could predict the set of circumstances that would arise twenty years later — of real prices of feedstock greatly increased, of over-capacity in the industry, of stagnant or reduced world demand, and of artificiality in energy pricing in the United States. And Ulster in the early 1980s would suffer grievously from that throttling combination of adverse factors.

But in 1962, things were booming. Standard Telephones were establishing a pilot factory at Monkstown; the Michelin tyre factory was opening at Hydepark and would employ seven-hundred people, going rapidly to two-thousand; Richardson's had built a fine new factory in the Harbour Estate for the manufacture of fertilisers; the BP refinery at Sydenham, costing £8 million, was nearing completion; work was in progress at Aldergrove to provide a modern civil airport in replacement of Nutt's Corner; the first stretch of the M1 motorway, from Belfast to Lisburn, was opened in July; the President of the Chamber was encouraged by the results of a promotional tour that he had made to the United States in May; and, as if to reflect the rapid expansion of industry in the Province and the improvement in the infrastructure, the Chamber journal was increased in size and upgraded in style. The title of that publication — "Northern Ireland Progress" — epitomised the dynamic state of the regional economy; and Minister of Commerce, J L O Andrews (now Sir John), must have been quietly pleased with the achievements of the Development Council and of his Ministry during his two years as their political head.

Those two years came suddenly to an end in March 1963, with the retirement of Lord Brookeborough from the Premiership. In the re-arrangement that followed, Captain Terence O'Neill emerged as Brookeborough's successor; and Andrews became Minister of Finance and Deputy Prime Minister. That in turn provided the opportunity for the rising star of the Ulster political scene, Brian Faulkner, to become Minister of Commerce following his success in Home Affairs during a most stressful period. And there was a warm welcome for the appointment in the Chamber, where the new Minister was well-known as a co-opted Council member, a successful businessman in his own right, and a foundation member of the Junior Chamber fourteen years previously,

As Brian Faulkner took over Commerce from an Andrews, another Andrews — David, cousin of the Comber family and Chairman of Isaac Andrews & Sons, the Belfast millers — took over the Presidency of the Chamber from A T Robinson. Neither the new Minister nor the new President was in the slightest complacent in the wake of the industrial achievements of the previous two or three years; for the rundown of employment in Ulster's staple industries of agriculture, shipbuilding, and textiles was continuing at an alarming rate. The mid-1962 report of an inter-departmental working party chaired by Sir Robert Hall had reminded everyone that in the farming revolution that began with the outbreak of war in 1939, fifty-thousand jobs had gone while output soared. And that was only part of the story, for employment in shipbuilding and textiles had declined by over thirty-thousand in the post-war years. The Hall Committee had been divided on issues such as the introduction of a "tax holiday" for new businesses and a subsidy of ten shillings a week for every employee in manufacturing industry. But they succeeded in re-focussing attention on the severity of the unemployment problem and on the need for new policies, new structures, and new incentives, if the pace of change were to be quickened.

In accord with its tradition, the Chamber welcomed the Hall Report and analysed it thoroughly, with the help of Professors Black and Parkinson of Queen's University. The Chamber was therefore able to make a major contribution to the subsequent debate; and there were several meetings with Ministers in the spring and summer of 1963. Under David Andrews' leadership, the Chamber also contributed constructively to the resolution in 1964 of a long-standing problem of recognition of the Irish Congress of Trade Unions by the Government of Northern Ireland. This in turn cleared the way for the establishment in 1965 of the Northern Ireland Economic Council in accordance with the recommendations of the Hall Committee. The Council consisted of representatives of employers, trade unions, and other interest-groups meeting under the chairmanship of Brian Faulkner as Minister of Commerce; and its role was to review aspects of the regional economy and to recommend change.

Meanwhile Faulkner had made several promotional visits to the United States; the liberally-minded Terence O'Neill had formally opened ICI Kilroot; an old Ulster linen company with a modern image — Samuel Lamont & Sons — had moved from Linenhall Street to the Stranmillis Embankment and been visited by Princess Margaret; another royal lady — Princess Beatrix of the Netherlands — had opened the huge Enkalon factory at Antrim; the Government itself had built a towering office-block — Dundonald House — on the outskirts of the city to house the very progressive Ministry of Agriculture and other sections of the greatly-expanded Civil Service; a start had been made on the construction of a new bridge across the Lagan from Donegall Quay to Queen's Quay (in approximately the position where the 19th Century Chamber had wanted a tunnel); the Queen Mother had formally opened the new Civil Airport at Aldergrove; the Northern Ireland Government had appointed the Lockwood Committee to review tertiary education in the Province (and prominent Chamber man, R B Henderson, Managing Director of Ulster Television Ltd, was a member of it); Autolite had made its decision to join the increasing number of companies investing in Northern Ireland; and Short's new strategic freighter had flown for the first time.

David Andrews as President of the Chamber had had some contact with many of these events; but it also fell to him to progress the Chamber reaction to the Benson Report on the future of the railways. This was a very thorough and courageous document which faced up to some unpalatable facts on the need for closures and better co-ordination between road and rail. On the other hand, the Belfast Chamber seems to have played little or no part in the great debate in London about the better co-ordination of business representation at national level; and there were neither cheers nor tears in Belfast when the Association of British Chambers of Commerce decided in September 1964 to stay outside the new Confederation of British Industry, leaving it to encompass only the Federation of British Industry, the British Employers Federation, and the National Association of British Manufacturers.

By then David Andrews had long since been succeeded as President by George B Howden, a life-time transport man who had just finished a stressful spell as Chairman of the Ulster Transport Authority. But David Andrews would be remembered at every formal event during Howden's year of office and in every subsequent year; for it was he who donated the handsome Badge of Office designed by James Warwick of the Belfast College of Technology and worn by every successive President since that day

Faces of the Chamber in Donegall Square West

The entrance to the Scottish Provident Buildings where the Chamber had its offices from November 1911 till January 1967.

W G Buchan MA, Secretary of the Chamber from September 1960 till July 1969 when he returned to his native Scotland.

The Presidential Badge of Office presented in 1964 by David Andrews, President 1963.

in March 1964 when its presentation came as a complete surprise to Howden. By then, Scotsman Bill Buchan was well established as the highly professional Secretary of the Chamber; and his many friends in Northern Ireland were delighted when he was invited by the American Ambassador in London to make a two-month tour of the United States in the spring of 1964 under the State Department's Foreign Leader Programme. And as Buchan travelled in the New World, his President George Howden guided the Chamber skilfully through the tortuous "old world" paths of transport re-organisation and the respective priorities of road and rail.

Later that year Harland & Wolff announced that the next stage in their modernisation programme would be the construction of a huge dry-dock. The earlier stages of their re-equipment programme began to bear fruit in August with the launch of their first large tanker, the TEXACO MARACAIBO, a vessel of nearly ninety-thousand tons; and by November, the yard was in the news again as they secured an order for a huge floating oil-rig for the North Sea. Meanwhile the Northern Ireland Hospitals Authority had confirmed a £66 million building programme covering the entire Province; the new Ministry of Development, with William Craig at the helm as Minister, was pushing on with other large infrastructure projects including the extension of the motorway system and the planning of a new city between Lurgan and Portadown; Carreras were planning a cigarette factory at Whiteabbey, which was expected to employ about two-thousand people; the Ministry of Commerce was planning a programme of Ulster Weeks in Great Britain; the Ulster Weaving Company had broken all records by selling three-hundred-and-sixty-thousand of their latest tea-towel, featuring the Beatles; and the great British electorate had decided to have its second Labour administration since the War, featuring Harold Wilson and George Brown.

Nearer home the Chamber had one of its now-rare flirtations with politics when the President personally welcomed the controversial meeting between Prime Minister Terence O'Neill and the Taoiseach of the Irish Republic, Sean Lemass, in January 1965. Shortly afterwards the Council unanimously ratified Howden's unqualified endorsement of the summit meeting; and the liberal spirit of 1783 again strode the corridors of the Chamber. In more practical terms, the Chamber used the

O'Neill/Lemass meetings as the stimulus for the initiation of a series of cross-Border commercial discussions involving the Dundalk, Dublin, Newry, and Belfast Chambers; and those discussions have continued periodically till the present day, with beneficial results for trade in both directions.

It was shortly after the O'Neill/Lemass meeting that the Government published a further economic plan for the Province. This had been prepared by Professor Wilson of Glasgow University; and it was under intense debate in business circles in March 1965 as the Chamber made history by installing its first and so-far only lady President. She was Mrs Irene Calvert, an executive director of the Ulster Weaving Company and former Independent MP for Queen's University.

As in her many other activities on behalf of the community, Mrs Calvert's contribution to the Chamber not only during her year as President but also in her earlier years as Vice-President and Committee Chairman was immense. And as she took up the Presidency in March 1965 her vision of the future — both its opportunities and its problems — was revealed in a message of welcome that she sent to delegates from many countries who were attending a World Economic Conference in Belfast organised by the Junior Chamber:

"We live in a world where scientific advance and technological innovation almost seem to make the possibility of material prosperity for all a foreseeable reality. Yet the impact of industrialisation creates many problems, human, social, economic, political, aesthetic, and moral: problems of human nature and social organisation; problems of ends as well as means".

But in Northern Ireland the "ends" for the next five years were clear, for Professor Wilson in his Development Plan had set targets of thirty-thousand new jobs in manufacturing industry, with an equal number in the service sector and a further five-thousand in the building industry; and the Chamber agreed that these were realistic targets, especially if industrial development policy gave just a little more attention to indigenous industry and to the creation of small businesses.

Irene Calvert's historic year in office coincided with a flood of historic issues for the Northern Ireland community; and she and her colleagues on the Council and in several of the standing committees had a busy time. On top of the Wilson Plan for the Province came the Matthew Plan for the Belfast area; the creation of a whole new structure for industrial and commercial training, involving a Training Executive and a number of Training Boards; the winding-up of the Northern Ireland Development Council, as the Economic Council at last got under way; the gradual rundown of the Ulster Transport Authority and its replacement by new structures that encouraged a more commercial approach; and, above all, the recommendations by the Lockwood Committee on the need for a new university and for the establishment of a centre of excellence in vocational education, by the amalgamation of certain existing colleges and the addition of more. By far the most controversial issue in the Lockwood debate was the proposal to locate the new university at Coleraine; and the Chamber did not quite escape being caught in the cross-fire. *"The West's awake and Londonderry has seethed with revolt"*, wrote "Town Talk" in the Chamber journal of March 1965; and the Chamber had a larger letter-bag for the next few weeks! But the Chamber was universally acclaimed for providing a forum at the end of May for a major speech on Northern Ireland by George Brown, Minister of Economic Affairs in Harold Wilson's administration; and Brown made friends for himself and for his Government by his obvious sensitivity to the problems of the region.

Rt Hon Brian Faulkner MP, later Lord Faulkner of Downpatrick, speaking at the opening of an exhibition organised by the Belfast Junior Chamber of Commerce in April 1965. Brian Faulkner was then in his heyday as Minister of Commerce. On his left are Mrs Irene Calvert, President of the Chamber, and Samuel H Boyle, President of the Junior Chamber.
(Photo from Chamber of Commerce Journal).

Meanwhile new firms were continuing to set-up in the Province, for Brian Faulkner's personal efforts were beginning to bear fruit; and old firms such as J P Corry's were expanding and re-locating. The centre of the city was being transformed by new office blocks; Short's were taking their first orders for the Skyvan; new buildings were continuing to spring up at Queen's University; Harland & Wolff secured a £14 million order from Norway for five bulk carriers; the Dean of Belfast, the Very Rev C I Peacocke launched an appeal for £200,000 to enable Belfast Cathedral to be completed; Sir James Martin, the Crossgar-born inventor of the Martin-Baker aircraft ejector-seat, which had saved the lives of a thousand pilots, announced an improved version; and as Brian Faulkner attended a reception in Belfast in September to launch the new Confederation of British Industry in Northern Ireland, it was announced that unemployment was down to twenty-eight-thousand or just over five-and-a-half per cent of the insured population. In a period of twenty years, almost two-hundred new projects had been established in the Province and there had been nearly as many expansions. These developments had created fifty-five-thousand new jobs; and there were a further seventeen-thousand in the pipeline. These figures are worth emphasising today; for as Lord Chandos wrote in his 1966 report on ten years as Chairman of the Development Council:

"The extent of the industrial revolution in Nothern Ireland is not often realised outside the Province and not always appreciated within it."

In industrial, commercial, agricultural, educational, and infrastructure terms, devolution backed financially by Westminster had been an incredible success, particularly in the post-war years; and the Chamber had played its full part in the changed order of things. Now the Chamber itself was about to be changed radically; and the changed Chamber would have to operate in a changed environment, for Northern Ireland was approaching its most restless years.

Chapter 11

A CHANGED CHAMBER IN CHANGED TIMES 1966 - 1983

As the year 1966 dawned in Ulster the trouble-spots of the world were Vietnam, Nigeria, and Rhodesia; but there were those who realised that before it was out there could be moments of tension in Belfast as ancient passions were whipped up by the celebration of the 50th anniversary of the 1916 Easter Rising in Dublin, the traditional parades of the majority community, and niggling fears that the union with Great Britain was being imperilled by liberal attitudes and cross-Border talks. The tetchiness that had crept into the community was apparent too in the great furore that arose in February about the naming of a new bridge across the Lagan in the centre of Belfast. But there was no tetchiness in the Chamber, either about the name of the bridge or about anything else; for the Chamber was deeply involved in much more constructive things.

It was during George Howden's Presidency in 1964/65 that the need for a fundamental review of the constitution and committee structure of the Chamber was recognised; and the task was given to a special committee chaired by G H Dunlop, the Assistant Managing Director and Secretary of W H Dunlop & Co, wholesale warehousemen. As a Fellow of the Chartered Institute of Secretaries and a man meticulous on detail, Harry Dunlop was an ideal choice for the leadership of this important committee; and he made an immense personal contribution both to the committee's March 1965 report and to the subsequent reconstruction of the

Hubert Taggart OBE, a stalwart of the Chamber Movement in Ballymoney and North Antrim.

Mrs Margot Neill, Chairman of the Education, Training and Employment Committee in the early 1970's.

W V Hogg MBE, a stalwart of the Chamber Movement in Newry and South Down.

Memorandum and Articles of Association of the Chamber. But in return he had the satisfaction of seeing the vision of the organisation lift from the original objective of an improved structure for decision-making to the concept of a regional chamber for the whole of Northern Ireland, an organisation to which the provincial chambers would affiliate. And that prize was ultimately attained not only through the work of Harry Dunlop's committee and the efforts of the office-bearers and staff of the Belfast Chamber; but also through the selfless co-operation of men like W V Hogg of the Newry Chamber and Hubert Taggart of the Ballymoney Chamber and, above all, of J A Rodgers of the Newtownabbey Chamber, who was at that time President of the old Association of Northern Ireland Chambers, a potential rival to the proposed new organisation.

When all the delicate discussions had been completed the Chamber met on 3 February 1966 under Mrs Calvert's chairmanship to give formal approval to its changed name and status; and in the span of a few historic minutes the Belfast Chamber of Commerce established in 1783 became the Northern Ireland Chamber of Commerce and Industry established in 1966. The Association of Northern Ireland Chambers had acquiesced in the change and would later be wound up at a dinner in Newtownabbey attended by the Prime Minister, Captain Terence O'Neill; and the new mechanism for liaison with the provincial chambers — the Standing Committee of Presidents — would have been established in the meantime. At the inaugural meeting of that body on 4 April the membership was confirmed as W J Morrison (Armagh), W McCaughan (Ballycastle), H Taggart (Ballymoney), W E Holten (Banbridge), R Graham (Coleraine), T Creighton (Enniskillen), J D Johnston (Fivemiletown), D Hudson (Irvinestown), J Cunningham (Kilkeel), Dr J Robertson (Limavady), M Collins (Lisnaskea), D M Holmes (Londonderry), H Jordan (Lisburn), W S Milner (Newtownabbey), W V Hogg (Newry), and G Hyde (Portadown); and Hubert Taggart of Ballymoney was elected Chairman, with George Hyde of Portadown as Vice-Chairman and J A Rodgers of Newtownabbey as the third representative on the Council of the Northern Ireland Chamber. Thus the new regional organisation began with the support of sixteen affiliated chambers; and over the next seventeen years that number would increase to around twenty-five as chambers were formed or re-formed in Ballymena, Ballynahinch, Belleek, Cookstown, Dromore (Co Tyrone), Ederney, Gilford, Newcastle, Portrush, and Warrenpoint.

But the fundamental change in constitution was by no means the only change that the Chamber had in hand in 1966, as the Presidency passed in March from Mrs Calvert to her very able young lieutenant, R N Crawford, Deputy Managing Director of the McNeill Group (NI) Ltd. From about the same time as the constitution committee was established, Norman Crawford had been energetically chairing a parallel group concerned with re-housing the organisation and establishing a Northern Ireland Trade Centre; and the group had reported publicly at a press conference on 11 October 1965. The Ulster Scottish Friendly Society was erecting a ten-storey office-block in Great Victoria Street Belfast; it would be known as Chamber of Commerce House; the Chamber would take an area within it of almost eight-thousand square feet to house its offices and an exciting new trade centre; and a Furnishing and Development

Geoffrey Auret, Secretary since 1970, with the pre-1983 entrance to Chamber of Commerce House in the background. Top right: the Trade Centre in 1967, awaiting its first exhibits. Bottom right: the Boardroom 1967-1974. (Photos by Wilfred Green and from Chamber Journal).

Fund would be opened forthwith. The trade-centre concept had caught the imagination both of the Government and of the more progressive elements of the business community; for it was seen not only as a potential shop-window for industry and commerce in the Province but also as a new focus for business meetings, conferences, and trade exhibitions. In consequence, some seventy firms reacted positively and generously to the appeal, with the result that by June 1966 approximately half of the £50,000 required by the organisers had been raised.

Norman Crawford participated in the "topping out" of the new building on 22 August 1966; and the Chamber staff were scheduled to move from the Scottish Provident Building by 1 February 1967. Meanwhile a cash crisis had arisen at Harland & Wolff which had resulted in the first of a series of Government interventions, including the appointment of J F Mallabar, a London accountant, as Chairman and Financial Controller. In banking, on the other hand, the route to greater stability lay through amalgamations; and Allied Irish Banks emerged in August 1966 as the amalgam of the Provincial, the Royal, and the Munster & Leinster. Some two-and-a-half years earlier the oldest of the Belfast-based banks, the Northern, had become associated with the cross-channel Midland, just as the Ulster had done with the Westminster as far back as 1917. And four years after the emergence of the Allied Irish Banks in 1966, the last structural move on the local banking scene took place, when the historic Belfast Bank merged with the Northern; and its male staff as they reported for work in the "United Northern Banks" on 1 July 1970 had to choose between the red carnations supplied by the publicity department of their new-found partners and the black ties recommended by one of their own diehards.

But in the broader community of Northern Ireland there had in the meantime been all too many reasons for wearing black ties. A civil rights movement of 1968, protesting mainly about perceived misdemeanours in local government, had escalated into serious street violence in 1969; and by August of that year fires were burning in Belfast and the guns were out. Terence O'Neill had been displaced as Prime Minister some months earlier by James Chichester-Clark, for every conciliatory gesture by Stormont was seen by its detractors as not enough and by its supporters as a concession to violence; and there was confusion and disillusionment and blind fury in which innocent people on both sides of the growing divide suffered grievously. Local authority was undermined by distant decision; and troops stood guard between the communities while paramilitary organisations on both sides nonchalantly equipped and trained for future conflict. And there would be a heavy price to pay for the experimental policies of those years, a price indeed that is still being paid in 1983.

Inevitably the civil unrest and the violence had a profound effect on the Chamber; and the succession of able Presidents of the late 1960s and early 1970s all found themselves spending a considerable proportion of their time on direct and indirect consequences of "the troubles". The Trade Centre had been formally opened on 16 May 1967 by Sir Robert Maclean, President of the Association of British Chambers, with Harry Dunlop in the chair and Terence O'Neill looking on; and soon it was being extensively used both for permanent displays by member companies and for special meetings and exhibitions, including virtually all the activities of the Chamber itself. Admittedly there was from the beginning a cloud over the financial aspects, in that the appeal had raised only £30,000 of the £50,000 required, leaving the remainder to be borrowed at substantial cost. But the hope was that as the potential of the centre became better known its use would build up, and profits would be generated to liquidate the borrowings over a relatively short time.

The agricultural industry, in the shape of the Ulster Farmers Union, the Ulster Agricultural Organisation Society, and the Marketing Boards for Milk, Pigs, and Seed Potatoes, made a gesture of faith in the Trade Centre by organising a joint donation of £1,000 — a gesture that Harry Dunlop welcomed warmly as the first general identification of agriculture with the overall industrial and commercial scene. And the President and his colleagues had understanding support too from the then Governor of Northern Ireland, Lord Erskine of Rerrick, himself a former businessman and active member of the Edinburgh Chamber. The local Chamber was therefore pleased when the Governor in March 1968 agreed to join its illustrious roll of Honorary Life Members.

The President's Badge of Office after the 1967 modification commissioned by G H Dunlop to recognise the changed name and scope of the Chamber from 1966.

(Photo from Chamber of Commerce Journal)

As Harry Dunlop handed over the President's Badge of Office to Allan Gray in March 1968, the more observant members noticed that the badge like the Chamber itself had been changed, by the addition of a matching scroll embodying the new name of the organisation. Dunlop, the man for detail and good order, had arranged and paid for this personally, just as he subsequently presented a beautiful gavel for the President's use at Council meetings. By then he had also succeeded Mrs Calvert as the representative of the Chamber in the Senate of Queen's University, a role that he fills with distinction to this day. Allan Gray too brought distinction to the Presidency, for he was the first former President of the Junior Chamber to fill the top office in the Senior Chamber; while in business he had played a major part in the transport revolution on the Irish Sea, as the founder of Ulster Ferry Transport Ltd, later associated with Coast Lines Ltd. It was therefore no accident that in the course of Gray's year in office there was a major transport exhibition in the Trade Centre — "Transfreight 69", it was called — and that Ross Campbell of Containerway Ltd gave a most informative paper on the truly pioneering efforts of a number of entrepreneurs in the development of containerisation and roll-on/roll-off movements across the Irish Sea from 1948 onwards.

But there were many other events that marked that year, besides civil-rights marches and timely reminders of Northern Ireland's leading position in sea transport, a position that was in accord with the heritage handed down by the Head Line, Kelly's, Corry's, the Ulster Steamship Company, George Langtry, and the merchants of 1783. British Junior Chamber came to Belfast for its annual conference; and the President

277

entertained the delegates in the Trade Centre. The Chamber sent a trade mission to Austria, in succession to its pioneering foray to Sweden in the previous year. ICI announced a £2 million expansion at Kilroot; two-tier postage was introduced; the Chamber discussed an economic plan for 1970-75 with Professors Matthew, Parkinson and Wilson; Robert Stenuit discovered the Spanish galleon, GIRONA, on the sea-bed off the North Antrim Coast; and Terence O'Neill asked *"What kind of Ulster do you really want?"*

O'Neill's question came in the aftermath of marches and political acrimony; and the charged atmosphere was already beginning to be reflected in the income of the Trade Centre. The first warning notes were therefore struck gently, as Dr H S Corscadden, Senior Managing Director of the Ulster Bank, took over the Presidency in the spring of 1969 and thus became the first President from that important institution since Robert Grimshaw in 1857. In the latter part of his year, Harry Corscadden would be pre-occupied with community problems; but in the first instance he was determined to increase the membership, which then stood at about eight-hundred in the aftermath of sharp increases in subscription rates. He also had to cope with the problem of replacing the Secretary, as Bill Buchan announced in June that he would be leaving at the end of October to take up a new post in the Chamber movement in Scotland, after *"eight creative and satisfying years"* in Belfast. His replacement was J M Devlin, a qualified accountant and graduate of Trinity College Dublin who was serving with Bangor Borough Council, after previous experience both in industry and with other public bodies.

As Jim Devlin took up the Secretaryship at the beginning of August, the storm-clouds of sectarian violence were gathering in many parts of Ulster; and the situation erupted in Londonderry on 12 August and spread to other centres, particularly West Belfast, in the succeeding days. In the wake of the violence, Dr Corscadden was invited to join a committee of non-political persons charged with finding *"ways and means of restoring peace and communal understanding"*; and he also joined with the President of the Junior Chamber, Noel L Valentine, in issuing a thought-provoking and moderating statement on behalf of the business community, which evoked a warm response from Lord Grey of Naunton who had succeeded Lord Erskine as Governor. The message from the two Presidents received a wide circulation at home and abroad and did much to put the record straight on the situation in industry and to restore dented business-confidence.

As the Chamber entered the decade of the 70s, Harry Dunlop agreed to serve in the new Community Relations Commission; several Chamber members were helping to shape the plans for the proposed polytechnic; the Macrory review of local government was just getting underway; and Brian Faulkner, now Minister of Development, was promising tens of thousands of new houses in the course of the next five years. Such was the environment in which Dr Corscadden was succeeded as President by J A Rodgers, who had done so much to facilitate the establishment of the regional chamber. And Jim Rodgers, after many years of executive experience in the linen industry, brought innovation and flair to the Presidency of the Chamber despite the distractions and distresses of continued community tension and outbreaks of terrorism.

At the annual lunch in May 1970, a senior director of Courtaulds spoke of the company's commitment to Northern Ireland, with nine-thousand people employed in nineteen factories. Shortly afterwards, Derek Birley, Deputy Director of Education for Liverpool and a professional to his finger-tips, was appointed Director of the new polytechnic which would be known for a time as the Ulster College. Soon he would be planning the amalgamation of the existing vocational colleges; and setting out on the remarkable course that produced an educational revolution for the Province in the course of the next ten years. The Chamber would at all times be supportive of his efforts through its representatives on the Board of Governors, later known as the Council; and the combination of Birley, a progressive Department of Education, and W A McNeill, the ex linen-man and foundation member of the Junior Chamber who became the first and only Chairman of the new institution, would effect a miracle at Jordanstown in circumstances that were often far from conducive.

The year 1970, with Jim Rodgers firmly in the chair in Belfast, also saw a General Election and a change of Government nationally. Harold Wilson gave way to Edward Heath and the thrust of policies changed. But the move to decimalisation of the

The 1970 President and a group of Past-Presidents at a dinner in the Trade Centre, 29 September 1970.
Seated, left to right: Dr E Mayne-Reid (1960), J E Forde (1959), J A Rodgers (1970), Sir Robert McConnell (1954), R McD Coulter (1961).
Standing, left to right: G H Dunlop (1967), David Andrews (1963), A T Robinson (1962), R N Crawford (1966), Dr H S Corscadden (1969), J A Gray (1968).
(Photo by courtesy of J A Rodgers).

currency and equal pay for women continued at full speed; and the Chamber was involved in discussions on both, and also on another Northern Ireland development plan which included the formation of a Local Enterprise Development Unit to stimulate the establishment of small businesses. Tony O'Reilly, the golden boy of Irish business and of Irish rugby, was "Face to Face" with Bill Heaney at an evening function in the Trade Centre organised jointly with the British Institute of Management. And there was co-operation too with CBI Northern Ireland both in nominations to a reconstituted Economic Council and in the organisation of a joint dinner in the Boardroom for the Confederation's Director-General, Campbell Adamson, when he visited the Province in October. Above all the Boardroom saw three historic functions in the course of a few weeks involving the entertainment of the Governor, Lord Gray, who accepted the Honorary Life Membership; a dinner for surviving Past-Presidents of the Belfast and Northern Ireland Chambers; and a similar event for the Standing Committee of Presidents of the provincial chambers.

Coincidentally, it was immediately after these events that the Chamber had another change of Secretary. Jim Devlin left to become Finance Officer of the Polytechnic; and his replacement was Geoffrey L Auret from the Personnel Department of Short's. Auret was an Englishman who had come to live in Northern Ireland in 1958 after twenty-three years of distinguished service in the Indian Army and in the Royal Artillery. Retiring as a lieutenant-colonel he had worked for a time in a textile factory in the Dungannon area before joining Shorts; and he had represented his company in the Chamber from 1968. Thus he had an ideal background for the heavy task that he took up on 23 November 1970.

As Jim Rodgers approached the end of his Presidency, there was another upheaval at Harland & Wolff which saw the resignation of Sir John Mallabar from the Chairmanship and reputedly attracted interest from the Fred Olsen Line and Aristotle Onassis, the Greek shipping tycoon. The Province was still reflecting too on the recommendations of the Macrory Committee on local government which proposed the transfer of responsibility for most functions to Stormont and to appointed area-boards, and the restructuring of the various existing tiers into twenty-six district councils with limited powers. Ewart's were stopping flax-spinning, but staying in synthetics and blends; Desmond Lorimer was becoming Chairman of the Housing Executive; the Trustee Savings Bank of Northern Ireland was completing its branch computerisation programme ahead of any other bank in Western Europe; the package of aids for industrial development was being curtailed in line with Conservative policy nationally; and, a few days before the annual general meeting of the Chamber in March, James Chichester-Clark resigned the Premiership of Northern Ireland, making way for Brian Faulkner. It was a time of change, and James Rodgers in his valedictory speech on 25 March 1971 claimed a new record: *"It's not every President"*, he said, *"who in the course of his period of office sees the back of two Chamber Secretaries, two Prime Ministers, and the whole of the national currency!"*

As Raymond Thompson took up the Presidency in the spring of 1971, the youthful Robin Bailie, a former member of the Chamber Council, was settling in as Minister of

Commerce in Brian Faulkner's Cabinet. The Chamber had enjoyed an excellent relationship with Bailie's predecessor Roy Bradford; and it was during Bradford's time at Commerce that an arrangement was negotiated which was to be vitally important during Raymond Thompson's Presidency. Because of the importance which the Government placed on the use of the Trade Centre for the projection of the industrial face of Ulster, the Ministry of Commerce agreed to make an outright support grant of £7,500 in the year 1969/70, followed by a further sum of up to £9,500 on the basis of £1 for every £2 that the Chamber could raise from its members before 31 December 1971. By now the Trade Centre was wilting under the influence of "the troubles"; and the Chamber journal, "Northern Ireland Progress", was becoming an even greater problem as costs increased and advertising revenue fell. The new President therefore made an all-out effort to raise further subscriptions from members; and a number contributed generously to provide another £6,850. But that was just over a third of the amount that would have been required to secure maximum Government grant; and there was a deficit of nearly £4,000 on the year's workings to add to an already excessive overdraft.

But the Chamber was not permitted to dwell on its own problems, for the whole community was again in a state of ferment despite "Ulster 71", a pageant of achievement and change in fifty years of self-government. As the imported head of police continued his policy of policing Belfast like an English city mid the shires, the Chamber called for stronger security; and the distinguished Ulsterman, Sir Frederick Catherwood, in a speech to a business lunch seriously advocated the creation of a whole series of new towns to enable people to make a fresh beginning in peaceful segregation. Rafton Pounder, John Simpson, J T O'Brien, and Dr A Park talked about the Common Market; and Clement Wilson, founder of the Trust that had provided the Boardroom furniture for the Chamber, was elected to Honorary Life Membership. IRA terrorism was rife in the land; but manufacturing industry was relatively unaffected, as the President explained in a splendid letter to ninety chambers of commerce in Great Britain.

As Raymond Thompson prepared to hand on the torch to H M Gabbey, who was known for his wit, his sartorial elegance, and his prowess at bridge, as well as for his respected status as a Managing Director of the Northern Bank, the Chamber in February 1972 took on Deborah Kerr (now McCauley) to drum up advertising revenue for "Progress". The Chamber finances were in a critical state; but that was as nothing in the face of the problems that beset the Ulster community. Terrorism was reaching a crescendo and Stormont was about to be suspended, as Brian Faulkner refused to hand over responsibility for internal security and the Northern Ireland courts to Edward Heath's Government in London. The crunch came at the end of March when Faulkner and his colleagues resigned; the Northern Ireland Parliament was suspended for a year by a bewildered House of Commons at Westminster; and William Whitelaw arrived in Belfast as Secretary of State, supported by a small group of junior ministers who each became responsible for one or more Northern Ireland departments. Under Maurice Gabbey's leadership the Chamber refrained from comment either on these developments or on the short political strike which followed;

and when Whitelaw addressed the Council and representatives of affiliated Chambers in September, the calling notice reminded members that the movement was non-political and that political questions should not be raised with the distinguished visitor. In the meantime, however, other questions had been put to David Howell, one of Whitelaw's ministers, by Maurice Gabbey, Harry Dunlop, and the Secretary: they concerned the possibility of further Government aid for the ailing Trade Centre — and the response was very positive. The Ministry of Commerce would provide grants of £5,000 a year for the next two years in the hope that the project would by then have become viable — a move that was in accord with a generous aid-package being offered at that time to stimulate the economy generally.

Meanwhile the British nation was fast approaching one of the turning points in its history — accession to the European Economic Community on 1 January 1973. As a result partly of routine cross-Border discussions with sister organisations in the Republic, the Chamber became convinced that Northern Ireland must have direct representation in Brussels; and Gabbey pursued this vigorously with civil servants and ministers. They foresaw difficulties in Whitehall, but there was a moment when Willie Whitelaw seemed to say that he would not allow the bureaucracy there to interfere. But the reality was difficult; and in the end the best that could be achieved was for the Ministry of Commerce to establish an industrial development office in Brussels as a convenient centre for its European operations. The debate continues in 1983!

And another theme that is still around in 1983 was much to the fore in late 1972: it was the question of co-ordination between the business organisations at national and regional level through a Confederation of British Business, an issue raised by the Devlin Report on Business Representation. The Northern Ireland Chamber contributed to the national debate through Allan Gray; but it would have been unwise to be in the forefront when the Chamber because of its financial situation was paying very much less than its share to the national organisation. However neither financial stringency nor community tension prevented the Chamber and its guests from relaxing for a while at its first dinner dance in the Culloden Hotel at Craigavad on 14 October: the tickets were £2.60 each, and overnight accommodation was £3.75 for a single and £7.50 for a double.

Representation in the EEC and reaction to the Devlin Report provided threads of continuity between Maurice Gabbey and his entrepreneurial successor as President, Erik Utitz of United Chrometanners Killyleagh. Utitz had been the energetic Chairman of the Chamber's International Commerce Committee some years previously; and he had a particular interest in the effect of Common Market membership on export prospects. The Chamber had for some years been attempting to prepare its members for Community membership by seminars and articles; but Utitz felt that the organisation should also arrange for a small group of members to go to Brussels to see for themselves. Such a visit took place in July 1973, involving the President himself together with John C McDowell of the Milk Marketing Board and the Secretary; and it gave rise to a most valuable report which again came down on the side of Northern Ireland representation either through an office in Brussels or by frequent well-directed visits.

Meanwhile a small steering committee or "think tank" was working hard within the Chamber to produce new ideas for consideration by the Executive; and those brought forward included the institution of a group telex scheme and a group pension scheme; reduction in the frequency of issue of "Northern Ireland Progress" from monthly to quarterly; and the introduction of a simple Business Letter produced on a duplicator in the office and issued to members as frequently as circumstances dictated. The first Business Letter was issued on 10 January 1974; and it carried a foreword from Erik Utitz which indicated that "Progress" had been totally superceded by the new medium. But it was the second issue that aroused most interest that year, for it not only detailed the membership and role of the new power-sharing Executive that had been established a few weeks earlier to restore devolved government to the Province; but also indicated for the first time to the Chamber membership at large that the financial situation of the Trade Centre was such that the bold experiment must come to an end. The office-bearers were seeking to dispose of the Chamber's interest in the lease of the premises: "the troubles" had exacted another toll. But there was good news too, for John Hume of the Social Democratic and Labour Party, as Minister of Commerce, had just opened his department's new industrial development office in Brussels and spoken encouragingly of its role. The office was to be headed by a young man called Robert Ramsey, who had been Brian Faulkner's aide in earlier days.

Erik E Utitz OBE
President 1973

Robert D Rolston CBE
President 1975

Sir Ivan Ewart DSC
President 1974

Andrew B Copnall MBE
President 1976

A James Beale MA
President 1977

Stanley Craigs OBE
President 1978

Shortly afterwards Erik Utitz vacated the chair in favour of Sir Ivan Ewart, the sixth member of that very famous linen family to become President of the Chamber in the course of its history. Sir Ivan's first concern was about the security situation in the country, as it affected business people and business confidence; and a week after he was installed, his Senior Vice-President, R D Rolston, addressed a very firm and detailed letter on the subject to the Secretary of State on behalf of the President and Council. But soon the President would also have to cope with the appalling consequences for business of the political strike called by the Ulster Workers' Council in the middle of May, an action which cost industry £80 million in lost production and brought down the power-sharing Executive. Just before the strike Len Murray of the TUC was the guest of the Chamber at the annual lunch in the Culloden Hotel. He had high hopes that the Review Body on Industrial Relations in Northern Ireland, chaired by Dr George Quigley, would come up with a blueprint for the maintenance of industrial peace, political strikes excluded.

For the man who took over from Sir Ivan Ewart as President, the leadership role in a business organisation was not a new experience; for he had been twice President of Belfast Junior Chamber, two years Chairman of CBI Northern Ireland, and deeply involved in many other streams of Ulster's industrial and commercial life. That was the wealth of experience which Robert Dewar Rolston, more usually known as "Bob", brought to the Presidential chair. And he set himself two immediate tasks. The first was to ensure that businessmen in Northern Ireland understood the consequences of a negative vote in the referendum that was shortly to take place about continued membership of the European Community; and the second was to get the finances of the Chamber on the way to recovery by maximising the effects of the remedial measures that were already in hand or under discussion. These included the axing of the Trade Centre; the transfer of the Chamber offices to a less commodious area on the third floor of the building; the continued suspension of the Chamber journal; tight cost-control in which the staff co-operated sacrificially; and a further drive to increase membership, the area on which Deborah Kerr had been concentrating since the demise of the journal. This programme was facilitated by the co-operation of the Department of Commerce and of Desmond Lorimer (later, Sir Desmond) as Chairman of Lamont Life Assurance, the new landlords of Chamber of Commerce House, and by the generosity of the Northern Bank, which waived interest on the indebtedness and agreed an attainable repayment schedule. And the Chamber was particularly grateful to Boyd McClure who had been Honorary Treasurer in the period of greatest difficulty and was now succeeded by R N Bowman, the manager of the historic Waring Street branch of the Northern Bank, who subsequently became one of the Managing Directors of that institution.

Under Nick Bowman's genial stewardship (which would last until 1982 when he would be succeeded by the present Honorary Treasurer, Hugh Davis, also of the Northern Bank) the financial situation of the Chamber would be transformed. Apart from the withdrawal from the Trade Centre and from the Journal and the continued exercise of tight cost-control, there were other factors which aided recovery. Chief amongst these was an upsurge in the demand for export documentation, caused

Hugh Davis, Honorary Treasurer since 1982,
latest in a long line of Treasurers from the
Northern Bank and the Belfast Banking
Company.

H Maurice Gabbey President 1972.
Honorary Treasurer 1967-1971.

partly by new requirements of the customs authorities in the Republic of Ireland and
partly by enhanced export activity by Northern Ireland firms, particularly in the food
sector. But other helpful factors included the Chamber earnings from its servicing of
the Post Office Users' Council; a steady increase in membership in response to good
programmes and useful services; the annual alignment of membership subscriptions
with inflation; and the conduct of seminars and similar events on a profit-earning basis.
The result is that the Chamber in 1983 is much stronger financially than at any time in
its two-hundred-year history, despite the difficult economic circumstances of recent
years and the loss of many valued members as victims of the recession.

But if the road to financial recovery for the Chamber began in 1975/76, so too did a
pattern of activities that would remain relatively unchanged for the remainder of this
story. Each of the eight Presidents since Bob Rolston has made a distinctive personal
contribution and has introduced changes and stimulated new ideas. But the basic
framework has remained unchanged, for reasons that are not difficult to find. The first
is that the environment in which the Chamber has had to operate has continued to
comprise direct rule from Westminster through a succession of Secretaries of State; a
greater or lesser degree of terrorist activity and community tension; and severe
economic difficulty, coupled with low profitability, reduced investment, and high
unemployment. And the second reason for a relatively unchanged pattern of
Chamber activity is that members appear to have found it appropriate, as evidenced
by an increase in membership from six-hundred-and-fifty in 1975 to almost nine-
hundred in 1981 and by a relative absence of criticism.

Bob Rolston worked hard on promoting the views of the business community on the
issues of the day with the direct-rule Ministers of his time; and his successors have
done likewise with successive ministerial teams. He also worked hard on building up
the prestige of the Chamber with Ministers, senior civil servants, the professions, and
the heads of the various public services; and his successors have sought to do likewise.

Finally, he put renewed effort into maintaining the "Northern Ireland" as opposed to the "Belfast" image of the Chamber by visiting the provincial towns, calling on the mayors or chairmen of councils, and having meetings both with affiliated chambers and with local direct members of the Northern Ireland Chamber; and his successors have tried to do likewise, each through his own particular inclination or strength.

Similarly, over the past eight years the annual programme of the Chamber has varied only slightly from a well-established and well-tried pattern. Each year's general meeting in the spring has been followed by a reception to enable the new President to meet members and their families and friends socially; and the serious work of the session has then been tackled through a number of specialist committees that meet as required, a small Executive Committee that meets monthly, and a large Council that meets three or four times a year. Small working parties have also been appointed as required, to deal with specific issues by formulating a proposed Chamber attitude for endorsement or modification by the Executive. And the general membership has been informed, advised, and involved through the business services provided, the monthly Business Letter, an Annual Year Book, four or five business lunches a year, a programme of seminars, and a number of social events including a dinner dance and a golf outing.

In accordance with tradition dating back to the last quarter of the 19th Century, the Council of the Chamber has continued to include nominees from many other trade associations and professional bodies, together with representatives of Belfast City Council and the Belfast Chamber of Trade. In addition, and of more recent standing, there have been nominated representatives of the Belfast Junior Chamber of Commerce, the Standing Committee of Presidents of Affiliated Chambers, the Northern Ireland Tourist Board, and the Ulster Farmers Union; and the Junior Chamber has also been represented on the Executive Committee, by its President. Thus the Council of the Chamber has potentially provided a parliament of industry, commerce, agriculture, tourism, and the public and professional services of the Province, though it has seldom been seen in that light and seldom (if ever) used in that way. But the Chamber in practice has had another way in which to make the wishes of the business community known and to have its interests upheld: that has been through its seventy-five nominees on forty-two public bodies, committees, and tribunals ranging from the Lights Advisory Committee to the Northern Ireland Council on Alcohol, from the Value Added Tax Tribunal to the Design Council, from the Senate of Queen's University Belfast to the Governors of the Hotel and Catering College at Portrush. Thus the modern Chamber is an organisation of many strands and of great potential strength as a medium for ascertaining, co-ordinating, channelling, and promoting the views of the entire business and professional community in Northern Ireland on almost any subject.

Such is the background to the distinctive personal contribution of each of the Presidents since 1976. The first of that octet was Andrew B Copnall, Regional Sales Manager for ICI Ltd, who succeeded to the top office in the spring of 1976, after chairing the Chamber's Development and Transport Committee for three years at the beginning of the decade. His Presidential theme was *"Involvement"* and his advice to members: *"Make your voice heard"*. But he himself had the task of making the Chamber voice heard on the many business issues of the day, which included the effects or likely effects of new legislation on Fair Employment, Sex Discrimination, and Industrial Relations; the future role of the Ulster Office in London in the context of direct rule; the establishment of the Northern Ireland Development Agency in succession to the Northern Ireland Finance Corporation; new security arrangements at Aldergrove Airport; and the effects of transport costs on the viability and competitiveness of Northern Ireland manufacturers.

But Andrew Copnall's greatest task — a task in which he was helped by many members of the Chamber — was to make a thoughtful and effective contribution on behalf of the organisation to a review of the Government's economic and industrial strategy for Northern Ireland, which had been commissioned by the Labour Secretary of State, Roy Mason. The review was being undertaken by a team of senior civil servants headed by Dr George Quigley; and a Chamber group led by Andrew Copnall had a long discussion with them on 29 April 1976. In the course of that discussion Copnall and his colleagues advocated many points that would feature in Chamber policy in the succeeding years, such as the effect of energy and freight costs on competitiveness, the need to encourage added-value processing, the role of small business and indigenous industry, and the need for the provision of incentives to work and for curbing abuse of the social security system. The Chamber was therefore pleased when a number of these points featured directly or indirectly in Dr Quigley's magnificent report published in September 1976; and Andrew Copnall immediately established a working party comprising R D Rolston, A J Beale of PA Management Consultants, K T Sturgess of the Ulster Weaving Company, the Secretary, and himself to dissect and analyse the report and its recommendations. The outcome was almost total Chamber endorsement of the recommendations of that far-seeing and still relevant document.

As the towering Scot, A J Beale, came to the Presidential chair in March 1977 the Chamber had re-established an Export Committee, chaired first by Andrew Copnall and then by Dr George Chambers, Chief Executive of the Milk Marketing Board, who had for some time been representing the Chamber on the British Overseas Trade Advisory Council. A working party chaired by Angus Gordon, Managing Director of Robinson & Cleaver Ltd, was hard at work on industrial democracy and employee involvement in the context of the Bullock Report; another, led by M W S Maclaran of G Heyn & Sons Ltd, was doing a most thorough job on quantifying the effects of transport costs on Northern Ireland industry; and a third group, headed by Ross Campbell of Lawther & Harvey Ltd, was weighing up the pros and cons of the Red and the Blue Transportation Strategies for Belfast in the future. But Jim Beale was soon faced with a more immediate problem: the dreaded prospect of another political strike that would (as most Chamber members saw it) cripple industry, inconvenience the public, and achieve nothing. These views were shared by CBI Northern Ireland (where Beale's Senior Vice-President, Stan Craigs of Courtaulds, was Chairman) and by the Northern Ireland Committee of the Irish Congress of Trade Unions; and the three organisations issued a joint statement in strong terms. In the event the strike was poorly backed and damage to industry was minimal. But it was a heyday for the news media including Downtown, the new commercial radio station at Newtownards.

Roy Mason's firm stand against the strike was admired in business circles; but there was still greater admiration for a range of measures that he and his popular lieutenant, Don Concannon, introduced in the summer and autumn of 1977 to help the Ulster economy. Parallel to these measures, the Economic Council was re-established, but on a different basis: this time it was to be totally independent, with its own staff, its own Director, and its own independent Chairman. There would be fifteen members — five nominated by the trade unions, five by employers, and five by the Secretary of State — and the first Chairman would be Professor Charles F Carter (later Sir Charles), Vice-Chancellor of Lancaster University and former Professor of Applied Economics at Queen's University Belfast. The Chamber was deeply involved in prior discussion with the CBI about the constitution and role of the new Council; and there was general agreement that the outcome represented a significant advance.

Meanwhile the Chamber itself had been pursuing an economic initiative which resulted in the publication towards the end of the year of a report entitled "Operating a Business in Northern Ireland". This was based on surveys by working parties chaired by W Elliott and R M Gibson, which reported to a policy group chaired by the President. Many of the recommendations were still on the table as Jim Beale's busy year came to and end and as he installed his successor, Stan Craigs, an Englishman who was well-known in the economic life of Northern Ireland not only as the head of the huge Courtaulds operation at Carrickfergus, but also for his devotion to the best interests of his adopted Province.

Though he himself was involved in big business, Stan Craigs directed the attention of the Chamber to the importance of small business; and he soon established a working party, chaired by R Gordon Smyth of Smyths for Records, to research and publish a report entitled 'Stimulating Small Business in Northern Ireland". Concurrent with that project the Chamber under Stan Craigs' vigorous leadership was also deeply involved in preparing evidence for the Birley Committee on "Opportunities at Sixteen"; in considering electricity charges in the light of the Shepherd Report and the escalation in costs as a result of a succession of oil crises; in framing representations on the revision of Company Law, where a group chaired by J Mc C Creighton was doing valuable work; and in assessing the implications of the Health and Safety at Work Order which became law in the autumn. The small-business project received a great fillip from the visit of the Chancellor of the Duchy of Lancaster, the Rt Hon Harold Lever, to address the annual lunch in the presence both of the Secretary of State and of his Minister of State responsible for Commerce, Don Concannon. Harold Lever at that time had responsibility at Cabinet level for stimulating small business nationally.

The theme was also of interest to the next President though he too came from an organisation that was large by Northern Ireland standards. This was Dr George Chambers of the Milk Marketing Board, who succeeded Stan Craigs in the spring of

1979. Chambers had been Chairman of the Export Committee prior to his setting foot on the Presidential ladder; and he retained that office not only during his two years as Vice-President, but also during his Presidential year. Inevitably, therefore, the subject of marketing and of export marketing in particular came strongly to the fore during his time in office. Yet the more important task was to establish a good working relationship with the new team of Ministers that came to Northern Ireland in the summer of 1979, consequent upon Mrs Thatcher's Conservative victory in the British General Election. In this task, the organisation got off to a good start through the decision of the new Secretary of State, Humphrey Atkins, to make his first public appearance in the Province at a Chamber lunch: that took place at the Culloden Hotel at Cultra on 30 May and it attracted an embarrassingly large attendance of three-hundred-and-forty, a record for a Chamber lunch in recent times.

Later in the year the dialogue with Ministers was continued both through written submissions and in a series of meetings; and a particularly good relationship was established with Giles Shaw, the Minister responsible for Commerce. The Chamber applauded the Government's determination to bring inflation under control; but was extremely critical of Government inactivity as the man-made fibre industry — so vital to Ulster — began to collapse as a result of reduced demand, over-capacity, and American competition. Another notable development was the drawing together of a strong case for the establishment of a unified, independent, and commercial structure for the promotion of industrial development: this was submitted to Sir Robert Kidd, former Head of the Northern Ireland Civil Service, who had been asked to review structures, parallel to a review of incentives by Arthur Andersen & Co. Significant too was the reactivation of an Education and Training Committee in the Chamber, under the stimulus of R B Henderson, Managing Director of Ulster Television Ltd, as chairman. Later this committee also encompassed Employment, as in the earlier years when it had been most successfully led by Jim Beale and by Mrs Margot Neill, who had subsequently become Chairman of the Equal Opportunities Commission.

Though the Chamber had a high regard for Mrs Neill and the other members and staff of the Equal Opportunities Commission and similar bodies — which were by then known menacingly as QUANGOs (quasi-autonomous non-Governmental organisations) — there was a strong feeling that industry was being subjected to rather too much harassment on labour and sociological law from too many quarters. This was reflected in the decision by R B Henderson, as he became President in the spring of 1980, to add the control of quangos to his chosen themes of *"Education and Communication"*. The new President came to office with heritage on his side; for several of his paternal ancestors had been active in the Chamber from the middle of the previous century, and his maternal grandfather — R B Henry — had been President in 1925. His chosen themes of education and communication were also in the mould of the man; for he had been a member of the Lockwood Committee which had stimulated a revolution in education in the Province in the 1970s, and communication ran deep in his veins as an eloquent speaker, a colourful writer, an experienced journalist, and the executive head of commercial television in Ulster for over twenty years.

Like his predecessors, Brum Henderson (as he is generally known) maintained the heavy programme of traditional activities, including liaison with the affiliated chambers and with sister organisations in the Republic of Ireland (in the course of his year he had the unique distinction of addressing the Dublin, Galway, Limerick, and Waterford Chambers). Reacting quickly to the marketing message of changed requirements, he also led the Chamber into such areas as improved industry/school liaison (where A C Brooke made notable contributions in his retirement from the higher reaches of the Civil Service); the great debate on industrial relations legislation (where the Government was undoing some of the measures introduced by its predecessors and seeking to curb trade-union power); and the whole energy scene (where the issues involved and the options available were steadily becoming more complex, as confirmed by John Gault's Chamber working party which reported in September 1980). These and many other issues were pursued not only through the Standing Committees and working parties, but also through business lunches where the list of distinguished speakers was headed by former Northern Ireland Minister, David Howell, who had become Secretary of State for Energy in Mrs Thatcher's administration. The GOC of the Army in Northern Ireland, Lt General Sir Richard Lawson, also made a welcome return visit to the Chamber, following his debut some twelve months earlier during George Chambers' Presidency. Thus Brum Henderson maintained a very high profile for the organisation, a situation that was apparent too in the reinvigoration of the long-standing *"meeting of seven"* under his chairmanship, these being occasions when representatives of seven business organisations meet informally with Westminster and European MPs to discuss current business issues.

Brum Henderson's successor was J R Fetherston, who had been local head of Albion Ltd for many years and was deeply steeped in the traditions and problems of the clothing industry — an industry which had long been one of Ulster's largest but less glamorous employers and was at that moment suffering grievously from world recession, intense competition from the developing countries, and the side-effects of the Government's remedies for the nation. Total industrial output in Northern Ireland was falling sharply as the recession, compounded by local factors, bit deeply; factory closures and massive redundancies were almost a daily occurrence; there was a great cloud again overhanging the future of the Belfast shipyard; and unemployment was approaching a hundred-thousand, representing over seventeen per cent of the insured population. In such circumstances it was essential that the Chamber should leave the Government in no doubt about the urgent need for new initiatives to save what was left of Ulster's industry and to stimulate investment. Jack Fetherston articulated that concern clearly and forthrightly; and he was reflecting deep feelings of despair in the Chamber at that time.

But as the hard-working and grimly determined President took office in March 1981 and began his interaction with the Hon Adam Butler, who had replaced Giles Shaw as Minister responsible for Commerce, the first ray of hope was already peeping over the horizon: it stemmed from a visit of the Prime Minister, Mrs Thatcher, to the Province some weeks earlier when she had promised that electricity prices in Northern Ireland would despite the greater dependence on expensive oil-fired generation be pegged to the level applying in the highest-cost region in Great Britain. And soon there would be further welcome news as the Government finally acceded to pressure from the Economic Council, ICTU, and all the business organisations including the Chamber on the need for new structures for the promotion of industrial development. The Northern Ireland Development Agency and the Industrial Development Organisation of the Department of Commerce were to be merged in a new Industrial Development Board that would have a substantial degree of independence, with its own board drawn from industry and commerce and key staff recruited or seconded from the private sector. LEDU, the highly-successful small business organisation would retain its independence and have its remit widened; and the Departments of Commerce and Manpower Services would in due time be merged into a new Department of Economic Development.

Meanwhile Jack Fetherston was energetically involved in the routine programme of Chamber activities, which again made heavy demands both on the President and on the staff. Behind the many meetings and public events there was as usual an immense amount of preparation; and that had to be dovetailed with the "bread-and-butter" activities of the Chamber such as dealing with up to six-thousand commercial enquiries a year, issuing five-thousand export documents, and processing over four-thousand messages in the group telex scheme. The Secretary's supporting staff of nine (including part-timers), headed by David Campbell as Administration Manager and Deborah McCauley as Public Relations Manager, had therefore few dull moments in this or in any other year in the recent past.

But Jack Fetherston's year was also marked by many non-routine features; and four will be chosen for brief mention. The first was the introduction at the President's personal initiative of a new-style business lunch, with the theme *"Let's get down to business"*. These were occasions when small groups of Chamber members gave presentations on their own business problems and the solutions adopted. The second non-routine feature was an ambitious publicity project spearheaded by Immediate Past-President Brum Henderson, involving the production by Ulster Television Ltd of an audio-visual presentation entitled *"There must be two places called Northern Ireland"*. This was intended for use by Ulster businessmen in their overseas trips as a means of projecting a more balanced image of the Province and its amenities as well as its problems. Another initiative worthy of special mention was the President's letter to over a hundred chambers of commerce in Great Britain and in the United States, putting Northern Ireland's security and political problems in perspective and seeking their understanding and help in the solution of its economic difficulties. In the event these two publicity initiatives were most timely, for there were serious community problems in the autumn and winter of 1981 which further distorted the image of Northern Ireland around the world. And the fourth non-routine feature of Jack Fetherston's year was also timely, for it offered another escape route for local business: this was the report *"Marketing for Economic Recovery"* produced by the Export Committee under the leadership of Dr George Chambers.

Several of the recommendations of that marketing report were still being debated as Jack Fetherston handed over the reins of office to the genial Sir Myles Humphreys in the spring of 1982. But the business scene was dominated by the tragic and bizarre collapse of De Lorean Motor Cars Ltd, which affected many Chamber members. For that reason the Chamber had agreed to service a committee representing the unsecured creditors; and to provide a channel for representations to the Secretary of State, who was now James Prior, one of the most experienced and respected figures in the whole British political scene.

Likewise Sir Myles Humphreys, as he came to the Presidential chair of the Chamber, was one of the best-known public figures in Northern Ireland. As Lord Mayor of Belfast in 1975-77, he had been a popular ambassador for the city at home and abroad; and in subsequent years, he had given further public service as Chairman both of Northern Ireland Railways and of the Police Authority, as well as maintaining his other business interests. His declared aims as President of the Chamber were to maintain the existing pattern of Chamber activities but with greater involvement of the affiliated chambers and with more attention to import substitution as a contributor to economic recovery. And he was soon busy on the first of these tasks by organising meetings with the Presidents of many of the provincial chambers.

However as the year progressed — a year in which unemployment climbed to over twenty per cent — Sir Myles and his colleagues inevitably became involved in many other non-routine areas. For some time there had been intense debate in the Chamber on Government proposals and consultative documents on management education and training, youth training, and industrial training generally — areas in which the Chamber's deliberations had been greatly assisted by the experience and leadership of Bill Slinger, a former Permanent Secretary in the Civil Service who was heading the personnel function in Carreras Rothmans (NI) Ltd; and several facets of the subject came to decision point in Government circles in the course of 1982. Amongst the consequences was the introduction of a most ambitious and imaginative Youth Training Programme in the autumn, with the full encouragement and assistance of the Chamber. There was consultation too on the membership and guidelines of the Industrial Development Board; and the office-bearers had an early meeting with the new Chief Executive of the Board, Saxon Tate of Tate & Lyle Ltd. Above all, as the year ended, Sir Myles led the Chamber into close discussion with Nicholas Scott, the member of Mr Prior's ministerial team responsible for publicity aspects of the Northern Ireland situation; and this resulted in a commitment of the Chamber to play a major part in the IDB's image campaign in 1983 — a commitment that represented the fulfillment of a dream for one Chamber member who had for several years been advocating greater involvement of the organisation in community leadership and in the restoration of confidence in Northern Ireland's ability and of pride in its heritage. That was C V Edmunds of Edmunds Catering Equipment, whose enthusiasm and ingenuity knew no bounds.

And so the Chamber came to its Bicentenary Year, the year which was so ingrained in the minds of a small group of members who had spent many hours in the course of 1982 discussing and planning how it should be celebrated. But first there were other notable events to take place — events which each in different ways also pointed both to the future and to the past. On 9 February John Gaston, the Chairman of the

The Bicentenary President with a group of Past-Presidents 1983. Seated, left to right: J A Gray (1968), R N Crawford (1966), R T Jordan (1983), R E Thompson (1971), J A Rodgers (1970), Dr H S Corscadden (1969). Standing, left to right: Dr George Chambers (1979), J R Fetherston (1981), Dr R B Henderson (1980), Sir Myles Humphreys (1982), G H Dunlop (1967). (Photo by Noel Quinn).

Northern Ireland Electricity Service, gave a milestone address to a business lunch on the theme *"Generation Strategy in Northern Ireland"*, which summarised an important report published by the Service at that time. Twelve days earlier the great and the good had assembled yet again, in the lofty Great Hall of Queen's University, for a truly historic occasion: this was the celebration of the tenth anniversary of the enlargement of the European Community, an event honoured by the presence of EC Commissioner Christopher Tugendhat, Irish Prime Minister Dr Garret FitzGerald, and former British Prime Minister Edward Heath. And five weeks later to the day, the Chamber staged its own historic occasion in the form of a splendid dinner in the offices of the Belfast Harbour Commissioners when Sir Myles Humphreys, himself a Harbour Commissioner, presided over a gathering of some two-hundred members and their guests, and when David Mitchell, the Environment Minister, proposed the toast to the Chamber. That evening, Sir Myles was wearing a magnificent new chain of office to accompany the Insignia presented by David Andrews in 1964 and modified by Harry Dunlop in 1967. Sir Myles himself had generously presented that chain to the Chamber; and fifteen days later he would pass it on to Robert T Jordan, as the former Esso man began a momentous twelve months as President of the Chamber in its Bicentenary Year.

Bob Jordan was an ideal man for that role, for he had just retired at an early age from his demanding position as Branch Manager of Esso Ltd. In his twenty-six years in the oil business — which followed five with Belfast Corporation — he had progressed steadily to his company's top post in Northern Ireland; and he had for many years acted as part-time oil-adviser to Government departments. Despite a serious illness in 1982, he tackled the Bicentenary Year with zest and aplomb; and he attracted goodwill and co-operation wherever he went, for his approach evoked that kind of response. That goodwill was exhibited too in the generosity of many firms in their contributions towards Bicentenary events; and an early expression of very substantial support from Ulster Television Ltd gave a particular uplift to the Bicentenary Committee, for it offered the prospect that the anniversary could be celebrated with expansiveness and style.

As the new President took up office in March, he announced that his priorities (apart from marking the Bicentenary appropriately) would be employment, the Northern Ireland image, the work of the Industrial Development Board, and energy conservation. These subjects would indeed occupy his attention as the months progressed; and he was soon able to confirm that the Chamber would make a strong input to a promotional mission to the United States and Canada in the autumn, which was being arranged by the Northern Ireland Partnership, the new grouping formed by IDB to enable local business people to play a part in correcting the image of Northern Ireland overseas, as well as mobilising the support of expatriates and other friends of the Province around the world. And as the Secretary of State in April announced a number of significant additions to the range of aids that IDB could offer to potential investors — aids that in part were previously thought to be impossible constitutionally — the Chamber too broke new ground. First, there was a seminar at the beginning of May on product development, under the leadership of the new Second Vice-President, H V Shimmons, Managing Director of RFD Ltd, who had chaired the Business Affairs Committee for several years. And second, there was a most useful interaction with the Merseyside Chamber when thirty of its members spent a day in Northern Ireland, by courtesy of Manx Airlines. Several business contacts were established and the various aids to economic development were reviewed, including the Enterprise Zone concept which the Government had introduced some years earlier to stimulate rejuvenation of run-down areas in regions such as Merseyside and Northern Ireland. In Belfast the concept was enjoying modest success; and there was satisfaction later when it was announced that Londonderry too was to have an Enterprise Zone. But neither Enterprise Zones nor Kinsale gas, nor even the prospect of learning Cantonese at the Ulster Polytechnic (which was advertised in the Business Letter), could divert the Chamber in 1983 from its determination to mark its origins in 1783 in a way that history would remember.

With the assistance of Bob Jordan's old firm, Esso Ltd, the Bicentenary was first brought to the attention of the public early in the year by the wide circulation of a colourful leaflet containing snippets of the history, glimpses of some of the personalities, and an outline of the programme of celebratory events. As a further trailer for the main activities in the autumn, the Chamber in association with the

Northern Ireland Electricity Service had a magnificent float in the Lord Mayor's Show in Belfast on 14 May, where it was awarded the Lord Mayor's Trophy for turn-out. The timing was appropriate, for it was in May 1783 that the merchants of Belfast met on several occasions to make preliminary plans for their Chamber of Commerce.

But in the next series of events it was the mode of travel that was appropriate: it was the historic Directors' Coach of the GNR, hauled by an authentic steam locomotive, by courtesy of the Railway Preservation Society, Northern Ireland Railways, and the Ulster Bank. This striking cavalcade — complete with Chamber and railway dignatories, ladies in ancient and modern costume, and an array of flags specially commissioned by the Commercial Union — travelled from Belfast to Lisburn and Portadown, to Ballymena, and to Coleraine and Londonderry on three successive days at the beginning of September; and at each venue, the President of the Northern Ireland Chamber and his party were received by the Presidents and other office-bearers of the affiliated chambers in the surrounding area, and mementos were exchanged. In this way the provincial chambers were fully associated with the Bicentenary Celebrations, and the breadth of the Chamber's interests was widely portrayed.

Fashion had come into the "Chamber on Tour", for the tour party had included two models in contrasting styles, and the men were all wearing the striking Bicentenary Tie commissioned on behalf of the Chamber by C V Edmunds. But fashion had a night of its own immediately afterwards, when Deborah McCauley on behalf of the Chamber and in association with Robinson & Cleaver, Hairlines of Great Victoria Street, and BP Oil organised a huge charity event in the Forum Hotel — "The Changing Face of Fashion" followed by a cheese and wine supper — which realised £2,000 for cardiac research.

The "Chamber on Tour" at Lisburn Station 5 September 1983.

Dr W A Maguire, keeper of local history at the Ulster Museum, preparing for the opening of the "Captains of Commerce" Exhibition, 17 October 1983.   (Photo by courtesy of the Belfast News Letter).

Next the emphasis switched to a more profound aspect of history: a "Captains of Commerce Exhibition" in the Ulster Museum, which ran from its opening by Adam Butler on 17 October till the end of the year. Sponsored by Carreras Rothmans (NI) Ltd and organised by Dr W A Maguire, keeper of local history at the museum, in consultation with Dr George Chambers of the Chamber, this fascinating exhibition featured industry and commerce in Belfast in 1783, 1883, and 1983, together with some of the early Chamber personalities and memorabilia.

Four days after the opening of the exhibition at the Ulster Museum, the scene changed to the Ulster Hall, venue for business lunches of the Chamber in the 1920s and for other memorable events in the organisation's history in earlier decades. But on this occasion the hot air and the vibrating tones came from the ensemble of the Ulster Orchestra under its conductor Bryden Thomson, in a splendid performance from a number of the works of Sir Hamilton Harty, the distinguished Ulster composer. And

296

the audience included many members of the Chamber and of other organisations that had helped in various ways with the Bicentenary. For them, it was a memorable evening, rounded off by an "Old Bushmills" reception in a nearby hostelry.

Sunday 23 October 1983 — and once again the scene is changed, to Saint Anne's Cathedral, for an inter-denominational service of praise and thanksgiving, conducted by the Dean of Belfast, the Very Reverend Samuel B Crooks. In that lovely temple of the 20th Century — standing on the spot where earlier had stood the 18th Century Parish Church of Saint Anne's and earlier still a centre of commerce in unbleached linen — a congregation of more than a thousand business people and their friends were uplifted by beautiful music, dignified ceremony, earnest prayers, and the thoughtful address of Dr Robin Eames, the Church of Ireland Bishop of Down and Dromore. The Queen was represented by Her Lieutenant, Lord Glentoran, former Minister of Commerce at Stormont and member of the Dixon family who were active in the Chamber over many decades; the Government by the Earl of Mansfield, Minister of State responsible for Agriculture (who read one of the lessons); and the City by the Lord Mayor, Councillor Alfred Ferguson. The procession included the Moderator of the Presbyterian Church in Ireland, a former President of the Methodist Church in Ireland, and the Roman Catholic Director for Ecumenism in Down and Connor. The President of the Chamber read the first lesson; members of the Chamber acted as ushers and collectors; and the proceedings began and ended with a fanfare from the trumpeters of the 1st Battalion of the Royal Highland Fusiliers. The service was televised by Ulster Television and transmitted nationally; and as the cameras ceased zooming, the microphones were switched off, and the great congregation dispersed, it was a proud moment for Val Edmunds who had been the chief organiser on the Chamber side.

Thus dignified by worship and remembrance, the Bicentenary reached its climax in a great banquet in Belfast City Hall on the evening of Tuesday 25 October, the 200th anniversary of that first Council meeting in 1783 when Waddell Cunningham was elected President of the Chamber. It was a function that historians will in due time compare with the extravaganza laid on by the Chamber in 1899 for the delegates to the annual conference of the British Chamber Movement, but with the 19th Century role of Robert Lloyd Patterson taken on by Leslie M McAlpine, the chief organiser and convenor of the 1983 Banquet Committee. A glittering attendance of almost four hundred, enlivened by a champagne reception and slightly startled by the clarion notes of the authentically-attired Trumpeter Silcock from Hillsborough, sat down to one of the best meals ever served in Belfast. Afterwards the Hon Adam Butler MP, Minister of State responsible for the new Department of Economic Development, proposed the toast to the Chamber; the President replied in appropriate terms; the Secretary, Geoffrey Auret, thanked Dr George Chambers for researching and writing the Chamber history and handed over a presentation of a Rowel Friers caricature, which Dr Chambers acknowledged; and Dr R B Henderson CBE proposed the toast to the guests, who included the Lord Mayor and Lady Mayoress, the Deputy Lieutenant (Sir Robin Kinahan) and his Lady, and representatives of many British and Irish Chambers, of kindred organisations, and of the Civil Service. The chief guest

At the Bicentenary Banquet 25 October 1983.

Minister of State, Adam Butler, and the President, R T Jordan, examining a memento while the Lord Mayor, Councillor Alfred Ferguson looks on.

Leslie McAlpine (right), Banquet Convenor, supervises the cutting of the Bicentenary Cake by the President and Mrs Jordan.

Alastair Burnet, star of the small screen and distinguished in business journalism and current affairs, replied amusingly and perceptively. And the Bicentenary Banquet was over, save for the memories of an occasion that had all the frills thanks to the generous sponsorship of the Trustee Savings Bank, the thoughtfulness of the Ulster Weaving Company (which provided gift napkins), and the meticulous organisation of Leslie McAlpine and his colleagues, backed up by the Chamber staff.

Four days later it was meticulous preparation and finely-tuned choice of word and phrase that the audience in the lecture theatre of the Social Sciences block at Queen's University admired when the Vice-Chancellor, Dr Peter Froggatt, gave the Bicentenary Lecture entitled *"Belfast: Some Reflections of Prospect and Retrospect".* Drawing on his deep understanding of the influences abroad in Belfast in the late 18th and early 19th Centuries as they involved and affected the pioneers of medicine in the town, the speaker enthralled his audience with a perceptive analysis of the reasons for gradual change in political thought and in attitudes within the Ulster business community over the past two-hundred years. He found it difficult, however, to project unequivocally from the experience of the past, though his brief prospective was in the main optimistic. Dr Froggatt was thanked by Bill Slinger who had been the chief organiser on behalf of the Chamber. The lecture will be published as a pamphlet, by courtesy of Century Newspapers Ltd.

Just as the Chamber in 1849 asked the Town Council to *"consider the propriety of making arrangements for the exhibition of suitable fireworks"* as Queen Victoria and her Consort sailed out of Belfast, so the Chamber in 1983 decided that the Bicentenary week should go out with a bang, in a fireworks display at Windsor Park Football Grounds. The event was held on Hallowe'en; and the proceeds were devoted to charity thanks to the co-operation of the Belfast Telegraph and generous sponsorship from Gallaher Ltd.

John D Coyle, President of the Galway Chamber of Commerce (left), and Connor V Connolly, Past-President of Galway (2nd left), handing over an inscribed decanter to the President (right) and Secretary of the Northern Ireland Chamber during a goodwill visit to Belfast to mark the Bicentenary.
(Photo by Wilfred Green).

A notable feature of the Bicentenary celebrations was the way in which members of the Chamber rallied round to provide generous financial support for the various projects and events, just as they had done at other great moments in the illustrious history of the organisation. That support continued till the very end, with the Bank of Ireland (which was itself celebrating its 200th anniversary in the same year) joining with its Investment Bank in sponsoring an audio-visual presentation on the changing face of industry and commerce in the Province, and one of the newer and most progressive firms in the country — Norbrook Laboratories of Newry who make pharmaceuticals and veterinary medicines — putting in a substantial contribution to meet residual expenses on various fronts. Generosity and thoughtfulness were apparent too in the many mementos handed over to the Chamber by individual firms and by other chambers of commerce in Northern Ireland, in Great Britain, and in the Republic of Ireland. In time these will become part of the fabric of the history of the

Wilson Ervin, Managing Director of the Northern Bank (centre), handing over the Bicentenary candelabra to the President, R T Jordan (left), and the Immediate Past-President, Sir Myles Humphreys, while G L Auret, Secretary (right), and R N Bowman, Managing Director of the Bank and former Honorary Treasurer of the Chamber, look on. The venue was the Waring Street branch, formerly the Exchange and Assembly Room.
(Photo by Ivan Lyttle).

Chamber, none more so than a splendid candelabra presented by the Northern Bank at a ceremony in its historic Waring Street branch on Wednesday 30 November 1983. In that magnificent building, which in its 18th Century days as the Exchange and Assembly Room had been the very centre of commercial life in Belfast and the venue for the Harp Festival of 1792 and the trial of Henry Joy McCracken in 1798, the Chamber was provided with a symbolic light to lead it into the next two-hundred years. And indeed that march to new initiatives and to further change had already begun, for the Senior Vice-President of the Chamber, John Stringer of Wade (Ireland) Ltd, the Secretary, Geoffrey Auret, and Edward Haughey, Managing Director of Norbrook Laboratories Ltd, had been torch-bearers for the Chamber and for industry and commerce in the Province in the Northern Ireland Partnership's exhaustive and highly successful promotional tour of the United States and Canada between 29 October and 11 November 1983.

There is no more suitable point at which to leave this story of a remarkable organisation that has endured for two-hundred years — an organisation which has been the vent for sacrificial public service by thousands of men and women working together for good — an organisation which has played a major part in changing the

The beginning of the next two hundred years! John Stringer, President-elect of the Chamber, speaking at a Northern Ireland Partnership presentation in the United States. Edward Haughey (top right) also played an important part in the mission. Robert Brett, 1983 President of the Belfast Junior Chamber (bottom right) leads an organisation that may contain the Waddell Cunningham of tomorrow.

face of Ulster. It would be tedious here to list even a fraction of the instances in which the changing faces of the Chamber of Commerce laboured long and laboured successfully for changes in their community — for improved public services, for new institutions, for a better infrastructure, for new industries, for new markets, for new policies. Suffice to say that they did and that Ulster has been much the better for it.

Now, as the Chamber starts out on its next two-hundred years, there are serious problems in the Ulster community, as there have been periodically in the past. But it is important for the world — and for the people of Ulster themselves — to see those problems in proper perspective. That is understandably impossible for that small proportion of the population that has been directly and tragically affected by the violence of recent years. It is difficult too for those who are so immersed in political manoeuvring that they may sometimes be in danger of forgetting that the objective is to devise and operate, to the benefit of all the people, stable political structures and systems that will command the respect and support of the vast majority of the people. And it is more difficult still for those who want to work and cannot find a job — and there are at least a hundred-thousand of them in Northern Ireland today. Yet those serious problems must not be allowed to obscure the fact that the people of Northern Ireland live in a country that is an incomparably better country today in almost every way than at any time in the two-hundred-year history of the Chamber of Commerce.

It would be wonderful to be able to end this work with a confident assessment that Northern Ireland now stood on the threshold of another great boom period in its economic and social history comparable to the second half of the 19th Century or the middle years of the 20th. Though that is not possible, there are in fact many harbingers of hope and sources of encouragement. The last few years have seen the establishment of a springboard for economic progress that can take this community forward again. There are many components in that springboard, such as the establishment of the Industrial Development Board; the improvements in the investment incentives and support services available both to incoming investors and to indigenous industry; the determination to project a more balanced picture of Northern Ireland in the outside world through the Northern Ireland Partnership; the broadening of the remit of the Local Enterprise Development Unit; the review and improvement of the whole fabric of industrial training; the decision to establish a new Management Centre; the huge effort that has been devoted to choosing the right energy options for the future, including the development of the lignite resource at Crumlin and the insertion of Kinsale gas into the energy-mix; and the more effective mobilisation of the resources of the Universities and the Polytechnic to the cause of industrial regeneration and commercial progress.

Within industry itself there is also a new spirit and a new determination. Two of the largest industries in the country are led by men who are imbued with a spirit of enterprise and determination that shines as strongly as the light of entrepreneurial flair shed by the great figures of the 18th and the 19th Centuries. At Short's, Sir Philip Foreman and his team have found a niche in the world market for aircraft which they are filling to perfection with fine products, the SD 330 and the SD 360; and at Harland & Wolff there is a new vibrancy radiating from John Parker, the dynamic young

301

Ulsterman who has recently taken over as Chairman and Chief Executive, with a deep insight of world shipbuilding. There is hope too in the residues of the man-made fibre, textile, clothing, engineering, and artificial-rubber industries that have survived the recession; in the obvious signs of further development of food-processing; in the high-technology Lear Fan jet; in the greater degree of market-orientation that is apparent across the face of Ulster industry, old and new; and in the continued success story of LEDU in the establishment and fostering of small businesses.

But if those hopes are to be realised, the spirit of the merchants of 1783 who founded the Chamber of Commerce and the spirit of the industrial giants of the 19th Century who established the basic fabric of industry in the Province will need to be abroad in the land. Things have changed immeasurably since the merchants of 1783 set out in their frail craft to trade with the world; but many of their virtues are unchanging in their fundamental importance. Reflect, therefore, on the words of Nicholas Breton, written in the reign of the first Queen Elizabeth, and come in spirit if not in fact with the 20th Century "Heirs of Adventure" as they set out on the second two-hundred years of industrial and commercial development in Northern Ireland:

"A worthy Merchant is the Heir of Adventure, whose hopes hang much upon the Winds.

He is a discoverer of countries and a finder-out of commodities, resolute in his attempts and royal in his Expenses.

He is the Exercise of the Exchange, the honour of Credit, the observation of time, and the understanding of thrift.

His study is Number, his Care his accounts, his Comfort his Conscience, and his Wealth his good name.

He fears not Scylla and sails close by Charybdis, and having beaten out a storm rides at rest in a harbour.

He plants the Earth with foreign fruits, and knows at home what is good abroad.

He is neat in apparel, Modest in demeanour, dainty in diet, and Civil in his Carriage.

In sum, he is the pillar of a City, the enricher of a country, the furnisher of a Court, and the Worthy Servant of a Queen."

A BICENTENARY SHARED

The immediate stimulus for the establishment of the Belfast Chamber of Commerce in the autumn of 1783 was the formation of the Dublin Chamber some months previously. It was therefore fitting that the Bicentenary year should end with a meeting between representatives of the two Chambers. This took place in Dublin on 7 December 1983.

The President of the Dublin Chamber, Niall Crowley, receives the President of the Northern Ireland Chamber, Robert T Jordan, outside the offices of the Dublin Chamber.

Council members of the two Chambers. Seated (left to right): John Vaughan, Deputy Vice-President Dublin; Desmond Miller, Vice-President Dublin; the two Presidents; Harry Shimmons, Deputy Vice-President Northern Ireland; and Declan Lennon, Immediate Past-President Dublin.

(Photos by Lensmen, Dublin).

PRESIDENTS OF THE BELFAST AND NORTHERN IRELAND CHAMBERS OF COMMERCE AND INDUSTRY 1783-1983

1783-1790	Waddell Cunningham	1881	Robert H S Reade DL
1791-1794	Alexander Orr	1882	James P Corry MP
1802-1803	Hugh Montgomery	1883	John Jaffe
1804-1806	William Sinclaire	1884	Sir Edward P Cowan DL
1807-1819	Robert Bradshaw	1885	Robert Megaw
1820	Narcissus Batt	1886	J Theodore Richardson
1821-1832	John S Ferguson	1887	Francis D Ward
1833	William Boyd	1888	William Q Ewart
1834	Robert Callwell	1889	Charles C Connor
1835-1842	William Boyd	1890	Adam Duffin
1843-1848	Robert McDowell	1891	William C Mitchell
1849	James Bristow	1892	David B Lytle
1850	James Steen	1893	John Greenhill
1851	John F Ferguson	1894	Herbert O Lanyon
1852	William Coates	1895	R Lloyd Patterson FLS
1853	William Valentine	1896	6th Marquis of Londonderry KG
1854	James Kennedy	1897	R Kyle Knox LL D
1855	James Bristow	1898	Gustav W Wolff MP
1856	John Thomson	1899	Frederick L Heyn
1857	Robert Grimshaw DL	1900	William Crawford
1858	Thomas McClure	1901	Robert Thompson
1859	James Bristow	1902	Rt Hon Thomas Sinclair DL MA
1860	John Herdman	1903	James Wilson ME
1861	John Hind	1904	Walter H Wilson
1862	Thomas Sinclair	1905	Alexander Cooke
1863	William Ewart	1906	Robert H S Reade DL
1864	Robert Henderson	1907	9th Earl of Shaftesbury KCVO
1865	James Macauley	1908	Sir Charles H Brett
1866	Charles Duffin	1909	George S Clark MP
1867	John Lytle	1910	John Rogers
1868	Sir Edward Coey DL	1911	J Milne Barbour DL
1869	Finlay McCance	1912	Robert A Mitchell LL B
1870	James Hamilton	1913	G Herbert Ewart MA
1871	William Spotten	1914	R Ernest Herdman DL
1872	Alexander Johns	1915	Samuel C Davidson MIMechE
1873	John Preston	1916	James H Stirling
1874	Elias H Thompson	1917	Hugh M Pollock DL
1875	Thomas Valentine	1918	Hugh M Pollock DL
1876	Thomas Sinclair MA	1919	Hugh L Garrett
1877	James Musgrave	1920	7th Marquis of Londonderry KG
1878	Alexander Johns	1921	William McMullan
1879	John Young	1922	W Hubert Webb DL
1880	R Lloyd Patterson	1923	Sir William F Coates Bart DL

1924	Sir Samuel Kelly	1954	Sir Robert McConnell Bart VRD
1925	Robert B Henry	1955	Victor F Clarendon CBE MA
1926	John E Wellwood	1956	Robert H Murphy OBE
1927	Hugh L McCready MA	1957	Sir Graham Larmor
1928	Frank Anderson MBE	1958	Sir James Norritt DL LL D
1929	Rt Hon Sir Edward M Archdale MP	1959	J Elliott Forde CBE DL
1930	Malcolm Gordon	1960	E Mayne Reid BSc PhD FRIC
1931	Thomas Somerset MP	1961	Robert McD Coulter LL B
1932	David D Reid BL DL MP	1962	A Thomas Robinson
1933	Henry H Stewart	1963	David Andrews OBE MSc
1934	Andrew C Marshall	1964	George B Howden CBE MInstCE
1935	Robert P C Gotto OBE	1965	Irene Calvert BA
1936	Rt Hon John M Andrews DL MP	1966	R Norman Crawford BComSc ACA
1937	Sir Joseph McConnell Bart DL MP	1967	G Henry Dunlop BComSc FCIS
1938	Capt D Cecil Lindsay DL	1968	J Allan Gray
1939	Lt Col D Cecil Lindsay DL	1969	Henry S Corscadden LL D
1940	Frank N Cooke	1970	James A Rodgers
1941	John G Michaels	1971	Raymond E Thompson
1942	Charles S Neill	1972	H Maurice Gabbey
1943	Sir Thomas W McMullan	1973	Erik E Utitz OBE
1944	Arthur F Shillington MIMechE	1974	Sir Ivan Ewart Bart DSC
1945	Sir Walter Smiles CIE DSO MP	1975	Robert D Rolston CBE
1946	Archibald Scott	1976	Andrew B Copnall
1947	Richard de B Chamberlain	1977	A James Beale MA
1948	Rt Hon Sir Harry Mulholland Bart OL	1978	Stanley Craigs OBE
1949	Sir Frederick E Rebbeck DSc DL	1979	George Chambers BSc PhD
1950	Col Samuel G Haughton DL	1980	R Brumwell Henderson CBE MA
1951	Col L Sydney Henshall DSO	1981	John R Fetherston
1952	Senator Herbert Quin CBE FCA	1982	Sir Myles Humphreys
1953	Senator Herbert Quin CBE FCA	1983	Robert T Jordan MBE CEng MIMechE

SECRETARIES OF THE BELFAST AND NORTHERN IRELAND CHAMBERS OF COMMERCE AND INDUSTRY 1783-1983

1783-1794 Robert Bradshaw
1802-1804 John Tisdall
1807-1812 Robert Callwell
1812-1817 James Luke
1817-1821 James Goddard
1821-1833 Samuel Bruce
1833-1847 C B Grimshaw
1847-1897 Samuel Vance

1898   B W Caughey
1899-1927 W J P Wilson
1927-1948 M R Whitham
1949-1960 Frank Coop
1960-1969 W G Buchan MA
1969-1970 J M Devlin BA FCA
1970-   G L Auret MBE FCIS

HONORARY TREASURERS OF THE BELFAST AND NORTHERN IRELAND CHAMBERS OF COMMERCE AND INDUSTRY 1853-1983

Prior to 1853 the Treasurership was usually combined either with the Presidency or with the Secretaryship.

1853-1873 Sir Edward Coey
1873-1880 E H Thompson
1880-1890 Sir John Preston
1891-1913 R H S Reade
1913-1927 David McKee
1927-1939 Samuel Johnston
1940-1951 R de B Chamberlain

1952-1956 S K Neill, OBE
1956-1967 G B Smyth
1967-1970 H M Gabbey
1971-1974 F B McClure
1975-1981 R N Bowman
1982-   Hugh Davis

PRESIDENTS OF THE ASSOCIATION OF NORTHERN IRELAND CHAMBERS OF COMMERCE 1923-1966

1923	H W Webb DL (Belfast)
1924,1925	F D Russell (Newry)
1926	J E Wellwood (Belfast)
1927,1928	W M Irons (Londonderry)
1929,1930	W McMullan (Belfast)
1931,1932	J Logan (Portadown)
1933,1934	W Cameron (Ballymena)
1935,1936	W Jackson (Coleraine)
1937-1948	No records available
1949	J Goligher (Londonderry)
1950	Col S G Haughton DL (Belfast)
1951	Col S G Haughton DL (Belfast)
1952	Col S G Haughton DL (Belfast)
1953	E Hodgett (Newry)
1954	Senator H Quin CBE FCA (Belfast)
1955	D H Stevenson (Portadown)
1956	F Storey CBE (Belfast)
1957	R B Price (Ballymoney)
1958	R H Murphy OBE (Belfast)
1959	J M Wilson (Armagh)
1960	R McD Coulter LL B (Belfast)
1961	C D Stewart-Liberty (Londonderry)
1962	A T Robinson (Belfast)
1963	W V Hogg (Newry)
1964	D Andrews OBE MSc (Belfast)
1965	G B Howden CBE MInstCE (Belfast)
1966	J A Rodgers (Newtownabbey)

PRESIDENTS OF THE BELFAST JUNIOR CHAMBER OF COMMERCE
1949-1983

1949 Neville Martin
1950 Morton McClure
1951 James H Casson
1952 William A McNeill
1953 Robert D Rolston
1954 J Allan Gray
1955 Robert D Rolston
1956 Col Henry J Porter OBE TD
1957 William H Wilson
1958 William M McCaughey
1959 John McK Boyle
1960 George S O'Neill
1961 Trevor C Dickey
1962 Desmond W Anderson
1963 W Stanley Hill
1964 R E Myles Humphreys
1965 Samuel H Boyle
1966 Herbert A Hadden
1967 R Robin Dunbar
1968 James McG Greig
1969 Noel L Valentine
1970 G Peter C Thompson
1971 F J Derek Falkiner
1972 John C Quinn
1973 J Campbell Morton
1974 C T Hogg
1975 J L Courtenay Thompson
1976 Leslie M McAlpine
1977 Douglas M Simpson
1978 Robert T Ferris
1979 C Stanley Myers
1980 H William R Kohner
1981 Cecil W Johnston
1982 David L Smyth
1983 Robert Brett

SELECTED SOURCES OF INFORMATION

On Chambers of Commerce

"Parliament of Commerce: The Story of the Association of British Chambers of Commerce: 1860-1960", by A R Ilersic and P F B Liddle (ABCC and Newman Neame, 1960).

"Our Illustrious Forbears: The Glasgow Chamber of Commerce 1783-1983", by C A Oakley (Blackie & Son, 1980).

"Princes and Pirates: The Dublin Chamber of Commerce 1783-1983", by L M Cullen (Dublin Chamber of Commerce, 1983).

Minute books, copy correspondence, and numerous other documents of the Belfast Chamber of Commerce held in the Public Records Office of Northern Ireland. With a few frustrating gaps, the minute books cover the period from 1783 till 1930. The copy correspondence extends till 1947; and there are a few other items relating to 1948 and 1949. The general PRONI reference number is D1857; and there is a catalogue to guide the researcher through the huge mass of material.

Bound volumes of the *"Journal of the Belfast Chamber of Commerce"*, April 1923 — March 1937, and of its ultimate successor, *"Northern Ireland Progress"*, April 1950 — December 1971; the *Year Books* of the Northern Ireland Chamber of Commerce and Industry, 1969-1983; and the monthly *Business Letters* of the Chamber, January 1974 — October 1983. This material is held at the Chamber offices, 22 Great Victoria Street, Belfast BT2 7BJ.

Files of the Milk Marketing Board for Northern Ireland on the Chamber of Commerce and its Committees, 1962-1983, held at 456 Antrim Road, Belfast BT15 5GD.

On the Economic and Social History of Belfast

"A History of the Town of Belfast from the Earliest Times to the Close of the 18th Century", by George Benn (Marcus Ward, 1877).

"A History of the Town of Belfast from 1799 till 1810", by George Benn (Marcus Ward, 1880).

"The Town Book of the Corporation of Belfast 1613-1816", edited by R M Young (Marcus Ward, 1892).

"Belfast and the Province of Ulster in the 20th Century", by R M Young (W T Pike & Co, 1909).

"A Short History of the Port of Belfast", by D J Owen (Mayne, Boyd & Son, 1917).

"History of Belfast", by D J Owen (W & G Baird, 1921).

"The Drennan Letters", edited by D A Chart (HMSO Belfast, 1931).

"Sidelights on Belfast History", by S S Millin (W & G Baird, 1932).

"Additional Sidelights on Belfast History", by S S Millin (W & G Baird, 1938).

"Old Belfast", by A S Moore (Carter Publications, 1951).

"Belfast in its Regional Setting: A Scientific Survey", edited by E E Evans et al (British Association, 1952).

"A Social Geography of Belfast", by Emrys Jones (Oxford University Press, 1960).

"Belfast and its Charitable Society: A Story of Urban Social Development", by R W M Strain (Oxford University Press, 1961).

"Belfast: The Origins and Growth of an Industry City", edited by J C Beckett and R E Glasscock (BBC, 1967).

"Buildings of Belfast 1700-1914", by C E B Brett (Weidenfeld & Nicholson, 1967).

"Belfast: Approach to Crisis: A Study of Belfast Politics", by Ian Budge and Cornelius O'Leary (Macmillan, 1973).

"The Business Community and Trade of Belfast 1767-1800", by N E Gamble (PhD Thesis to the University of Dublin 1978, opened January 1983).

"Belfast: An Illustrated History", by Jonathan Bardon (Blackstaff Press, 1982).

"Belfast: The Making of the City: 1800-1914", by J C Beckett et al (Appletree Press, 1982).

On Commercial and Industrial Development in the North of Ireland

"The Industrial Archaeology of Northern Ireland", by W A McCutcheon (HMSO Belfast, 1980).

"The Economic History of Ireland in the Eighteenth Century", by George O'Brien (Maunsel & Co, 1918).

"With Plunkett in Ireland: The Co-op Organiser's Story", by R A Anderson (Macmillan, 1935).

"The Lagan Valley 1800-50", by E R R Green (Faber & Faber, 1949).

"Irish Linen Halls", by E R R Green (Carter Publications, 1951).

"Northern Ireland 1921-1971", by Hugh Shearman (HMSO Belfast, 1971).

"The Irish Co-operative Movement: Its History and Development", by Patrick Bolger (Institute of Public Administration Dublin, 1977).

"Ireland's Eye: The Photographs of Robert John Welch", by E E Evans and B S Turner (Blackstaff Press, 1977).

"Once Upon the Lagan: The Story of the Lagan Canal", by May Blair (Blackstaff Press, 1981).

"Shipbuilding in Belfast", by Fred Heatley in *"Northern Life"*, Vol 2, 1981.

On Families and Firms

"The Centenary Volume of the Northern Banking Company Ltd Belfast", by E D Hill (McCaw, Stevenson, and Orr, 1925).

"Harland & Wolff's Shipyards and Engine Works at Belfast", by Denis Rebbeck in *"Engineering"*, Sep 19 & 26, 1952.

"Romantic Suffern", by S V Penfold (Rockland County Historical Committee, Tallman, New York, 1955).

"Nine Generations: A History of the Andrews' Family, Millers of Comber", by Sydney Andrews (Isaac Andrews & Sons, 1958).

"The Sirocco Story", by E D Maguire (Davidson & Co, 1958).

"The Life and Times of Mary Ann McCracken", by Mary McNeill (Allen Figgis & Co, 1960).

"Guinness's Brewery in the Irish Economy 1759-1876", by Patrick Lynch and John Vaizey (Cambridge University Press, 1960).

"Irish Linen: William Ewart & Son Ltd" by J M Gray (William Ewart & Son, 1964).

"Decades of the Ulster Bank 1836-1964", by W J Knox (Ulster Bank, 1964).

"Seize then the Hour: A History of James P Corry & Co Ltd and of the Corry Family 1123-1974", by John Caughey (J P Corry & Co, 1974).

"Cautious Belfast: The Story of the First Fifty Years of Harris, Marrian & Co Ltd 1925-75", by T S Duncan (Harris Marrian & Co 1975).

"The Belfast Bank 1827-1970", by Noel Simpson (Blackstaff Press/Northern Bank, 1975).

"Long Shadows Cast Before: Nine Lives in Ulster, 1625-1977", by C E B Brett (John Bartholomew & Son, 1978).

"A Dictionary of Irish Biography", by Henry Boylan (Gill & MacMillan, 1978).

"Root and Branch: Allied Irish Banks Yesterday, Today, Tomorrow", (Allied Irish Banks, 1979).

"Absentees, Architects, and Agitators: The Fifth Earl of Donegall and the Building of Fisherwick Park", by W A Maguire, *Proceedings of Belfast Natural History and Philosophical Society*, Second Series, Vol 10, 1981.

"Things Phoenix 1782-1982" (Phoenix Assurance Co, 1982).

"Malone House: Owners and Occupants", by W A Maguire (Architectural Heritage Society, 1983).

"Bank of Ireland Bicentenary 1783-1983" (Bank of Ireland, 1983).

"Spirit of the Age: The Story of Old Bushmills", by Alf McCreary (Old Bushmills Distillery Co/Blackstaff Press, 1983).

On Churches and Churchmen

"An Historical Account of the Diocese of Down and Connor", Vol 2, by James O'Laverty (Gill & Son, 1880).

"History of Methodism in Ireland", by C H Cruickshank (Allen, 1885).

"Historic Memorials of the First Presbyterian Chuch in Belfast" (Marcus Ward, 1887).

"History of the Second Congregation of Protestant Dissenters in Belfast", by S S Millin (W & G Baird, 1900).

"Rosemary Street Presbyterian Church: A Record of the Last Two-Hundred Years", by J W Kernohan ("Witness" Office, 1923).

"The Church of Ireland in Belfast: Its Growth, Condition, Needs: The Story of the Churches 1779-1931", by J F McNeice (Belfast Newsletter, 1931).

"The Seceders in Ireland with Annals of Their Congregations", by David Stewart (Presbyterian Historical Society, 1950).

"Kilraughts: A Kirk and It's People", by S A Blair (First Kilraughts Presbyterian Church, 1973).

"Ballyroney: Its Church and People", by J W Lockington (Ballyroney Presbyterian Church, 1979).

"Presbyterianism in Killead", by W D Weir and H Campbell (Killead Presbyterian Church, 1980).

"The Heritage of Drumbo", by J F Rankin (Drumbo Parish Church, 1981).

"A History of Congregations in the Presbyterian Church in Ireland 1610-1982, (Presbyterian Historical Society, 1982).

"Gravestone Inscriptions", by R S J Clarke, selected volumes (Ulster-Scot Historical Foundation, various dates).

On the Linen Hall Library and Educational Establishments

"History of the Belfast Library and Society for Promoting Knowledge: The Linen Hall Library", by John Anderson (McCaw, Stevenson & Orr, 1888).

"Belfast Royal Academy 1785-1935", by Hugh Shearman (Wm Strain & Sons, 1935).

"The History of the Royal Belfast Academical Institution 1810-1960", by John Jamieson (RBAI/Wm Mullan & Son, 1959).

"Queen's University Belfast 1845-1949", by T W Moody and J C Beckett (Faber & Faber, 1959).

"Methodist College Belfast: The First 100 Years 1868-1968, (MCB/W & G Baird, 1968).

On Politics and Politicans

"Personal Narrative of the Irish Rebellion of 1798", by C H Teeling (1828).

"History of the Irish Rebellion in the Year 1798", by Samuel McSkimmin (John Mullan, 1853).

"Craigavon: Ulsterman", by St John Ervine (George Allen & Unwin, 1949).

"Carson", by H M Hyde (William Heinemann, 1953).

"The Ulster Crisis", by A T Q Stewart (Faber & Faber, 1967).

"The Autobiography of Terence O'Neill: Prime Minister of Northern Ireland 1963-1969" (Rupert Hart-Davis, 1972).

"The Ulster Unionist Party 1882-1973", by J F Harbinson (Blackstaff Press, 1973).

"Northern Ireland 1968-73: A Chronology of Events", Vol 1 1968-71, by R Deutsch and V Magowan (Blackstaff Press, 1973).

"The United Irishmen", Education Facsimiles 61-80 (PRONI, 1974).

"The Volunteers, 1778-84", Education Facsimiles 141-160 (PRONI, 1974).

"The '98 Rebellion", Education Facsimiles 81-100 (PRONI, 1976).

"A Stable Unseen Power: Dr William Drennan and the Origins of the United Irishmen", by A T Q Stewart in *"Essays Presented to Michael Roberts"* (Blackstaff Press, 1976).

"Memoirs of a Statesman", by Brian Faulkner (Weidenfeld & Nicholson, 1978).

"Ireland: A History", by Robert Kee (Weidenfeld & Nicholson, 1980).

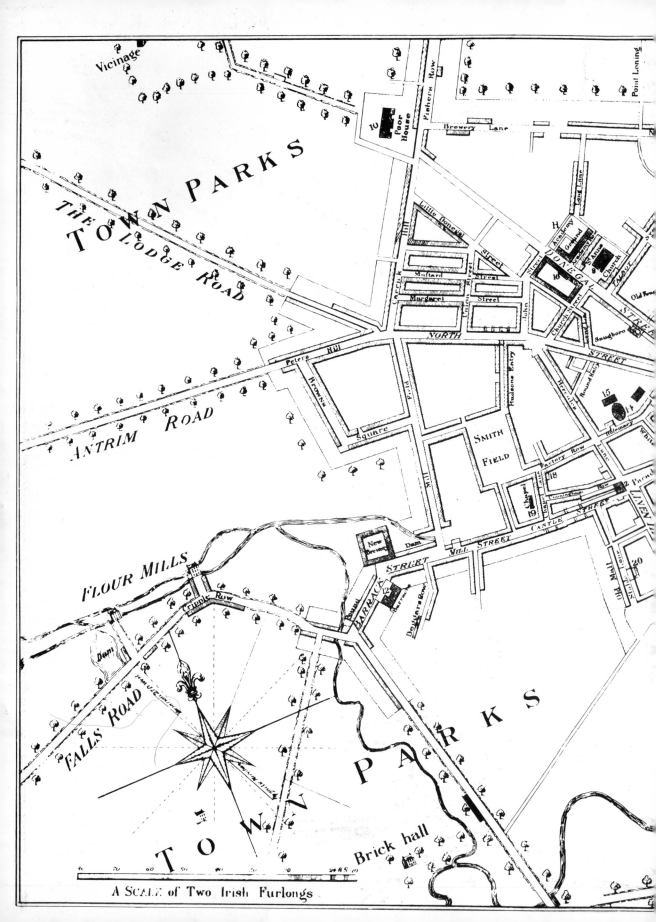

A SCALE of Two Irish Furlongs